CD GUIDE
TO POP
& ROCK

To my wife Claudia with love
for bringing me out of
rock's 'medieval' period.

First published 2001

Printed in England
by Bookmarque

for the Publishers
B.T. Batsford Ltd
9 Blenheim Court
Brewery Road
London N7 9NY

A member of the Chrysalis Group plc

A CIP catalogue record for this book is available from the British Library

ISBN 0 7134 8638 4

Chrysalis

CD GUIDE TO POP & ROCK

PAUL ROLAND
National Music Press Reviewer

Acknowledgements

The author would like to express his
thanks to the following for supplying
review copies:

Jo Pratt (EMI)
Carlos Anaia (Warners)
Andy Street (Deram)
Sam White (Mercury)
John Coyne and Liz Fraser (Virgin)
Andy Fraser (Mute)
Angela (Polydor)
Chris Sharpe (Beggars Banquet)
Sara (Sony Music)
Kaz (Mercenary PR)
Nigel Woodbine (Quite Great PR)

When I began buying records in the mid-seventies my initial excitement at finding a new album was always tempered by a certain anxiety. In those pre-digital days LPs were notoriously prone to what were euphemistically called 'pressing problems' and would jump at the slightest provocation.

Being a finicky and rather intense adolescent I spent as much time 'scratching and sampling' my collection in the truest sense of the term and bathing my records in anti-static fluid as I did listening to the music. It was only when I could finally afford to invest in some real Hi-Fi (for the cost of a small property in Bermuda) that I could buy new records with a reasonable expectation of being able to hear them right through to the fade.

And then, in the late eighties, came CDs. No more scratches, no more skating stylus, no more singers stuck in the wrong sort of groove. No, compact discs were marketed as being indestructible and for once the marketing men weren't being 'economical with the truth'. Nine out of ten releases played perfectly on even the most modest player and the sound quality did not deteriorate no matter how many times I played 'Smoke On The Water'.

There were initial rumblings of discontent from audiophiles (Hi-Fi fanatics to you and me) concerning the highly questionable merits of analogue over digital and from collectors who enjoyed the feel of 'a real record'. But these were probably the same people who wanted to go 'back to mono'. As far as the average punter was concerned Compact Discs were the Creator's second gift to the music lover (the first being either Mozart or Motorhead depending on your taste) and they proved to be the perfect medium for whatever turned you on, musically speaking.

Unfortunately, in their rush to re-issue their entire back catalogue on CD the record companies weren't always as conscientious as they might have been and many albums were mastered from whatever tapes were to hand. These were often second, or even third generation copies, which meant that some classic albums such as 'Led Zeppelin IV' were issued with noticeable distortion and with a sound quality that did not do justice to the digital format.

More recently these mistakes have been corrected as record companies have made an effort to locate the original master tapes and re-master the old albums using the new, superior 24-bit technology, adding previously unreleased bonus tracks whenever possible. By doing so they have managed to persuade some of us to buy a favourite album for the third time and even tempt our teenage kids to dip into what is now known rather derogatively as 'dad rock'. Unfortunately, some of the original inferior issues are still clogging up the racks of your local record store, while some third generation releases have confused the situation even more by claiming to supersede all previous versions in terms of sound quality and packaging. But these frequently offer less value for money because copyright issues have forced the new owners of these albums to drop the bonus tracks. The late-nineties Hendrix re-issues, which are authorised by the late guitarist's estate, and EMI's Bowie re-issues are prime culprits.

This book is intended to clarify all this confusion by identifying the best buys on the market for the casual as well as the committed music fan.

This is not another selective collector's list of essential albums – although several hundred certified classics are included – but a reasonably comprehensive buyer's guide (given the space) which I believe balances informed and entertaining reviews with a consumer journalist's appreciation of sound quality, content and value for money.

It has been my intention to do for rock and pop what other CD guides have done for classical and jazz, namely highlighting the most representative albums by the major and most significant artists in every genre. And if that means recommending a 'greatest hits' collection instead of a 'legitimate' album, then so be it. I have given the titles of at least one and sometimes several albums by the same artist if you want to sample more of the same, plus there is a useful 'If you like this, why not try...' feature which offers more avenues for exploration. In addition, there are supplementary lists at the back of the book to help build the foundation of the essential CD collection, or for you to compare lists and argue the merits of your choices over mine.

You won't find catalogue numbers, chart placings and the name of the session musician who played the nose flute solo on an individual track, or any other trivia, but I hope this guide will help you to make a more informed choice that ensures you get the CD you really wanted. And it will also save you money.

It's almost impossible to keep personal preferences out entirely and I make no excuse for my enthusiasm for certain 'old classics' and those new artists that move me in mysterious ways, but I have tried to be fair and impartial when considering artists that I personally have no feeling for.

I hope too that you will discover some of the cult independent artists that the High Street chains don't stock and maybe re-discover what might be rather grandly described as rock's rich heritage, as I did during the writing of this guide. Whether you enjoy browsing through the racks at your local record emporium or shopping on the Internet, good hunting and happy listening.

Paul Roland

Artist/Band name

AC / DC

Album title

'IF YOU WANT BLOOD, YOU'VE GOT IT'

Record label (current issue)

Original date of album release

(Atlantic) 1978

Full track listing

Track listing: Riff Raff • Hell Ain't A Bad Place To Be • Bad Boy Boogie • The Jack • Problem Child • Whole Lotta Rosie • Rock 'N' Roll Damnation • High Voltage • Let There Be Rock • Rocker

Synopsis/critique

The best songs from their early albums in a steaming live setting. The band excelled as a live act where their irrepressible energy could spark off the crowd like ball lightning and Angus could bludgeon their bleeding ears with finger blistering solos and bone-crunching slabs of sound. Stick your head in the speaker during his feedback frenzy on 'Bad Boy Boogie' and you'll know why they call an electric guitar an axe! A raw, sweaty celebration of laddish indulgence and testosterone overload. One of the great heavy rock albums of all time.

Rating for content
Rating for sound quality in CD form

Rating:
Sound ★★★★☆   Content ★★★★★

Also recommended:

Recommended Albums by same artist/band

'High Voltage' (ATCO/Warners) a less bombastic set of tunes with an insidious, bluesy feel and 'Let There Be Rock' (Atlantic), which is arguably their strongest studio album boasting four headbanging anthems ('Bad Boy Boogie', 'Problem Child', 'Whole Lotta Rosie' and the title track).

If you like this, why not try:

Further listening suggestions

AC/DC 'Live' 1992 with Brian Johnson (available in single and double disc editions), George Thorogood, Ozzy Osbourne & Guns 'n' Roses.

Cross reference

A Certain Ratio

'FORCE'

(Rev-Ola/Factory) 1994

Track listing: Only Together • Bootsy • Fever 103 Degrees • Naked And White • Mickey Way • And Then She Smiled • Take Me Down • Anthem • Si Fermi O Gredo

Before techno the underground clubs of Northern Britain reverberated to the sound of what can best be described as industrial disco supplied by the likes of Sheffield's A Certain Ratio. This experimental indie collective mixed jazz-funk and ambient sounds to create an urban soundscape that was sufficiently black to make an impression on the Billboard R&B chart, but also eclectic enough to be embraced by the nascent Manchester dance scene. 'Force' was recorded after founder members Peter Terrell (keyboards) and Simon Topping (vocals/percussion) had been replaced by singer Carol McKenzie and saxophonist Tony Quigley, a move which helped secure a major label deal with A&M and their belated absorption into the mainstream. Unfortunately, the album doesn't include their final Factory single 'Wild Party' which was their most substantial indie hit to date.

Rating:
Sound ★★★☆☆ Content ★★★☆☆
Also recommended:
'Up In Downsville' (Robsrecords), one of their most accessible albums featuring vocals by Denise Johnson of Primal Scream, and 'Looking For A

Certain Ratio' (Creation), an album of selective remixes.
If you like this, why not try:
New Order, Joy Division.

Abba

'GOLD'

(Polydor) 1992

Track listing: Dancing Queen • Knowing Me, Knowing You • Take A Chance On Me • Mama Mia • Lay All Your Love On Me • Super Trouper • I Have A Dream • Winner Takes It All • Money, Money, Money • SOS • Chiquitita • Fernando • Voulez Vous • Gimme, Gimme, Gimme • Does Your Mother Know • One Of Us • Name Of The Game • Thankyou For The Music • Waterloo

Abba

'MORE ABBA GOLD'

(Polydor) 1999

Track listing: Summer Night City • Angel Eyes • The Day Before You Came • Eagle • I Do I Do I Do I Do • So Long • Honey Honey • The Visitors • Our Last Summer • On And On And On • Ring Ring • I Wonder • Lovelight • Head Over Heels • When I Kissed The Teacher • I Am The City • Cassandra • Under Attack • When All Is Said And Done • The Way Old Friends Do

At the peak of their popularity the Swedish supergroup ran a close third to Elvis and The Beatles in terms of sales, their royalty payments dwarfing the export earnings of their country's national steel industry. Volume 1 of this indispensable compilation of ear candy collects all their essential early hits including their chirpy Eurovision winner from 1974, 'Waterloo', and leaves their more introspective, melancholic and mature work for volume 2. The latter offers their less immediate, but ultimately more enduring and satisfying songs such as the wistful 'The Day Before You Came'.

With their irresistible hooks, mellow close-harmony vocals and simple lyrics these songs have a universal appeal that defies musical boundaries, bringing the group praise from such unlikely admirers as Elvis Costello and Bono of U2. Lightweight though they may be, these tracks exemplify the art of the three-minute pop song; each perfectly crafted and guaranteeing a good time. Flawless.

Rating:
Sound ★★★★★ Content ★★★★☆
Also recommended:
'Voulez Vous', 'Supertrouper' and 'The Visitors' (all on Polydor).
If you like this, why not try:
The Beatles, **The Beach Boys**, **Erasure** and the various Eurodisco acts of the seventies produced by Giorgio Moroder.

ABC

'LEXICON OF LOVE'

(Mercury) 1996

Track listing: Show Me • Poison Arrow • Many Happy Returns • Tears Are Not Enough • Valentine's Day • Look Of Love (Pt 1) • Date Stamp • All Of My Heart • 4 Ever 2 Gether • Look Of Love (Pt 2) • Tears Are Not Enough • Poison Arrow • Look Of Love • Alphabet Soup • Theme From 'Mantrap' • Look Of Love

Sheffield is a grimly dark steel town whose contribution to British culture is limited to having produced a glut of heavy metal acts with the subtlety of a steam hammer. So, when glamorous dancefloor darlings ABC sashayed onto stage and screen in 1982 with the funk and flair of a black soul group the critics cried 'phony'. But with this, their first album, all but the most cynical were won over. The combination of Martin Fry's honest, wide-eyed romanticism, a clutch of finger-snapping songs – which seamlessly married a string-driven pop pastiche to a pneumatic beat – and Trevor Horn's lush, melodramatic production made this debut offering a certified club choice for most of the decade.

This is the remastered version burnished with a digital gloss to give a greater clarity and sheen to such sophisticated eighties dancefloor favourites as 'Poison Arrow', 'Look Of Love' and 'Tears Are Not Enough'. Better still, it also boasts six extra tracks featuring extended remixes and live tracks. The only regret is that you will have to look elsewhere to add the fabulous 'When Smokey Sings'.

Rating:
Sound ★★★★☆ Content ★★★☆☆
Also recommended:
The Collection (Spectrum) a comprehensive budget-priced hits package.
If you like this, why not try:
Spandau Ballet, Heaven 17, **Frankie Goes To Hollywood**.

AC/DC

'LET THERE BE ROCK'

(Atlantic) 1977

Track listing: Go Down • Dog Eat Dog • Let There Be Rock • Bad Boy Boogie • Problem Child • Overdose • Hell Ain't A Bad Place To Be • Whole Lotta Rosie

AC/DC had no pretensions towards subtlety and thankfully they never compromised their repertoire of heavy riffs with the now obligatory ballad. This is arguably their strongest studio set boasting four headbanging anthems, 'Bad Boy Boogie', 'Problem Child', 'Whole Lotta Rosie' and the title track. The titles tell all you need to know about their brand of swaggering bar room boogie. Each supplying a healthy dose of sex, drink and r-e-a-l rock and roll. What more could a red-blooded adolescent ask for?

The complete AC/DC catalogue has been remastered at a premium price and all offer a significant improvement on the sound quality of the original 1980s releases.

Rating:
Sound ★★★★☆ Content ★★★★☆

AC/DC

'IF YOU WANT BLOOD, YOU'VE GOT IT'

(Atlantic) 1978

Track listing: Riff Raff • Hell Ain't A Bad Place To Be • Bad Boy Boogie • The Jack • Problem Child • Whole Lotta Rosie • Rock 'N' Roll Damnation • High Voltage • Let There Be Rock • Rocker

The best songs from their early albums in a steaming live setting. The band excelled as a live act where their irrepressible energy could spark off the crowd like ball lightning and Angus could bludgeon their bleeding ears with finger-blistering solos and bone-crunching slabs of sound. Stick your head in the speaker during his feedback frenzy on 'Bad Boy Boogie' and you'll know why they call an electric guitar an axe! A raw, sweaty celebration of laddish indulgence and testosterone overload. One of the great heavy rock albums of all time.

Rating:
Sound ★★★★☆ Content ★★★★★

AC/DC

'HIGHWAY TO HELL'

(Atlantic) 1979

Track listing: Highway To Hell • Girls Got Rhythm • Walk All Over You • Touch Too Much • Beating Around The Bush • Shot Down In Flames • Get It Hot • If You Want Blood • Love Hungry Man • Night Prowler

This was the last studio album from Australia's premier hard rock outfit to feature gravel-voiced frontman Bon Scott, who died just as the single 'Touch Too Much' was climbing the charts. For many fans of the band their later albums with replacement Brian Johnson are a pale imitation of 'the real thing' and most wouldn't give a XXXX for the po-faced posturing and catalogue of clichés of those later offerings. Bon sings as if he's got his tongue wedged firmly in his cheek, which gives their blatantly sexist lyrics a veneer of impish charm, an impression emphasized by guitarist Angus Young's habit of dressing up as a demented, overgrown schoolboy complete with cap, short trousers and satchel. Ironically, the title track is arguably the weakest cut on the album, typifying the type of neanderthal stomp many lesser heavy rock outfits are often criticized for making. However, the remainder bite down on memorable meaty riffs and guitar breaks that are uncharacteristically economical for an act of their musical persuasion.

Rating:
Sound ★★★★☆ Content ★★★★☆
Also recommended:
'High Voltage' (ATCO/Warners) a less bombastic set of tunes with an insidious, bluesy feel plus 'Flick Of The Switch' (Atlantic), 'Stiff Upper Lip' (EMI) and the box set of Bon Scott era unreleased tracks and rarities 'Bonfire' (Atlantic).
If you like this, why not try:
George Thorogood, Ozzy Osbourne and **Guns 'N' Roses.**

Bryan Adams

'WAKING UP THE NEIGHBOURS'

(A&M) 1991

Track listing: Is Your Mama Gonna Miss Ya • Hey Honey, I'm Packin' You In • Can't Stop This Thing We Started • Thought I'd Died And Gone To Heaven • Not Guilty • Vanishing • House Arrest • Do I Have To Say The Words • There Will Never Be Another Tonight • All I Want Is You • Depend On Me • Everything I Do (I Do It For You) • If You Wanna Leave Me (Can I Come Too) • Touch The Hand • Don't Drop That Bomb On Me

The Canadian singer/writer/guitarist entered the stadium league with this monster commercial platter. It spawned a staggering five hit singles, including the somewhat overwrought ballad 'Everything I Do', which featured in the Kevin Costner costume adventure *Robin Hood*. Adams's consistent success with mediocre material continues to confound the critics, but has proven ideal radio fodder and it evidently satisfies the mainstream music buyer for whom one suspects Springsteen might prove too demanding. None of the tracks are as wistfully nostalgic as his best song, 'Summer Of '69', indeed several suggest that the four-chord formula is beginning to wear rather thin, but there is plenty of passion to please the AOR audience whose loyalty appears to intensify the blander his material becomes.

Rating:
Sound ★★★★☆ Content ★★★☆☆
Also recommended:
'Cuts Like A Knife', 'Reckless' featuring three tracks with Tina Turner, 'Unplugged' and '18 Til I Die' (all on A&M), each of which are comparatively more rocky and less blatantly commercial than 'Waking Up The Neighbours'.
If you like this, why not try:
Bruce Springsteen, Bon Jovi.

The Adverts

'CROSSING THE RED SEA WITH THE ADVERTS'

(Essential) 1978

Track listing: One Chord Wonders • Bored Teenagers • New Church • On The Roof • New Boys • Bombsite Boys • No Time To Be 21 • Safety In Numbers • Drowning Men • On Wheels • Great British Mistake • Gary Gilmore's Eyes • We Who Wait • New Day Dawning

The two opening tracks of this archetypal 'amateurs R us' album sums up the apathetic, 'up yours' attitude which the punks personified. Frontman TV Smith had evidently read the infamous article in punk zine *Sniffin' Glue* which showed the only three guitar chords its readers would need to learn before forming a band. But he rarely used more than one. The group's infectious enthusiasm and evident delight in their inexperience more than compensates for the ragged free-for-all scramble that characterizes just about every track on the album and the inconsistency of the material. Completing the unholy trinity of essential three-minute thrash classics is the brief but brilliant 'Gary Gilmore's Eyes', a lurid homage to schlock horror movies inspired by the execution of the American killer who offered to donate his eyes to science.

Rating:
Sound ★★★☆☆ Content ★★★☆☆
Also recommended:
The Adverts 'Radio Sessions' (Burning Airlines) as a sample of their endearingly shambolic live set.

If you like this, why not try:
The Angelic Upstarts, **The Sex Pistols**, **The Damned**, TV Smith's Explorers.

Aerosmith

'ROCKS'

(Columbia) 1976

Track listing: Back In The Saddle • Last Child • Rats In The Cellar • Combination • Sick As A Dog • Nobody's Fault • Get The Lead Out • Lick And A Promise • Home Tonight

With a cocksure swagger and a fistful of bluesy metal riffs Aerosmith are the missing link between The Stones, James Brown and Guns 'N' Roses. 'Rocks' is by far the most consistent album that the band made in their pre-MTV days before the collaboration with Run DMC introduced them to a new generation and ensured them stadium stacking status. On the strongest songs ('Rats In The Cellar', 'Sick As A Dog' and the opener) frontman Steve Tyler's Jaggeresque drawl is complemented by Joe Perry's indolent lead licks and sweetened by Beatle-styled vocal harmonies before the belligerent rhythm section delivers its blows well below the belt. This isn't stock metal, it's fast and funky and untainted by the kind of flabby soft-rock anthems that undermined contemporaries Bon Jovi, Foreigner and the like. 'Like real good boogie?' asks Tyler on 'Get The Lead Out'. Well, if you do, here's where you'll find it.

Rating:
Sound ★★★☆☆ Content ★★★★☆

Also recommended:
'Pump' (Geffen) and 'Greatest Hits 1973–1988' (Columbia), 17 stadium-shaking classics plus one previously unreleased item.
If you like this, why not try:
Guns 'N' Roses, The Rolling Stones, The Black Crowes, **RUN DMC.**

Tori Amos

'LITTLE EARTHQUAKES'

(East West/Warners) 1992

Track listing: *Crucify • Girl • Silent All These Years • Precious Things • Winter • Happy Phantom • China • Weather • Mother • Tear In Your Hand • Me And A Gun • Little Earthquakes*

Singer-songwriter Tori Amos turned her back on a promising career as a classical pianist because she found the repertoire as stale as 'stinky cheese'. Her own songs draw on influences as diverse as Joni Mitchell and Led Zeppelin (in their more reflective, folksy moments) and are presented in a traditional rock context with occasional colouring from acoustic instruments. On this, her debut album, she can be wilfully obtuse, both rhythmically and lyrically, a trait which distinguishes Tori from her early influences Joni Mitchell, Laura Nyro and Janis Ian. There are intimate confessions that attempt to reconcile fey romanticism with a cynical look at life. 'Crucify', for example, contains a typically sour and self-deprecating observation in the line, 'Got enough guilt to start my own religion', while 'Me And A Gun' describes her ordeal at the hands of a rapist with chilling candor.

Rating:
Sound ★★★★☆ Content ★★★★★

Tori Amos

'UNDER THE PINK'

(East West/Warners) 1994

Track listing: *Pretty Good Year • God • Bells For Her • Past The Mission • Baker Baker • Wrong Band • Waitress • Cornflake Girl • Icicle • Cloud On My Tongue • Space Dog • Yes, Anastasia*

The comparisons with Kate Bush are again obvious (particularly in the breathy vocal performances and penchant for fanciful themes), but it's a comparison which is not entirely justified. While Kate delighted in creating characters to voice her often whimsical fantasies, Tori is more concerned with stripping away the masks to reveal the paradox at the core of the human psyche. For that reason, her albums can be as fascinating and cathartic as a session in analysis, but at a fraction of the cost of going to a shrink.

This million seller includes the hit single 'Cornflake Girl' and the typical oddball 'God' in which she wrestles with the demons from her fundamentalist upbringing.

Rating:
Sound ★★★★☆ Content ★★★★☆
Also recommended:
'Boys For Pele' (Atlantic), her third solo outing which has been favourably compared with Joni Mitchell's 'Blue'.
If you like this, why not try:
Kate Bush, Joni Mitchell, Joan Osborne.

Ash

'FREE ALL ANGELS'

(Infectious) 2001

Track Listing: Walking Barefoot • Shining Light • Burn Baby Burn • Candy • Cherry Bomb • Submission • Someday • Pacific Palisades • Shark • Sometimes • Nicole • There's A Star • World Domination

Ash, Northern Ireland's answer to chill-out rockers Stereophonics, evidently believe that the good things are worth waiting for. In 94 they had no regrets about turning down the chance to tour with Pearl Jam and Soul Asylum in order to concentrate on their A levels. And they were clearly in no hurry to make a definitive statement in the studio. The first two albums demonstrated that they had both the hard edge and the hooks to give their rivals a run for their money. But it wasn't until 'Angels' that they jettisoned the retro punk and grunge influences for more subtle shadings, as on stand out tracks 'Someday' and 'Candy' which recall classic Sixties symphonic pop (the latter featuring a Walker Brothers sample).

Psych pop, Brit pop and lashings of power chords mix with Tim Wheeler's wistful melodies to make 'Angels' one of the strongest offerings from the province since the innocent days of The Undertones.

Rating:
Sound ★★★★☆ Content ★★★★☆
Also recommended:
'Trailer', '1977' and 'Nu Clear Sounds' (all on Infectious).

If you like this, why not try:
Travis, Stereophonics, Feeder, REM.

Atomic Kitten

'RIGHT NOW'

(Innocent) 2001

Track Listing: Right Now • Follow Me • Whole Again • Eternal Flame • Tomorrow & Tonight • Get Real • Turn Me On • Hippy • You Are • Cradle • Bye Now • Stragers • See Ya • I Want Your Love

These girls may look like cute and cuddly tabbies and sound much like the rest of the pack on soulful smoochers such as 'Whole Again' and 'Cradle', but when they get their claws into feisty dance tracks of the calibre of 'Turn Me On' and 'Follow Me' they make the Spice Girls and S Club 7 sound like pampered pussies. The secret lies in their stronger, more assertive vocals and their commitment to hauling pop out of the playground and back onto the dance floor. Only 'Bye Now' and 'Hippy' seem superfluous to requirements, lacking any real sense of identity or purpose. Otherwise this is a surprisingly strong set of tunes featuring their first four singles 'See Ya', 'I Want Your Love', Right Now' and 'Follow Me'. Don't knock it till you've tried it.

Rating:
Sound ★★★★☆ Content ★★★☆☆
Also recommended: n/a
If you like this, why not try:
Destiny's Child, The Sugar Babes, Steps, Hear'Say.

Bad Company

'BAD COMPANY'

(Swan Song/Warners) 1974

Track listing: Can't Get Enough • Rock Steady • Ready For Love • Don't Let Me Down • Bad Company • The Way I Choose • Movin' On • Seagull

When Paul Rodgers formed Bad Company in 1973 with his buddies from Mott The Hoople, King Crimson and his former outfit, Free, any financial institution would have been happy to underwrite the risk as it promised to be the start of another lucrative franchise. The formula was not that dissimilar to the sparse, muscular music made by Free with the emphasis on Rodgers' abrasive sandpaper vocals, a supple, sinewy spine running through ballads and rockers alike and a set list of soulful Beatlesque tunes with backbone. The trouble was that the group's songwriting skills were not always up to scratch. The title track with its outlaw imagery and a handful of others are admirably lean and mean, with Rodgers raging against a wall of power chords, but the remainder are strictly second rate makeweights. But then, that's what the track search button on your CD player was made for.

Rating:
Sound ★★★☆☆ Content ★★★☆☆

Bad Company

'STRAIGHT SHOOTER'

(Swan Song/Warners) 1975

Track listing: Good Lovin' Gone Bad • Feel Like Makin' Love • Weep No More • Shooting Star • Deal With The Preacher • Wild Fire Woman • Anna • Call On Me

An album which aims for greatness with the soft metal singles 'Good Lovin' Gone Bad' and 'Feel Like Makin' Love', but pitches a few shots short of the target thanks to a couple of rather crass crowd pleasers. It's obvious that the band's songwriting talents are already overstretched and that even their commitment, stamina and musicianship are not enough to sustain interest through the mediocre material that pads out what was originally side two of the LP.

But if you're still interested, be sure to look out the remastered version as the original CD release is marred by a dull, boxy sound.

Rating:
Sound ★★★☆☆ Content ★★★☆☆
Also recommended:
The 'Original' Bad Company Anthology (Elektra), a 2CD set featuring several previously unreleased recordings and a couple of songs recorded specially for this collection.
If you like this, why not try:
Bon Jovi, **Free**, or **Paul Rodgers'** 'Tribute To Muddy Waters', a 2CD set featuring celebrity guest guitar stars.

The Band

'MUSIC FROM BIG PINK'

(Capitol/EMI) 1968

*Track listing: Tears Of Rage •
To Kingdom Come • In A Station •
Caledonia Mission • The Weight •
We Can Talk • Long Black Veil • Chest
Fever • Lonesome Susie • Wheels On Fire
• I Shall Be Released*

Having paid their dues with Ronnie
Hawkins and then Bob Dylan, The
Band took one bemused look at the
hash-shrouded hippie paradise that
the US had become in the late Sixties
and headed west in search of their
roots and the 'real' America. There,
in the rural backwaters they
discovered a rich heritage of tall
tales, traditional country tunes and
larger-than-life small town characters
that they were to describe with a
writer's keen eye for detail.

Rejecting the current fad for multi-
tracked recording, The Band went
back to basics, recording all the
songs live and dividing the vocals
between the three leads who traded
lines in an impromptu call-and-
response gospel-cum-country style.
The overall impression is of
eavesdropping on a backwoods story-
telling and guitar-picking session in
the days before the West was won.

Rating:
Sound ★★★☆☆ Content ★★★★☆

The Band

'THE BAND'

(Capitol/EMI) 1969

*Track listing: Across The Great Divide • Rag
Mama Rag • The Night They Drove Old
Dixie Down • When You Awake • Up On
Cripple Creek • Whispering Pines • Jemima
Surrender • Rockin' Chair • Look Out
Cleveland • Jawbone • Unfaithful Servant •
King Harvest (Has Surely Come)*

The Band were once described as the
only rock outfit who could have
warmed up the audience for Abraham
Lincoln. Their self-titled second album
boasts such a strong selection of songs
it's doubtful that old Abe would have
been able to command the crowd's
attention long enough to deliver even
the celebrated 'Gettysburg Address'.
'The Night They Drove Old Dixie
Down' is perhaps their best known
song thanks to Joan Baez's reasonably
faithful cover version, but there are a
wealth of strong tunes here for those
with time to explore the backwoods of
rock's rich heritage. This is the album
that kick started and defined country
rock and 30 years later it stands as one
of the finest examples of the genre.

Rating:
Sound ★★★☆☆ Content ★★★★☆
Also recommended:
'Rock Of Ages' (Capitol) a definitive
live recording from '72 without the
glad handing and over indulgence
which marred 'The Last Waltz'.
If you like this, why not try:
**Bob Dylan, Creedence Clearwater
Revival, Neil Young.**

The Beach Boys

'PET SOUNDS'

(Capitol) 1967

Track listing: Wouldn't It Be Nice • You Still Believe In Me • That's Not Me • Don't Talk (Put Your Head On My Shoulder) • I'm Waiting For The Day • Let's Go Away For Awhile • Sloop John B • God Only Knows • I Know There's An Answer • Here Today • I Just Wasn't Made For These Times • Pet Sounds • Caroline No

Bonus tracks: Unreleased Backgrounds • Hang On To Your Ego • Trombone Dixie

It is one of the great ironies of pop that the Beach Boys' resident genius, Brian Wilson, hated surfing and was so self-conscious that he became a recording studio recluse rather than risk having sand kicked in his face.

In 1967, having captured the sound of a mythical Californian summer in a string of close-harmony sun 'n' surfing classics, Brian was determined to mature as an artist and stretch the boundaries of pop. Taking The Beatles 'Rubber Soul' album as his inspiration he spent the spring of 1967 creating one of the most perfectly realized pop records ever made with an obsessive attention to detail. The songs on 'Pet Sounds' replace the innocence and escapism of 'California Girls' and 'I Get Around' with a wistful longing for love and acceptance, each meticulously orchestrated track being conceived as a sophisticated three-minute pop symphony gilded by the group's seamless ethereal harmonies. Although it spawned two massive hit singles in 'God Only Knows' and

'Wouldn't It Be Nice' at the time the album was seen by insiders and outsiders alike as too introspective and self-indulgent, with Brian Love of the band referring to it dismissively as 'Brian's ego music'. However, in retrospect it stands as a landmark recording and as significant an album as 'Sgt Pepper'. Brian later confessed that he sensed that the angels were watching over these sessions and listening back to them now it's difficult to disagree with him. Bliss.

Rating:
Sound ★★★★☆ Content ★★★★★

The Beach Boys

'20 GOLDEN GREATS'

(Capitol) 1987

Track listing: Surfin' USA • Fun, Fun, Fun • I Get Around • Don't Worry Baby • Little Deuce Coupe • When I Grow Up (To Be A Man) • Help Me Rhonda • California Girls • Barbara Ann • Sloop John B • You're So Good To Me • God Only Knows • Wouldn't It Be Nice • Good Vibrations • Then I Kissed Her • Heroes And Villains • Darlin' • Do It Again • I Can Hear Music • Break Away

This 24-carat compilation charts the evolution of one of the greatest pop acts of the Sixties, or indeed any other era, from the sweet innocence of their sun 'n' surf singles to Brian's sun-kissed 'pocket symphonies' with their Spector-inspired 'Wall of Sound'. It begins by celebrating the myth of an endless summer of sun, surf and cruising Sunset Strip then gradually shifts into a minor key as youthful idealism becomes somewhat soured by experience and too many drugs. Every track is a poignant reminder of just how great pop can be.

As an alternative, consider the more comprehensive 2CD set 'The Best Of The Beach Boys' which digs deeper into the golden era, lifts a few choice cuts from 'Pet Sounds' and adds their finest recordings from the otherwise not-so-golden seventies. These compilations are arguably the best way to savour the Beach Boys as their early albums were padded out with obvious fillers, while the later outings were frustratingly inconsistent.

Rating:
Sound ★★★★☆ Content ★★★★★
Also recommended:
'Good Vibrations – 30 Years Of The Beach Boys' (Capitol) a 4CD box set which includes tantalizing fragments from the aborted 'Smile' sessions. And 'Pet Sounds' 4CD set (Premier/EMI) a completist's dream – the original album plus alternate mixes, unreleased backing tracks and out-takes.
If you like this, why not try:
Jan & Dean, Phil Spector's sixties productions or the various Doo Wop collections.

The Beastie Boys

'LICENSED TO ILL'

(Def Jam) 1986

Track listing: Rhymin' & Stealin' • The New Style • She's Crafty • Posse In Effect • Slow Ride • Girls • Fight For Your Right • No Sleep Till Brooklyn • Paul Revere • Hold It Now, Hit Hit • Brass Monkey • Slow And Low • Time To Get Ill

The mainstream music business was as wary of rap in the early eighties as they had been of punk in the mid-seventies, but the shrewd crew behind Def Jam were eager to exploit its potential appeal among the affluent white audience. In The Beastie Boys they found a white act with the right in-your-face attitude and street cred to take rap out of the ghettos and into the suburbs. Mike D, Ad-Rock and MCA may have been middle-class kids pretending to be attention-seeking, hyper-active high school brats, but 'License To Ill' proved that their baggy jeans, baseball caps and bragging were merely accessories. Their audacious mix of black beats and adolescent anthems was spiked with self-effacing humour and laced with a judicious sampling of hard rock riffs to ensure that it was as marketable as a Big Mac. The hardcore rappers may have sneered at their boorish 'fight for your right to party' philosophy, but they had to admire their cheek.

'Fight For Your Right' gatecrashed every bash on both sides of the pond to become the mega-selling single of '86 and the album subsequently became a surprise US number one. The party may be over for the Beasties but the goofy comic strip humour of 'She's Crafty', 'Girls' and 'No Sleep Till Brooklyn' remains as sharp as Bart Simpson's shorts.

Rating:
Sound ★★★★☆ Content ★★★★★

The Beastie Boys

'PAUL'S BOUTIQUE'

(Capitol) 1989

Track listing: To All The Girls • Shake Your Rump • Johnny Ryall • Egg Man • High Plains Drifter • The Sound of Science • 3 Minute Rule • Hey Ladies • 5 Piece Chicken Dinner • Looking Down The Barrel Of A Gun • Car Thief • What Comes Around • Shadrach • Ask For Janice • B-Boy Bouillabaisse Medley: A Year And A Day • Hello Brookly • Dropping Names • Lay It On Me • Mike On The Mic • AWOL

After an enforced three-year lay off (during which they spent more time in court than in the recording studio) it looked like the Beasties had blown it, but against all expectations they returned with an ambitious and impressive offering. In contrast to the sparse linear grooves of the first album they created a dense, almost psychedelic, collage of inner-city sounds and kitsch pop culture soundbites to give an impression of hedonist heaven in the Big Apple.

The Dust Brothers can be credited with giving the brats from Brooklyn a more sophisticated sound and insisting that there was less reliance on a riff, but any pretence towards sophistication was swiftly rebutted by track titles such as 'Lay It On Me' and 'Shake Your Rump'.

Rating:
Sound ★★★★☆ Content ★★★★☆
Also recommended:
'Check Your Head' (Capitol) on which the Beasties augmented sampled sounds with real instruments and stirred jazz, funk and punk into the mix. 'Ill Communication' (Capitol) offers more of the same.
If you like this, why not try:
Public Enemy, Grandmaster Flash, **RUN DMC**, LL Cool J.

The Beatles

'RUBBER SOUL'

(Parlophone) 1965

Track listing: Drive My Car • Norwegian Wood • You Won't See Me • Nowhere Man • Think For Yourself • The Word • Michelle • What Goes On • Girl • I'm Looking Through You • In My Life • Wait • If I Needed Someone • Run For Your Life

While The Beatles' early LPs recreated the excitement of their live set with a mixture of covers and self-penned songs, 'Rubber Soul' marked their first step toward realizing the untapped potential of pop.
Each successive album revealed new aspects of the group's multi-faceted persona. On 'Rubber Soul' we glimpse Lennon's disillusionment in the enigmatic narrative of 'Norwegian Wood', his world-weary cynicism on 'Nowhere Man' and his attempt to reconcile the realist and the romantic on the reflective 'In My Life'. In contrast, McCartney casts himself in the role of a Tin Pan Alley songsmith for 'Michelle' and a handful of other memorable tunes, while George Harrison is allowed just one shot from the wings with 'If I Needed Someone'.

Fired by a desire to outclass each other and ever eager to discover new sounds, Lennon and McCartney experimented with a diverse range of musical sounds and styles, knowing that their producer George Martin would be capable and willing to supply whatever their muse required. When they fancied strings Martin obliged with the orchestration, when they brought in exotic instruments such as the sitar for 'Norwegian Wood', Martin dutifully recorded it without question and when Lennon asked for a baroque solo on 'In My Life' it was Martin who hired the harpsichord and played the part. It was his classical training, technical expertise and encouragement which made it possible for the group to evolve from the teen beat combo of 'Please Please Me' to the maturity of 'Rubber Soul' in just three short years. The album remains a superlative example of pop craftsmanship, but more significantly it suggests that from this point on anything was possible.

Rating:
Sound ★★★★☆ Content ★★★★☆

The Beatles

'REVOLVER'

(Parlophone) 1966

Track listing: Taxman • Eleanor Rigby • I'm Only Sleeping • Love You Too • Here, There And Everywhere • Yellow Submarine • She Said, She Said • Good Day Sunshine • And Your Bird Can Sing • For No One • Dr Robert • I Want To Tell You • Got To Get You Into My Life • Tomorrow Never Knows

It is the bitter-sweet contrast between McCartney's winsome sentimentality and Lennon's caustic wit and wordplay which gave both their collaborations and individual contributions such an enduring appeal, a contrast which finds its apotheosis on 'Revolver'. It is an album that marries the pop sensibilities of 'Rubber Soul' with the first flowering of psychedelia, a synthesis that was to culminate with 'Sgt Pepper'. Harrison rants on 'Taxman' to a clipped riff that was later appropriated by The Jam, then allows himself to muse on the meaning of life in 'Love You Too' to the languorous strains of a droning sitar. McCartney goes as soft as a marshmallow on 'Here, There And Everywhere' in an effort to win over the mums and the middle-aged, then redeems himself with the string-driven 'Eleanor Rigby' before dusting off his blues to the Tamla-tinted 'Got To Get You Into My Life'. Lennon, meanwhile, struggles between lethargy and artistic ambition on 'I'm Only Sleeping', rousing himself for 'Dr Robert' and then sinking into a blissful brown study on the mantra-styled 'Tomorrow Never Knows' with its exhortation to 'turn off your mind, relax and float down stream'. From the band that had incited hordes of pre-teens to scream themselves hoarse to the tune of 'She Loves You' only three years earlier, this was more mind-blowing than dropping acid.

Rating:
Sound ★★★★★ Content ★★★★☆

The Beatles

'SGT PEPPER'S LONELY HEARTS CLUB BAND'

(Parlophone) 1967

Track listing: Sgt Pepper's Lonely Hearts Club Band • With A Little Help From My Friends • Lucy In The Sky With Diamonds • Getting Better • Fixing A Hole • She's Leaving Home • Being For The Benefit Of Mr Kite • Within You Without You • When I'm Sixty-Four • Lovely Rita • Good Morning, Good Morning • Sgt Pepper (Reprise) • A Day In Life

In the summer of '67, the so-called 'Summer of Love', 'Sgt Pepper' marked pop's rite of passage from adolescent indulgence to a state of lucid self awareness. It was the highlight in a year of significant 'happenings'. People still remember where they were and what they were doing when they first heard it, just as they recall the day Kennedy was assassinated and the day the first men landed on the moon. Although its status as the first 'concept album' doesn't stand up to scrutiny and its initial impact has inevitably declined over the decades, it remains a delirious celebration of pop as a cultural phenomenon and a consummation of The Beatles artistic ambitions.

With 'Sgt Pepper' they set the standard for multi-track pop production for decades to come, simultaneously flirting with psychedelia, but eschewing its excesses. While the acid rock outfits indulged in extensive instrumental explorations of inner space the Beatles grounded their flights of fantasy in wry Northern humour,

presenting the songs as a series of contrasting music hall 'turns' or circus acts tinted with the vibrant hues of a drug-induced dream.

Following Pepper's invitation to 'sit back and let the evening go', the curtain rises on Ringo's cuddly crooner ('With A Little Help From My Friends'), continues with John's surreal stream of consciousness ('Lucy In The Sky'), adds Paul's programme of comic and sentimental songs ('Fixing A Hole', 'She's Leaving Home'), before Lennon's carnival barker brings the first act to an end with his homage to fairground acrobat 'Mr Kite'. George provides the obligatory exotic eastern interlude ('Within You, Without You'), then more light relief from Paul ('Lovely Rita', 'When I'm Sixty-Four') leads into a jaunty reprise of Pepper's theme tune before the show closes with the majestic 'A Day In The Life', on which Lennon entreats the listener to share a 'trip' with the band. If it's a mind-expanding experience, it has less to do with the chemicals that its creators were consuming at the time and more to do with the breadth of the band's imagination and their willingness to experiment with a kaleidoscope of sounds. 'Revolver' may, in retrospect, be the stronger album, but 'Sgt Pepper' finally justified pop's claim to be taken seriously.

Digital remastering has revealed a degree of clarity and depth of detail in the recordings that was previously unheard by owners of the original vinyl version.

Rating:
Sound ★★★★★ Content ★★★★★

The Beatles

'THE WHITE ALBUM'

2 CDs (Parlophone) 1968

Track listing: Back In The USSR • Dear Prudence • Glass Onion • Ob-La-Di, Ob-La-Da • Wild Honey Pie • The Continuing Story Of Bungalow Bill • While My Guitar Gently Weeps • Happiness Is A Warm Gun • Martha My Dear • I'm So Tired • Blackbird • Piggies • Rocky Racoon • Don't Pass Me By • Why Don't We Do It In The Road? • I Will • Julia • Birthday • Yer Blues • Mother Nature's Son • Everybody's Got Something To Hide Except Me And My Monkey • Sexy Sadie • Helter Skelter • Long, Long, Long • Revolution 1 • Honey Pie • Savoy Truffle • Cry Baby Cry • Revolution 9 • Good Night

Unsure of which route to pursue after the unprecedented success of 'Sgt Pepper' John, Paul and George pulled in different directions leaving Ringo marking time back at base camp. As a consequence they produced a curate's egg of half-baked ideas with occasional moments of brilliance and the unmistakable bouquet of bad vibes.

Despite the conspicuous lack of continuity 'Back In The USSR', 'Yer Blues' and 'Helter Skelter' confirmed that they could still come together in the interests of the firm. Even by their own high standards 'Dear Prudence', 'Glass Onion', 'Cry Baby Cry', 'Revolution' and 'I'm So Tired' were vital additions to their catalogue. And, as always, McCartney kept the mums happy with 'Martha My Dear', 'Blackbird', 'Honey Pie' and the excruciatingly coy 'I Will'. In addition George contributed what is

arguably his finest song, 'While My Guitar Gently Weeps' and even Ringo did his bit with the amiable 'Don't Pass Me By'. There was even one for the kids to join in with, 'Ob-La-Di, Ob-La-Da'.

It could so easily have been a classic single LP, but no one wanted to sacrifice their songs for the common good, and so it remains a flawed masterpiece. At least it proves that the Fab Four were fallible.

Rating:
Sound ★★★★★ Content ★★★★☆

The Beatles

'ABBEY ROAD'

(Parlophone) 1969

Track listing: Come Together • Something • Maxwell's Silver Hammer • Oh! Darling • Octopus's Garden • I Want You (She's So Heavy) • Here Comes The Sun • Because • You Never Give Me Your Money • Sun King • Mean Mr Mustard • Polythene Pam • She Came In Through The Bathroom Window • Golden Slumbers • Carry That Weight • The End • Her Majesty

After the squabbling which wrecked 'The White Album' sessions The Beatles agreed to put themselves under the patriarchal eye of George Martin and trust to his commercial judgement in the event of any dispute. The result was one of the finest pop albums the group ever made with a cache of strong songs performed with the conviction that it was likely to be their last recording together. The mix of Lennon and McCartney tunes is much as before, although McCartney thankfully subdues his predisposition to mawkish sentimentality and Lennon rediscovers his passion for straight-ahead rock with lyrics which hint at a love of Lewis Caroll. With 'Something' and 'Here Comes The Sun' George delivers two of his finest songs, as if in preparation for his solo career, and Ringo gets another children's favourite in 'Octopus's Garden' to rival the perennially popular 'Yellow Submarine'. George Martin seamlessly stitched together a number of unfinished fragments for the extended medley that ends the album and with it one of the most productive musical marriages in pop.

Rating:
Sound ★★★★★ Content ★★★★☆

The Beatles

'LET IT BE'

(Parlophone) 1970

Track listing: Two Of Us • Dig A Pony • Across The Universe • I Me Mine • Dig It • Let It Be • Maggie Mae • I've Got A Feeling • One After 909 • The Long And Winding Road • For You Blue • Get Back

Recorded before 'Abbey Road', but released after the band's acrimonious split, this scrappy set offers little more than a coda to their incredible career. The initial idea was for The Beatles to get back to basics by recording live in the studio in the hope of rekindling their enthusiasm, but it only served to put their fragile friendship under greater strain. Instead of bringing them together, it documents their disintegration. Matters aren't helped by the inclusion of fragments of the

group fooling around on throwaways 'Dig It' and 'Maggie Mae', nor by Phil Spector's post-production interference which artificially sweetened 'Across The Universe' and 'The Long And Winding Road' to the distaste of George Martin and the group. But after the poignant performance of 'Let It Be' and the rooftop finale all is forgiven.

Rating:
Sound ★★★☆☆ Content ★★★☆☆

The Beatles

'1962–1966'

(Apple/EMI) 1993

Track listing: Love Me Do • Please Please Me • From Me To You • She Loves You • I Want To Hold Your Hand • All My Loving • Can't Buy Me Love • A Hard Day's Night • And I Love Her • Eight Day's A Week • I Feel Fine • Ticket To Ride • Yesterday • Help! • You've Got To Hide Your Love Away • We Can Work It Out • Day Tripper • Drive My Car • Norwegian Wood • Nowhere Man • Michelle • In My Life • Girl • Paperback Writer • Eleanor Rigby • Yellow Submarine

The Beatles

'1967–1970'

(Apple/EMI) 1993

Track listing: Strawberry Fields Forever • Penny Lane • Sgt Pepper's Lonely Hearts Club Band • With A Little Help From My Friends • Lucy In The Sky With Diamonds • A Day In The Life • All You Need Is Love • I Am The Walrus • Hello, Goodbye • The Fool On The Hill • Magical Mystery Tour • Lady Madonna • Hey Jude • Revolution • • Back In The USSR • While My Guitar Gently Weeps • Ob-La-Di, Ob-la-Di • Get Back • Don't Let Me Down • The Ballad Of John

And Yoko • Old Brown Shoe • Here Comes The Sun • Come Together • Something • Octopus's Garden • Let It Be • Across The Universe • The Long And Winding Road.

Between their first recording session in 1963 and their final impassioned performance on the roof of the Apple offices seven years later, The Beatles evolved at a pace that astonished both themselves and their fans. With each new album Lennon and McCartney confirmed their position as the most prolific and commercially successful songwriting partnership in pop by accumulating a catalogue of deceptively simple and diverse songs with a universal appeal. From their days as cute Northern mop tops to their transformation as bearded gurus of Sixties counter culture they covered all the bases, creating something for everyone, but without seeming to compromise their credibility.

The first disc of the '1962–66' set gathers the hits from the days of Beatlemania and Merseybeat when the group embodied the optimism of post-war prosperity, while the second betrays the influence of Bob Dylan and The Byrds as well as recording their increasing disillusionment and disintegration as a group.

The Beatles created the core soundtrack to the Sixties, but you won't find them on any of the many 'various artists' compilations. So, these comprehensive collections are the only way to fill those gaps in your collection. The other reason that this double CD set and its companion is an essential purchase is that many of The Beatles' classic singles (and their equally brilliant B-sides) were not included on

their official albums as it was thought that fans wouldn't buy an LP if they had already bought a track as a single.

And if that isn't enough to convince you, consider the fact that careful painstaking remastering has burnished these tracks with a sheen that makes them sound as if they were freshly minted yesterday.

Thirty years on, these tracks remain a seminal influence on just about every artist that has emerged since The Beatles broke up. Together these two compilations represent the greater part of The Beatles bequest to 20th-century popular music. Can you afford to be without them?

Rating:
Sound ★★★★★ Content ★★★★★

The Beatles

'ANTHOLOGY VOLUME I'

2 CDs (Apple/EMI) 1995

Track listing: Free As A Bird • That'll Be The Day • In Spite Of All The Danger • Hallelujah • I I Love Her So • You'll Be Mine • Cayenne • Ain't She Sweet • My Bonnie • Cry For A Shadow • Searchin' • Three Cool Cats • Sheik Of Araby • Like Dreamers Do • Hey Little Girl • Besame Mucho • Love Me Do • How Do You Do It • Please Please Me • One After 909 • Lend Me Your Comb • I'll Get You • I Saw Her Standing There • From Me To You • Money • You Really Got A Hold On Me • Roll Over Beethoven • She Loves You • Till There Was You • Twist And Shout • This Boy • I Want To Hold Your Hand • Moonlight Bay • Can't Buy Me Love • All My Loving • You Can't Do That • I Love Her • Hard Day's Night • I Wanna Be Your Man • Long Tall Sally • Boys • Shout • I'll Be Back • I'll Be Back • You Know What To Do • No Reply • Mr Moonlight • Leave My Kitten Alone • No Reply • Eight Days A Week • Hey Hey Hey • Kansas City • Eight Days A Week

An alternate history of the Fab Four as revealed through rehearsals, false starts, fragments and previously unreleased performances from the period 1963–65 plus the reconstructed, posthumous hit 'Free As A Bird'. Fascinating for hardcore fans, although not essential for the casual listener.

Listening to this ragbag of unfinished recordings and alternative versions confirms Lennon's claim that they were as vulnerable, flawed and fallible as the rest of us. But it also reveals that the group never took themselves as seriously as everybody else seemed to at the time. They may have been intuitively clever, but they were never self-consciously so and their songs remain at the pinnacle of popular music.

Rating:
Sound ★★★☆☆ Content ★★★☆☆
Also recommended:
The Beatles Anthology Vol 2 & 3, 'The Beatles At The BBC' a 2CD set of early radio sessions and interviews, 'Past Masters Vol 1 & 2' and 'No. 1', an alternative hits collection. Plus the first five albums, 'Please Please Me', 'With The Beatles', 'A Hard Day's Night', 'Beatles For Sale','Help!' and 'Yellow Submarine' (Parlophone/EMI). Although the soundtrack to this animated film is largely taken up with George Martin's orchestral passages several essential tracks ('Only A Northern Song' and 'Hey Bulldog') are unavailable elsewhere (all on EMI).
If you like this, why not try:
The Beatles' solo albums, **The Byrds, Oasis, Blur, Paul Weller**.

The Jeff Beck Group

'BECK-OLA/TRUTH'

2 albums on 1 CD (EMI) 1969

Track listing: All Shook Up • Spanish Boots • Girl From Mill Valley • Jailhouse Rock • Plynth (Water Down The Drive) • The Hangman's Knee • Rice Pudding • Shapes Of Things • Let Me Love You • Morning Dew • You Shook Me • Ol' Man River • Greensleeves • Rock My Plimsoul • Beck's Bolero • Blues De Luxe • I Ain't Superstitious

These two late sixties outings by the ex-Yardbird guitarist preserve his restlessly inventive fret work as well as some raw vocal performances by the young Rod Stewart. On both sessions Beck flirts with the heavy blues 'n' boogie style which was later refined by Jimmy Page as the blueprint for Led Zeppelin, but aside from a powerful reworking of 'You Shook Me' (later covered by Zeppelin) and a handful of other blues standards both albums suffer from a crippling inconsistency and a lack of commitment to any particular style.

On 'Truth' Beck attempts to rework such unlikely items as 'Ol' Man River' and almost carries it off thanks to Rod's emotive delivery, but even he can't rescue 'Greensleeves', a perfunctory re-recording of The Yardbirds' 'Shapes Of Things' and a leaden attempt at the traditional folk tune 'Morning Dew'. More successful is the showcase instrumental 'Beck's Bolero' (written not by Beck but by 'rival' Jimmy Page), on which he wrings every conceivable sound from his guitar via a battery of effects pedals, and a heavied-up cover of the Howling Wolf classic 'I Ain't Superstious' which was featured on the soundtrack of the Martin Scorsese movie 'Casino'.

Remastering benefits the first album with a clarity it lacked on vinyl, but careless remastering of the second creates a boomy, indistinct, bottom-heavy sound. There is noticeable distortion on 'Girl From Mill Valley', while the closing jam, 'Rice Pudding', is abruptly cut off when the album hits the maximum 71 minutes running time! Bizarre.

Rating:
Sound ★★★☆☆ Content ★★★☆☆
Also recommended:
'Blow By Blow' and 'Wired' (CBS), two mid-seventies instrumental outings which found Beck developing jazz-rock fusion.
If you like this, why not try:
Rod Stewart's early Seventies solo albums, The Faces, **The Yardbirds**, Jeff Beck's solo albums.

The Bee Gees

'VERY BEST OF...'

(Polydor) 1990

Track listing: You Win Again • How Deep Is Your Love • Night Fever • Tragedy • Massachusetts • I've Gotta Get A Message To You • You Should Be Dancing • New York Mining Disaster 1941 • Children Of The World • First Of May • Don't Forget To Remember • Saved By The Bell • Run To Me • Jive Talkin' • More Than A Woman • Stayin' Alive • Too Much Heaven • Ordinary Lives • To Love Somebody • Nights On Broadway

The Brothers Gibb began as a Beatles-like close harmony trio in the mid-Sixties with a string of mawkish pop ballads, of which 'Massachusetts' and 'I've Gotta Get A Message To You' are prime examples. But by the end of the decade they were sounding decidedly dated. In '74 R&B producer Arif Mardin saved them from cabaret circuit obscurity and gave them a second lease of life as disco divas with a leaner, funkier sound featuring Barry's trademark falsetto. At the peak of their popularity the critics derided the brothers as camp and contrived and their sound as sickly sweet as candyfloss. But while tracks such as 'More Than A Woman' and 'How Deep Is Your Love' certainly qualify as breathlessly smoochy muzak, the more upbeat 'Stayin' Alive', 'Night Fever' and 'Jive Talking' are as insidiously memorable as anything pop has to offer.

The 'Very Best Of...' contains six US number one hits from that latter era as well as the cream of their pre-disco period in pristine, digital sound.

Rating:
Sound ★★★★☆ Content ★★★☆☆
Also recommended:
'Mr Natural', 'Children Of The World', 'Main Course', 'Spirits Having Flown' (all on Polydor).
If you like this, why not try:
'Saturday Night Fever' original soundtrack and its sequel 'Stayin' Alive' (Polydor), Frankie Valli And The Four Seasons.

George Benson

'ABSOLUTE BENSON'

(Universal) 2000

Track listing: The Ghetto • El Barrio • Jazzenco • Deeper Than You Think • One On One • Hipping The Hop • Lately • Come Back Baby • Medicine Man • El Marrio

After more than a decade of taking it easy as an MOR artist George Benson bounced back into mainstream pop with this largely instrumental album of classy chill-out tunes laced with a twist of funk and an R&B chaser. Only three songs feature the man himself on the mike; the Latin flavoured 'El Barrio', a soulful interpretation of Ray Charles' 'Come Back Baby' and an invigorating cover of Donny Hathaway's club classic 'The Ghetto'. On the other tracks the legendary jazz-rock guitarist lets his guitar do the talking, and very eloquently it does too. Play loud and party!

Rating:
Sound ★★★★☆ Content ★★★☆☆
Also recommended:
'The George Benson Collection' (WEA) and 'The Best Of Benson' (Columbia).
If you like this, why not try:
Lionel Richie, Herbie Hancock, Wes Montgomery.

Chuck Berry

'HAIL! HAIL! ROCK 'N' ROLL'

(Chess) 1988

Track listing: Maybellene • Thirty Days • No Money Down • Roll Over Beethoven • Brown Eyed Handsome Man • Too Much Monkey Business • You Can't Catch Me • School Day • Rock 'n' Roll Music • Sweet Little Sixteen • Reelin' And Rockin' • Johnny B. Goode • Around And Around • Beautiful Delilah • Carol • Sweet Little Rock And Roller • Almost Grown • Little Queenie • Back In The USA • Memphis, Tennessee • Let It Rock • Bye Bye Johnny • I'm Talking About You • Come On • Nadine • No Particular Place To Go • You Never Can Tell • Promised Land.

This indispensable compilation serves a blueprint for fifties rock and roll, gathering many of the essential songs from the era when rock was raw, spontaneous and exciting. Elvis may have embodied the music's restless spirit, but Chuck was its most eloquent spokesman and one of its genuine innovators. These deceptively simple tales of teenage angst, aspiration and frustration constitute the cornerstones of the rock repertoire not only because they boast memorable hooks and a certain wry, self-mocking humour, but also because they rarely use more than three chords, a fact that would encourage successive generations of teenagers to have a go themselves. Chuck's solos were short, sweet and straight to the point, making these tracks exercises in economy and a seminal influence on generations of guitar stars and singer-songwriters.

The impressive sound quality suggests that most of these tracks have been transferred from first- or second-generation masters.

Rating:
Sound ★★★★☆ Content ★★★★★
Also recommended:
'The London Chuck Berry Sessions' and 'Rock 'N' Roll Rarities' the latter featuring 32 previously unreleased alternative takes or mixes (both on Chess/Ace).
If you like this, why not try:
Bo Diddley, **Eddie Cochran, George Thorogood,** early **Rolling Stones.**

Björk

'DEBUT'

(One Little Indian) 1993

Track listing: Human Behaviour • Crying • Venus As A Boy • There's More To Life Than This • Like Someone In Love • Big Time Sensuality • One Day • Aeroplane • Come To Me • Violently Happy • The Anchor Song • Play Dead

An astonishing showcase for the highly individual vocal gymnastics of the ex-Sugarcubes singer who may have looked like a hippie pixie but who sang with the irrepressible energy of a hyperactive tot. Fortunately for her, producer Nellee Hooper was more than up for the gig with a sampler full of techno beats and cutting edge club sounds to trick up the mix of jazz and indie-dance tracks.

Idiosyncratic, eclectic and ingenious. It has the icy beauty of a glacier and is equally treacherous if you're unprepared for its twists and turns. If you don't already own a copy, buy one. And if you do, buy another for a friend.

Rating:
Sound ★★★★☆ Content ★★★★☆

Also recommended:
'Post' and 'Homogenic' (both on One Little Indian).
If you like this, why not try:
The Sugarcubes, Altered Images, **PJ Harvey.**

Black Sabbath

'BLACK SABBATH'

(Essential/Castle) 1970

Track listing: Black Sabbath • The Wizard • Behind The Wall Of Sleep • N.I.B. • Evil Woman • Sleeping Village • Warning

Bonus track: Wicked World

Metal merchants don't come much heavier than Black Sabbath, the Birmingham band who virtually invented the brand with the malevolent title song to this, their first album. From the distant rumble of thunder and ominously tolling bells with which it opens we're drawn into a nightmare world of lurid, low-budget schlock-horror movies and comic-strip occultism whose soundtrack screams at a volume that's likely to induce severe migraine. But cacophony can be fun!

On the more lumbering tracks Ozzy Osbourne makes a virtue of his limited vocal range, which assumes an almost monotonous tone as he invokes diabolical forces from the bottomless pit of his fevered imagination, while his acolyte Tony Iommi draws from a vault of bone-crunching riffs that were to make Sabbath the undisputed princes of darkness. 'The Wizard' and 'Behind The Wall Of Sleep' are stiff and uninspired, but the title track, 'N.I.B.' (aka 'Nativity In Black') and

'The Warning' make eternal damnation sound very tempting indeed.

If, as one of their album titles suggests, the group 'sold their souls for rock and roll', the devil definitely got the best tunes and we got a great deal.

Rating:
Sound ★★★★☆ Content ★★★★☆

Black Sabbath

'PARANOID'

(Essential/Castle) 1970

Track listing: War Pigs • Paranoid • Planet Caravan • Iron Man • Electric Funeral • Hand Of Doom • Rat Salad • Fairies Wear Boots

Their satanic majesties raise yet another monolithic monument in the dark history of heavy rock with this celebration of sonic chaos and general insanity.

Beginning with the wailing wartime sirens of 'War Pigs' it signals a merciless blitz on the brain that is leavened only by the inclusion of the atmospheric 'Planet Caravan' and by the suspicion that the band had their tongues firmly in their cheeks. Anyone that can write a song called 'Fairies Wear Boots' and include the line 'Are you from my brain?' in another can't be taken too seriously. Rarely has a group walked the fine line between pretension and self-parody with such self-assurance.

This 1996 release has been remastered from the original master tapes and offers a significant improvement in sound over the original mid-eighties CD issue.

Rating:
Sound ★★★★☆ Content ★★★☆☆

Black Sabbath

'TECHNICAL ECSTASY'

(Vertigo) 1976

Track listing: Back Street Kids • You Won't Change Me • It's Alright • Gypsy • All Moving Parts (Stand Still) • Rock 'N' Roll Doctor • She's Gone • Dirty Women

Just when it seemed that Sabbath might be in danger of being declared extinct in the mid-seventies they surprised critics and fans with this multi-layered and more mature offering featuring strings, layered acoustic guitars and that spawn of Satan – synthesizers! The lush production may have angered Ozzy who split soon afterward, but it added a vital new dimension to their sound. Besides, it was done without compromising their hard rock credentials. There was still a thick wad of grinding overdriven guitars and enough fat 'n' fruity solos to appease the hardcore headbangers as well as faster tempos in an attempt to shake off the image of the band as ponderous, musical primitives.

Unfortunately careless digital remastering has dulled its edge.

Rating:
Sound ★★★☆☆ Content ★★★★☆
Also recommended:
'Master Of Reality', 'Vol 4', 'Sabbath Bloody Sabbath' and the compilation 'We Sold Our Souls For Rock And Roll' (all on Essential).

If you like this, why not try:
Metallica, **Def Leppard**, **Iron**
Maiden, **Motorhead**, Mercyful Fate
and **Ozzy**'s solo albums.

Blondie

'PLASTIC LETTERS'

(Chrysalis) 1978

Track listing: Fan Mail • Denis • Bermuda Triangle Blues • Youth Nabbed As Sniper • Contact In Red Square • (I'm Always Touched By Your) Presence Dear • I'm On E • I Didn't Have The Nerve To Say No • Love At The Pier • No Imagination • Kidnapper • Detroit 442 • Cautious Lip

Bonus tracks: Poets Problem • Denis (alternative version)

In the aftershock of punk Blondie offered spunky sixties pop sensibilities with an inoffensive New Wave attitude. Their best songs had hooks that dug deep under the skin and wouldn't let up, but their greatest attribute was peroxide pin-up Debbie Harry, an ex-Playboy bunny who came on like a Barbie doll on speed to complete an image made in marketing heaven. 'Plastic Letters', boasts a collection of radio-friendly power-pop inspired by kitsch Sixties comic strips and tacky B movies. But when they are coloured by Debbie Harry's wistful voice they take on a distinctive cartoonish quality. Two of the strongest songs, 'Fan Mail' and 'I Didn't Have The Nerve To Say No', are unapologetically retro, complete with a cheesy Farfisa organ beloved by the garage bands who were the protopunks of their day. And there's a self-confident cover of the old Randy

And The Rainbows hit 'Denis' which became Blondie's breakthrough single. The addition of the alternative mix of 'Denis' with its girly group harmony vocals and lashings of reverb shows how much more the group owed to Phil Spector than they did to punk.

Rating:
Sound ★★★☆☆ Content ★★★☆☆

Blondie

'ATOMIC – THE VERY BEST OF'

(Chrysalis) 1998

Track listing: Atomic • Heart Of Glass • Sunday Girl • Call Me • The Tide Is High • Denis • Dreaming • Rapture • Hanging On The Telephone • (I'm Always Touched By Your) Presence, Dear • Island Of Lost Souls • Picture This • Union City Blue • War Child • Rip Her To Shreds • One Way Or Another • X-Offender • I'm Gonna Love You Too • Fade Away And Radiate

Bonus tracks: Atomic '98 (Xenomania mix) • Atomic '98 (Tall Paul Remix)

Kicking off with the Giorgio Moroder produced 'Atomic' this appealing collection of Blondie's biggest hits and selected album tracks revolves around their five number one million-selling singles. By this point in their career the ragged, engaging amateurism and tongue-in-cheek humour of the earlier albums has given way to a slick, polished production propelled by a repetitive metronomic pulse and gilded with tasteful synthesizer fills. But if Blondie had sold-out their nominal New Wave credentials in order to dominate the dancefloors they did it with considerable style. Disco didn't leave us with much that was memorable, but these tracks demonstrate what could be done with driving dancefloor rhythms if you could add a catchy tune or two and a voice oozing sex appeal. But you'll still need 'Blondie' and 'Plastic Letters' to get the whole picture.

Rating:
Sound ★★★★★ Content ★★★★☆
Also recommended:
'Blondie' (Chrysalis), 'Parallel Lines'
If you like this, why not try:
The Pretenders, The Eurythmics, The Cars, Sixties girl groups.

Blur

'PARKLIFE'

(EMI) 1994

Track listing: Girls And Boys • Tracy Jacks • End Of A Century • Park Life • Bank Holiday • Bad Head • The Debt Collector • Far Out • To The End • London Loves • Trouble In The Message Centre • Clover Over Dover • Magic America • Jubilee • This Is A Low • Lot 105

Blur may have lost out in the sales stakes to Oasis since the mad summer of 1994 when the comparative merits of the two bands seemed to obsess the entire nation, but of the two Blur have proven the more consistently interesting. Otherwise the only thing the two bands shared, apart from their public loathing of each other, was their preoccupation with the sixties, with the former attempting to re-write the entire Beatles back catalogue while Blur revived the archetypal English

whimsy and art school artifice of The Kinks.

However, Blur's admiration of The Kinks isn't as blatant nor as slavishly obvious as their rivals' fixation with the Fab Four. The ghost of Ray Davies can be heard on the character sketch 'Tracy Jacks' and there are echoes of the similarly styled Small Faces in the title track on which Phil Daniels lends his broadest 'sarf London' accent. Damon Albarn even manages a fair stab at Syd Barrett on 'Far Out', but elsewhere the influences are less apparent. From the fairground-styled embellishments and novelty instrumentation to the flirtations with punk and psych-pop, 'Parklife' constantly surprises with its diversity of material and infectious good humour. The mock-cockney jollity may have been a pose, but the songs are strong enough to outlast the hype.

Rating:
Sound ★★★★☆ Content ★★★★☆

Blur

'BEST OF'

(Food/Parlophone) 2000

Track listing: Beetlebum • Song 2 • There's No Other Way • The Universal • Coffee And TV • Parklife • End Of A Century • No Distance Left To Run • Tender • Girls And Boys • Charmless Man • She's So High • Country House • To The End • On Your Own • This Is A Low • For Tomorrow

Blur's ascent from the anonymity of the indie-dance circuit at the beginning of the nineties to national celebrity was long and tortuous. Few fans will have stayed the course, so this collection is to be welcomed as a chance to catch up on those early singles. Beginning with the 'baggy' Mancunian anthems 'She's So High' and 'There's No Other Way' through Britpop biggies 'Country House', 'Girls And Boys' and 'Charmless Man' to the attempts to reinvent themselves on the more recent releases. It also serves to showcase the range and depth of Damon Alburn's talent as a wordsmith and wit.

Rating:
Sound ★★★★☆ Content ★★★★☆
Also recommended:
'The Great Escape' (Parlophone).
If you like this, why not try:
The Kinks, The Small Faces, **The Smiths**.

Booker T And The MGs

'THE BEST OF'

(Atlantic) 1984

Track listing: Green Onions • Mo' Onions • Jelly Bread • Tic-Tac-Toe • Soul Dressing • Terrible Thing • Can't Be Still • Boot-Leg • Summertime • Be My Lady • Red Beans And Rice • My Sweet Potato • Booker-Loo • Hip Hug-Her • Slim Jenkins Place • Groovin'

Booker T And The MGs (aka The Memphis Group) oiled the gears and stoked the furnace at the soul factory they called Stax. This much-respected interracial group led by organist Booker T Jones and guitarist Steve Cropper served as the label's house band during the sixties, providing a lean and seamless rhythm track for a succession of singers including Wilson Pickett and Otis Redding. The pick of their 'solo' outings are collected on this superbly remastered compilation which showcases Cropper's incisive lead licks and Booker's ability to make the organ swing. Unfortunately, neither 'Time Is Tight' nor 'Hang Em High', their other big hits, are included on this collection, but there are enough funky 12-bar variations to keep the dancefloors crowded till the last note fades.

Rating:
Sound ★★★★☆ Content ★★★★☆
Also recommended:
'Best Of' (Stax), another compilation with the same name, but this one includes the 'missing' hits.
If you like this, why not try:
Wilson Pickett, **Otis Redding** and 'Quadrophenia' (the original soundtrack).

David Bowie

'THE MAN WHO SOLD THE WORLD'

(EMI) 1971

Track listing: The Width Of A Circle • All The Madmen • Black Country Rock • After All • Running Gun Blues • Saviour Machine • She Shook Me Cold • The Man Who Sold The World • The Supermen

Bonus tracks: Lightning Frightening • Holy Holy • Moonage Daydream • Hang On To Yourself

'MWSTW' is frequently overlooked as being inferior to Bowie's later albums and even to its predecessor 'Hunky Dory'. But while it's true that 'Black

33

Country Rock', 'Running Gun Blues', 'Saviour Machine' and 'She Shook Me Cold' haven't aged well, it's a mistake to hear the album as Bowie in 'metal machine music' mode, or even as the artist in transition. The opener is dark theatre at its most unsettling with its protagonist searching the blackest recesses of his soul for fundamental answers and finding only his own uncertainty. 'All The Madmen' takes us into the soul-less corridors of the asylum to which Bowie feared he might one day be confined after having witnessed his mother and his brother descend into madness, while 'After All' conjures up a carnival of freaks and the title track describes a man haunted by his alter ego. The addition of the four bonus tracks (one previously unreleased, two demos and a rare B-side) renders the original issues obsolete.

Rating:
Sound ★★★★☆ Content ★★★☆☆

David Bowie

'HUNKY DORY'

(EMI) 1971

Track listing: Changes • Oh You Pretty Things • Eight Line Poem • Life On Mars? • Kooks • Quicksand • Fill Your Heart • Andy Warhol • Song For Bob Dylan • Queen Bitch • The Bewlay Brothers

Before Bowie assumed the role that made him famous, that of the self-destructive hedonistic rock god Ziggy Stardust, he experimented with a variety of personas. 'Hunky Dory' finds him in the guise of an early

seventies singer-songwriter paying his dues to Dylan, Andy Warhol, Jacques Brel and Lou Reed and flirting with the amoral philosophy of occultist Aleister Crowley. The SF element is minimal, but just enough to imbue his most potentially popular songs ('Oh You Pretty Things' and 'Life On Mars?') with a distinctive quality that hints at what is to come. 'Hunky Dory' speaks of a man in search of himself and finding only aspects, a suspicion that is confirmed by the modest nature of the production which relies on layered acoustic guitars and piano. It's suggestive of a dress rehearsal with Ziggy waiting impatiently in the wings for his understudy to vacate the stage. Though Bowie addicts would doubtless disagree.

Rating:
Sound ★★★☆☆ Content ★★★☆☆

David Bowie

'THE RISE AND FALL OF ZIGGY STARDUST AND THE SPIDERS FROM MARS'

(EMI) 1972

Track listing: Five Years • Soul Love • Moonage Daydream • Starman • It Ain't Easy • Lady Stardust • Star • Hang Onto Yourself • Ziggy Stardust • Suffragette City • Rock 'n' Roll Suicide.

Bonus tracks: John I'm Only Dancing • Velvet Goldmine • Sweet Head • Ziggy Stardust (demo) • Lady Stardust (demo)

Bowie brought an innate sense of theatre, a splash of lurid colour and high camp cabaret to the gloom of post-Beatles Britain with this examination of a preening, pouting, androgynous futuristic teen idol. But Bowie didn't just sing the role, he lived it, made up and kitted out like a space-age drag queen in figure-hugging lurex and precariously perched upon skyscraper-high platform boots.

In stark contrast to the brooding introspection of 'The Man Who Sold The World' and the cautious optimism which characterized 'Hunky Dory', Ziggy exudes sensuous self-confidence and a brash sense of style. Ziggy is seen as self-absorbed in 'Star', seduced by his own image in 'Moonage Daydream' and worshipped by adoring fans as the 'leper messiah' on the hit single 'Starman'. He savours fame and its excesses on 'Lady Stardust' and 'Hang On To Yourself', then becomes fatally ensnared in a myth of his own making on the title track before finally committing 'rock and roll suicide' in squalid isolation after his band and fans have deserted him. And all to the strains of 11 of the most deliciously decadent gender bender anthems ever committed to tape.

This particular edition of the album is beefed up by the addition of five extra tracks, two demos, a couple of superior B-sides and the out-take 'Sweet Head' which was unwisely whipped off the album at the last minute.

Rating:
Sound ★★★★★ Content ★★★★★

David Bowie

'ALADDIN SANE'

(EMI) 1973

Track listing: Watch That Man • Aladdin Sane • Drive-In Saturday • Panic In Detroit • Cracked Actor • Time • The Prettiest Star • Let's Spend The Night Together • Jean Genie • Lady Grinning Soul

If Ziggy was the flamboyant face of the glam rock era then Bowie's next incarnation could be seen as the ultimate icon of the fragmented and self-analytical Seventies. Whilst 'Ziggy' was pure pantomime, 'Aladdin Sane' introduced a considerably more tortured creation fleshed out by the artist's personal experience of having been the main attraction in rock's own freak show, further blurring the distinction between the creator and his creation.

As if to mirror the lightning flash across the face on the cover the music is an edgy, schizophrenic mix of rock and Berlin-styled cabaret. The amphetamine rush of 'Watch That Man' and 'Panic In Detroit' contrasting with the decadent neuroticism of the more theatrical numbers, 'Time', 'Lady Grinning Soul' and the title track. While Bowie stalks the stage in the guise of the 'cracked actor' Mick Ronson and the band recreate the cocksure swagger of the Stones for the space age, allowing guest Mike Garson to fracture piano lines with the gleeful abandon beloved by Thelonious Monk. 'Who will love Aladdin Sane?' sighs Bowie with a wearied smile. We will.

Rating:
Sound ★★★★☆ Content ★★★★☆

David Bowie

'DIAMOND DOGS'

(EMI) 1974

Track listing: Future Legend • Diamond Dogs • Sweet Thing • Candidate • Sweet Thing (Reprise) • Rebel Rebel • Rock 'n' Roll With Me • We Are The Dead • 1984 • Big Brother • Chant Of The Ever Circling Skeletal Family

Bonus tracks: Dodo • Candidate (demo)

'And in the death... red mutant eyes gazed down on Hunger City.' Bowie sets the scene for a post-apocalyptic vision with a monologue in which the survivors are stalked by scavengers through an Orwellian landscape and where drugs and rock music offer only a temporary respite from reality.

'Diamond Dogs' marks Bowie's last legitimate rock album before years of restless experimentation. From the opening bars to the decaying grandeur of '1984' and its companion piece 'Big Brother' this is rock theatre as grand guignol, the only concession to convention being the Stones-styled 'Rebel Rebel' and the title track.

'This isn't rock and roll, this is genocide,' he sings and by God, you'll believe it.

Again, he evidently had a surfeit on superior songs as one of the strongest tracks, 'Candidate' is consigned to the bonus bin.

Rating:
Sound ★★★★★ Content ★★★★★

David Bowie

'LOW'

(RCA) 1977

Track listing: Speed Of Life • Breaking Glass • What In The World • Sound And Vision • Always Crashing In The Same Car • Be My Wife • A New Career In A New Town • Warszawa • Art Decade • Weeping Wall • Subterraneans

After a brief flirtation with white soul music on 'Young Americans' and 'Station To Station' Bowie was mentally and physically exhausted. He complained of being treated like the freak attraction in the rock circus. And so, in an effort to find himself he cast off the mantle of the 'Thin White Duke', his 'plastic soul' persona, and retired to Berlin to begin experimenting with electronics in the company of ex-Roxy Music keyboard wizard Brian Eno and King Crimson guitarist Robert Fripp. 'Low' was the first of a trio of bleak, atmospheric albums recorded in the shadow of the Berlin Wall and on which he kept the vocals to a minimum in order to reflect his increasing alienation and uncertain sense of identity. There is a strange beauty in the surreal ambient soundscapes and a palpable sense of desperation in the sparser songs which was to have a significant and lasting influence on a generation of eighties electronic groups from Joy Division to Depeche Mode.

Rating:
Sound ★★★★☆ Content ★★★☆☆
Also recommended:
'Heroes', the second instalment in

Bowie's Berlin trilogy, 'David Live', 'Scary Monsters' and 'The Singles Collection' (EMI).
If you like this, why not try:
Philip Glass, **Brian Eno**, **Suede**.

Billy Bragg

'VICTIM OF GEOGRAPHY'

(Cooking Vinyl) 1993

Track listing: Greetings To The New Brunette • Train Time • Marriage • Ideology • Levi Stubbs' Tears • Honey, I'm A Big Boy Now • There Is Power In A Union • Help Save The Youth Of America • Wishing The Days Away • Passion • Warmest Room • Home Front • She's Got A New Spell • Must I Paint You A Picture • Tender Comrade • Price I Pay • Little Time Bomb • Rotting On Remand • Valentine's Day Is Over • Life With The Lions • Only One • Short Answer • Waiting For The Great Leap Forwards

A reissue of two essential albums on one CD from Barking's answer to Bruce Springsteen, though it's arguable that Billy exhibits more integrity on a song such as 'There Is Power In A Union' than The Boss has done in his entire back catalogue (with the honourable exception of 'Tom Joad'). A more fitting comparison might be with Woody Guthrie whose unpublished poetry Billy has recently set to music with the blessing of the great man's daughter. Both men find more humanity in the struggles endured by ordinary people than in any fictional figures and they do so without indulging in heart-tugging contrivances, cliches or sickly sweet sentiment.

'Victim Of Geography' repackages two of Billy's most accomplished albums, the politically astute 'Talking With The Taxman About Poetry' and the more personal, introspective 'Worker's Playtime'. The former features Johnny Marr on the opening track and one of Billy's most poignant narrative tales, 'Levi Stubbs' Tears', while the latter finds one of our most erudite and honest artists reflecting on such diverse subjects as self-destructive relationships and the brutality of prison life. Both albums are blessed with his unvarnished vocal and a sincerity which puts the majority of 'pop' performers to shame.

Rating:
Sound ★★★★☆ Content ★★★★★
Also recommended:
Also recommended: 'William Bloke', 'Don't Try This At Home' (featuring Peter Buck and Michael Stipe of REM) and 'Mermaid Avenue', his reworking of Guthrie's songs with the band Wilco (all on Cooking Vinyl).
If you like this, why not try:
Paul Weller.

James Brown

'SEX MACHINE – THE VERY BEST OF...'

(Polydor) 1991

Track listing: Please Please Please • Think • Night Train • Out Of Sight • Papa's Got A Brand New Bag • I Got You (I Feel Good) • It's A Man's Man's Man's World • Cold Sweat • Say It Loud, I'm Black And I'm Proud • Get Up (I Feel Like Being A) Sex Machine • Hey America • Make It Funky • I'm A Greedy Man • Get On The Good Foot • Get Up Offa That Thing • It's Too Funky In Here • Living In America • I'm Real • Hot Pants • Soul Power (Live)

After leaving a southern gospel quartet in the mid-fifties the gravel-voiced godfather of funk re-baptized himself 'Soul Brother Number One' and cast his band as ardent worshipers whose role was to whip their leader and the audience into an ecstasy of excitement that was unmistakably secular. The early hits ('Please Please Please' and 'Night Train') betray a gospel influence as Brown runs the gamut of emotions from impassioned whisper to a hoarse holler that can still make the hairs on the nape of your neck stand up and beg. But the late Sixties club classics such as 'Sex Machine', 'Say It Loud, I'm Black And I'm Proud' and 'Cold Sweat' are unashamedly fat and funky. The rhythm section locks into a push 'n' pull groove and the melody takes a back seat while J.B. and the horns trade lines punctuated by Jimmy Nolen's trademark 'chicken scratch' guitar. As the brass section turns on the heat Brown incites his audience to strut their stuff and shake parts of their anatomy that they didn't even know had rhythm! The Godfather of Soul was clearly no longer preaching from the 'Good Book'.

If you want to know where Prince, Madonna, Public Enemy and a whole generation of hip hop acts found their inspiration look no further. Get down and get funky!

Rating:
Sound ★★★★☆ Content ★★★★★
Also recommended:
'Star Time', a 4CD box set (Polydor).
If you like this, why not try:
Prince, Parliament, **Funkadelic**.

Jeff Buckley

'GRACE'

(Columbia) 1994

Track listing: Mojo Pin • Grace • Last Goodbye • Lilac Wine • So Real • Hallelujah • Lover • You Should've Come Over • Corpus Christi Carol • Eternal Life • Dream Brother

Jeff Buckley inherited his late father's appetite for risky musical gambles, his extraordinary vocal agility and range and also sadly, his predisposition for self-destruction. Both father and son died just either side of thirty, with Jeff having barely hinted at the promise to come on this, his debut album. But while Tim Buckley's music was firmly rooted in the Greenwich Village folk tradition his son's influences were infinitely more diverse. 'Grace' finds him attempting to exorcise his demons through the confessional and blending a precious amalgam of seemingly disparate styles often within the structure of a single song. 'Mojo Pin' sees him effecting a slow-burn on a track that appears to have been distilled from folk, blues and indie-guitar pop; his multi-octave voice dropping from a heavenly high to an earthy snarl in a single line. But he was equally adept at sustaining a meditative mood as demonstrated on the wistful 'Corpus Christi Carol' by Benjamin Britten and the cover of Leonard Cohen's 'Hallelujah', on both of which he reveals the fragile, translucent tone of an incorruptible choirboy. It's an album which affirms that Jeff was born with talent to spare, but with precious little time to develop it.

Rating:
Sound ★★★★☆ Content ★★★★☆
Also recommended:
'My Sweetheart The Drunk'
(Columbia).
If you like this, why not try:
Tim Buckley, **Nick Drake, Leonard Cohen**.

Kate Bush

'THE KICK INSIDE'

(EMI) 1978

Track listing: Moving • The Saxophone Song • Strange Phenomena • Kite • Man With The Child In His Eyes • Wuthering Heights • James And The Cold Gun • Feel It • Oh To Be In Love • L'Amour Looks Something Like You • Them Heavy People • Room For The Life • Kick Inside

With her pre-Raphaelite looks, winsome voice and a portfolio of highly imaginative songs Kate Bush charmed the critics, mesmerized most of the male population and proved that female artists didn't have to sell themselves short to succeed. Her debut album and strikingly original single 'Wuthering Heights' made an instant impact in an era dominated by derivative disco acts and those chasing the dog-end of punk. Most of these tracks were drawn from a stockpile of songs that she had written in her teens and together proved the perfect showcase for her precocious talent. The hits 'Wuthering Heights' and 'The Man With The Child In His Eyes' remain obvious highlights, but even the earliest songs betray a highly developed imagination, a rare erudition and an innate sense of theatre.

Rating:
Sound ★★★★☆ Content ★★★☆☆

Kate Bush

'HOUNDS OF LOVE'

(EMI) 1985

Track listing: Running Up That Hill • Hounds Of Love • The Big Sky • Mother Stands For Comfort • Cloudbusting • The Ninth Wave: And Dream Of Sheep • Under Ice • Waking The Witch • Watching You Without Me • Jig Of Love • Hello Earth • The Morning Fog.

Bonus Tracks: The Big Sky • Running Up That Hill • Be Kind To My Mistakes • Under The Ivy • Burning Bridge • My Lagan Love

'Hounds Of Love' marked a belated return to form for Kate after the indulgent and over-produced album 'The Dreaming'. Generally regarded as her masterwork, 'Hounds Of Love' sees her expanding both her musical vocabulary and sound palette thanks largely to the introduction of the Fairlight synthesizer which she programs to perform like an orchestra-in-a-box. It features prominently on 'Running Up That Hill' (which became her biggest hit since 'Wuthering Heights' and was the single which finally introduced her in America), providing a wash of soft-focus sound through which her vocal soars and smoulders. And there is heavy reliance too on computerized Linn drums, which provide a pattern to propel the tracks along, but there are enough ethnic instruments and real strings to save the songs from sinking into a morass of artificial instrumentation.

Throughout Kate uses technology and studio trickery subtly and sparingly as if it was another instrument, most effectively on the song cycle 'The Ninth Wave', which depicts the last moments in the life of a drowning woman. Altogether this proves to be her strongest collection of songs with the second single 'Cloudbusting' being another obvious highlight. 'Hounds' is clearly the work of a maturing talent, a multi-layered album that rewards repeated listening.

Rating:
Sound ★★★★☆ Content ★★★★★

Kate Bush

'THE SENSUAL WORLD'

(EMI) 1989

Track listing: The Sensual World • Love And Anger • The Fog • Reaching Out • Heads We're Dancing • Deeper Understanding • Between A Man And A Woman • Never Be Mine • Rocket's Tail • This Woman's Work • Walk Straight Down The Middle

A densely textured album 'The Sensual World' marks the full flowering of Kate's talent, but it is also a 'difficult' album to love unconditionally. The sheer scale of its ambition and impenetrable subject matter is a lot to take in at one sitting. Aside for the title track the songs are less accessible than previous outings, but if its riches are not immediately apparent they are gradually revealed on subsequent plays.

The instrumental mix is much as before, but various celebrity guests provide much needed tonal colour. Dave Gilmour of Pink Floyd contributes a scorching guitar solo on 'Rocket Trail', piper Davey Spillane

adds a traditional Irish tone to the title track, while Nigel Kennedy tempers the synthesizer strings with a yearning violin solo and the Trio Bulgarka bring an earthy spirituality to several tracks, although they are conspicuously misplaced on 'Deeper Understanding', Kate's love song to her new computer!

Rating:
Sound ★★★★☆ Content ★★★☆☆

Kate Bush

'THE WHOLE STORY'

(EMI) 1989

Track listing: Wuthering Heights (new vocal version) • Cloudbusting • Man With The Child In His Eyes • Breathing • Wow • Hounds Of Love • Running Up That Hill • Army Dreamers • Sat In Your Lap • Experiment IV • Dreaming • Babooshka • Big Sky

Opening with an inferior re-recording of the mock-Gothic 'Wuthering Heights' this slender hits package charts Kate's development as one of the most eloquent and eclectic artists of the eighties. Although she toned down the high-strung vocal histrionics and theatrical artifice of the earlier songs it's clear that her talent for turning a memorable tune rarely deserted her. But what made these recordings unique was her enhancement of those melodies with a fey, alluring romanticism and an often fanciful theme that would have appeared twee and contrived in the hands of a lesser talent.

Although this is a useful summary of Kate's career as a singles artist, it only scratches the surface.

Rating:
Sound ★★★★☆ Content ★★★★★
Also recommended:
'Lionheart', 'Never Forever', 'The Dreaming' (all on EMI).
If you like this, why not try:
Tori Amos, Peter Gabriel, Joan Osborne, Dido.

Buzzcocks

'SINGLES GOING STEADY'

(EMI) 1990

Track listing: Orgasm Addict • What Do I Get • I Don't Mind • Love You More • Ever Fallen In Love (With Someone You Shouldn't Have Fallen In Love With) • Promises • Everybody's Happy Nowadays • Harmony In My Head • Whatever Happened To • Oh Shit • Autonomy • Noise Annoys • Just Lust • Lipstick • Why Can't I Touch It • Something's Gone Wrong Again

Manchester's answer to The Sex Pistols had no interest in inciting anarchy in the UK, nor did they profess an interest in politics as did The Clash. Frontman Pete Shelley was more preoccupied with adolescent angst than anarchy and besides, his Woolworth's guitar wouldn't have stood a battering at the barricades. Instead, the Buzzcocks merely bitched about being bored teenagers whose pent-up energy and emotions were more likely to lead to an unsightly rash than a riot. And they did so with an impulsive urgency and sense of irony that ensured that their compact adrenaline anthems were seen as significant as the sloganeering of their more seditious southern counterparts. This essential compilation collects both sides of their first eight singles, which

appear to be powered by a cocktail of rampant hormones and raw energy.

Rating:
Sound ★★★★☆ Content ★★★★☆
Also recommended:
Their first album 'Another Music In A Different Kitchen' and the 3CD set 'Product' (Premier/EMI).
If you like this, why not try:
The Sex Pistols, Magazine, **The Only Ones**.

The Byrds

'THE VERY BEST OF...'

(Columbia/Sony) 1997

Track listing: Mr Tambourine Man • All I Really Want To Do • Chimes Of Freedom • I'll Feel A Whole Lot Better • Turn Turn Turn • Times They Are A'Changing • World Turns All Around Her • It Won't Be Wrong • He Was A Friend Of Mine • Eight Miles High • 5D • Mr Spaceman • So You Want To Be A Rock And Roll Star • My Back Pages • Renaissance Fair • Goin' Back • Wasn't Born To Follow • Dolphin's Smile • You Ain't Going Nowhere • One Hundred Years From Now • You're Still On My Mind • Hickory Wind • Ballad Of Easy Rider • Jesus Is Just Alright • It's All Over Now Baby Blue • Lay Lady Lay • Chesnut Mare

The Byrds named themselves in homage to The Beatles whose vocal harmonies they imitated as closely as their Californian accents would allow, but their sound and choice of material initially owed more to Bob Dylan. This synthesis of styles would emerge as the first rumblings of folk-rock and would in turn inspire The Beatles to feature The Byrds' trademark twangy guitar sound on 'Rubber Soul' and would also encourage Dylan to forsake folk for an electric band. But although The Byrds benefited from this creative cross-fertilisation, and enjoyed considerable commercial success with a number of amplified Dylan covers (all of which are included on this definitive history), it wasn't until they added eastern influences on the acid rock anthem 'Eight Miles High' that they really took flight. The psychedelic era was arguably their most productive period, but their experiments were inevitably prone to self-indulgence and excess. When the hash haze cleared the group returned to the simplicity of their country roots and it is with these timeless images of Americana that this generously filled disc concludes.

Rating:
Sound ★★★★☆ Content ★★★★★
Also recommended:
'The Notorious Byrd Brothers' (Columbia).
If you like this, why not try:
Crosby, Stills, Nash and Young, **Neil Young, REM.**

Cabaret Voltaire

'EIGHT CREPUSCULE TRACKS'

(Crepuscule) 1988

Track listing: Slugging For Jesus Pts 1 & 2 • Fools Game • Slugging For Jesus Pt 3 • Yashar • Your Agent Man • Gut Level • Invocation • Shaft

A disturbing collage of electronic instrumentation, tape loops and distorted verbal soundbites from a trio who anticipated sampling by several years and were an incalculable influence on techno and their more commercially successful dance-orientated contemporaries. Dadaesque surrealism meets Bowie and Eno in an East European industrial soundscape. Yes, it's that bleak, although the Ofra Haza sample on 'Yashar' gave them an indie dancefloor hit.

Rating:
Sound ★★★☆☆ Content ★★★☆☆
Also recommended:
'Groovy, Laid Back And Nasty' and 'Code' redefine the meaning of art-house (both on Parlophone).
If you like this, why not try:
Can, **Kraftwerk, Joy Division, New Order.**

Captain Beefheart

'SAFE AS MILK'

(Castle/BMG) 1967

Track listing: Sure Nuff 'N' Yes I Do • Zig Zag Wanderer • Call On Me • Dropout Boogie • I'm Glad • Electricity • Yellow Brick Road • Abba Zaba • Plastic Factory • Where There's A Woman • Grown So Ugly • Autumn's Child

Bonus tracks: Safe As Milk • On Tomorrow • Big Black Baby Shoes • Flower Pot • Dirty Blue Gene • Trust Us • Korn Ring Finger

Captain Beefheart seems to exist in a parallel universe where music is rarely intentionally melodic and where lyrics are assembled to sound as impenetrable and meaningless as possible. But just before Beefheart took his leave of the real world he made one of the most extraordinary albums in the history of rock. His unique brand of boogaloo borrows heavily from R&B, but adds a generous measure of psychedelic psychosis which seems to bring out both the genius and the beast in the one-time painter and child prodigy. A young Ry Cooder on guitar helps ground the Captain's more bizarre lyrical diversions and keeps the music more or less in key. Later efforts would unleash the beast and give it its head entirely, but here Beefheart bays at the moon like Howling Wolf.

With a host of previously unreleased bonus tracks and the benefit of remastering, this revised version of the legendary debut album from the eccentric Captain and his crew is an essential purchase, even if you already own the original issue.

Rating:
Sound ★★★★☆ Content ★★★★★

Captain Beefheart

'TROUT MASK REPLICA'

(Warners) 1969

Track listing: Hair Pie Bake 2 • Pena • Well • When Big Joan Sets Up • Fallin' Ditch • Sugar 'N' Spikes • Ant Man Bee • Orange Claw Hammer • Wildlife • She's Too Much For My Mirror • Hobo Chang Ba • Blimp (Mousetrapreplica) • Steal Softly Through Snow • Old Fart At Play • Veteran's Day Poppy

While the rest of California was basking in the dying rays of the Summer of Love, Captain Beefheart and his old buddy Frank Zappa retired to a grim, psycho-styled house on the coast to record this avant-garde free-jazz freakout in which they subject the blues to some serious electric shock therapy. Their hack-and-slash method of music

therapy exerts much the same mixture of fear and fascination as Hitchcock's schlock-horror movie, but in place of Norman Bates it's Zappa and Beefheart who perform a post-mortem on the remains of their songs until only the grisly innards are left. This is the soundtrack to a very disturbing movie indeed. Its similarity to a movie soundtrack is further emphasized by the addition of snippets of abstract dialogue between the tracks giving the impression that the recording studio has become a substitute for the asylum. The line between genius and madness has never been so brilliantly blurred. Audition 'Ant Man Bee' to get a taste of what's on offer, but give the other customers in the store fair warning!

Rating:
Sound ★★★★☆ Content ★★★★★
Also recommended:
'Doc At The Radar Station' (Virgin/EMI) 1980 and 'Spotlight Kid'/'Clear Spot' (Warners) 2 albums on 2CD set.
If you like this, why not try:
Howling Wolf, The Fall, Sonic Youth, Public Image Ltd.

Caravan

'IN THE LAND OF GREY AND PINK'

(Deram/Polygram) 1971

Track listing: Golf Girl • Winter Wine • Love To Love You • In The Land Of Grey And Pink • Nine Feet Underground: Nigel Blows A Tune • Love's A Friend • Make It 76 • Dance Of The Seven Paper Hankies – Hold Grandad By The Nose • Honest I Did – Disassociation • 100% Proof

In the autumn of 1970 this Canterbury quartet, led by cousins Richard and David Sinclair, sojourned a while in the pastel-tinted land of the title where they shared magic mushrooms with the vertically challenged inhabitants. They returned from their reverie with this whimsical collection of soft-focused psychedelia which invites comparison with early Pink Floyd, although its irregular time signatures owes more to jazz and its unusual instrumentation to folk-rock. Flute, tenor sax and piccolo complement the languid vocals to evoke a child-like realm somewhere on the border between Tolkien's Middle Earth and Alice's Wonderland.

'Winter Wine' and 'Love To Love You' are inconsequential souvenirs of an era too often spaced-out to focus on the real world, while the side-long suite 'Nine Feet Underground' suggests that they sampled rather too much of the pernicious puckweed than was good for them. But both 'Golf Girl' and the quaintly charming title track have enough effervescent appeal to earn a place on the fun shelf.

Rating:
Sound ★★★★☆ Content ★★★★☆
Also recommended:
'For Girls Who Grow Plump In The Night' (Deram).
If you like this, why not try:
Soft Machine, early **Pink Floyd**, Syd Barrett.

The Cardigans

'GRAN TURISMO'

(Stockholm Records) 1998

Track listing: Paralyzed • Erase — Rewind • Explode • Starter • Hanging Around • Higher • Marvel Hill • My Favourite Game • Do You Believe • Junk Of The Hearts • NIL

Pop is a notoriously difficult genre to define and the same can be said for its more creative exponents, as few stay strictly within the terms of their remit. The Cardigans are typical of the type of band whose songs are stamped from the classic mould, but who are distinguished from their predecessors by selective sampling and assimilation of the sounds of their time. Although of Swedish origin their musical language is post-Britpop, guitar-based, but fed through more auxiliary processors than even Brian Eno could get to grips with until the backing sounds like its coming at you down a dodgy phone line. Only Nina Pearson's winsome vocal remains firmly in focus, as precious and beguiling as that of Debbie Harry or Shirley Manson of Garbage with whom The Cardigans can be favourably compared. Contains the hits 'Erase-Rewind' and 'My Favourite Game'.

Rating:
Sound ★★★★☆ Content ★★★★☆
Also recommended:
'Life' and 'First Band On The Moon' (Stockholm/Polygram).
If you like this, why not try:
Garbage, **Smashing Pumpkins**, Echobelly.

Mariah Carey

'MARIAH CAREY'

(Columbia) 1990

Track listing: Vision Of Love • There's Got To Be A Way • I Don't Wanna Cry • Someday • Vanishing • All In Your Mind • Alone In Love • You Need Me • Sent From Up Above • Prisoner • Love Takes Time

Mariah Carey may be the best-selling artist of the nineties, but anyone over the age of ten could be forgiven for thinking that she gives pop music a bad name. She has been described as 'yelling her own bad songs accurately', of 'pointless pyrotechnics', 'never using one note when ten will do' and of making a 'brutal assault' upon songs which a more mature and sensitive artist would know requires a certain degree of restraint. In short, she doesn't seem to know the meaning of the word subtlety. Or one could be kind and say that having a five-octave vocal range she naturally tires of singing puerile playground ballads straight and needs to exercise her vocal chords until stronger material comes along. Her work on the multi-platinum 'Music Box' recorded a couple of years later suggests that the latter conclusion might be nearer the truth. Sample 'You Need Me' to discover which side of the argument you agree with.

Rating:
Sound ★★★☆☆ Content ★★★☆☆
Also recommended:
'Emotions', 'Music Box' and 'Daydream' (Columbia).
If you like this, why not try:
Whitney Houston, Celine Dion.

The Cars

'THE CARS'

(Elektra) 1978

Track listing: Good Times Roll • My Best Friend's Girl • Just What I Needed • I'm In Touch With Your World • Don't Cha Stop • You're All I've Got Tonight • Bye Bye Love • Moving In Stereo • All Mixed Up

The Cars made little impact in Europe where their so-called 'New Wave' image was seen as artificial and contrived. But in the States the Boston-based group became a lucrative and leading brand name after having been shrewdly marketed with a series of limited edition picture disc singles. Their first big hit, 'My Best Friend's Girl', is included on this strong, self-titled debut along with half a dozen similarly styled college radio-friendly pop songs penned by their anorexic-looking frontman, Ric Ocasek. All are propelled by chugging guitars, subtle synth lines and beefy drums (courtesy of Roy Thomas Baker who also produced Queen) with impeccable harmony vocals supplied as an optional accessory.

Rating:
Sound ★★★★★ Content ★★★★☆

The Cars

'CANDY-O'

(Elektra) 1979

Track listing: Let's Go • Since I Held You • It's All I Can Do • Double Life • Shoo Be Doo • Candy-O • Night Spots • You Can't Hold On Too Long • Lust For Kicks • Got A Lot On My Head • Dangerous Type

When writing about The Cars it's tempting to run out a lot of automobile metaphors; comparing the group to a mass-produced model that rolled off the production line polished to perfection, but which soon lost its sheen. It's true that after a promising start they hit a few bumps and limped along in second gear, but 'Candy-O', their second album, injected enough refined four-star fuel into the power pop formula to leave the rest of the American AOR acts standing at the starting line.

'Let's Go', 'Double Life', 'Dangerous Type' and the title track provide perfect cruising music for the post-punk generation and enough insidious hooks to forgive their shameless clinical recycling of other people's riffs and even those ridiculous skinny ties.

Rating:
Sound ★★★★★ Content ★★★★☆

The Cars

'HEARTBEAT CITY'

(Elektra) 1984

Track listing: Hello Again • Looking For Love • Jackie • It's Not The Night • Drive • Shooting For You • Why Can't I • Magic • You Might Think • I Do Refuse • Stranger Eyes

By the time they came to record 'Heartbeat City' the rust had set in and they began cruising rapidly downhill in neutral. They bottomed out with this album which could offer only the opener 'Hello Again' and 'You Might Think' as evidence

that Ocasek was still in the driving seat. But by the fade it was obvious that he was asleep at the wheel. Clearly they weren't the same sporty model that their fans thought they had bought years before. However even as the revamped family friendly saloon they got more mileage out of their music than their less credible contemporaries could have hoped for. The bland 'Drive' sold faster than a Big Mac and fries after it was featured (incongruously) on the soundtrack accompanying shots of starving Ethiopians during the Live Aid telecast.

Rating:
Sound ★★★★★ Content ★★★☆☆
Also recommended:
'Panorama', 'Greatest Hits', 'Shake It Up'(all on Elektra).
If you like this, why not try:
Television, Tom Petty, the dB's, Blondie.

Nick Cave And The Bad Seeds

'YOUR FUNERAL... MY TRIAL'

(Mute) 1986

Track listing: Your Funeral…My Trial • Stranger Than Kindness • Jack's Shadow • The Carny • She Fell Away • Hard On For Love • Sad Waters • Long Time Man • Scum

Cave is the High Priest of Goth. His bible-black lyrics are steeped in religious symbolism and proclaimed in a sepulchral tone which makes every album sound like a funeral oration. But even after he has laid the bodies of his victims in the ground – to the Bad Seeds brooding, macabre accompaniment and a chorus of moaning souls – their restless spirits return to haunt him and us. 'I am a crooked man and I've walked a crooked mile,' he intones on the title track as the band stagger like drunken pallbearers from the charnel house to the graveside. And from that morbid introduction the long tortuous journey to the little black hole in the middle of the disc just gets darker and darker. Along the way we meet deranged murderers ('Jack's Shadow'), the exhibits of a fairground freak show ('The Carny') and a homicidal religious fanatic ('Hard On For Love'). Disturbing, but utterly compelling.

Rating:
Sound ★★★★☆ Content ★★★★☆

Nick Cave And The Bad Seeds

'TENDER PREY'

(Mute) 1988

Track listing: Mercy Seat • Up Jumped The Devil • Deanna • Watching Alice • Mercy • City Of Refuge • Slowly Goes The Night • Sunday's Slave • Sugar Sugar Sugar • New Morning

'Who's that hanging from the gallow tree, his eyes are hollow but he looks like me,

Who's that swinging from the gallow tree, up jumped the devil and took my soul from me.'

For once the words 'dark' and

'densely textured' are inadequate to describe this mock-Gothic soundtrack whose heart is blacker than a Stephen King novel.

It appears that Nick wants to confess to his crimes before he is ready to walk that last mile in the company of the granite-faced Warden and the sorrowful priest. So hear him out, but be warned, this is not for the ears of the innocent or those of a nervous disposition. He will lead us down some very dark alleys and strip away the veneer of respectability on which we depend to keep the demons from our doors.

'Oh poor heart I was doomed from the start, doomed to play the villain's part,' he sings and he isn't kidding. There's bloody murder, incest and much worse in these tracks and no redemption for the sinner. But boy, does he make temptation sound enticing.

If the condemned could hear this before they went to meet their maker they might walk that last mile with a broad grin on their face.

Rating:
Sound ★★★☆☆ Content ★★★★☆

Nick Cave And The Bad Seeds

'MURDER BALLADS'

(Mute) 1996

Track listing: Song Of Joy • Stagger Lee • Henry Lee • Lovely Creature • Where The Wild Roses Grow • Curse Of Millhaven • Kindness Of Strangers • Crow Jane • O'Malley's Bar • Death Is Not The End

'Those lunatic eyes, that hungry kitchen knife.' Yep, we're hitchin' another nightmare ride with the devil's favourite minstrel, Nick Cave. Nick's lifelong obsession with notorious criminals and their nefarious crimes culminated in this chilling collection of ten traditional tales of 'bad seeds' who remain unrepentant, even in the face of 'old sparky' or the hangman's noose. PJ Harvey, Shane MacGowan and Kylie Minogue (of all people) are among the guests cast as his various accomplices or victims. Curiously enough, it's Kylie who makes the most memorable contribution as the ill-fated Elisa Day on the haunting 'Where The Wild Roses Grow', a track which gave Nick the nearest he ever came to a hit single.

Despite the grim theme this is the most accessible of his albums thanks partly to the folk flavourings, but also because of the sparse production which sets the narrative centre stage. Pleasant dreams.

Rating:
Sound ★★★★☆ Content ★★★★☆
Also recommended:
'Let Love In', 'The Good Son' and 'Henry's Dream' (all on Mute).
If you like this, why not try:
The Birthday Party, Bauhaus, Leonard Cohen.

The Chemical Brothers

'EXIT PLANET DUST'

(Freestyle Dust/Virgin) 1995

Track listing: Leave Home • In Dust We Trust • Song To The Siren • Three Little Birdies Down Beats • Fuck Up Beats • Chemical Beats • Life Is Sweet • Playground For A Wedgeless Firm • Chico's Groove • One Too Many Mornings

In their laboratory of sound The Chemical Brothers created artificial life from the DNA of modern music, cloning breakbeats for clients Primal Scream, Prodigy and The Manic Street Preachers. All pretensions towards art were abandoned in the service of the pure science of sound. Their aim? To produce a stream of consciousness distilled in a dance groove with traces of hip hop and house, but one chemically altered to resist infection. Once they had patented the formula it was distributed to addicts and the effects were immediate and extraordinary. Limbs that previously exhibited no signs of life were seen to twitch uncontrollably, body temperatures rose and the life-threatening condition known as terminal boredom was banished from the planet. What chance the Nobel Prize for aural chemistry now?

Demo the stand-out tracks 'Life Is Sweet' and 'Alive Alone', featuring Tim Burgess of The Charlatans and Beth Orton respectively, to sample the soundtrack to the new century.

Rating:
Sound ★★★★☆ Content ★★★☆☆

Also recommended:
'Dig Your Own Hole' (Freestyle
Dust/Virgin).
If you like this, why not try:
Orbital, **The Orb**, Prodigy, Dust
Brothers.

Alex Chilton

'LIKE FLIES ON SHERBERT'

(Cooking Vinyl) 1976

Track listing: Boogie Shoes • My Rival • Hey Little Child • Hook Or Crook • I've Had It • Rock Hard • Girl After Girl • Waltz Across Texas • Alligator Man • Like Flies On Sherbert

Chilton began his erratic career as the 16-year-old lead singer of The Box Tops, the group who scored a hit in 1967 with 'The Letter'. But to serious record collectors he is revered as a cult figure who became a significant influence on every indie/alternative rock act from REM through The Soft Boys to Teenage Fanclub. This celebrated solo album captures Alex in the white heat of creativity as he tempers the belligerence of The Who with the free spirit of The Byrds, adding shadings of psychpop and white soul to four originals and some inspired covers. If ever an album made a case for the overthrow of corporate rock and the award of reparations to the criminally neglected this is it. Trivia fans take note: 'Alligator Man' was featured in the cult Hammer horror movie *Dracula AD1972*.

Rating:
Sound ★★★★☆ Content ★★★★☆

Also recommended:
'19 Years – A Collection' (Rhino) 1991.
If you like this, why not try:
Big Star, **Robyn Hitchcock**, **The Soft Boys**, REM, Teenage Fanclub, The Cramps.

Eric Clapton

'THE CREAM OF ERIC CLAPTON'

(Polydor) 1994

Track listing: Layla • Badge • I Feel Free • Sunshine Of Your Love • Crossroads • Strange Brew • White Room • Bell Bottom Blues • Cocaine • I Shot The Sheriff • After Midnight • Swing Low Sweet Chariot • Lay Down Sally • Knockin' On Heaven's Door • Wonderful Tonight • Let It Grow • Promises • I Can't Stand It

Eric 'Slowhand' Clapton couldn't truly be said to be an innovator, but in staying faithful to his first love, the blues, and being its most eloquent spokesman he has ensured that it remains the mother lode of modern music. He is a musican's musician, a supreme soloist who can wring every ounce of emotion from a single solo and, most important of all, make every note count.

If you haven't sampled Clapton to date, this is the ideal primer, although it doesn't cover the earthy early recordings with John Mayall or The Yardbirds, nor the extended improvisational workouts with Cream in concert.

However, the better known studio recordings with that seminal supergroup are all included on which

Clapton's emotive solos are fired with a stridency and authority that he was later to subdue for his muted mid-seventies mainstream material. Of the latter 'Lay Down Sally', 'Wonderful Tonight' and the cover of JJ Cale's 'After Midnight' are prime examples; at once soulful and soft-centred, but raised from the mediocre by a tender turn of phrase. The blues may be a universal music, but Clapton has articulated the ecstasy and the heartache that it communicates in a voice that is uniquely his own.

Rating:
Sound ★★★★☆ Content ★★★★★

Eric Clapton

'FROM THE CRADLE'

(Reprise/Warners) 1994

Track listing: Blues Before Sunrise • Third Degree • Reconsider Baby • Hoochie Coochie Man • Five Long Years • I'm Tore Down • How Long Blues • Goin' Away Baby • Blues Leave Me Alone • Sinner's Prayer • Motherless Child • It Hurts Me Too • Someday After Awhile • Standing Around Crying • Drifting • Groaning The Blues

A return to roots and a welcome return to form for old 'Slowhand' after a dispiriting number of bland, over-produced AOR albums during the eighties and nineties. Few of his older fans could believe that he would ever pay his dues to the blues again, but when he did, he did it in style. The booklet proclaims that these are all live-in-the-studio recordings without any overdubs or editing of any kind. But behind the perceptible sense of

pride and the pleasure in once again being in the company of old friends, one also senses the sadness which drove him to seek solace in the bitter-sweet beauty of the blues.

Rating:
Sound ★★★★☆ Content ★★★★★

Eric Clapton

'UNPLUGGED'

(Warners) 1992

Track listing: Signe • Before You Accuse Me • Hey Hey • Tears In Heaven • Lonely Stranger • Nobody Knows You (When You're Down And Out) • Layla • Running On Faith • Walking Blues • Alberta • San Francisco Bay Blues • Malted Milk • Old Love

Before MTV's 'unplugged' showcase became an excuse for every 'name' act to recycle their set in an acoustic setting, Eric Clapton used the opportunity to get back to his blues roots and in doing so set the standard for the series. Stripped of the stodgy over-production which had weighed down his solo albums old 'Slowhand' positively shone in the subdued setting as he honoured the immortals and gave vent to his grief over his young son's death in the genuinely moving 'Tears In Heaven'.

Here is incontrovertible proof that the blues is not just for the bad times, but is the best non-alcoholic pick-me-up known to man.

Rating:
Sound ★★★★☆ Content ★★★★☆
Also recommended:
'Crossroads' (Polydor) 4CD box set drawing upon choice cuts, rarities and

previously unreleased items from The Yardbirds era to the mid Eighties; 'Crossroads Vol 2 – Live In The 70s' (Polydor) 2CD box set; and 'August' (Warners) an R&B set produced by Phil Collins.

If you like this, why not try: **Cream**, Blind Faith, **Derek And The Dominoes**, **Rory Gallagher**.

The Clash

'THE CLASH'

(CBS) 1977

Track listing: Janie Jones • Remote Control • I'm So Bored With The USA • White Riot • Hate And War • What's My Name • Deny • London's Burning • Career Opportunities • Cheat • Protex Blue • Police And Thieves • 48 Hours • Garageland

It's ironic to listen to 'I'm So Bored With The USA' in the light of subsequent events, namely the group's eager embracing of the Big Mac dream across the pond. Where was their bitter contempt for rapacious commercialism just a few years later when they began filling arenas across the States? But back in '77 their first communiqué declared punk's Year Zero with the slogan 'No Elvis, no Beatles, no Stones', as the Notting Hill revolutionaries waged war on everything they considered contrived, counterfeit or corrupt. Their music had all the subtlety of a kick in the nuts and the verbal graffiti could have been scraped off the tenement walls where they claimed to have cultivated their contempt for capitalism. But it was

the sound of the times. Their political credentials and East End accents may have been suspect, but their commitment was unquestionable. Who needs expensive stress therapy when you can crank up 'White Riot' and get out your pent-up aggression for free?

Rating:
Sound ★★★☆☆ Content ★★★★☆

The Clash

'LONDON CALLING'

(CBS) 1979

Track listing: London Calling • Brand New Cadillac • Jimmy Jazz • Hateful • Rudie Can't Fail • Spanish Bombs • The Right Profile • Lost In The Supermarket • Clampdown • Guns Of Brixton • Wrong 'Em Boyo • Death Or Glory • Koka Kola • The Card Cheat • Lover's Rock • Four Horsemen • I'm Not Down • Revolution Rock • Train In Vain

From his vantage point in the high-rise hell of a Notting Hill Gate squat Joe Strummer claimed to be able to hear punk, R&B and reggae from the open windows of the surrounding flats. Once The Clash had established their punk credentials they felt free to indulge their passion for these other influences on this flawless double album, which the group shrewdly insisted should be sold for the price of a regular LP.

With its mixture of urban rock, rockabilly and Rasta rhythms it marked the transmutation of punk into the nebulous category commonly known as 'alter native rock', whose themes were universal rather than personal and more persuasively articulated. But whatever label you apply to it, this is a remarkably consistent and significant album.

'Death Or Glory' summed up their attitude to the sessions which saw guide vocals and mistakes make it to the finished mix in the cause of authenticity. But it was the belligerent title track and 'Train In Vain' which gave the group their biggest hits to date.

Rating:
Sound ★★★★☆ Content ★★★★★

The Clash

'THE STORY OF THE CLASH VOLUME I

2 CDs (Columbia) 1999

Track listing: CD I – The Magnificent Seven • Rock The Casbah • This Is Radio Clash • Should I Stay Or Should I Go • Straight To Hell • Armagideon Time • Clampdown • Train In Vain • Guns Of Brixton • I Fought The Law • Somebody Got Murdered • Lost In The Supermarket • Bank Robber

CD 2 – (White Man) In Hammersmith Palais • London's Burning • Janie Jones • Tommy Gun • Complete Control • Capital Radio • White Riot • Career Opportunities • Clash City Rockers • Safe European Home • Stay Free • London Calling • Spanish Bombs • English Civil War • Police And Thieves

'The Story Of The Clash' is really the story of two bands, or a band with two faces, if you're a cynic. The earlier incarnation gobbed all over the enervated, incestuous establishment and incited the great unwashed to join a popular uprising against unemployment, the American cultural domination of Europe and crass, commercial pop in such scathing songs as 'London's

Burning', 'White Riot', 'Career Opportunities' and 'Capital Radio'. But then 'Train In Vain' brought them an unexpected breakthrough in America and they swallowed their bile, made their peace with pop's past and diversified into dub, rap and an updated dance-friendly version of 'rude boy' rock.

This is the one to own, assuming of course that you don't already have the original albums. (Shame on you if you don't!)

Rating:
Sound ★★★★☆ Content ★★★★★
Also recommended:
The single CD retrospective 'The Singles', and 'Sandinista!' their 1980 Triple album now on 2 CDs (both on Columbia).
If you like this, why not try:
Angelic Upstarts, Big Audio Dynamite, **Sex Pistols**.

Eddie Cochran

'THE VERY BEST OF aka THE ANNIVERSARY ALBUM'

(Fame/EMI) 1990

Track listing: C'mon Everybody • Three Steps To Heaven • Weekend • Skinny Jim • Completely Sweet • Milk Cow Blues • Cut Across Shorty • Hallelujah I Love her So • Something Else • Blue Suede Shoes • Eddie's Blues • Sittin' In The Balcony • Summertime Blues • Twenty Flight Rock • Three Stars • Cherished Memories

Before the advent of pop videos, songs had to tell a story in under three minutes. If it wasn't in the grooves then it wouldn't capture the imagination or heart of the singles-buying teen. The songs of fifties rocker Eddie Cochran more than satisfied on all counts and they also capture the lost innocence of that era.

Eddie was one of the few early stars who not only wrote his own songs but also played, sang and produced them himself; multi-tracking so that he could play several instruments without using session men. He looked like Elvis' cute younger brother, but he rocked harder, played a mean guitar and could encapsulate what it meant to be a teenager in the early fifties. Songs such as 'Summertime Blues', 'Twenty Flight Rock' and 'C'mon Everybody' described the fun and frustrations of cruising, partying and courting when you didn't have the car, the money or the girl. Whether at school, at home or at work Eddie's characters were at the mercy of grown ups who were determined to put the boy down and spoil his fun. When he was killed in a car crash at the age of 21 he'd left just eight gems and some substandard country songs, less than would fill an LP, but these are more than enough to justify his place on that great jukebox in the sky.

Rating:
Sound ★★★★☆ Content ★★★★☆
Also recommended:
'The Eddie Cochran Box Set' (Liberty/EMI) 4 CDs, 'The EP Collection' (See For Miles) and 'The Best Of' (MFP). The latter is a budget-priced sampler covering most of the hits but also including the terrific 'Nervous Breakdown' which is not included on the 'The Very Best Of'.
If you like this, why not try:
Chuck Berry, Link Wray, **Carl Perkins**, the various Sun rockabilly compilations.

Cocteau Twins

'TREASURE'

(4AD) 1984

Track listing: Ivo • Lorelei • Beatrix • Persephone • Pandora • Amelia • Aloysius • Cicely • Otterley • Domino

Like their namesake, the film director, poet and painter Jean Cocteau, the Twins' music has a surreal cinematic quality that prompted many reviewers to talk in terms of 'grand cathedrals of sound'. Elizabeth Fraser's hallucinatory vocals drift on layers of translucent guitars that would have provided the perfect soundtrack to 'La Belle et la Bete', a film once described as being 'diamond cold and lunar bright'. A perfect description of this album. Cocteau would have adored them.

Rating:
Sound ★★★★☆ Content ★★★★☆

Cocteau Twins

'HEAVEN OR LAS VEGAS'

(4AD) 1990

Track listing: Cherry Coloured Funk • Pitch The Baby • Iceblink Luck • Fifty-Fifty Clown • Heaven Or Las Vegas • I Wear Your Ring • Fotzepolitic • Wolf In The Breast • Road, River And Rail • Frou Frou Foxes In Midsummer Fires

If 'Treasure' mirrored the fanciful dream-like imagery of 'La Belle et la Bete' then the more conventional, song-orientated 'Heaven' aspires to underscore 'Orphée', the film director Cocteau's modern version of the Orpheus myth. It's as enigmatic and multi-layered as the movie that the director himself likened to 'a petrified fountain of thought.' Transpose the word 'sound' for 'thought' and you have a perfect description of this album. Gorgeous.

Rating:
Sound ★★★★☆ Content ★★★★☆
Also recommended:
'Victorialand' (4AD) 1986. After the lush production of 'Treasure' their fourth album is an exercise in New Age ambient music using only acoustic instruments. Plus 'Four Calendar Café' (Fontana) and 'Garlands' (4AD).
If you like this, why not try:
This Mortal Coil, **Everything But The Girl**.

Leonard Cohen

'GREATEST HITS'

(Columbia) 1975

Track listing: Suzanne • Sisters Of Mercy • So Long Marianne • Bird On A Wire • Lady Midnight • The Partisan • Hey, That's No Way To Say Goodbye • Famous Blue Raincoat • Last Year's Man • Chelsea Hotel No 2 • Who By Wire • Take This Longing

Something of a misnomer this, as the morose Canadian singer-songwriter, poet and sometime novelist has fewer certified hits under his belt than boxer Frank Bruno. It's nevertheless a welcome summary of his 30-year career as one of the more erudite bedsit balladeers, although it inevitably ignores as many essential items as it includes. Cohen, whose songs have been covered with more commercial success by others, chooses to use his songs for self-analysis through the use of metaphor and quasi-religious symbolism. But he also manages to get under the skin of his often tortured subjects if he has an empathy with them, as he does when remembering Janis Joplin in 'Chelsea Hotel No 2'. However, even when he is contented he still manages to sound like he's carving the lyrics on a tombstone, which might account for his enduring popularity with the likes of Nick Cave and Andrew Eldritch who named his band The Sisters Of Mercy after Cohen's song of the same title. If you're unfamiliar with his work, take a listen to the muted, brooding 'Suzanne', but keep the Prozac handy.

Rating:
Sound ★★★★☆ Content ★★★★★
Also recommended:
'Songs Of Leonard Cohen' 1968, 'Songs From A Room' 1969, 'Songs Of Love And Hate' 1971, 'Recent Songs' 1979 and 'I'm Your Man' 1988.
If you like this, why not try:
Jennifer Warnes' collection of Cohen covers 'Famous Blue Raincoat', and the Various Artists Cohen tribute project 'I'm Your Fan'.

Coldplay

'PARACHUTES'

(Parlophone) 2000

Track listing: Don't Panic • Shiver • Spies • Sparks • Yellow • Trouble • Parachutes • High Speed • We Never Change • Everything's Not Lost

Classic songwriting for the new millennium, or dull AOR ballads for the undiscerning? Coldplay scored a massive hit with 'Shiver', but the jury is still out considering their long-term prospects. Singer Chris Martin wrests every ounce of emotion from a set of comparatively slight songs on the theme of unrequited love against a lavish orchestral backdrop. It sounds significant, soulful and sincere, but as an album it's also unusually short. The problem is that too many of the songs cruise in low gear and rely too heavily on Chris Martin's fragile vocal to sustain interest when they should have been concentrating on dynamic contrast and instrumental colour. The comparisons with Radiohead are unwarranted, although there is promise in the stronger songs, 'Spies', 'Shiver' and 'Yellow'. Whether there is more to Coldplay than this well-crafted set only time will tell.

Rating:
Sound ★★★★☆ Content ★★★☆☆
Also recommended:
n/a
If you like this, why not try:
U2, Dido, Stereophonics.

Phil Collins

'FACE VALUE'

(Virgin) 1981

Track listing: In The Air Tonight • This Must Be Love • Behind The Lines • The Roof Is Leaking • Droned • Hand In Hand • I Missed Again • You Know What I Mean • Thunder And Lightning • I'm Not Moving • If Leaving Me Is Easy • Tomorrow Never Knows

Twenty years after playing the Artful Dodger as a child actor in the original stage production of *Oliver!* Phil Collins was still hawking the cheeky cockney image for all it was worth in a series of increasingly bland solo albums, although his irrepressible optimism is tempered on this uncharacteristically downbeat debut with pained resignation as he reflects on an acrimonious divorce. The experience brings an acidity to an otherwise shallow set of heavily orchestrated middle-aged rock songs which confounded the critics but nevertheless kick-started his highly successful solo career and bolstered his bank balance by another few million. And still he held down his day job with Genesis. 'Leaving Me Is Easy' was a minor hit despite being one of the more substantial and serious tracks, whereas the comparatively vacuous 'In The Air Tonight' became a monster smash.

Rating:
Sound ★★★★☆ Content ★★★☆☆
Also recommended:
'Hello, I Must Be Going' and 'No Jacket Required' (Virgin).
If you like this, why not try:
Genesis, Peter Gabriel solo albums, **Eric Clapton.**

Sam Cooke

'THE MAN AND HIS MUSIC'

(RCA) 1986

Track listing: Meet Me At Mary's Place • Good Times • Shake • Sad Mood • Bring It On Home To Me • That's Where It's At • That's Heaven To Me • Touch The Hem Of His Garment • You Send Me • I'll Come Running Back To You • Win Your Love For Me • Wonderful World • Cupid • Just For You • Chain Gang • Only Sixteen • When A Boy Falls In Love • Rome Wasn't Built In A Day • Everybody Loves To Cha Cha • Nothing Can Change This Love • Love Will Find A Way • Another Saturday Night • Having A Party • Twistin' The Night Away • Somebody Have Mercy • Ain't That Good News • Soothe Me • Change Is Gonna Come

Sam brought the rich, mellifluous phrasing of gospel to pop and in doing so fully justified the title of one of the many posthumous collections of his work, 'the man who invented soul'. His vocal agility, innate sense of harmony and perfect pitch breathed warmth into even the most unpromising material. When the music called for it his voice soared with the aspiration of a minister, testifying with the intensity and conviction of one who has sinned and returned to the fold. Moreover, he never sold a song short. There is no trace of artifice in these peerless performances, no contrived stylizing or grand empty gestures. Sam made every note count. Though frequently short-changed by mundane material his silken voice exuded sheer class from first note to last. The gospel standard 'Touch The Hem Of His Garment' would make even the most

wicked sinner repent, while the secular hits 'Wonderful World', 'Cupid' and 'Bring It On Home' are irradiated with a warmth that penetrates right down to the soul.

Rating:
Sound ★★★★☆ Content ★★★★☆
Also recommended:
'In The Beginning' (Ace) and 'Sam Cooke With The Soul Stirrers' (Ace), two superlative gospel showcases for Cooke's honey-like tone lovingly remastered from the original tapes.
If you like this, why not try:
Jackie Wilson, **Dion**, Ray Charles, Al Green, early **Rod Stewart**.

Alice Cooper

'SCHOOL'S OUT'

(Warners) 1972

Track listing: School's Out • Luney Tune • Gutter Cat Vs The Jets • Street Fight • Blue Turk • My Stars • Public Animal No 9 • Alma Mater • Grande Finale

One can only imagine what the Reverend Furnier thought of his son's transformation from God-fearin' church-goer to the ghoul of Glam Rock. Alice's on-stage antics included the decapitation of dolls, mock executions and the re-enactment of his own nightmares, acts which made Ozzy Osbourne look like Mother Teresa by comparison. Alice's albums were equally over-the-top, bringing shock-rock tactics and a macabre sense of theatre to songs on which he dragged America's sacred cows to the slaughter. 'School's Out' brought his brand of anarchy to academia with parodies of 'West Side Story' and its troubled teen stereotypes plus a fistful of adolescent anthems that would inspire a generation of glam-metal copyists in the eighties.

Unfortunately, the sound quality of this first CD issue suffers from the over-use of compression (a process which was designed to reduce tape hiss, but which also limits the dynamic range of the recording until it sounds claustrophobic). There is also noticeable distortion at the beginning of the title track and a dull boxiness which cries out for remastering.

Rating:
Sound ★★★☆☆ Content ★★★☆☆

Alice Cooper

'BILLION DOLLAR BABIES'

(Warners) 1973

Track listing: Hello Hooray • Raped And Freezin' • Elected • Billion Dollar Babies • Unfinished Sweet • No More Mr Nice Guy • Generation Landslide • Sick Things • Mary Ann • I Love The Dead

Roll up, roll up the rock and roll circus is back in town featuring America's main attraction, Alice Cooper. Tonight before your very ears the cadaverous Alice will wrestle a live boa constrictor, guillotine innocent cuddly toys and perform various unspeakable acts with live chickens. We kid you not.

'Hello Hooray' raises the curtain on more acts of delicious depravity with a touch of high camp and its tongue firmly in its cheek. The title track is shameless schlock-horror in the 'Rocky Horror Picture Show' vein and features uncredited appearances by Donovan and Marc Bolan, whose combined incomes gave the album its name. Other highlights include the hit singles 'Elected' and 'No More Mr Nice Guy' plus the deceptively charming 'Mary Ann', which turns out to be a love song to a transvestite. Only Alice Cooper could top that – and he does with the typically tasteless 'I Love The Dead' which serves as both a fitting finale and a preview of his next provocative performance.

The sound quality offers a significant improvement over its predecessor with bite in the treble and plenty of beef in the bottom end. Also available as a special-priced double disc featuring live tracks.

Rating:
Sound ★★★★☆ Content ★★★★☆

Alice Cooper

'WELCOME TO MY NIGHTMARE'

(Atlantic) 1975

Track listing: Welcome To My Nightmare • Devil's Food • The Black Widow • Some Folks • Only Women Bleed • Department Of Youth • Cold Ethyl • Years Ago • Steven • The Awakening • Escape

Back in the early seventies Alice was every parent's nightmare and their offspring's idea of gross-out, escapist entertainment. His black humour and extravagant sense of theatre reached its extreme with this staging of their collective fears, which featured an appearance by Vincent Price as the sinister curator of a travelling freak show.

By this time Alice's act was beginning to lose its shock value, but 'Devil's Food', 'The Black Widow' and 'Cold Ethyl' still carry a delicious frisson, while the uncharacteristically tender 'Only Women Bleed' provides much needed relief – and, incidentally, gave him one of his biggest hits. The three tracks on the theme of mental illness, beginning with 'Years Ago', suggest that he was already looking for a way out of the artistic straitjacket that he had wrapped himself in, but it was clearly too late to effect an escape.

He may have been a sickie, but he was fun. Who else but Alice Cooper could extol the virtues of poisonous spiders, slip in references to necrophilia and namecheck Donny Osmond all on the same record!

Unfortunately the digital remastering is bottom heavy making for a dense, unfocused sound with insufficient bite.

Rating:
Sound ★★★☆☆ Content ★★★★☆
Also recommended:
'Muscle Of Love', 'The Beast Of Alice Cooper' (all on WEA).
If you like this, why not try:
Twisted Sister, Marilyn Manson, Ozzy Osbourne, Motley Crue.

Julian Cope

'WORLD SHUT YOUR MOUTH'

(Mercury) 1984

Track listing: Brandy's First Jump • Greatness And Perfection Of Love • Elegant Chaos • Kolly Kibber's Birthday • Head Hang Low • Metranii Vavin • Sunshine Playroom • Lunatic And Fire Pistol • Strasbourg • Quizmaster • Pussyface • Wreck My Car • High Class Butcher • Eat The Poor

After professional eccentric Cope split The Teardop Explodes in 1983 he retired to the shed at the bottom of his garden with reels of recording tape and a stock of spliffs to assemble the first in a series of solo albums with a distinctly English psychedelic tinge. Some of the songs had been left over from the final Teardrop sessions, but others were the expression of his new-found freedom, inspired by sources as diverse as Graham Greene ('Kolly Kibber's Birthday') and Syd Barrett ('Sunshine Playroom'). Fortunately, Jools hadn't taken quite as many mind-mangling drugs as the ex-Floyd frontman which ensured that the songs were kept in focus, underpinned by the precision playing of ace guitarist Steve Lovell and ex-Teardrop drummer Gary Dwyer. By the time he had added a touch of oboe to the more picturesque tracks even the gnomes at the bottom of his garden were beaming.

Rating:
Sound ★★★☆☆ Content ★★★★☆

Julian Cope

'PEGGY SUICIDE'

(Island) 1991

Track listing: Pristeen • Double Vegetation • East Easy Rider • Promised Land • Hanging Out And Hung Up On The Line • Safesurfer • If You Loved Me At All • Drive She Said • Soldier Blue • You... • Not Raving But Drowning • Head • Leperskin • Beautiful Love • Western Front 1992 • Hung Up And Hanging Out To Dry • American Lite • Las Vegas Basement

After a serious of disjointed and disappointing offerings Jools returned to form with this sprawling double album which boasted a more traditional rock and roll feel. He'd obviously spent the preceding months holed up in the now celebrated shed with copies of Iggy And The Stooges 'Raw Power' whose influence was evident on songs such as 'Hanging Out'. Also on the menu were extended guitar freak outs underscoring songs with serious ecological, social and political themes. But there were also intervals of stoned serenity, as on 'Beautiful Love', which became a minor hit single.

Rating:
Sound ★★★☆☆ Content ★★★★☆
Also recommended:
'Jehovahkill' (Island), 'Saint Julian' (Island), 'Fried' (Mercury) and 'Floored Genius Vol:1 The Best Of Julian Cope' (Island).
If you like this, why not try:
The Teardrop Explodes, Syd Barrett, Bevis Frond, **Robyn Hitchcock**.

The Corrs

'FORGIVEN, NOT FORGOTTEN'

(Atlantic) 1995

Track listing: Erin Shore • Forgiven, Not Forgotten • Heaven Knows • Along With The Girls • Someday • Runaway • The Right Time • The Minstrel Boy • Toss The Feathers • Love To Love You • Secret Life • Carraroe Jig • Closer • Leave Me Alone • Erin Shore

The Corr clan (three sisters and their brother) create a sound as smooth as a glass of Guinness. But for some it's a rather sickly sweet brew of MOR pop seasoned with traditional Celtic flavourings and topped with a frothy head of close-harmony vocals aimed at the 'Riverdance' audience and incurable, soft-centred romantics. The Corrs wear their hearts on their sleeves and every song seems to involve confessions to cuddly teddy bears rather than real relationships, but the instrumental interludes demonstrate able musicianship and there are just enough production tricks and overdriven guitars to stop it sinking into a sticky morass.

Rating:
Sound ★★★★☆ Content ★★☆☆☆
Also recommended:
'In Blue', 'Unplugged' and 'Talk On Corners'. The latter is also available in a special edition with additional remixes (all on Atlantic.)
If you like this, why not try:
Horslips, Sinead O'Connor, Van Morrison.

Elvis Costello

'MY AIM IS TRUE'

(Demon Records) 1977

Track listing: Welcome To The Working Week • Miracle Man • No Dancing • Blame It On Cain • Alison • Sneaky Feelings • Red Shoes • Less Than Zero • Mystery Dance • Pay It Back • I'm Not Angry • Waiting For The End Of The World • Watching The Detectives.

Bonus Tracks: Radio Sweatheart • Stranger In The House • Imagination • Mystery Dance • Cheap Reward • Jump Up • Wave A White Flag • Blame It On Cain • Poison Moon

Rating:
Sound ★★★☆☆ Content ★★★★★

Elvis Costello

'THIS YEAR'S MODEL'

(Radar/Demon) 1978

Track listing: No Action • This Year's Girl • The Beat • Pump It Up • Little Triggers • You Belong To Me • Hand In Hand • (I Don't Want To Go To) Chelsea • Lip Service • Living In Paradise • Lipstick • Vogue • Night Rally

Bonus tracks: Radio Radio • Big Tears • Crawling To The USA • Running Out Of Angels • Green Shirt • Big Boys

Recorded in just 24 hours on a shoestring budget of £2,000 'My Aim Is True' stands as one of the most significant personal statements on the state of the nation and of one Declan Patrick McManus (aka Costello) towards the end of the seventies.

Costello's barbed wire commentaries on popular culture, 'uncomfortable' contemporary topics (ie domestic violence, fascism) and personal obsessions are frequently disguised by wily wordplay, wrapped in deceptively agreeable tunes and discharged in an abrasive nasal whine that made the crossover from New Wave to the mainstream inevitable. But although these songs are as contemptuous, angry and intense as any that the punks spat forth the year this album was released, the punk element is minimal as Elvis reveals the influence of fifties rockabilly and sixties pop in tracks such as 'Mystery Dance' and 'Red Shoes'. The collection of outtakes and demos, which incidentally almost double the original running time, betray an unfashionable affection for country music.

Costello's talent for penning pithy pop songs on a wide range of themes – from the intimately personal to the universal and political – was once again allied to his prickly personality on this second outing which also saw the arrival of The Attractions as his resident band. Their presence ensured that 'This Year's Model' sounded more assured, while the benefit of an increased budget can be heard in the more densely textured, professional sound defined by Steve Nieve's 'cheesy' retro Farfisa organ.

Like its predecessor this album is positively bursting with great songs which just get better and better with successive plays. Most immediately appealing are the singles 'Pump It Up', '(I Don't Want To Go To) Chelsea' and 'Radio Radio' (the latter had been inexplicably excluded from the original vinyl version), but it's no glib exaggeration to say that there isn't a weak track here.

The addition of six bonus tracks including a demo of 'Green Shirt' demands immediate purchase.

Rating:
Sound ★★★★☆ Content ★★★★★

Elvis Costello

'ARMED FORCES'

(Demon) 1979

Track listing: Accidents Will Happen • Senior Service • Oliver's Army • Big Boys • Green Shirt • Party Girl • Goon Squad • Busy Bodies • Sunday's Best • Moods For Moderns • Chemistry Class • Two Little Hitlers • (What's So Funny About) Peace, Love And Understanding

Bonus Tracks: My Funny Valentine • Tiny Steps • Clean Money • Talking In The Dark • Wednesday Week • Accidents Will Happen • Alison • Watching The Detectives

The original title of Elvis' third offering was 'Emotional Fascism', which suggested that the emphasis had shifted from tales of failed romance and caustic social comment to the overtly political with Costello discharging his bitter indignation at every form of intolerance within range.

Despite the pervading pessimism and a slight downgrade in quality control the album remains his best-seller to date, primarily because of the inclusion of the hit 'Oliver's Army'. It also proved to be the last record for some considerable time to feature the classic Attractions sound as Elvis felt the urge to indulge his eclectic taste and passion for soul and country music on subsequent sets.

Rating:
Sound ★★★★☆ Content ★★★★☆

Elvis Costello

'IMPERIAL BEDROOM'

(Demon) 1982

Track listing: Beyond Belief • Tears Before Bedtime • The Long Honeymoon • Shabby Doll • Man Out Of Time • Almost Blue • The Loved Ones • ...And In Every Home • Human Hands • Town Cryer • You Little Fool • Pidgin English • Boy With A Problem • Little Savage • Kid About It

With his thick horn-rimmed glasses and sharp suits Elvis may have borne a superficial similarity to Buddy Holly, but one only needed to lend an ear to this mid-career milestone to appreciate how far pop had progressed since the fifties. Not since Lennon's primal scream session, 'The Plastic Ono Band' album, had music been used so effectively as an emotional catharsis as Elvis subjects himself to scathing self-analysis in effort to exorcise his demons. The frequently painful revelations are partly alleviated by the balm of sixties' pop sophistication applied by ex-Beatles engineer Geoff Emerick, although the lush orchestrations aren't allowed to smother the confession with sentiment.

Another indispensable album from one of the most consistently creative artists of the era and one which demands to be played straight through.

Rating:
Sound ★★★★★ Content ★★★★☆
Also recommended:
'King Of America', 'Almost Blue', 'Blood And Chocolate', 'Get Happy!',

'Almost Blue', and 'The Very Best Of Elvis Costello' (all on Demon) plus 'Spike' and 'Brutal Youth' (both on Warners).

If you like this, why not try:
Nick Lowe, Squeeze, **Billy Bragg**, **Paul Weller**.

Country Joe And The Fish

'ELECTRIC MUSIC FOR THE MIND AND BODY'

(Vanguard/Ace) 1967

Track listing: Flying High • Not So Sweet Martha Lorraine • Death Blues • Porpoise Mouth • Section 43 • Superbird • Sad And Lonely Times • Love • Bass Strings • The Masked Marauder • Grace

This album was as essential to the Woodstock generation as a well thumbed copy of *Lord Of The Rings*. Country Joe could be sly and satirical, poking fun at the naïveté of the peace and love fraternity, but he could also be po-faced, provocative and political which seemed highly significant if you were stoned, but tiresome if you were sober. However, when he was on form and the band were blissed-out they saturated the senses in the cool, vivid colours of the acid-rock sound experience.

A truly narcotic album. 'Not So Sweet Martha Lorraine' is one of several jug band blues numbers, 'Grace' is Joe's tribute to the lead singer of Jefferson Airplane and the re-recording of 'Section 43' (which had originally appeared on an EP) is archetypal acid rock. But the track which almost makes up for the excess of hippie noodling is the epic 'Bass Strings' which was

reputed to have spiritual qualities, provided of course that you'd taken liberal quantities of chemicals before the track began.

Rating:
Sound ★★★☆☆ Content ★★★★☆
Also recommended:
'The Collected Country Joe' (Vanguard).
If you like this, why not try:
The Grateful Dead, Love, Jefferson Airplane.

Crass

'STATIONS OF THE CRASS'

(Crass/SRD) 1990

Track listing: Stations Of The Crass • Mother Earth • White Punks On Hope • You've Got Big Hands • Darling • System • Big Man • Hurry Up Gary • Gas Man Cometh • Democrats • Contaminational Power • Time Out • I Ain't Thick It's Just A Trick • Fun Going On • Crutch Of Society • I Heard Too Much About • Chairman Of The Board • Tired • Walls • Upright Citizen • System • Big Man • Banned From The Roxy • Hurry Up Gary • Middle Class, Working Class • Fight War Not Wars • Shaved Women • Fun Going On • Unknown Songs • Do They Owe Us A Living • Punk Is Dead

Punk was not the monotonous discordant thrash and scramble for cash that the popular press described. The Crass were sincere in their commitment to anarchy as a means of undermining the system and not simply as a provocative slogan for securing tabloid headlines. This live album captures them in typically vitriolic mood; raging at their allegedly less committed contemporaries such as The Clash, as well as the establishment and orthodox religion with earsplitting feedback, lashings of distorted guitar and military drum beats that called on the faithful to storm the barricades, rather than rush the record shops. Anger and integrity. Not for the fainthearted.

Rating:
Sound ★★★☆☆ Content ★★★☆☆
Also recommended:
'Feeding Of The 5000' (Crass), 'Penis Envy' (Crass) and 'Yes Sir, I Will' (Crass).
If you like this, why not try:
The Clash, Angelic Upstarts, The Fall.

Cream

'DISRAELI GEARS'

(Polydor) 1967

Track listing: Strange Brew • Sunshine Of Your Love • World Of Pain • Dance The Night Away • Blue Condition • Tales Of Brave Ulysess • We're Going Wrong • Outside Woman Blues • Take It Back • Mother's Lament • SWLABR

By the mid-Sixties the legend 'Clapton is God' was to be seen spray-painted on walls the length and breadth of Britain. So naturally expectations were high when the all-mighty guitar guru formed the first so-called 'supergroup' with the equally revered Jack Bruce and Ginger Baker. Bruce had ambitions to raise the bass from a supporting role to that of a lead instrument, while Baker shared the aim of extending the boundaries of rock through extended improvisations based on the blues. This first album however, is more concerned with establishing the group's credentials as a commercial concern, rather than showcasing their instrumental virtuosity. Only 'Strange Brew', 'Sunshine Of Your Love' and 'Tales Of Brave Ulysses' are distinctively different, but these three tracks alone are worth the price of admission. 'Tales' boasts one of the most readily identifiable riffs in rock and also some of the most intoxicating imagery ever set to music.

'Disraeli Gears' is the sound of 'swinging London' in the first flush of psychedelic euphoria.

Rating:
Sound ★★★☆☆ Content ★★★☆☆

Cream

'WHEELS OF FIRE'

2 CDs (Polydor) 1968

Track listing: White Room • Sittin' On Top Of The World • Passing The Time • As You Said • Pressed Rat And Warthog • Politician • Those Were The Days • Born Under A Bad Sign • Deserted Cities Of The Heart • Crossroads • Spoonful • Train Time • Toad

An uneven, but nevertheless indispensable 2CD set comprising live and studio recordings by the first so-called 'supergroup' who were intent on redefining the art of improvisation. The band were at their best reworking the blues and here they give a masterclass in musical architecture while refashioning three foundation stones of the rock repertoire, 'Sittin' On Top Of The World', 'Born Under A Bad Sign' and 'Spoonful'. Less successful is Bruce's harmonica solo 'Train Time' which never really picks up sufficient steam to pull out of the station, but Clapton's solo flights take off as elegantly as a bird, soaring into previously uncharted territory while the rhythm remains tighter than the skin on Baker's snare.

Baker was the band's back-seat driver and a man with a mission to prove that a drum kit is not merely an instrument to keep time. His 16-minute solo 'Toad' must be the most skipped track on CD, but if you have the stamina to stick with it then it will reveal a level of invention equal to that of the two leads. However, if all you want are the two 'hits', 'White Room' and 'Crossroads', you'll find them on various compilations.

Rating:
Sound ★★★☆☆ Content ★★★★☆
Also recommended:
'Live Cream Vol 1 & 2' (Polydor) and 'The Very Best Of Cream' (Polydor) plus 'Those Were The Days' (Polydor) 4CD box set.
If you like this, why not try:
Eric Clapton solo albums, Blind Faith, **Derek And The Dominoes**, Rory Gallagher, **George Thorogood**.

Creedence Clearwater Revival

'CHRONICLE'

(Fantasy) 1987

Track listing: *Suzie Q* • *I Put A Spell On You* • *Proud Mary* • *Bad Moon Rising* • *Lodi* • *Green River* • *Commotion* • *Down On The Corner* • *Fortunate Son* • *Travellin' Band* • *Who'll Stop The Rain?* • *Up Around The Bend* • *Run Through The Jungle* • *Lookin' Out My Back Door* • *Long As I Can See The Light* • *I Heard It Through The Grapevine* • *Have You Ever Seen The Rain?* • *Hey Tonight* • *Sweet Hitch-Hiker* • *Someday Never Comes*

The cover of CCR's 'Green River' album shows the band standing in a sunlit grove attired in chequered working-men's shirts, looking like lumberjacks on their lunch break. It sums up their music perfectly. What you see, is what you get; straightforward Creole country rock that sounds as if it had been distilled on the banks of the bayou. It's tightly focused on lead singer-songwriter John Fogerty's gruff, compelling vocal. Fogerty was a Californian who had never been south of Berkley, but he virtually invented 'swamp rock' which became a favourite with Vietnam GIs.

Here are all the essential tracks including eight gold singles and the pick of six platinum albums which were the perfect antidote to prog-rock excess.

Rating:
Sound ★★★★☆ Content ★★★★★
Also recommended:
'Chronicle Vol 2' (Fantasy) and for the completists a 10CD set, 'The Collection' (Fantasy).
If you like this, why not try:
John Fogerty solo albums, **The Byrds**, **REM**, **Giant Sand**, **Patty Griffin**.

Sheryl Crow

'TUESDAY NIGHT MUSIC CLUB'

(A&M) 1993

Track listing: *Run, Baby, Run* • *Leaving Las Vegas* • *Strong Enough* • *Can't Cry Anymore* • *Solidify* • *The Na Na Song* • *No One Said It Would Be Easy* • *What I Can Do For You* • *All I Wanna Do* • *We Do What We Can* • *I Shall Believe*

After one-time session singer Sheryl Crow rejected her debut album as sounding 'too perfect' she recorded a second during informal after hours jam sessions, hence the title of this multiple Grammy award winner. 'Tuesday Night Music Club' arrived at a time when FM radio and the more adult-orientated rock press were hungry for something meaty to sink their teeth into. As a consequence the album and accompanying single, the untypical 'All I Wanna Do', were over-played to the point where they sounded like they had been on the menu for decades, but somehow they retained their spontaneity. It's easy to forget how fresh and mature sounding her mix of new country and acoustic indie rock sounded back in '93, but with familiarity comes a deeper appreciation of her mordant back-porch perspective and singular slant on the darkening of the American dream.

Rating:
Sound ★★★★☆ Content ★★★★☆
Also recommended:
'Sheryl Crow' (A&M).
If you like this, why not try:
Suzanne Vega, Madonna, Patty Griffin, Joan Osborne, Beth Orton.

The Cult

'LOVE'

(Beggars Banquet) 1985

Track listing: Nirvana • Big Neon Glitter • Love • Brother Wolf, Sister Moon • Rain • Phoenix • Hollow Man • Revolution • She Sells Sanctuary • Black Angel

The Cult emerged roughly unscathed from the wreckage of punk-indie Goth rockers Southern Death Cult with an unapologetically retro sound that borrowed wholesale from the late sixties and a neo-hippy image taken from the Native Americans. At a time when the only options appeared to be between effete electro-pop and ragged DIY bedsit bands, The Cult sounded like the real thing. They created a sound as sparse and expansive as U2 with strong echoes of Cream, Led Zeppelin and Jimi Hendrix. It was a move which elicited derision from the critics, but the audience were too young to make the connection. The singles 'She Sells Sanctuary' and 'Rain' enabled the group to accumulate a sufficiently deep war chest for an assault upon the States and from then they never looked back (unless it was for inspiration).

Rating:
Sound ★★★★☆ Content ★★★★☆

The Cult

'ELECTRIC'

(Beggar's Banquet) 1987

Track listing: Wild Flower • Peace Dog • Lil' Devil • Aphrodisiac Jacket • Electric Ocean • Bad Fun • King Contrary Man • Love Removal Machine • Born To Be Wild • Outlaw • Memphis Hipshake

The perfect title for an album that worships the wah-wah pedal and kneels at the altar of a monolithic Marshall stack. From the first crunching chord, clouds of dry ice descend upon a wall of overdriven guitars and awaken a rhythm section who sound like they've been partying all night with the Prince of Darkness (actually it was their producer Rick Rubin of Def Jam Inc). Then singer Ian Astbury lets rip with a full- throated vocal that betrays long nights listening to old Deep Purple records and it's off to lay siege to Stonehenge.

Power comes from the direct, highly disciplined, uncompromising approach and lashings of volume. These boys' amps go all the way up to 11. Oh, and by the way the songs are uniformly excellent. Crank it up and dry your hair in the slipstream.

Rating:
Sound ★★★★☆ Content ★★★★☆

The Cult

'SONIC TEMPLE'

(Beggars Banquet) 1989

Track listing: Sun King • Fire Woman • American Horse • Edie (Ciao Baby) • Sweet Soul Sister • Soul Asylum • New York City • Automatic Blues • Soldier Blue • Wake Up Time For Freedom • Medicine Train

The Cult's ambition to replicate the stripped down sound of Cream, Led Zeppelin and AC/DC was fully realised with the recording of 'Sonic Temple', but by the time the album was in the can deep fissures had rendered the group structurally unsound.

It is a record conceived to please American FM rock radio with slam bang hooks, short, sharp solos, an outrageously expansive drum sound and vocals that recall Jim Morrison at his brooding best. Few bands of the post-punk/pre-grunge era managed to rock as

hard as The Cult without losing their grip and descending into full blown metal. File under 'Rock'.

Rating:
Sound ★★★★☆ Content ★★★★☆
Also recommended:
'The Cult', 'Dreamtime' and 'Pure Cult – The Best Of' (all on Beggars Banquet).
If you like this, why not try:
Southern Death Cult, **Sisters Of Mercy**, **The Mission**, Killing Joke.

Culture Club

'THE BEST OF'

(Virgin) 1994

Track listing: Do You Really Want To Hurt Me • White Boy • Church Of The Poison Mind • Changing Everyday • War Song • I'm Afraid Of Me • It's A Miracle • Dream • Time Clock Of The Heart • Dive • Victims • I'll Tumble 4 Ya • Miss Me Blind • Mistake No 3 • Medal Song • Karma Chameleon

Boy George was one of the most colourful pop stars of his day, an exotic preening peacock in dreadlocks and dresses who charmed critics and parents alike with his effusive personality. He was the personification of the upwardly mobile eighties, one of those rare party animals who had a seemingly limitless repertoire of witty one-liners and sensational stories for the press. But like the 'New Romantics' who came before him he spent more time in front of the mirror perfecting his make-up than he did on his music. His greatest creation was not the succession of hit singles collected on this CD, but his own outrageous image and in the end he was consumed by the excesses of the lifestyle that he had given everything to possess. He wasn't a musician and when his private life began to fall apart, the life inevitably went out of his music.

His most enduring songs recycled the best of the past, specifically seventies soul and Motown, to provide a non-stop soundtrack to the perfect party. They were George's meal ticket to chat show celebrity and were not expected to outlast their 'sell-by' date. The fact that they do is due almost entirely to his larger-than-life personality, rather than the merits of the music itself.

Rating:
Sound ★★★★☆ Content ★★★☆☆
Also recommended:
The original albums from which these tracks were taken, 'Waking Up With The House On Fire' (Virgin), 'Kissing To Be Clever' (Virgin) and 'Colour By Numbers' (Virgin).
If you like this, why not try:
Simply Red, **ABC**, Bow Wow Wow.

The Cure

'STARING AT THE SEA'

(Fiction) 1986

Track listing: Killing An Arab • 10.15 Saturday Night • Boy's Don't Cry • Jumping Someone Else's Train • A Forest • Play For Today • Primary • Other Voices • Charlotte Sometimes • Hanging Gardens • Let's Go To Bed • Walk • Love Cats • I'm Cold • Caterpillar • In Between Days • Another Journey By Train • Close To Me • Descent • Night Like This • Splintered In Her Head • Mr Pink Eyes • Happy The Man • Throw Your Foot • Exploding Boy • Few Hours After This • Man Inside My Mouth • Stop Dead • New Day

Chapter One of The Cure saga opens with our indie heroes courting controversy back in '78 with the much misunderstood 'Killing An Arab' single, and closes with their enthronement as clown princes of Goth.

It plays like a psychotherapist's session tape on which our angst-ridden patient relives his nightmares in grisly detail until the doctor is sent screaming for the straitjacket. Throughout, Robert Smith reveals his neurosis in a tone that suggests that he really believes that suicide is a reasonable solution to a bad hair day. Although this serves as a useful primer for late-comers the more significant singles were still to come.

Rating:
Sound ★★★★☆ Content ★★★★☆

The Cure

'WISH'

(Fiction) 1992

Track listing: Open • High • Apart • From The Edge Of The Deep Green Sea • Wendy Time • Doing The Unstuck • Friday I'm In Love • Trust • Letter To Elise • Cut • To Wish Impossible Things • End

'Wish' is the perfect antidote to the heavy opiate dirges of their previous outing to Goth City, 'Disintegration', although the tempos remain stubbornly sluggish. With the exception of the despairing 'Open', 'Apart' and 'Cut', its songs have been mixed from a palette of vibrant colours in a studio now illuminated by sunlight after years of being shrouded in cobwebs, much like Miss Haversham's mansion. The highpoint, 'Friday I'm In Love', has to be one of the most disarmingly charming songs to grace the charts in a decade.

'Wish' was The Cure's most commercial record to date and for once that term is not intended as an insult.

Rating:
Sound ★★★★☆ Content ★★★★★
Also recommended:
'Kiss Me, Kiss Me, Kiss Me'. Alternatively the weighty 16CD box set 'The Cure Box' and the album of inventive remixes 'Mixed Up' (all on Fiction).
If you like this, why not try:
Various Artists '100 Years – A Tribute To The Cure' (Cleopatra/Cargo), **Siouxsie And The Banshees**, The Glove (Smith's collaboration with Steve Severin).

Cypress Hill

'CYPRESS HILL'

(Ruff House/Columbia) 1989

Track listing: Pigs • How I Could Just Kill A Man • Hand On The Pump • Hole In The Head • Ultraviolet Dreams • Light Another • The Phunky Feel One • Break It Up • Real Estate • Stoned Is The Way Of The Walk • Psychobetabuckdown • Something For The Blunted • Latin Lingo • The Funky Cypress Hill Shit • Tres Equis • Born To Get Busy

'Some say that life is a bitch' sing Cuban-American crew Cypress Hill and then proceed to leave you in no doubt that they know what they're talking about by reeling off a litany of scary inner-city stories and bum

dope deals. They might plunder frisky P-Funk and soul tracks for samples, but all their tracks are drenched in the sweet smell of the weed and underscored by the ominous presence of violence and death. Frequently unsettling, but curiously compelling.

Rating:
Sound ★★★★☆ Content ★★★★☆
Also recommended:
'Black Sunday' (Columbia) and 'Cypress Hill III – Temples Of Boom' (Columbia).
If you like this, why not try:
Public Enemy, Pearl Jam, Sonic Youth.

The Damned

'DAMNED DAMNED DAMNED'

(Demon) 1977

Track listing: Neat Neat Neat • Fan Club • I Fall • Born To Kill • Stab Your Back • Feel The Pain • New Rose • Fish • See Her Tonite • One Of The Two • So Messed Up • I Feel Alright

The Damned were the first punk band to release a single and the first to record an album, two ambitions they were desperate to fulfil before they had time to learn more chords and risk spoiling the effect. Both were produced by Nick Lowe whose stated philosophy was 'bang it down and tart it up later', although in the case of his delinquent protégés he didn't bother to burnish the ragged edges.

'New Rose' compresses their nihilistic philosophy into one frantic three-minute thrash with Vanian quoting from 'Leader Of The Pack' to give a nod to those in the know that we're into schlock-horror B movie territory and not the serious stuff perpetrated by The Clash. The tracks sound like they are on the verge of disintegrating as the band speed on their own adrenaline in a mad dash for the exit, while Vanian spits out the words. The Damned may have seemed like a bunch of buffoons in comparison with The Pistols and The Clash, but they were the genuine article. They took a perverse pleasure in their instrumental ineptitude and delighted in destroying their equipment while the tapes were still rolling. But above all, they were enthusiastic. And that's worth more than knowing a fourth chord.

Rating:
Sound ★★★☆☆ Content ★★★★☆

The Damned

'PHANTASMAGORIA'

(MCA) 1991

Track listing: Street Dreams • Shadow Of Love • There'll Come A Day • Sanctum Sanctorum • Is It A Dream • Grimly Fiendish • Edward The Bear • Eighth Day • Trojans • I Just Can't Be Happy Today

By the time they came to record 'Phantasmagoria' Dave Vanian's Dracula obsession had possessed him entirely. The punk element had all but dissipated leaving the group looking like the illegitimate offspring of the Addams family and sounding

as if they would be happier cranking out soundtracks for a Hammer horror. 'Grimly Fiendish', a track typical of their new direction, is based on a children's comic character and became one of their biggest hits along with 'Shadow Of Love' and a melodramatic cover of Barry Ryan's 'Eloise' from the same sessions. Their transformation from cartoon punks to cartoon Goths was complete.

Rating:
Sound ★★★★☆ Content ★★★☆☆
Also recommended:
'Best Of' (Big Beat), 'BBC Radio 1 Sessions' (Strange Fruit), 'Eternally Damned – The Very Best' (MCI), 'Light At The End Of The Tunnel' (MCA) 2CD set of rarities and out-takes, 'Machine Gun Etiquette' (Big Beat) and 'The Black Album' (Big Beat).

If you like this, why not try:
The Cramps, The Adverts, Dead Kennedys.

De La Soul

'3 FEET HIGH AND RISING'

(Big Life) 1989

Track listing: Intro • The Magic Number • Change In Speak • Cool Breeze On The Rocks • Can U Keep A Secret • Jenifa Taught Me • Ghetto Thang • Transmitting Live From Mars • Eye Know • Take It Off • A Little Bit Of Soap • Tread Water • Say No Go • Do As De La Does • Plug Tunin' • De La Orgee • Buddy • Description • Me Myself And I • This Is A Recording 4 Living In A Full Time Era • I Can Do Anything • D.A.I.S.Y Age • Potholes In My Lawn

At a time when rap was becoming increasingly militant, aggressively macho and tediously monosyllabic, De La Soul produced a mellow, chill-out classic by sampling smoochy R&B, soft rock and psychedelia to create an aural collage that they called Daisy Age soul (Da Inner Sound Y'all).

The Long Island innovators present the album in the form of a game show soundtrack with sketches and soundbites between the tracks to evoke a comic strip suburbia, but like the characters in 'Pleasantville' they prove to be subversive in a subtle way. Songs such as the singles 'Me Myself I' and 'The Magic Number' keep the faith with the hip hop hardcore, but expand its vocabulary with humour and the acknowledgement that there is no substitute for a good tune.

Their cleverness, however, proved their undoing after their liberal use of samples got industry lawyers in a feeding frenzy. The resulting regulations effectively put the 'cuffs on their creativity, but the album remains a delight and they should be credited with raising the cultural awareness of their younger fans with their 'afro-centric' image and for giving them an alternative to the self-destructive 'gangsta' lifestyle.

Rating:
Sound ★★★★☆ Content ★★★★☆
Also recommended:
'De La Soul Is Dead' (Big Life).
If you like this, why not try:
Funkadelic, Parliament, Soul ll Soul.

Dead Can Dance

'WITHIN THE REALM OF A DYING SUN'

(4AD) 1986

Track listing: Anywhere Out Of The World • Windfall • In The Wake Of Adversity • Xavier • Dawn Of The Iconoclast • Cantara • Summoning Up The Muse • Persephone

Dead Can Dance were assumed to be a Goth band by those who hadn't actually bothered to listen to their albums and as ambient New Age artists by those who did, but who didn't understand what it was that they were listening to. However, those who listened *and* understood were often no nearer to defining the duo than anyone else. Over the course of their eclectic career Lisa Gerrard and partner Brendan Perry explored Celtic, Medieval and Middle Eastern music in the search for a sound that expressed an inner reality, rather than commenting on the physical world around them. No surprise then that they remained a cult and that Gerrard eventually found fulfilment as a film composer, initially with *The Insider* and then with her contribution to *Gladiator*. Those who were struck by the ethereal beauty of the latter will find much to enjoy here.

'Within The Realm Of A Dying Sun' is the duo's classical album with the traditional instruments augmented by samplers and computers and of course, Gerrard's heavenly vocal.

Rating:
Sound ★★★★☆ Content ★★★★☆

Dead Can Dance

'AION'

(4AD) 1990

Track listing: Arrival And The Reunion • Mephisto • Fortune Presents Gifts Not According • End Of Woods • Wilderness • Garden Of Zephirus • Satarello • Song Of Sibyl • As The Bell Rings The Maypole Sign • Black Sun • Promised Womb • Radharc

Brendan Perry has described his method of composition as being capable of producing 'dangerously beautiful music', which is an apt description of 'Aion'. It's an album rooted in the Renaissance and featuring authentic instruments layered with Gregorian chants and droning guitars to evoke a lush pastoral landscape of the inner mind.

Rating:
Sound ★★★★☆ Content ★★★★☆
Also recommended:
'A Passage In Time' (Warners) Well chosen compilation which acts as an ideal introduction plus 'Into The Labyrinth' (4AD).
If you like this, why not try:
This Mortal Coil, **Cocteau Twins**.

Dead Kennedys

'FRESH FRUIT FOR ROTTING VEGETABLES'

(Alternative Tentacles) 1980

Track listing: Kill The Poor • Forward To Death • When Ya Get Drafted • Let's Lynch The Landlord • Drug Me • Your Emotions • Chemical Warfare • California Uber Alles • I Kill Children • Stealing People's Mail • Funland At The Beach • Ill In The Head • Holiday In Cambodia • Viva Las Vegas

Jello Biafra has been described as a political performance artist whose self-righteous scattergun sarcasm was aimed at conservative middle-aged hippies and fascists alike. He was evidently angered as much by the failure of liberals to confront the fascists as by the extremists themselves. 'Fresh Fruit' finds him urinating over the manicured lawns of suburbia and the self-centred New Age cults of the sunshine state, while the band hammer home their message with nagging guitars, rumbling bass and drums that appear to be in the process of being flayed alive. Unfortunately, the production of this first album is poor, dampening the impact of 'California Uber Alles' and 'Holiday In Cambodia', two of the most pugnacious songs that hardcore punk produced.

Rating:
Sound ★★★☆☆ Content ★★★☆☆

Dead Kennedys

'PLASTIC SURGERY DISASTERS'

(Alternative Tentacles) 1982

Track listing: Government Flu • Terminal Preppie • Trust Your Mechanic • Well Paid Scientist • Buzzbomb • Forest Fire • Halloween • Winnebago Warrior • Riot • Bleed For Me • I Am The Owl • Dead End • Moon Over Marin • In God We Trust

With the loss of The Pistols, and The Clash having been accused of selling out, it was down to the Dead Kennedys to carry the black flag of punk into the eighties. Their second album is as fierce and derisive as the first but with a vastly improved sound. Their targets are kept more clearly in focus and are hit squarely where it hurts. It's just a pity that the best songs were on the earlier record. Although little more than a footnote in the history of hardcore it's now a considerably more desirable item thanks to the inclusion of the 8 tracks from the 'In God We Trust' EP.

Rating:
Sound ★★★★☆ Content ★★★☆☆
Also recommended:
'Frankenchrist' (Alternative Tentacles) and the compilation 'Give Me Convenience Or Give Me Death' (Alternative Tentacles).
If you like this, why not try:
Various Artists 'Virus 100' (Alternative Tentacles) another 'tribute' project, The Damned, The Adverts, Green Day.

Deep Purple

'IN ROCK'

Anniversary Edition (EMI) 1970

Track listing: Speed King • Bloodsucker • Child In Time • Flight Of the Rat • Into The Fire • Living Wreck • Hard Lovin' Man

Bonus tracks: Black Night • Speed King • Cry Free • Jam Stew • Flight Of The Rat • Speed King • Black Night

It is hard to imagine how a classic album of this stature could be improved upon, but it has been by the addition of previously unreleased out-takes, selected remixes and a wholesale clean-up of the original masters. It's an understatement to say

that these tracks have never sounded so good. Restoration has had the effect of significantly expanding the heavily compressed sound of the original to lend a real wallop to hot-wired hard rock classics 'Living Wreck', 'Black Night' and 'Speed King' that fully justifies revisiting these old albums and burnishing them anew. From the thunderous cacophony which opens 'Speed King' to the slow burn of 'Child In Time' this is the album that defined hard rock at the beginning of the Seventies and now its restoration has set the standard for the art of remastering.

Rating:
Sound ★★★★★ Content ★★★★★

Deep Purple

'FIREBALL'

25th Anniversary Edition (EMI) 1971

Track listing: Fireball • No No No • Demon's Eye • Anyone's Daughter • The Mule • Fools • No One Came

Bonus tracks: Strange Kind Of Woman • I'm Alone • Freedom • Slow Train • Demon's Eye • The Noise Abatement Society Tapes • Fireball • Backwards Piano • No One Came

Purple once held the record for being the loudest band in the world, an achievement which tended to obscure the tensile strength and suppleness in their songs; qualities which were lacking in their more , riff-orientated rivals. 'Fireball' shows them to be masters of belligerent blues-rock with tracks burning on a short fuse before swiftly building to a screaming climax.

Ian Gillan may have lacked the subtlety of Zeppelin's Robert Plant, but these tracks prove that he had the lung capacity to be heard over the barrage of power chords and could hold his own centre stage with one of the most formidable rhythm sections in rock.

This revamped reissue adds a remix of the single 'Strange Kind Of Woman' and enough bonus material to compensate for the comparatively stilted and second-rate fillers which padded out the second side of the original album. And as with all the other Purple remasters the CD includes a 28-page booklet telling the full story of these historic sessions illustrated with rare photos.

Rating:
Sound ★★★★☆ Content ★★★★☆

Deep Purple

'MACHINE HEAD'

2 CD Anniversary Edition (EMI) 1972

Track listing: CD 1 1997 Remixes – Highway Star • Maybe I'm A Leo • Pictures of Home • Never Before • Smoke On The Water • Lazy • Space Truckin'

Bonus track: When A Blind Man Cries

CD 2 Remasters – Highway Star • Maybe I'm A Leo • Pictures Of Home • Never Before • Smoke On The Water • Lazy • Space Truckin'

Bonus tracks: When A Blind Man Cries • Maybe I'm A Leo • Lazy

Uncertain whether to remix the entire 'Machine Head' album or remaster it, EMI opted to do both, hence this 2CD set offering the remixes on the first disc and the remasters on the second. What more can be said about an album which gave the world 'Smoke On The Water' and the most frequently played riff in rock, not to mention the screaming salvo of 'Highway Star', the belligerent blues labouring under the name of 'Lazy' and the almighty 'Space Truckin'. Roger Glover's remixes have wiped away layers of grime to reveal the masterwork beneath.

Rating:
Sound ★★★★☆ Content ★★★★★

Deep Purple

'LIVE IN JAPAN'

Remastered Edition 3CDs (EMI) 1993

Track listing: CD 1 – Highway Star • Child In Time • The Mule • Strange Kind Of Woman • Lazy • Space Truckin' • Black Night

CD 2 – Highway Star • Smoke On The Water • Child In Time • The Mule • Strange Kind Of Woman • Lazy • Space Truckin'

CD 3 – Highway Star • Smoke On The Water • Child In Time • Smoke On The Water • Lazy • Space Truckin' • Speed King

What could be better than 'Made In Japan', one of the all-time classic live albums? Answer: 'Live In Japan', an expanded and remastered triple CD version culled from the same tour. Hardcore fans will relish the chance to hear all three shows, even though the set list is almost identical, because there's no such thing as too much of a good thing. The first Osaka show, taped at the ungodly hour of 6.30 in the evening, betrays no sign of jet lag as the group punish their instruments to the evident bemusement of 13,000 stunned children of the rising sun. The second show sees them delivering a performance of awesome power and intensity, while the third offers versions of 'Strange Kind Of Woman' and 'Speed King' which are even better than the ones chosen for the original album with ferocious solos from Blackmore and a considerably more confident vocal from Gillan.

Digitally remixed from the original tapes, 'Live In Japan' is a testament to the musical muscle of one of the greatest rock bands captured at the very peak of their powers.

Rating:
Sound ★★★★☆ Content ★★★★★
Also recommended:
'Made In Japan' (EMI) the original double live album on 1 CD, plus 'Burn', 'Who Do We Think We Are' and the solid 'hits' package 'Deepest Purple' (all on EMI).
If you like this, why not try:
Whitesnake, **Ritchie Blackmore's Rainbow, The Cult.**

Def Leppard

'PYROMANIA'

(Vertigo) 1983

Track listing: Photograph • Too Late For Love • Comin' Under Fire • Foolin' • Die Hard The Hunter • Rock! Rock! • Billy's Got A Gun • Action! Not Words • Stage Fright • Rock Of Ages

'Women to the left, women to the right. There to entertain and take you thru the night.' Yes, it's another heavy metal manifesto, this time from England's answer to AC/DC. Sheffield is renowned for its steel, but this particular compound sounds like it's been recycled from substandard material. Part of the blame lies with Robert 'Mutt' Lange whose highly polished production smooths the rougher edges until the group sounds as bland as his former clients, The Cars. But that was evidently the intention. From the moment they rode in on the New Wave of British heavy metal, Leppard had their sights set on the lucrative American market which meant packaging their adolescent macho-posturing in an AOR, radio-friendly wrapping.

British critics found the band crass and commercial, but fans on both sides of the Atlantic lapped it up, while heavy rotation of their videos ensured that it was shipped to the States by the tanker load. Leppard still hold the record for being the first band to sell over seven million copies of successive albums Stateside, the second being 'Hysteria' which racked up a staggering 14 million. But some might say that they still sound like an adolescent AC/DC who have spent too much time in front of the mirror perfecting the pose instead of practising their riffs. Includes the hits 'Photograph' and 'Rock Of Ages', both of which became staples of their live set.

Rating:
Sound ★★★★☆ Content ★★★☆☆

Def Leppard

'HYSTERIA'

(Vertigo) 1987

Track listing: Women • Rocket • Animal • Love Bites • Pour Some Sugar On Me • Armageddon It • Gods Of War • Don't Shoot Shotgun • Run Riot • Hysteria • Excitable • Love And Affection

Even the loss of their drummer's left arm in a car crash was not enough to limit Leppard's insatiable appetite for conquest. A specially customized kit was built which allowed Rick Allen to trigger fills with his feet before the band could embark on a mission to market their particular brand of metal-lite alloy to kids who were too young to have seen Sabbath or Motorhead. 'Hysteria' was three years in the making at a cost of a cool million. Yet, the mix is much as before – only more so. It's loud, proud and bombastic, but serious metal heads would rather have the real thing.

Rating:
Sound ★★★★☆ Content ★★★☆☆
Also recommended:
The rawer 'Retro-Active' which has a live-in-the-studio feel and 'Slang' which audaciously updated their sound all on Bludgeon Riffola).
If you like this, why not try:
Metallica, **Iron Maiden**, Samson.

Depeche Mode

'THE SINGLES 81–85'

(Mute) 1998

Track listing: Dreaming Of Me • New Life • Just Can't Get Enough • See You • The Meaning Of Love • Leave In Silence • Get The Balance Right • Everything Counts • Love In Itself • People Are People • Master And Servant • Blasphemous Rumours • Somebody • Shake The Disease • It's Called A Heart

Bonus tracks: Photographic • Just Can't Get Enough (Remix)

This is the first instalment in the continuing success story of the boys from Basildon who swapped their rinky-tink Casio keyboards and pre-programmed, push-button pop for AOR American rock and subsequent stadium-packing success. 'The Singles' was originally released in 1985. The early hits, 'Dreaming Of Me', 'New Life' and 'Just Can't Get Enough' exemplify the soulless, Kraftwerk-styled synth-pop of the early eighties with its 'futurist' trappings, but the latter singles dabble with darker subject matter without obstructing their steady stream of success.

This remastered edition adds a remix of 'Just Can't Get Enough' and the original version of 'Photographic', issued on the Some Bizarre label.

Welcome to the machine.

Rating:
Sound ★★★★☆ Content ★★★☆☆
Also recommended:
'Music For The Masses', 'Violator' and 'Songs Of Faith And Devotion', their more intense, mature work from the 1990s (all on Mute).
If you like this, why not try:
Kraftwerk, **The Human League**, Thompson Twins.

Derek And The Dominoes

'LAYLA AND OTHER ASSORTED LOVESONGS'

(Polydor) 1970

Track listing: I Looked Away • Bell Bottom Blues • Keep On Growing • Nobody Knows You When You're Down And Out • I Am Yours • Anyday • Key To The Highway • Tell The Truth • Why Does Love Got To Be So Sad? • Have You Ever Loved A Woman • Little Wing • It's Too Late • Layla • Thorn Tree In The Garden

Clapton's deification had become such a burden to him by 1970 that he felt forced to seek anonymity in this studio band formed with the ill-fated Duane Allman.

Clapton's status as a guitar god and the subsequent success of the single 'Layla' has led to the album's inflated reputation. 'Key To The Highway' used to rock harder when Clapton played it with John Mayall, while 'Bell Bottom Blues' and 'Nobody Knows You' appear to anticipate the mellow, mainstream rock that Clapton was to coast along with through the Seventies. In essence it's a buddy session with old slowhand and Allman trading licks on a set of laid-back blues and soft-centred rockers with little quality control to weed out the prunes from the plums. But it's got the full, unedited version of 'Layla' and that alone makes it a must.

Rating:
Sound ★★★★☆ Content ★★★★☆
Also recommended:
'Crossroads' (Polydor), 4CD Clapton retrospective featuring previously unreleased tracks from what would have been the Dominoes' second album.

If you like this, why not try:
The Allman Brothers, **Cream**, **Clapton**'s solo albums, Albert King.

Dexy's Midnight Runners

'SEARCHING FOR THE YOUNG SOUL REBELS'

(Parlophone) 1980

Track listing: Burn It Down • Tell Me When My Light Turns Green • The Teams That Meet In Caffs • I'm Just Looking • Geno • Seven Day's Too Long • I Couldn't Help If I Tried • Thankfully Not Living In Yorkshire It Doesn't Apply • Keep It • Love Part One • There There My Dear

There's a scene in Alan Parker's caustic musical comedy *The Commitments* when the all-white Dublin soul band are stunned into silence by their manager's declaration that the Irish are the 'blacks of the Western world' and that, as such, they should proclaim that they're black and they're proud. One can imagine Kevin Rowland giving a similar pep talk to his young soul rebels in the summer of '78 when he was trying to convince them that it was prime time for a soul revival. Back then Britain was still absorbing the aftershocks of punk and the slick sound of Stax was as unfashionable as kaftans and flares. But Rowland drilled Dexy's until they were so sharp that all resistance was futile.

The band was his creation and he ran a tight ship. His quavering vocal and indomitable personality dominates this first album, while the band break out the brassiest riffs since Geno Washington packed the ballrooms of the Northern Soul circuit. But Rowland's predominance is occasionally to its detriment. 'Searching' is an intense but erratic album partially undermined by pretentious padding (Rowland's rant on 'Thankfully Living In Yorkshire..' being a prime example), but it burns with a passion that James Brown would have been proud of.

Rating:
Sound ★★★★☆ Content ★★★★☆

Dexy's Midnight Runners

'TOO-RAY-AY'

(Mercury) 1982

Track listing: The Celtic Soul Brothers • Let's Make This Precious • All In All • Jackie Wilson Said • Old • Plan B • I'll Show You • Liars A To E • Until I Believe In My Soul • Come On Eileen

Had anyone of lesser commitment made a switch from Northern soul to traditional Irish folk they would have been accused of commercial cynicism, or premature senility. But such was Kevin Rowland's personal conviction that few protested when he recruited fiddle trio The Emerald Express and swapped the group's street gang image for gypsy chic and dungarees. The combination of rasping brass and sweeping fiddles created an unlikely hybrid which Kevin coined 'Celtic Soul', but it was one that worked. While the self-celebratory 'Celtic Soul Brothers' failed to penetrate the higher

regions of the chart when released as a single, the ebullient 'Come On Eileen' was number one on both sides of the Atlantic and a cover of Van Morrison's 'Jackie Wilson Said' racked up very respectable sales. Rowland later admitted that he took an unfair share of the credit for Dexy's distinctive sound which should have been shared equally with guitarist Al Archer, but it's Rowland's conviction that is the real heart and soul of the band.

Rating:
Sound ★★★★☆ Content ★★★★☆
Also recommended:
'Very Best Of' (Mercury)
If you like this, why not try:
Van Morrison, The Pogues, Geno Washington.

Dido

'NO ANGEL'

(Arista) 2001

Track listing: Here With Me • Hunter • Don't Think Of Me • My Lover's Gone • All You Want • Thank You • Honestly OK • Slide • Isobel • I'm No Angel • My Life

Bonus tracks: Take My Hand • Here With Me (Video) • Thank You (Video)

With Dido's debut, quality songwriting returns to grace the dancefloors. Produced by her brother Rollo and techno-alchemist Youth, 'No Angel' synthesizes trip-hop and pop into a confection that's as smooth as whipped cream to redefine the term 'easy listening'. Acoustic guitar, tasteful synths, mellow mid-tempo grooves and

Dido's lucid, intimate vocal make this the perfect soundtrack for stress-busting or snuggling up to someone special. Sample 'My Lover's Gone' with eyes closed and be transported to the desert island of your choice complete with circling seagulls and the sound of waves lapping gently on the shore.

Rating:
Sound ★★★★☆ Content ★★★★☆
Also recommended: n/a
If you like this, why not try:
Sinead O'Connor, Beth Orton, **Portishead**.

Dion

'BEST OF DION AND THE BELMONTS'

(Music For Pleasure) 1999

Track listing: Teenager In Love • I Wonder Why • Where Or When • Every Little Thing I Do • Lover's Prayer • No One Knows • That's My Desire • Don't Pity Me • In The Still Of The Night • Will You Love Me Still • Runaround Sue • Lonely Teenager • Sandy • Lovers Who Wander • Runaway Girl • Queen Of The Hop • Lonely World • King Without A Queen • Kissin' Game • Tonight, Tonight • The Wanderer

Dion might be little more than a 'golden oldie' to the majority of daytime radio DJs, but he had a voice as rich and smooth as melted butterscotch and he sang with a fluid, soulful style that would have brought a tear to the eye of the great Sam Cooke. During the late fifties and early sixties he enriched a string of classic teen dream tunes that defined the soulful street corner, close harmony, a cappella singing style known as Doo Wop. Most of the white Doo Wop vocal groups

were bland, but Dion and The Belmonts were the exception.

These 40-year-old recordings exude a warm, nostalgic glow that is enhanced by remastering which is little short of a revelation. This is the demonstration quality sound that your CD player has been waiting for.

Rating:
Sound ★★★★★ Content ★★★★☆
Also recommended:
'Lovers Who Wander'/'So Why Didn't You Do That Before?', 2 albums on 1 CD, the latter being a collection of outtakes (Ace)
If you like this, why not try:
Jackie Wilson, Sam Cooke.

Celine Dion

'FALLING INTO YOU'

(Epic) 1996

Track listing: It's All Coming Back To Me Now • Because You Loved Me • Falling Into You • Make You Happy • Seduces Me • All By Myself • Declaration Of Love • Natural Woman • Dreamin' Of You • I Love You • If That's What It Takes • I Don't Know • River Deep, Mountain High • Your Light • Call The Man

The temptation to compare the music of Celine Dion to that of the film which gave her the biggest hit of her career is irresistible and not entirely gratuitous. Above the waterline it's a classy production designed to impress, but puncture its pretensions and it'll sink faster than a lead lifeboat. Its tidal wave of gushing emotions would serve as a suitable soundtrack for an old-fashioned Barbara Cartland romance, overwrought, overdressed and overrated. But unlike the iceberg which sank *The Titanic* there is little substance below the surface. The only thing keeping this album afloat is the quality of the musicianship (no pun intended).

Rating:
Sound ★★★★☆ Content ★★☆☆☆
Also recommended:
'Celine Dion' and 'The Colour Of My Love' (both Epic).
If you like this, why not try: Whitney Houston, Janet Jackson, Mariah Carey, Annie Lennox.

Dire Straits

'BROTHERS IN ARMS'

(Vertigo) 1985

Track listing: So Far Away • Money For Nothing • Walk Of Life • Your Latest Trick • Why Worry • Ride Across The River • Man's Too Strong • One World • Brothers In Arms

When the clamour of punk began to die down at the beginning of the eighties ex-pub rockers Dire Straits emerged with a lucrative brand of laid-back rock tailor-made for the more mature end of the market and the fledgling CD format. This, their fifth studio album, sold on such a scale that industry insiders suggested that there was a point when everyone who owned a CD player also owned a copy of this disc.

The key to The Straits success was that their music wasn't too dynamic, nor demanding. It fitted unobtrusively into the listener's lifestyle like a well-behaved pet dog. You could clean the car, do the chores and entertain friends without having to adjust the volume every time the guitar solo came along and it was suitably impressive for showing off the hi-fi. But like the proverbial pet it also had the right pedigree. Knopfler's laid-back guitar licks looked back to Clapton, Rory Gallagher and Martin Barre of Jethro Tull, while his mid-Atlantic drawl reminded older fans of JJ Cale, Springsteen and Bob Dylan.

The singles 'Money For Nothing' (featuring Sting) and 'Walk Of Life' may have ensured heavy rotation on MTV and subsequent sales beyond 20 million (eclipsing even Michael Jackson's 'Thriller'), but it's the semi-acoustic folk-rock tracks that have an enduring and unassuming appeal.

Rating:
Sound ★★★★★ Content ★★★★☆

Dire Straits

'ALCHEMY – LIVE'

(Vertigo) 1984

Track listing: Once Upon A Time In The West • Expresso Love • Private Investigations • Sultans Of Swing • Two Young Lovers • Telegraph Road • Solid Rock • Going Home • Romeo And Juliet

By this point in their career the group's studio albums were becoming increasingly bland, but in performance they could still cut it, particularly when allowed the luxury of a broader canvas, as on the epic 'Telegraph Road' and 'Once Upon A Time'. Knopfler strolls through the songs in a laid-back, leisurely manner evoking the romance of the wide open spaces with images that would have done Dylan proud. He gives the impression that he's going to take his own sweet time getting to the point, (assuming that there is one), underscoring his wry observations with an understated, economical guitar style which invites comparison with Clapton and delivers them in a drawl that sounds like Springsteen during a late-night session for the introspective 'Nebraska'.

This is one Dire Straits album that even the critics wouldn't be embarrassed to own.

Rating:
Sound ★★★★☆ Content ★★★★☆

Dire Straits

'MONEY FOR NOTHING'

(Vertigo) 1988

Track listing: Sultans Of Swing • Down To The Waterline • Portobello Belle • Twisting By The Pool • Romeo And Juliet • Where Do You Think You're Going • Walk Of Life • Private Investigations • Money For Nothing • Tunnel Of Love • Brothers In Arms • Telegraph Road

The inevitable 'greatest hits' package provides a veritable blueprint for the Dire Straits sound opening with 'Sultans Of Swing', the song that mythologized their pub-rock origins and in doing so, launched the careers of innumerable copy-cat bands. Everything you could possibly want to know about Dire Straits can be heard between the intro and fade of that one song. But if you want more, there's the urban romance of 'Romeo And Juliet', complete with distinctive Dobro guitar picking, the Springsteen-

styled 'Tunnel Of Love', Yuppie favourites 'Twisting By The Pool' and 'Walk Of Life', plus a 12-minute live version of 'Telegraph Road'.

Rating:
Sound ★★★★★ Content ★★★★☆
Also recommended:
'Communique', 'Love Over Gold', 'On Every Street' and 'Making Movies' (all on Vertigo).
If you like this, why not try:
Eric Clapton, **Rory Gallagher**, Chris Rea, Notting Hillbillies.

Dr Feelgood

'SINGLES – THE UA YEARS'

(Liberty/EMI) 1989

Track listing: Roxette • She Does It Right • Back In The Night • Going Back Home • Riot In Cell Block 9 • Sneakin' Suspicion • She's A Wind Up • Baby Jane • Down At The Doctors • Milk And Alcohol • As Long As The Price Is Right • Put Him Out Of Your Mind • Hong Kong Money • No Mo Do Yakamo • Jumping From Love To Love • Violent Love • Waiting For Saturday Night • Monkey • Trying To Live My Life Without You • Crazy About Girls • My Way • Madman Blues • See You Later Alligator • Hunting, Shooting, Fishing • Don't Wake Up • Milk And Alcohol

Need a shot of rhythm and blues with a little rock and roll on the side, just for good measure? Whatever ails you Dr Feelgood can fill the prescription. There's no queue to be seen at this surgery and no waiting list for an op. The doc dispenses his remedy the instant the needle hits the groove guaranteeing to have you back on your feet before morning. Although you'll have to work up a fever first. His therapy may be rough 'n' ready, but it'll galvanize the disheartened and make the lame boogie. So, inoculate yourself against the blues this winter, or any other time of the year for that matter, with Dr Feelgood's cure-all: 26 of the most potent restoratives on the market.

Rating:
Sound ★★★★☆ Content ★★★★☆
Also recommended:
'Down By The Jetty' (Grand/Vital), 'Sneakin' Suspicion' (Grand/Vital), 'Stupidity' (Liberty), their classic live album, plus the ultimate tribute, 'Looking Back' a 5CD box set (EMI) featuring 104 tracks including many rare and unreleased items plus recorded interviews.
If you like this, why not try:
John Lee Hooker, Elmore James, Muddy Waters, **George Thorogood**.

Fats Domino

'BEST OF'

(MFP) 1988 Budget price

Track listing: Blueberry Hill • Whole Lotta Lovin' • Fat Man • Blue Monday • I'm Walking • I'm In Love Again • Be My Guest • When My Dreamboat Comes Home • Let The Four Winds Blow • I'm Gonna Be A Wheel Someday • Walking To New Orleans • Ain't That A Shame • I Want To Walk You Home • My Blue Heaven • Valley Of Tears

Fats may not have been the most dynamic performer during the pioneering days of pop, but he was one of the most commercially successful and best loved artists of the era. In contrast to the rebellious icons of the fifties he was an amiable,

avuncular figure who managed to stay the distance, proving to be a consistent hitmaker for almost 20 years with over 60 top 100 hits to his credit. With his first national hit, 'The Fat Man', he established an unmistakable style which put a strong back beat to a boogie woogie piano figure and added a rasping sax and a rich bluesy vocal with a trace of a Creole accent.

His later recordings tend to sound bland and rather similar as he diluted the highly successful formula with schmaltzy strings, but some of these early hits are steeped in the New Orleans R&B tradition with a sprinkling of voodoo gumbo for good measure.

Rating:
Sound ★★★☆☆ Content ★★★☆☆
Also recommended:
'Walking To New Orleans' (Bear Family) box set.
If you like this, why not try:
Little Richard, **Jerry Lee Lewis**, Smiley Lewis.

Donovan

'GREATEST HITS AND MORE'

(EMI) 1991

Track listing: Sunshine Superman • Wear Your Love Like Heaven • Jennifer Juniper • Barabajagal • Hurdy Gurdy Man • Epistle To Dippy • To Susan On The West Coast Waiting • Catch The Wind • Mellow Yellow • There Is A Mountain • Happiness Runs • Season Of The Witch • Colours • Superlungs My Supergirl • Lalena • Atlantis • Preachin' Love • Poor Cow • Teen Angel • Aye My Love

Rating:
Sound ★★★☆☆ Content ★★★☆☆

Donovan

'THE TRIP'

(EMI) 1991

Track listing: The Trip • Lullaby Of The Spring • Sunny South Kensington • Sand And Foam • Someone Singing • Guinevere • Celeste • Widow With Shawl • Writer In The Sun • Entertaining Of A Shy Girl • The Land Of Doesn't Have To Be • Skip-A-Long-Sam • Hampstead Incident • Mad John's Escape • Three Kingfishers • Little Boy In Corduroy • Isle Of Islay • Young Girl Blues • Museum • As I Recall It • Legend Of A Young Girl Linda • House Of Jansch • Oh Gosh • There Was A Time

Donovan began in the early sixties as an earnest imitation of Bob Dylan, scoring hits with the sparse, acoustic, folk-flavoured 'Colours' and 'Catch The Wind'. (The versions included on this compilation are the superior latter re-recordings with additional instrumentation.) But as soon as he discarded his political hang-ups and his harmonica to embrace the hippy ideal of free love and flower power, he found himself on a more artistically rewarding trip.

Protest gave way to the soft focus psych-pop of 'Sunshine Superman' and 'Mellow Yellow' enriched by sounds and instrumentation borrowed freely from jazz, classical and ethnic Indian music. 'Sunshine Superman', for example, finds his soft Scottish brogue drifting on an exotic magic carpet of sound woven by an ensemble comprising harpsichord, flute and fretless acoustic bass.

Though redolent with the musty scent of incense, Donovan's songs had a child-like simplicity, a quality enhanced by his lyrics that were firmly rooted in the Celtic fairy-tale tradition. But as the optimism of the late sixties became soured, Donovan's innocence and idealism appeared dated and even naïve. Songs such as the simplistic 'There Is A Mountain' and 'Happiness Runs' revealed him to be more in tune with children and as such his music was considered too precious for the increasingly cynical seventies.

NB: In deference to his status as troubadour to the flower-power generation, several of these tracks feature uncredited guest appearances by leading players of the period, including Paul McCartney, Graham Nash and future members of Led Zeppelin and Cream, as well as the Jeff Beck group.

'The Trip' is a companion piece to 'Greatest Hits' and could be subtitled 'The Best And The Worst Of Donovan' as it includes some of his most contrived and twee titles as well as a few rare gems such as 'Hampstead Incident', 'Museum', 'Guinevere' and 'Young Girl Blues'. Together, these two CDs comprise some of the finest music to come out of the sixties.

Rating:
Sound ★★★☆☆ Content ★★★★☆
Also Recommended:
'Troubadour – The Definitive Collection', a 2CD set (EMI.
If you like this, why not try:
Dr Strangely Strange,
Tyrannosaurus Rex, **Nick Drake**,
The Incredible String Band.

The Doors

'THE DOORS'

(Elektra) 1967

Track listing: Break On Through • Soul Kitchen • The Crystal Ship • Twentieth Century Fox • Alabama Song • Light My Fire • Back Door Man • I Looked At You • End Of The Night • Take It As It Comes • The End

While the youth of America basked in the blissful ignorance of the Summer of Love, Jim Morrison and The Doors took a bum trip down the dark alleys of the American dream, encountering the flip side of free love, serial killers and a society at war with itself in Vietnam and on the streets of the US.

Morrison couldn't bring himself to subscribe to the hippies' happy-ever-after philosophy. He had taken the group's name from Aldous Huxley's 'The Doors Of Perception', in which the writer described his mind-expanding experiences with LSD, but when Morrison unlocked the doors of his mind with hallucinogenics he was overwhelmed with visions of a world where violence festered just beneath the surface and where the spectres of sex and death went hand in hand. His self-destructive rock god persona and pre-dilection for morbid poetry combined with the band's sense of theatre to create some of the most intense experiences on record. Their self-titled debut contrasted baroque pop ('Light My Fire'), earthy blues ('Back Door Man'), the dark cabaret of Kurt Weill ('Alabama Song') and several acts in an unfolding drama culminating in the creeping malevolence of 'The End' with a sound that defined the late Sixties.

Rating:
Sound ★★★☆☆ Content ★★★★★

The Doors

'STRANGE DAYS'

(Elektra) 1967

Track listing: Strange Days • You're Lost Little Girl • Love Me Two Times • Unhappy Girl • Horse Latitudes • Moonlight Drive • People Are Strange • My Eyes Have Seen You • I Can't See Your Face In My Mind • When The Music's Over

'Strange Days' sees The Doors leaving their dark theatre of Bacchanalian rites for a stroll among the 'freaks' on Sunset Strip. Instead of indulging in orgiastic excess as he did on the first album, Morrison appears content on this occasion to preside over the spectacle, savouring the vicarious pleasures like a beatific pagan god in black leather. Only on the pretentious 'Horse Latitudes' does he over-reach himself, indulging in fifth-form poetry and screaming against the instruments. Otherwise the overall tone is generally lighter, less intense, a celebration of unbridled hedonism with Krieger's classical styled guitar spiraling around Manzarek's reedy Vox Continental organ and harpsichord as John Densmore demonstrates how free jazz drum patterns can enable a rock band to escape the conventions of rigid four-to-the-bar rhythms.

This may not be The Doors' strongest set, but it helped shape the archetypal sound of the Sixties and it boasts one of the decade's defining moments during 'When The Music's Over' when

Morrison declares, 'We want the world and we want it… now!'.

Rating:
Sound ★★★★☆ Content ★★★★☆

The Doors

'WAITING FOR THE SUN'

(Elektra) 1968

Track listing: Hello I Love • Love Street • Not To Touch The Earth • Summer's Almost Gone • Wintertime Love • The Unknown Soldier • Spanish Caravan • My Wild Love • We Could Be So Good Together • Yes, The River Knows • Five To One

Another comparatively subdued set from a band who were then attempting to straddle two contrasting camps, namely teen-friendly top 40 radio and the acid-dropping longhairs who were frequently too stoned to find their radios, never mind tune the dial. 'Hello, I Love You', 'Wintertime Love' and the languorous ecstasy of 'Love Street' appeased the AM radio audience, while 'The Unknown Soldier' and 'Five To One' ensured that the group's leftwing credentials remained unsullied by their commercial success.

The overall impression however, is of a band who have more than their music on their collective mind and who have allowed Morrison's escalating personal problems to force them to take their eye off the ball.

If you can find a compilation with 'Hello I Love You', 'Love Street', 'Summer's Almost Gone' and 'Five To One' then you can cheerfully give this one a miss.

Rating:
Sound ★★★★☆ Content ★★★☆☆

The Doors

'LA WOMAN'

(Elektra) 1971

Track listing: The Changeling • Love Her Madly • Been Down So Long • Cars Hiss By My Window • LA Woman • L'America • Hyacinth House • Crawling King Snake • The Wasp • Riders On The Storm

Shortly before his death at the age of 27, the lizard king, now bearded and bloated almost beyond recognition, got his act together for one last session with the band that had given form to his tortured visions and in so doing, had defined the sound and spirit of the late sixties. In an attempt to reclaim past glories they opted to record a set of venomous roadhouse rockers, including a baleful cover of John Lee Hooker's 'Crawling King Snake', live in the studio with minimal ornamentation. The fragmented feel of the previous albums was replaced by a palpable sense of lithesome, licentious menace that seemed to have emerged from the surrounding swamplands as the band sought to summon up the restive spirit of their former greatness. But it is the quiet, haunting 'Riders On The Storm' which ensured that even after Morrison had vacated the stage for the last time The Doors would be a permanent fixture of classic rock radio playlists for decades to come. They were indeed 'stoned immaculate'.

Rating:
Sound ★★★★☆ Content ★★★★★

Also recommended:
'The Soft Parade', 'Morrison Hotel', 'The Best Of The Doors' and the 4CD box set 'The Doors' (all on Elektra).
If you like this, why not try:
Echo And The Bunnymen, Love, The Velvet Underground.

Nick Drake

'FIVE LEAVES LEFT'

(Island) 1969

Track listing: Time Has Told Me • River Man • Three Hours • Day Is Done • Way To Blue • Cello Song • The Thoughts Of Mary Jane • Man In A Shed • Fruit Tree • Saturday Sun

Nick Drake died at the age of 26 from an overdose leaving behind just three albums of wistful acoustic folk in the Tim Buckley/Van Morrison mould. Although the title of his debut album refers to the number of cigarette papers that he had left at the final session, it might just as easily have been an allusion to the first flush of autumn, the season that his music so effortlessly evokes. 'Five Leaves' sees Drake, the tragic romantic poet, surveying the world from his Cambridge garret and longing for the beauty beyond the boundaries of the physical world.

Drake's music is less strident than Van Morrison, more fragile even than Buckley and far less winsome than Donovan, with whom there are only superficial similarities. Both his voice and his music are quintessentially English, modest and understated, enriched with tasteful string arrangements and jazz-styled bass lines that complement his delicate guitar

playing. Although the sound is rooted in the late sixties the songs have a timeless quality. 'Fruit Tree' is particularly affecting as it has Nick musing on the posthumous acquisition of fame.

Rating:
Sound ★★★★☆ Content ★★★★☆

Nick Drake

'BRYTER LATER'

(Island) 1970

Track listing: Introduction • Hazey Jane II • At The Chime Of A City Clock • One Of These Things First • Hazy Jane I • Bryter Layter • Fly • Poor Boy • Northern Sky • Sunday

Producer Joe Boyd has described this album as the most perfect record that he ever made. Unfortunately, his belief in his protégé was never matched by the record's commercial success and Nick remains a cult figure 30 years after his untimely death. 'Bryter Layter' finds him in a less subdued mood than on 'Five Leaves' with backing from John Cale and members of Fairport Convention on three elegant instrumentals and a collection of exquisite impressionistic sketches. The blending of music and poetry has rarely been more fully realized than on this record.

Rating:
Sound ★★★★☆ Content ★★★★☆
Also recommended:
'Pink Moon' (Island) and 'Fruit Tree' a box set.
If you like this, why not try:
Jeff Buckley, Tim Buckley, Cat Stevens, Kevin Ayers.

Duran Duran

'GREATEST'

(EMI) 1998

Track listing: Is There Something I Should Know? • The Reflex • A View To A Kill • Ordinary World • Save A Prayer • Rio • Hungry Like The Wolf • Girls On Film • Planet Earth • Union Of The Snake • New Moon On Monday • Wild Boys • Notorious • I Don't Want Your Love • All She Wants Is • Electric Barbarella • Serious • Skin Trade • Come Undone

Most of Duran Duran's designer disco hits had the gloss and shelf life of a Sunday supplement fashion feature. In fact, their slick and lavishly expensive videos were little more than exotic photo shoots in motion, complete with lithesome, glossy-lipped models. They made a virtue of excess and extravagant emotions while marketing dreams for their screamage fans, but had an unnerving knack of penning some genuinely memorable pretty-boy pop. Both the naff and the nuggets are included on this 20-track hits package which also includes one of the memorable pop songs written for the James Bond franchise ('A View to a Kill').

'Emotionless and cold as ice, all of the things I like,' sings Simon Le Bon on 'Electric Barbarella'. At least they were honest about it.

Rating:
Sound ★★★★★ Content ★★★☆☆
Also recommended: 'Seven And The Ragged Tiger' (EMI).
If you like this, why not try:
Spandau Ballet, ABC, Power Station, **Japan**.

Ian Dury

'NEW BOOTS AND PANTIES'

(Stiff) 1977

Track listing: Wake Up And Make Love With Me • Sweet Gene Vincent • I'm Partial To Your Abracadabra • My Old Man • Billericay Dickie • Clevor Trever • If I Was With A Woman • Blockheads • Blackmail Man • There's Nothing With It!

According to the late Ian Dury, 'there ain't half been some clever bastards'. And he should know, because he was one of them himself. A former art school teacher, he brought a touch of British music hall humour and saucy seaside postcard innuendo to the overly earnest punk scene. But Ian Dury and The Blockheads were no novelty act. Dury was a populist poet with a unique sense of the absurd and a touching empathy for his eccentric creations. He delighted in taking the mickey out of himself as much as he did out of a collection of cockney cartoon characters that included 'Billericay Dickie' and 'Clevor Trever'. But while his lyrics were as caustic and concise as a limerick, the music (by partner Chas Jankel) was as nimble as a tea leaf on the old apples and pears.

Dury's most endearing songs on this album are the naughty ones, but he could also be romantic when the mood took him, as he is on 'Wake Up And Make Love', or sentimental, as on 'My Old Man'. Or both, as when eulogizing his idol on 'Sweet Gene Vincent'. As the saying goes, if the man hadn't been made, they'd have had to invent him. He was one of a kind.

Rating:
Sound ★★★☆☆ Content ★★★★☆
Also recommended:
'Juke Box Dury' (Stiff) later reissued on MFP as a budget-priced compilation under the title 'Greatest Hits'.
If you like this, why not try:
Nick Lowe, Wreckless Eric, **Elvis Costello**.

Bob Dylan

'BRINGING IT ALL BACK HOME' aka 'SUBTERRANEAN HOMESICK BLUES'

(CBS) 1967

Track listing: Subterranean Homesick Blues • She Belongs To Me • Maggie's Farm • Love Minus Zero – No Limit • Outlaw Blues • On The Road Again • Bob Dylan's 115th Dream • Mr Tambourine Man • Gates Of Eden • It's Alright Ma • It's All Over Now, Baby Blue

This is the album which marked both rock's coming-of-age and the transformation of little Robert Zimmerman, the earnest young folk singer with the nasal whine and Woody Guthrie fixation, to Bob Dylan, the prophetic street poet. On hearing the first chords of 'Subterranean Homesick Blues' the folk fraternity accused him of selling out, but their cries of 'Judas' were swallowed up in the one collective intake of breath made by those who never dreamed that pop would find such an articulate spokesman.

Whether performing solo on the four songs beginning with 'Mr Tambourine Man', or when backed by the Paul Butterfield Blues Band on the remainder, Dylan channels a stream of consciousness that swiftly turns into a tidal wave of ideas fuelled by a diet of amphetamines and the alternative realities described by William Blake and the Beat poets.

It doesn't matter now that his verse is seen as equal parts pretentious and profound. This was the album that suggested that there could be more to pop than the boy-meets-girl comic book cliches of early rock. It was honest, imaginative and intelligent. But more significantly, it promised greater things to come.

Rating:
Sound ★★★★☆ Content ★★★★★

Bob Dylan

'HIGHWAY 61 REVISITED'

(CBS) 1967

Track listing: Like A Rolling Stone • Tombstone Blues • It Takes A Lot To Laugh, It Takes A Train to Cry • From A Buick 6 • Ballad Of A Thin Man • Queen Jane Approximately • Highway 61 Revisited • Just Like Tom Thumb's Blues • Desolation Row

With robust backing from a bona fide rock band the one time political dissenter re-channels his passion into wryly amusing descriptions of provincial America ('Tombstone Blues'), youthful privilege ('Like A Rolling Stone') and the polarization of the generations ('Ballad Of A Thin Man'). Being a shrewd observer, Dylan slyly avoids direct references to the real world, and instead recasts his creations as if they were players in a travelling medicine show to give scenes that incorporate elements of American mythology, Biblical fable and Dadaesque dream symbolism as on the highly descriptive 'Desolation Row'.

In a surging stream of consciousness fed by liberal doses of black coffee, cigarettes and speed Dylan psyches himself up to mock the world that he considers too surreal to take seriously. The early influences are still in evidence – specifically the languid romanticism of Rimbaud, the obtuse imagery beloved of the Beat poets and the spectre of Robert Johnson – but these are now subservient to Dylan's personal vision and a narrative that seems to take on a momentum of its own.

Rating:
Sound ★★★★☆ Content ★★★★★

Bob Dylan

'JOHN WESLEY HARDING'

(CBS) 1968

Track listing: John Wesley Harding • As I Went Out One Morning • I Dreamed I Saw St Augustine • All Along The Watchtower • The Ballad Of Frankie Lee And Judas Priest • Drifter's Escape • Dear Landlord • I Am A Lonesome Hobo • I Pity The Poor Immigrant • The Wicked Messenger • Down Along The Cove • I'll Be Your Baby Tonight

Considering that Dylan is lauded as one of the most eloquent artists of his generation it might come as a

shock for the uninitiated to hear some of the painfully contrived and awkward couplets on this otherwise amiable collection of rustic country tunes. 'As I Walked Out One Morning' suffers the most from Dylan's off-the-cuff rhyming which suggests that the quality of his poetry could be as erratic as his harmonica playing. That aside, this is an album of modest ambitions and considerable charm. If it wasn't so subdued it might rate higher with the casual consumer, but if they checked it out they'd be rewarded with the genuinely moving 'I Pity The Poor Immigrant', the blackly humorous 'The Wicked Messenger', a coy country love song 'I'll Be Your Baby Tonight' and the master's original version of 'All Along The Watchtower'.

Rating:
Sound ★★★☆☆ Content ★★★★☆

Bob Dylan

'BLOOD ON THE TRACKS'

(CBS) 1975

Track listing: Tangled Up In Blue • Simple Twist Of Fate • You're A Big Girl Now • Idiot Wind • You're Gonna Make Me Lonesome When You Go • Meet Me In The Morning • Lily, Rosemary And The Jack Of Hearts • If You See Her Say Hello • Shelter From The Storm • Buckets Of Rain

'Blood On The Tracks' finds bitter, broken-hearted Bob crawling from the wreckage of a broken marriage and baring his wounds for all the world to see. The sparse arrangements offer no emollient for his emotional scars, only a stark setting for his sober philosophical reflections. There's anger, regret and sharp recriminations for the betrayals of trust, specifically in 'Idiot Wind', but no one can turn pain into poetry quite as eloquently as Dylan who substitutes his usual allegories for harsh, honest realism. But this return to form also includes one last shot at the mythic American narrative in the story of 'Lily, Rosemary and the Jack of Hearts' which revisits 'Desolation Row' with a new cast of characters.

'Blood On The Tracks' was Bob's last serious artistic statement before his inevitable decline into mediocrity and occasionally self-parody. And it remains one of the most significant albums of the seventies.

Rating:
Sound ★★★★☆ Content ★★★★★

Bob Dylan

'THE BEST OF BOB DYLAN'

(Columbia) 1997

Track listing: Blowin' In The Wind • The Times They Are A-Changin' • Don't Think Twice, It's All Right • Mr Tambourine Man • Like A Rolling Stone • Just Like A Woman • All Along The Watchtower • Lay Lady Lay • I Shall Be Released • If Not For You • Knockin' On Heaven's Door • Forever Young • Tangled Up In Blue • Oh, Sister • Gotta Serve Somebody • Jokerman • Everything Is Broken • Shelter From The Storm

'THE BEST OF BOB DYLAN VOL 2'

(Columbia) 2000

Track listing: Things Have Changed • A Hard Rain's A-Gonna Fall • It Ain't Me Babe • Subterranean Homesick Blues • Positively 4th Street • Highway 61 Revisited • Rainy Day Women • I Want You • I'll Be Your Baby Tonight • Quinn The Eskimo • Simple Twist Of Fate • Hurricane • Changing Of The Guards • License To Kill • Silvio • Dignity • Not Dark Yet

Two well-chosen compilations to supplement the official albums, the second of which is made all the more tempting by the addition of two previously unreleased tracks ('Things Have Changed' and 'Dignity').

The first charts Dylan's development from flat-capped folkie with the dirt of the dustbowl still fresh on his harmonica, through the mid-sixties when he played guru of Greenwich Village to The Beatles and The Byrds before winding up with the best from his bible-bashing 'born again Bob' period. The second harvests the windfalls, some of which are not essential, but which serve to fill the gaps if you don't own the barely adequate albums that he made from the late seventies to date. The selection process appears to have been rather arbitrary with such essential items as 'Masters of War', 'My Back Pages' and 'Talking World War 3 Blues' conspicuously absent. But most of the 'popular' hits are here and they're fine if you take them as tasters for the official albums rather than as representative retrospectives.

Rating:
Sound ★★★★☆ Content ★★★★★

Also recommended:
'Blonde On Blonde', 'Desire', 'The Basement Tapes', 'Before The Flood' and the 3CD set 'Biograph' (all on CBS) plus 'Greatest Hits' Vol 1–3 (Columbia) and 'The Bootleg Series' Vol 1–3 (Columbia).
If you like this, why not try:
The Band, Bruce Springsteen, Woody Guthrie, Billy Bragg.

Earth, Wind And Fire

'LET'S GROOVE – THE BEST OF'

(Columbia) 1997

Track listing: Let's Groove • Boogie Wonderland • Saturday Nite • In The Stone • I've Had Enough • Can't Let Go • Fall In Love With Me • Star • September • Jupiter • Got To Get You Into My Life • Fantasy • Evil • That's The Way Of The World • You Can't Hide Love • Reasons • After The Love Has Gone

EWF were one of the few 'progressive' jazz funk outfits of the seventies whose music outlasted the disco fad. They were the flip side of Funkadelic's sensual boogie, marrying soul and showbiz to a 'spiritual philosophy' that embraced Egyptian mythology and New Age mysticism. The only aspect of their act that the CD can't capture is their visual impact, the brash exuberance and SF-inspired spectacle of their live shows and also their notoriously outrageous costumes. But 'Let's Groove' takes in all the essential hits up to and including 'That's The Way of The World'. In fact, there's enough funky brass in the box to get the most listless individual to work off

a few extra pounds with the promise of some class. A chill-out tunes for after-session relaxation.

Rating:
Sound ★★★★★ Content ★★★★☆
Also recommended:
'The Eternal Dance' (Columbia) 3CD set and 'Boogie Wonderland' (Telstar), an alternative 'best of' collection.
If you like this, why not try:
Parliament, Funkadelic, Sly Stone.

Echo And The Bunnymen

'CROCODILES'

(Korova/WEA) 1980

Track listing: Going Up • Stars Are Stars • Pride • Monkeys • Crocodiles • Rescue • Villiers Terrace • Pictures On My Wall • All That Jazz • Happy Death Men

At a time when punk had become a parody of itself and synths were being pressed into the service of poseurs with increasingly silly haircuts, The Bunnymen pulled the plug on Echo, their drum machine, and looked to the past for inspiration. They found it in tracks by The Doors, The Velvet Underground and The Thirteenth Floor Elevators which they duly updated for the eighties, adding prowling bass lines, sparse guitar work and atmospheric electronic embellishments which gravitated around Ian McCulloch's often brooding and frequently melodramatic vocal.

'Crocodiles', their astonishing debut, is often described as dark-hued psychedelia for the eighties, but beneath the superficial similarities it has more in common with Jacques Brel or Joy Division than Jim Morrison. Its combination of melancholic intensity and gloomy grandeur appealed to a generation of art-school intellectuals and painfully self-conscious adolescents who saw themselves as tragic romantic heroes. While the band create a real sense of Gothic theatre on such tracks as 'Monkeys' and 'Rescue' Mac articulates the fears and anxieties of a generation who were determined to feel sorry for themselves, just so long as they looked the part with their wild Byronic hair, ankle-length raincoats and a permanent pout.

Rating:
Sound ★★★★☆ Content ★★★★☆

Echo And The Bunnymen

'PORCUPINE'

(Korova/WEA) 1983

Track listing: The Cutter • Back Of Love • My White Devil • Clay • Porcupine • Heads Will Roll • Ripeness • Higher Hell • Gods Will Be Gods • In Bluer Skies

With 'Porcupine' and its hit single 'The Cutter', The Bunnymen moved from cult icons to mainstream popstars without lightening the mood or easing up on the intensity. There's little doubt that this is a 'difficult' album to like, unless you're a manic depressive who craves a daily fix of doom and despondency. Part of the problem is the heavy orchestration which stifles the songs leaving them gasping for air. But taken in moderation it can be as efficacious as Prozac.

Rating:
Sound ★★★★☆ Content ★★★★☆
Also recommended:
'Ocean Rain' and the compilations 'Songs To Learn And Sing' and 'Ballyhoo – The Best Of' (Sire/Korova/WEA).
If you like this, why not try:
The Doors, Jacques Brel, **The Cure**.

Electric Light Orchestra

'FIRST MOVEMENT'

(EMI) 1987

Track listing: First Movement • Look At Me Now • 10538 Overture • Queen Of The Hours • The Battle Of Marston Moor • Mr Radio • Kuiama • Roll Over Beethoven • From The Sun To The World • Momma • In Old England Town • Showdown

The concept behind ELO was to continue where The Beatles had left off in their experiments with rock band and orchestra. But occasionally homage came uncomfortably close to blatant imitation.

The band were the brainchild of Roy Wood, enfant terrible of sixties psych-pop group The Move, who wanted to create symphonic rock for the emerging album market. It was a worthy ambition, but one fated to fail because the rigid rock rhythms and the more fluid classical structure simply didn't mix. The tracks which work best ('10538 Overture', 'Showdown' and 'Roll Over Beethoven') are those on which the strings simply augment the songs, whereas the attempts to integrate rock group and orchestra as one unit fall flat on their aspirations.

'First Movement' is a mixed bag of tracks from their first two albums recorded before Wood lost interest and left to form Wizard and is infinitely preferable to the unwieldy folly that it became under the leadership of Jeff Lynne in the late seventies.

Rating:
Sound ★★★☆☆ Content ★★★☆☆

Electric Light Orchestra

'OUT OF THE BLUE'

(Epic) 1977

Track listing: Turn To Stone • It's Over • Sweet Talkin' Woman • Across The Border • Night In The City • Starlight • Jungle • Believe Me Now • Steppin' Out • Standing In The Rain • Summer And Lightning • Mr Blue Sky • Sweet Is The Night • The Whale • Birmingham Blues • Wild West Hero

It's hard to believe that this Cecil B De Mille-sized production was created at the height of punk and that it outsold both The Pistols and The Clash at the time. The year of its release ELO toured with a spectacular laser show whose centrepiece was a Star Wars-styled spaceship, though it might have been more appropriate had they used a hot air balloon. The songs are pure bubblegum, inflated to outlandish proportions by a production that Hollywood would have been proud of. Only four tracks ('Turn To Stone', 'Sweet Talkin' Woman', 'Mr Blue Sky' and the clumsy 'Wild West Hero') retain any interest, which for a double album doesn't offer a good return on the investment.

Rating:
Sound ★★★☆☆ Content ★★★☆☆
Also recommended:
'The Best Of' (Epic). Alternatively a 3CD set consisting of three original albums – 'Eldorado', 'New World Record' and 'Out Of The Blue' (Epic)
If you like this, why not try:
Abba, The Beatles.

Emerson, Lake And Palmer

'ELP'

(Atlantic) 1971

Track listing: The Barbarian • Take A Pebble • Knife-Edge • The Three Fates • Tank • Lucky Man

For a time in the early seventies this three-man symphonic 'supergroup' held court as the crown princes of pomp rock, committing musical GBH on a string of classical pieces, including Mussorgsky's 'Pictures At An Exhibition', in the belief that nothing succeeds like excess. They must have seemed the height of sophistication to sixth formers throughout the kingdom, but their music has dated more than most and remains stubbornly unfashionable with no hope of a revival, at least until the next millennium. But for those of a forgiving nature there is much to enjoy, if they can overlook the group's gross musical conceit, the dated synth sounds, their self indulgence, incomprehensible lyrics and occasional clumsy execution. Keith Emerson's virtuoso piano lines are one such reason for reassessment, Greg Lake's silken vocal on the uncharacteristically delicate 'Take A Pebble' another and the inclusion of 'Lucky Man' a third. The latter, incidentally, features one of the earliest appearances of the Moog synthesizer.

Rating:
Sound ★★★★☆ Content ★★★☆☆

Emerson, Lake And Palmer

'TARKUS'

(Atlantic) 1971

Track listing: Eruption • Stones Of Years • Iconoclast • Mass • Manticore • Battlefield • Aquatarkus • Jeremy Bender • Bitches Crystal • The Only Way • Infinite Space • A Time And A Place • Are You Ready Eddy?

Having murdered Mussorgsky, Bartòk and Janac̆ek on their previous albums, ELP used themes by Bach Snr. as scene setting passages for their epic futuristic SF fantasy which described a war between mutant armadillos, pterodactyls and lions with a scorpion's tale! We kid you not. Fortunately, the music isn't as preposterous as the theme, although there are plenty of references to 'the winds of time' and other prog-rock cliches. But generally the music is leaner, less musclebound and bullish enough to crush whatever criticism you care to level at it.

Replace the hideous cartoon cover with one of your own and you'll have a fine example of prog-rock excess with which to frighten the children.

Rating:
Sound ★★★☆☆ Content ★★★☆☆

Emerson, Lake And Palmer

'BRAIN SALAD SURGERY'

(Atlantic) 1973

Track listing: Jerusalem • Tocatta • Still…You Turn Me On • Benny The Bouncer • Karn Evil 9 1st Impression Pt 1 • 1st Impression Pt 2 • 2nd Impression • 3rd Impression

'Welcome back my friends, to the show that never ends…'

While it's true that ELP's extravagant showmanship, self indulgence and demonstrative displays of instrumental virtuosity have dated considerably, their musicianship has not.

The centrepiece of their most accomplished album, the 30-minute 'Karn Evil 9', reveals a wealth of music ideas executed with considerable flair and energy, after which one can almost overlook the shambolic cockney pub pleaser 'Benny The Bouncer'. Almost. But then there's Lake playing the troubadour on 'Still…You Turn Me On' in a similar style to his solo hit 'I Believe In Father Christmas', Emerson's solo piano party piece 'Toccata' and an audacious, but not entirely unsuccessful reworking of 'Jerusalem', which would have made the ideal encore.

Unfortunately the sound quality of the CD doesn't do the music justice. It's bottom heavy and lacking in top-end sparkle.

Rating:
Sound ★★★☆☆ Content ★★★★☆

Also recommended:
'Pictures At An Exhibition', 'Works Vol:1' and 'The Best Of' (both on Essential/BMG).
If you like this, why not try:
King Crimson, The Nice.

Eminem

'THE MARSHALL MATHERS LP'

(Interscope) 2000

Track listing: Public Service Announcement 2000 • Kill You • Stan • Paul (skit) • Who Knew • Steve Berman (skit) • I'm Back • Marshall Mathers • Ken Kaniff (skit) • Drug Ballad • Amityville • Bitch Please II • Kim • The Way I Am • The Real Slim Shady • Remember Me • Under The Influence • Criminal

The bad boy of rap has been castigated for his tiresome reliance on expletives, his explicitly violent scenarios and his homophobia, but for those who can overlook his more reprehensible traits there is much to relish on his second offering. His humour is as black as that of Lenny Bruce and his themes are an imaginative variation on the common cliches of gansta rap. But what makes his albums a cut above the rest is the periodic transformations that he makes between identities from the mild-mannered Marshall Mathers to the psycho-killer Eminem, much like the volatile character in the movie *American Psycho*. Love him or loathe him Eminem tells it like it is – the everyday story of mom's apple pie America with the ratings-winning ingredients of sex, violence, greed,

drugs and the obligatory dead body in the bedroom. Includes the controversial hit single 'Stan', which describes the murder of the narrator's pregnant girlfriend. Surely one of the most cinematic and unsettling songs ever to insinuate itself into the charts.

Rating:
Sound ★★★★☆ Content ★★★★☆
Also recommended:
'The Slim Shady LP' (Interscope).
If you like this, why not try:
Public Enemy, Dido, Limp Bizkit.

Eno

'HERE COME THE WARM JETS'

(Island) 1974

Track listing: Needles In A Camel's Eye • The Paw Paw Negro Blowtorch • Baby's On Fire • Cindy Tells Me • Driving Me Backwards • On Some Faraway Beach • Blank Frank • Dead Finks Don't Talk • Some Of Them Are Old • Here Come The Warm Jets

Eno was never likely to emulate the success of his ex-mates in Roxy Music once he had jumped ship, but few expected him to land on his feet in the way that he did. His first solo album was at least a critical, if not exactly a commercial, success, securing praise for a set of idiosyncratic songs with eccentric rhythms, a grim sense of humour and vibrant electronic textures. 'Baby's on Fire' sounds like the kind of song Marc Bolan might have made had he teamed up with Sparks.

It would be a mistake to underestimate the influence of this modest offering on the evolution of eighties electro-pop and its significance as a stepping stone to Eno's later ambient experiments. But what separates Eno from his acolytes is his impish sense of fun.

Rating:
Sound ★★★★☆ Content ★★★★☆

Eno

'ANOTHER GREEN WORLD'

(Island) 1975

Track listing: Sky Saw • Over Fire Island • St Elmo's Fire • In Dark Trees • The Big Ship • I'll Come Running • Another Green World • Sombre Reptiles • Little Fishes • Becalmed • Zawinul • Lava Everything Merges With The Night • Spirits Drifting

By the time he released this third album Eno had shed his gay oddball image and settled down to cultivate a career as the architect of ambient, avant-garde electronic soundscapes with the occasional eccentric art pop song serving as an arresting feature. Of the 14 tracks only five have lyrics, the remainder seemingly created organically as the tape loops blended with Eno's spontaneous improvisations.

Rating:
Sound ★★★★☆ Content ★★★★☆
Also recommended:
'Brian Eno Box Set Vol 1 & 2' two retrospective 3CD sets on Virgin.
If you like this, why not try:
Roxy Music, David Bowie 'Low' and 'Heroes'.

Erasure

'POP – THE FIRST 20 HITS'

(Mute) 1992

Track listing: Who Needs Love (Like That) • Heavenly Action • Oh L'Amour • Sometimes • It Doesn't Have To Be • Victim Of Love • The Circus • Ship Of Fools • Chains Of Love • A Little Respect • Stop! • Drama • You Surround Me • Blue Savannah • Star • Chorus • Love To Hate You • Am I Right? • Breath Of Life • Take A Chance On Me • Who Needs Love (Remix)

When keyboard whizz kid Vince Clarke left Depeche Mode at the height of their early success many thought that he had blown a circuit and didn't expect to hear from him again. However, he only needed his transistors tweaked and a replacement part(ner) – singer Andy Bell – then it was back to business. And what a lucrative business it turned out to be as the duo racked up 22 hit singles and four number one albums between the end of the eighties and the rise of Britpop, which effectively made them redundant overnight.

These tracks remind us that they were more cute than cutting edge with a passion for indigestible dollops of sacharine sweet synths and camp seventies disco, but there's little doubt that Clarke was a consummate songsmith and one of the few Brits to wring soul out of a synth.

Rating:
Sound ★★★★☆ Content ★★★☆☆
Also recommended:
'The Circus', 'Wild' and 'Chorus' (all on Mute).
If you like this, why not try:
Depeche Mode, Yazoo, **Abba.**

Eurythmics

'IN THE GARDEN'

(RCA) 1981

Track listing: English Summer • Belinda • Take Me To Your Heart • She's Invisible Now • Your Time Will Come • Caveman Head • Never Gonna Cry Again • All The Young People • Sing Sing • Revenge

Dave and Annie's debut album doesn't rank too high in their discography although the hypnotic drone that drives the melancholic 'Never Gonna Cry Again' is arguably one of their finest moments. But as a whole the album lacks the soul and sophistication of their later efforts and, perhaps more significantly, the hits. However, Dave's subtle use of second-generation synthesizer technology underscoring Annie's chillingly detached vocals makes for a modish, urbane and danceable record that put the New Romantic poseurs in the shade.

Rating:
Sound ★★★★☆ Content ★★★☆☆

Eurythmics

'SWEET DREAMS'

(RCA) 1983

Track listing: Love Is A Stranger • I've Got An Angel • Wrap It Up • Could Give You A Mirror • Walk • Sweet Dreams (Are Made Of This) • Jennifer • Somebody Told Me • This City Never Sleeps • This Is The House

In '83, when the budget for music videos was threatening to exceed the cost of the original recording, Dave and Annie recorded their breakthrough album on an ancient eight-track tape machine in a converted London flat next door to a timber factory. Before every take they had to wait until there was a break when the saws were shut down.

The critics' favourite catchphrase at the time was 'nice video, shame about the song', but the videos for the singles 'Love Is A Stranger' and 'Sweet Dreams' helped to establish the Eurythmics as one of the few acts who could use the new medium to enhance their music rather than as a mere marketing tool. The songs are more upbeat than on the first album, exploiting the hypnotic quality of the drum machine and the banks of pulsing keyboards, but there is still a trace of melancholy in the tunes and in Annie's androgynous vocal. The overall impression is of a singularly intelligent pair subjecting their thought processes and emotions to almost surgical scrutiny, a notion borne out by a sleeve credit to psychoanalyst Edward de Bono, the founding father of 'lateral thinking'.

Rating:
Sound ★★★★☆ Content ★★★★☆

Eurythmics

'TOUCH'

(RCA) 1983

Track listing: Here Comes The Rain Again • Regrets • Right By Your Side • Cool Blue • Who's That Girl • First Cut • Aqua • No Fear, No Hate, No Pain • Paint A Rumour

'Touch', the third album, was less robotic and more R&B than the preceding pair with Dave reprogramming their electronic backline to process more supple rhythms and Annie stretching out on soulful songs such as 'Right By Your Side' and 'First Cut'. Meanwhile the singles, 'Who's That Girl' and 'Here Comes The Rain Again', ensured they remained dancefloor darlings and at the cutting edge of contemporary pop.

The album also benefited from the move to a 24-track studio where the extra tracks and professional facilities produced a more spacious and detailed sound.

Rating:
Sound ★★★★★ Content ★★★★☆

Eurythmics

'BE YOURSELF TONIGHT'

(RCA) 1985

Track listing: Would I Lie To You • There Must Be An Angel • I Love You Like A Ball And Chain • Sisters Are Doin' It For Themselves • Conditioned Soul • Adrian • It's (Baby Coming Back) • Here Comes That Sinking Feeling • Better To Have Lost In Love

For their fifth album the dance and soul element was beefed up with good old-fashioned guitar; Dave's power chords providing the perfect foil for Annie's rasping vocal on 'Would I Lie To You?' The track was one of four hit singles to be taken from their most rootsy offering to date and one which signalled both a change in direction away from electro-pop and their elevation to superleague status, as emphasized by the roster of guests. Elvis Costello contributed to 'Adrian',

Stevie Wonder lent his harmonica to 'There Must Be An Angel' and Aretha Franklin demonstrated why she was called the 'Queen Of Soul' on the single 'Sisters Are Doing It For Themselves'.

Rating:
Sound ★★★★☆ Content ★★★★★
Also recommended: 'Greatest Hits', 'Savage' and 'Revenge' (all on RCA.)
**If you like this, why not try:
Annie Lennox** solo albums, **Human League, Depeche Mode**.

Everly Brothers

'GREATEST RECORDINGS'

(Ace) 1988

Track listing: Wake Up Little Susie • Problems • Take A Message To Mary • I Wonder If I Care As Much • Poor Jenny • Love Of My Life • Bird Dog • Like Strangers • Hey Doll Baby • Leave My Woman Alone • Till I Kissed You • Claudette • Should We Tell Him • All I Have To Do Is Dream • Rip It Up • When Will I Be Loved • Bye Bye Love • Let It Be Me

Don and Phil were clean-cut country boys whose seamless, close-harmony singing had been refined during years of touring the Southern states with their parents' hillbilly band. They may have looked like hayseeds in comparison with the wild men of rock, but they were the most consistent hit makers of the era and they introduced the idea that the sound of a record was as important, if not more so, than any other element. 'Greatest Recordings' gathers all the tracks you'll ever need, 18 perfectly pitched hits on which the brothers' voices melt into the mix of chiming guitars which strum so hard that they don't need drums to drive them.

If a group features close-harmony vocals you can bet that they acquired their inspiration here.

Rating:
Sound ★★★★★ Content ★★★★☆
Also recommended:
'Songs Our Daddy Taught Us' (Ace) and the 'Classic Everly Brothers' (Bear Family) box set.
If you like this, why not try:
The Byrds, Carl Perkins.

Everything But The Girl

'BABY THE STARS SHINE BRIGHT'

(Blanco Y Negro) 1986

Track listing: Come On Home • Don't Leave Me Behind • A Country Mile • Cross My Heart • Don't Let The Teardrops Rust Your Shining Heart • Careless • Sugar Finney • Come Hell Or High Water • Fighting Talk • Little Hitler

After ten years of being stereotyped as the agony aunts of the college campus and bedsit community Tracy Thorn and Ben Watt finally came of age with this candidly emotional album. The earnest amateur charm of their indie days gives way to a blend of country music and café jazz sophistication with Bacharach-inspired orchestrations by Watt, which just manage to avoid the cabaret clichés that he had feared might overtake them.

Rating:
Sound ★★★★☆ Content ★★★☆☆

Everything But The Girl

'WALKING WOUNDED'

(Virgin) 1996

Track listing: Before Today • Wrong • Single • The Heart Remains A Child • Walking Wounded • Flipside • Big Deal • Mirrorball • Good Cop Bad Cop • Wrong • Walking Wounded

By the mid-nineties the duo's music was in danger of becoming enervated and far too frail to last. But just when they appeared to be slipping into a creative stupor the injection of drum 'n' bass tracks restored their vital signs. It's clear that their collaborations with Massive Attack had stimulated them to action, although on none of the tracks do they risk straining themselves. The heart is evidently bruised but functioning, so draw close as Tracy confides her tales of lost love and loneliness with the intimate touch of a torch singer while Ben furnishes suitably lush orchestrations.

They may not be the most animated artists on Earth, but there's no doubt that they are a class act.

Rating:
Sound ★★★★☆ Content ★★★☆☆
Also recommended:
'Idlewind', 'Amplified Heart', 'The Best Of' and a second retrospective collection, 'Home Movies' (all on Blanco Y Negro/Warners)
If you like this, why not try:
Massive Attack, This Mortal Coil.

The Fall

'THE WONDERFUL AND FRIGHTENING WORLD OF'

(Beggars Banquet) 1984

Track listing: Lay of The Land • Two Times Four • Copped It • Elves • Oh Brother • Draygo's Guilt • God Box • Clear Off • Creep • Pat Trip Dispenser • Slang King • Bug Day • Stephen Song • Craigness • Disney's Dream Debased • No Bulbs

The long-suffering Mark E Smith must surely qualify as Manchester's most morose citizen and it's his neurotic nightmares, peopled with cutting caricatures, that make the Fall's music some of the most uncomfortable, but essential of our time. Smith takes a perverse pleasure in being different, disconcerting and difficult; three words which sum up this album as accurately as any that you're likely to get.

The Fall are the nearest thing 'popular music' has to Kafka. And in these days of corporate rock we need them even more. Includes the subversively sing-a-long single 'C.R.E.E.P' featuring Brix (the ex-Mrs Smith) on backing vocals and (presumably) unintentionally 'commercial' production values.

Rating:
Sound ★★★☆☆ Content ★★★☆☆

The Fall

'THIS NATION'S SAVING GRACE'

(Lowdown/Beggars Banquet) 1985

Track listing: Mansion • Bombast • Barmy • What You Need • Spoilt Victorian Child • LA • Gut Of The Quantifier • My New House • Paintwork • I Am Damo Suzuki • To Nkroachment Yarbies

The major labels may be running the show, but the dissenting voice of the indie artist can occasionally be heard berating them from the stalls. One of the most distinctive and persistent hecklers has been Mark E Smith of The Fall.

With 'This Nation's Saving Grace' Smith gives a two-fingered salute to the conventional perfections of pop. His songs are characterized by a reckless rhythmic experimentation and an exhilarating freedom from the beat that is the musical equivalent of watching a circus performer put his head in the lion's mouth. However, Smith can also be quirky, charming and playful in a perverse way when it suits him, as on 'Spoilt Victorian Child' and 'I Am Damo Suzuki', where his wry humour expresses itself in sly digs at the kind of cliches beloved by his contemporaries. It is this spontaneous, unpredictable, off-the-wall approach that endears The Fall to those who delight in music that sounds like it might bite back.

Rating:
Sound ★★★☆☆ Content ★★★☆☆
Also recommended:
'45 84 89 The A Sides', 'The Frenz Experiment' (all on Beggars Banquet).

If you like this, why not try:
Television Personalities, The Cure,
The Virgin Prunes.

Family

'MUSIC IN A DOLLS' HOUSE'

(Reprise) 1968

Track listing: The Chase • Mellowing Grey •
Never Like This • Me My Friend • Variation
On A Theme Of Hey Mr Policeman • Winter
• Old Songs, New Songs • Variation On A
Theme Of The Breeze • Hey Mr Policeman •
See Through Windows • Variation On A Theme
Of Me And My Friend • Peace Of Mind •
Voyage • The Breeze • 3XTime

Family were one of the few progressive
rock bands to take the term seriously.
In place of the interminable extended
solos in which their rivals indulged,
Family experimented with fragmented
rhythms, strange song structures,
unusual instrumentation, sound effects
and... ideas.

Consequently this minor classic has
dated rather better than its
contemporaries. Of course it helps that
they could write hit singles
('Burlesque', 'The Weaver's Answer')
and that despite the experimental edge
they still sound like a rock group led by
a singer with a demented vibrato who
would enjoy chewing the head off an
arty prog-rocker for the sheer hell of it.

Rating:
Sound ★★★☆☆ Content ★★★☆☆
Also recommended:
'Family Entertainment' (Reprise).
If you like this, why not try:
Traffic, Blind Faith, Jethro Tull.

Fatboy Slim

'HALFWAY BETWEEN THE GUTTER AND THE STARS'

(Skint) 2000

Track listing: Sunset (Bird Of Prey) • Ya
Mama • Talking Bout My Baby • Demons •
Song For Shelter • Retox • Weapon Of
Choice • Drop The Hate • Star 69 • Love
Life • Mad Flava

Married life and fatherhood may
have mellowed the Big Beatster, but
that doesn't mean that the only
parties he gets to these days offer
puppet shows and pass-the-parcel.
The speaker-splitting dance floor
fillers of yore with their symbolic
sexual structure (involving aural
foreplay, an orgasmic climax and the
obligatory post-coital chill-out
ciggy) have been largely replaced by
laid-back mellifluent grooves,
although 'Mad Flava' and 'Ya
Mama' are as fat and funky as
anything on his earlier, more
innovative offerings.

Bootsy Collins makes several
larger-than-life appearances on
'Halfway', while the vocal talent of
Macy Gray embellishes the
infectious 'Love Life' and 'Demons'.
The new Mr Ball even manages to
resurrect the ghost of Jim Morrison
for the single 'Sunset' which
demonstrates that he is still as
irreverent and fun to have around as
any DJ to have spliced and diced the
turntables at the Big Beat Boutique.

Rating:
Sound ★★★★☆ Content ★★★☆☆

Also recommended:
'Better Living Through Chemistry' and 'You've Come A Long Way Baby' (both on Skint).
If you like this, why not try:
Various Artists 'A Break From The Norm' mixed by Fatboy Slim.

Bryan Ferry

'THESE FOOLISH THINGS'

(EG/EMI) 1973

Track listing: Hard Rain's A Gonna Fall • River Of Salt • Don't Ever Change • Piece Of My Heart • Baby I Don't Care • It's My Party • Don't Worry Baby • Sympathy For The Devil • Tracks Of My Tears • You Won't See Me • I Love How You Love Me • Loving You Is Sweeter Than Ever • These Foolish Things

Ferry was still enjoying fame as the face and voice of Roxy Music when he made this disparate collection of covers, anticipating the fashion for similarly styled solo diversions by quite a few years. Bryan looks back with a nostalgic eye through his record collection with the hope of putting a new spin on Dylan, Smokey Robinson and The Stones, among others, but adds nothing to the originals other than his quavering voice and a languid lounge lizard chic. It's only when he gets into character to play the part of the crooner on the title track that he carries a real sense of conviction. He seduces this Tin Pan Alley standard as he would a classy dame, waltzing it around a little before turning on the charm until it surrenders to his tender but firm embrace. The incorrigible old smoothie.
Rating:
Sound ★★★☆☆ Content ★★★☆☆

Also recommended:
'Let's Stick Together' and 'Another Time, Another Place' (Virgin/EMI).
If you like this, why not try:
Roxy Music, Smokey Robinson, David Gray.

The Flamin' Groovies

'FLAMINGO'

(Buddha/RCA) 1970

Track listing: Gonna Rock Tonite • Comin' After Me • Headin' For The Texas Border • Sweet Roll Me On Down • Keep A' Knockin' • Second Cousin • Childhood's End • Jailbait • She's Falling Apart • Road House

Bonus tracks: My Girl Josephine • Around And Around • Rockin' Pneumonia And The Boogie Woogie Flu • Somethin' Else • Rumble • Going Out Theme

While their Californian contemporaries were blissed-out after interminable excursions into the uncharted regions of acid-rock the Groovies got their mojos working and breathed new life into the fossilized remains of R&B. Their early Stones-styled songs are fuelled by liberal quantities of bourbon and fired by a fierce love of British beat and old-style raunch and roll. Suitably stoned, in the traditional sense, the band loosened up, cranked their amps up to 11 and let loose with this frantic set that was to prove a major influence on a generation of punk rockers across the pond.

The CD reissue has been remastered and comes complete with extensive sleeve notes plus six bonus out-takes from the 'Teenage Head' sessions. Pop doesn't get much better than this.
Rating:
Sound ★★★☆☆ Content ★★★★★

The Flamin' Groovies

'TEENAGE HEAD'

(Buddha/RCA) 1971

Track listing: High Flyin' Baby • City Lights • Have You Seen My Baby? • Yesterday's Numbers • Teenage Head • 32:20 • Evil Hearted Ada • Doctor Boogie • Whiskey Woman

Bonus tracks: Shakin' All Over • That'll Be The Day • Louie Louie • Walking The Dog • Scratch My Back • Carol • Going Out Theme

The Groovies' second essential outing kicks off with a track that could have come from Captain Beefheart's finest hour, 'Sure Nuff N Yes I Do', then just gets better and better. Mick Jagger is rumoured to have rated it higher than 'Sticky Fingers', which was released the same year, and even if it isn't true, it ought to be. Without a doubt the Groovies made the more consistent record on which they ride the mystery train to rock and roll heaven while knocking out laid-back country boogie, sun-styled rockabilly and lean-limbed R&B. Whatever a mojo might be, these guys sounded like they were working it to death.

The CD reissue boasts seven bonus tracks including storming covers of 'Shaking All Over', 'Louie Louie' and the previously unreleased 'Scratch My Back'. Absolutely essential.

Rating:
Sound ★★★☆☆ Content ★★★★★
Also recommended:
'Shake Some Action' on which producer Dave Edmunds burnishes their rough edges until they positively glow. Power-pop perfection.

If you like this, why not try:
MC5, **Iggy & The Stooges**, **The Rolling Stones**, The Cramps.

Fleetwood Mac

'GREATEST HITS'

(CBS) 1989

Track listing: The Green Manalishi • Oh Well Pt 1 • Oh Well Pt 2 • Shake Your Moneymaker • Need Your Love So Bad • Rattle Snake Shake • Dragonfly • Black Magic Woman • Albatross • Man Of The World • Stop Messing Around • Love That Burns

Back in the sixties, long before the name Fleetwood Mac became synonymous with AOR stadium rock, Mick Fleetwood and John McVie were at the helm of one of the premium progressive blues groups in Britain. This compilation gathers the finest recordings from that period and also serves as a reminder of the talent of 'lost' guitar virtuoso Peter Green who was responsible for penning their perennially popular instrumental hit 'Albatross' as well as 'Black Magic Woman'(which was later covered by Santana), and half a dozen more that have since become blues standards.

Rating:
Sound ★★★☆☆ Content ★★★★☆
Also recommended:
'Live At The BBC' (Essential) on 2CDs and 'The Complete Blue Horizon Sessions' (Columbia) a 6CD set featuring 33 previously unreleased recordings.
If you like this, why not try:
Eric Clapton, **The Yardbirds**, John Mayall's Bluesbreakers.

Fleetwood Mac

'RUMOURS'

(Warners) 1977

Track listing: Second Hand News • Dreams • Never Going Back Again • Don't Stop • Go Your Own Way • Songbird • The Chain • You Make Loving Fun • I Don't Want To Know • Oh Daddy • Gold Dust Woman

More than 25 million people own a copy of 'Rumours', though it's hard to find many that will own up to the fact. It's one of those albums that you buy against your better judgement hoping that your friends won't find out, but then play when your personal prejudices, and your brain, has been put to sleep. Its easy-on-the-ear formula is often cited as defining branded AOR corporate rock, but its appeal lies is in its anonymity. It's the musical equivalent of the Big Mac, cooked up for mass consumption, but lacking the distinctive taste of a real meal.

Part of its appeal lies in its simplicity, its smooth blend of pop, rock, folk and country and its bland, inoffensive sound. Most of the songs use no more than four basic chords and if you could plot their dynamics you might be forgiven for thinking that you were looking at the medical chart of a comatose patient. But play the languid 'Dreams' or 'The Chain' in mixed company and see how slow everyone is to turn it off.

It's bubblegum for grown-ups and the kind of album that you either love, or love to hate.

Rating:
Sound ★★★★☆ Content ★★★★☆

Fleetwood Mac

'TUSK'

(WEA) 1979

Track listing: Over And Over • Ledge • Think About Me • Save Me A Place • Sara • What Makes You Think You're The One • Storms • That's All For Everyone • Not That Funny • Sisters Of The Moon • Angel • That's Enough For Me • Brown Eyes • Never Make Me Cry • I Know I'm Not Wrong • Honey Hi • Beautiful Child • Walk A Thin Line • Tusk • Never Forget

After the phenomenal success of 'Rumours' the group could stop watching the studio clock, but even they must have caught their breath when presented with the bill for the follow up. The final cost for recording 'Tusk' was a cool million bucks, making it the most expensive album at that time, although it soon recouped its budget many times over. Anxious not to repeat themselves they overdid the experimentation until the songs sank under the weight of ornamentation and embellishments. As with the Beatles' 'White Album' it aimed to give each member a platform for self-expression, but succeeded only in dissipating their energy and ideas. With the exception of Stevie Nicks' sorrowful 'Sara' and the anthemic title track it lacked the informality and bitter-sweet melancholia of the first two albums. Momentum rather than merit carried it.

Rating:
Sound ★★★★☆ Content ★★★☆☆
Also recommended:
'Fleetwood Mac' (Reprise) the new line-ups debut outing and 'Tango In The Night' (Warners).

If you like this, why not try:
Crosby, Stills, Nash and Young, Neil Young, Traffic.

Frankie Goes To Hollywood

'WELCOME TO THE PLEASURE DOME'

(Island) 1984

Track listing: Well... • The World Is My Oyster • Snatch Of Fury • Welcome To The Pleasure Dome • Relax • War • Two Tribes • Ferry • Born To Run • San Jose • Wish The Lads Were Here • Black Night White Light • The Only Star In Heaven • The Power Of Love • Bang

Frankie might have remained gay cult icons had it not been for the intervention of Radio One DJ Mike Reid who, legend has it, cut 'Relax' off in its prime on the grounds of 'good taste'. As a consequence the marketing machine went into overdrive ensuring that the group became the hottest act on the planet for a month or so and 'Relax' became the first of three consecutive number one singles. The other two, the similarly styled 'Two Tribes' and the emotive 'Power Of Love' are garish and overblown dancefloor teasers. The rest of the album is equally reliant on producer Trevor Horn's computer-generated tracks and a disproportionate amount of covers. It's fine if you were there, but if not you might wonder what all the fuss was about.

Rating:
Sound ★★★★☆ Content ★★★☆☆
Also recommended:
'Bang! – Greatest Hits' (ZTT).

If you like this, why not try:
ABC, Wham.

Aretha Franklin

'QUEEN OF SOUL'

(Rhino) 1994

Track listing: I Never Loved A Man (The Way I Love You) • Do Right Woman, Do Right Man • Dr Feelgood • Baby I Love You • (You Make Me Feel Like A) Natural Woman • Chain Of Fools • Since You've Been Gone • Ain't No Way • Save Me • House That Jack Built • Think • I Say A Little Prayer • Seesaw • Daydreaming • Call Me • Don't Play That Song • Border Song • You're All I Need To Get By • I'm In Love • Spanish Harlem • Rock Steady • Angel • Until You Come Back To Me

Throughout her 40-year career Aretha has been ill-served by substandard material and unsuitable settings, but she has informed every performance with the majesty of her four-octave vocal range and the passionate intensity of a background in gospel. Once you've heard the awesome Aretha in full flight the superficial stylings of such singers as Celine Dion and Whitney Houston will sound artificial and contrived by comparison.

Of all the compilations on the market this is the one to own as it concentrates on the classic recordings she made for Atlantic during the late sixties and early seventies when she was backed by one of the tightest, most soulful session bands in the business. Unfortunately, none of her gospel tracks from the period are included, but these secular sides carry sufficient conviction to redeem even the most unrepentant sinner.

Rating:
Sound ★★★★☆ Content ★★★★☆
Also recommended:
'30 Greatest Hits' (Atlantic) and 'Queen Of Soul: The Atlantic Recordings' (Rhino) a 4CD set.
If you like this, why not try:
Dinah Washington, **Annie Lennox**, **Whitney Houston**.

Free

'TONS OF SOBS'

(Island) 1968

Track listing: Over The Green Hills Pt 1 • Worry • Walk In My Shadow • Wild Indian Woman • Goin' Down Slow • I'm A Mover • The Hunter • Moonshine • Sweet Tooth • Over The Green Hills Pt 2

Free were hailed as masters of sparse, slowburning blues while the members were still in their teens, but the pressures of overnight success proved their undoing. However, during their brief tenure as 'the new Cream' they created some of the most intense and soulful tracks ever committed to tape. The brooding power of 'Going Down Slow', 'Walk In My Shadow' and 'Moonshine' plus the strutting bravado of 'The Hunter' affirms that real feeling comes from the gut and not from vocal histrionics, while strength stems from controlled intensity and not cranked-up powerchords. Paul Kossoff's expressive, economical solos speak volumes with comparatively few notes, while his simple chords leaves space for Rodgers to stalk the spaces in between, a technique which was intended to keep the songs

smouldering until the moment when the band finally released the pent-up tension.

It's a certainty that at any given moment someone is playing 'All Right Now' somewhere in the world, although it's equally certain that if the group's first album had enjoyed as much daytime airplay as that single these tracks would be just as popular.

Rating:
Sound ★★★★☆ Content ★★★★★

Free

'ALL RIGHT NOW – THE BEST OF FREE'

(Island) 1991

Track listing: Wishing Well • All Right Now • Little Bit Of Love • Come Together In The Morning • The Stealer • Sail On • Mr Big • My Brother Jake • The Hunter • Be My Friend • Travellin' In Style • Fire And Water • Travelling Man • Don't Say You Love Me

A 'best of' collection with a difference – all 14 tracks have not only been remastered, they have been remixed which means that the heavily compressed sound of the original albums has been supplanted by a far more spacious soundstage in which the instruments have more room to breathe and the tracks gain more impact as a result. The bass can now be heard prowling with almost feline agility around the bottom end; the piano fills which were muddied by a bad mix now ring out; Kossoff's lean, lyrical lead lines are sharply focused and Rodger's rasping vocal is given centre stage. But it's the drums which gain the most from this radical revamp, the clean up has had the effect of making them sound as if they'd been retuned from the flabby thump of yore to add real smack where it counts. Even the overly familiar 'All Right Now' comes up fresh and vibrant without losing its 'classic' feel.

Whatever reservations fans may have about having classic recordings 'tampered with' in this way, it's no exaggeration to say that these tracks have been born again. And although this CD doesn't include three of the essential tracks from 'Tons of Sobs' it still adds up to one hell of a package for lovers of hard rock, seventies style.

Rating:
Sound ★★★★★ Content ★★★★★
Also recommended:
'The Free Story' (Island).
If you like this, why not try:
Led Zeppelin, Bad Company, Deep Purple, Rory Gallagher, Ten Years After.

Fun-da-mental

'SEIZE THE TIME'

(Nation/Beggars Banquet) 1994

Track listing: Dog Tribe • Seize The Time • Mera Mazab • President Propaganda • No More Fear • Dollars Or Sense • Mother India • Mr Bubbleman • English Breakfast • Bullet Solution • Fatherland • New World Order • White Gold Burger • Back To Basix

Fun-da-mental have been described as 'the Asian Public Enemy', a collective of West Indian rappers, percussionists and turntable techno wizards whose aim has been to shake up the stagnant Western music industry with a militant political message wrapped in hardcore rap and ragga. The main weapon in their musical Intifada are soundbites from the speeches of Malcolm X, Nelson Mandela and Mahatma Ghandi welded to a belligerent dance beat and sweetened by samples from the soundtracks of Indian films. This first salvo came with the warning: 'Contains The Truth'.

Rating:
Sound ★★★★☆ Content ★★★☆☆
Also recommended:
'With Intent To Pervert The Course Of Injustice' (Nation).
If you like this, why not try:
Trans Global Underground, Loop Guru.

Funkadelic

'ONE NATION UNDER A GROOVE'

(Warners) 1978

Track listing: One Nation Under A Groove • Grooveallegiance • Who Says A Funk Band Can't Play Rock •Promentalshitbackwashpsychosis Enema Squad • Into You • Cholly • Lunchmeataphobia • P.E. Squad • Doodoo Chasers • Maggot Brain

Funkadelic was the creation of the diabolically cunning Dr Funkenstein, aka George Clinton, who stitched together this mother of all monsters using the remains of his R&B outfit

Parliament. He gave it the brain of a deranged B movie mogul and the soul of James Brown. Then he plugged it into the mains and brought to life the baddest brother of them all.

The title of the tracks should give a warning as to what's in store for the unwary; the squat, muscular sound of seventies soul psyched up with Hendrix-styled guitar histrionics and ground out to a groove high on illicit chemical substances. In effect, Prince for the pre-digital generation with sufficient explicit sexual and political content to put the moral majority into intensive care for the duration.

Now you too can reanimate your limbs with Dr Funkenstein's patent psych-funk fusion which, in the words of the good doctor himself, will 'free your mind and your ass will follow.'

Rating:
Sound ★★★★☆ Content ★★★☆☆
Also recommended:
'Free Your Mind And Your Ass Will Follow' (Pye).
If you like this, why not try:
Parliament, **Prince**, **Earth Wind And Fire**, **Sly Stone**.

When Peter Gabriel left Genesis at the peak of their popularity, few gave him much of a chance of carving out a solo career. Genesis had nurtured a large and loyal following with their pomp-rock epics, quirky English humour and highly theatrical stage shows, whereas Gabriel's first solo outing revealed a serious, self-absorbed artist who was clearly reluctant to play the part any longer. The obvious highlight, 'Solsbury Hill', described his feelings on leaving the group while others sound like the last act of a Genesis show in which the discontented singer strips off the masks one at a time and removes the greasepaint before laying his characters to rest in the prop box with the discarded costumes. In comparison with his more adventurous and eclectic albums of the next decade it's little more than a dress rehearsal for the forthcoming productions, but with a sufficient sense of melodrama and self-mockery to satisfy Genesis fans. An artist in transition.

Rating:
Sound ★★★★☆ Content ★★★☆☆

Peter Gabriel

'1'

(Virgin) 1977

Track listing: Moribund The Burgermeister • Solsbury Hill • Modern Love • Excuse Me • Humdrum • Slowburn • Waiting For The Big One • Down The Dolce Vita • Here Comes The Flood

Peter Gabriel

'III'

(Virgin) 1980

Track listing: Intruder • No Self Control • Start • I Don't Remember • Family Snapshot • And Through The Wire • Games Without Frontiers • Not One Of Us • Lead A Normal Life • Biko

Gabriel found his distinctive voice as a solo artist with his third self-titled album on which he banned drummers Phil Collins and Jerry Marotta from using cymbals in the hope of creating a more austere sound. His eagerness to break with conventional rock music was facilitated by the use of programmable percussion tracks and synchronized synthesizers, which meant that he could dispense with chords and instead build songs from layered melodic lines.

The album also marks a move away from the lyrical conceits of the Genesis era with several striking character sketches in 'Family Portraits', 'Intruder' and 'I Don't Remember' plus the archly cynical 'Games Without Frontiers' and the poignant tribute to the murdered anti apartheid activist Steve Biko.

Gabriel's public-school education had finally paid off with an unusually intelligent and articulate collection that was to have a profound influence on the evolution of popular music over the next decade.

Rating:
Sound ★★★★★ Content ★★★★☆

Peter Gabriel

'SO'

(Virgin) 1986

Track listing: Red Rain • Sledgehammer • Don't Give Up • That Voice Again • In Your Eyes • Mercy Street • Big Time • We Do What We're Told • This Is The Picture

By the mid-eighties Gabriel was no longer reliant on loyal Genesis fans to underwrite the risk on his musical ventures. By assimilating world music into rock he had created a market of his own and was running a virtual monopoly on music of quality and distinction.

Collaborators on the project included Laurie Anderson, Stewart Copeland, Jim Kerr and Kate Bush whose contribution to the empyreal 'Don't Give Up' ensured that it became one of the biggest hit singles of Gabriel's career. The album spawned three more massive hits, 'Sledgehammer', 'Red Rain' and 'Big Time', the former a powerhouse of percussive funk, the second incorporating authentic African tribal rhythms and the latter chewing on a brassy R&B riff. But it's the tender 'Mercy Street' (a tribute to the poet Anne Sexton) which proved that meticulous musicianship, articulate lyrics and precision production doesn't necessarily mean soulless sophistication.

'So' marked the peak of Peter Gabriel's powers as a solo artist, but there is still reason to hope that he may be able to repeat it.

Rating:
Sound ★★★★★ Content ★★★★☆
Also recommended: 'Peter Gabriel Vol:III' and 'Plays Live' (both on Virgin)
If you like this, why not try:
Genesis, **Kate Bush**, the various 'World Music' artists on his own Real World label.

Rory Gallagher

'DEUCE'

(Capo/BMG) 1971

Track listing: I'm Not Awake Yet • Used To Be • Don't Know Where I'm Going • Maybe I Will • Whole Lot Of People • In Your Town • Should've Learnt My Lesson • There's A Light • Out Of My Mind • Crest Of A Wave

Bonus track: Persuasion

They used to call the blues 'the devil's music' and for good reason. Not only did he have all the best tunes; he also had the most seductive salesmen in his employ. Celtic rocker Rory Gallagher was one of the most personable and persuasive brokers that the blues ever had. His modest, unassuming manner was mirrored in the music that he made which eschewed flashy fretboard fireworks for lucid expressions of the earthy power and beauty of the blues. On 'Deuce', his second solo session, his 'no frills' philosophy irradiates a set of deceptively simple songs all of which are embellished with his wistful Irish lilt and laid-back conversational solos. This is where Mark Knopfler nicked his best licks, but Rory did rocking blues better than any of his more commercially successful contemporaries. If this sounds like your thing, audition the opening track on your next visit to a record emporium and see what you've been missing all these years.

All of Rory's albums are now remixed, remastered and reissued with extra tracks.

Rating:
Sound ★★★☆☆ Content ★★★★☆

Rory Gallagher

'BBC SESSIONS'

2 CDs (Capo/BMG) 1999

Track listing: Calling Card • What In The World • Jacknife Beat • Country Mile • Got My Mojo Working • Garbage Man • Roberta • Used To Be • I Take What I Want • Cruise On Out • Race The Breeze • Hands Off • Crest Of A Wave • Feel So Bad • For The Last Time • It Takes Time • Seventh Son Of A Seventh Son • Daughter Of The Everglades • They Don't Make Them Like You • Toredown • When My Baby She Left Me • Hoodoo Man

Gallagher was perhaps too subdued a personality and too subtle a musician to make much impact on the self-indulgent, style-conscious seventies, but after his death his music has acquired the same timeless quality as that of the great bluesmen.

These previously unreleased in-concert and live-in-the-studio recordings preserve the prime period Gallagher band passing the performer's musical proficiency acid test. Rory refused to release singles so these sessions were the only way he could ensure his music got airtime and he poured every ounce of his being into them in an effort to convert non-believers to the redemptive power of the blues.

The 'studio' disc compiles early Gallagher favourites and rarities, while the in-concert disc is a reminder of how well he responded to a live audience, the very lifeblood of the blues. In the accompanying sleeve notes Rory's brother suggests that Rory was probably the finest electric guitar virtuoso of his generation and on the evidence of these recordings it is difficult to disagree with him.

Rating:
Sound ★★★☆☆ Content ★★★★☆

Rory Gallagher

'IRISH TOUR'

(Capo/BMG) 1974

Track listing: Cradle Rock • I Wonder Who • Tattoo'd Lady • Too Much Alcohol • As The Crow Flies • A Million Miles Away • Walk On Hot Coals • Who's That Coming? • Back On My Stompin' Ground • Maritime

It's a testament to Gallagher's consistency and commitment as a live performer that two of his three recommended recordings are live sets. This vital item (originally released as a double LP) is aflame with finger-blistering solos and also some of the finest acoustic blues performances on record. But Gallagher's appeal doesn't rest solely on demonstrative guitar solos. There's a tender soulfulness in his voice that gives his performances a quality that makes him very difficult to dislike.

Again, remastering has afforded a considerable improvement on the original CD issues, so take this opportunity to replace your old copies now, or introduce yourself to the simple pleasures of uncompromising rough 'n' ready rock.

Rating:
Sound ★★★☆☆ Content ★★★★☆

Also recommended:
'Rory Gallagher', 'Stage Struck', 'Photo Finish' plus the budget-priced compilation 'Edged In Blue' which serves as an ideal introduction to his music (all are on Capo/BMG).
If you like this, why not try:
George Thorogood, Eric Clapton, Cream.

Garbage

'GARBAGE'

(Mushroom/BMG) 1995

Track listing: Supervixen • Queer • Only Happy When It Rains • As Heaven Is Wide • Not My Idea • A Stroke Of Luck • Vow • Stupid Girl • Dog New Tricks • My Lover's Box • Fix Me Now • Milk

The Wisconsin quartet's choice of name belies the quality of their music which recycles techno, grunge and goth into a gleaming new music machine customized for the 21st-century consumer. The band was the brainchild of Nirvana producer Brian Vig who has brought the compressed steamhammer sound of Seattle to the service of dance music then laced it with a twist of black, fatalistic humour. This, their debut album, boasts no fewer than three hit singles ('Queer', 'Stupid Girl' and 'Only Happens When It Rains') plus nine more that could easily have charted, each featuring the dark, dry vocal tone of Shirley Manson.

Rating:
Sound ★★★★★ Content ★★★★☆
Also recommended:
'Garbage Version 2.0' (Mushroom).

If you like this, why not try:
The Cardigans, **Björk**, The
Cranberries, **Portishead**.

Marvin Gaye

'WHAT'S GOING ON'

(Tamla Motown) 1971

*Track Listing: What's Going On • What's
Happening Brother • Flyin' High • Save
The Children • God Is Love • Mercy Mercy
Me • Right On • Wholly Holy • Inner City
Blues*

Marvin Gaye had long been
disenchanted with the sanitized soul of
Motown, 'the hit factory' and with the
strict regime imposed by label boss
Berry Gordy who didn't want his artists
tackling serious subjects. Gaye's
frustration with this feel-good fantasy
life was compounded by tales of the
war in Vietnam that he had heard first
hand from returning GIs and by the
tragic death of his partner, Tammi
Terrell, who had died on stage in his
arms. In an effort to come to terms with
this emotional turmoil and fulfil his
artistic ambitions Gaye wrote this
seamless suite of songs covering
controversial issues from ghetto life to
ecology and crime. But although the
album addresses social issues that no
soul record had touched on before, it is
unable to offer any solutions.

The three hits 'Mercy Mercy Me',
'Inner City Blues' and the title track
dissolve subtle jazz shadings into a
sublime soul-funk groove as Marvin
muses on the state of the nation.

With 'What's Going On' Marvin
Gaye reinvented himself as an albums
artist and marked soul's coming of age

after its dance-dominated adolescence.
If you only own one soul album, then
this must be the one.
Rating:
Sound ★★★★☆ Content ★★★★☆
Also recommended:
'Let's Get It On' and 'Motown's
Greatest Hits: Marvin Gaye' (both on
Motown).
If you like this, why not try:
Al Green, Mary Wells, Tammi
Terrell, Diana Ross, **Smokey
Robinson**.

Genesis

'FOXTROT'

(Virgin) 1972

*Track Listing: Watcher Of The Skies •
Timetable • Get 'Em Out By Friday • Can-
Utility And The Coastliners • Horizon •
Supper's Ready*

Public-school prog-rockers Genesis
brought a quintessentially English
undergraduate humour to rock which
set them apart from their furrow-
browed contemporaries Yes and Pink
Floyd whose albums were
consequently very heavy going
indeed. This element is most clearly
in evidence on 'Get 'Em Out By
Friday' on which Gabriel and Collins
assume the roles of an avaricious
property developer and his elderly
victim. Diehard fans however prefer
'Watcher Of The Skies' and
'Supper's Ready' with their
grandiose sense of theatre, generous
stock of fragmented time signatures
and of course, the obligatory
Mellotron which gave these extended

song suites an epic quality.

Genesis' musical vocabulary has dated, but thanks to remastering their recordings have weathered well.

Rating:
Sound ★★★★☆ Content ★★★★☆

Genesis

'SELLING ENGLAND BY THE POUND'

(Virgin) 1973

Track listing: Dancing With The Moonlight Knight • I Know What I Like (In Your Wardrobe) • Firth Of Fifth • More Fool Me • The Battle Of Epping Forest • After The Ordeal • The Cinema Show • Aisle Of Plenty

'Selling England' sees the group streamlining their symphonic rock to yield an unlikely hit single in the form of the charmingly nonsensical 'I Know What I Like'.

'Dancing With The Moonlight Knight' is a suitably imperious opener, building majestically from a plaintive medieval introduction to a double-speed instrumental passage propelled by Phil's precision drumming that is soon awash with an ethereal choir and flecks of searing guitar. Gabriel and Collins share the vocals on 'Firth Of Fifth' which blossoms into a beautiful instrumental constructed around a rippling piano, breathy flute and soaring guitar solo recalling King Crimson in their more pastoral passages. Then Phil's solo vocal on the characterless 'More Fool Me' reveals just how closely he blended with Gabriel, leading some to believe that it was Gabriel alone

who sang and making Collins the obvious choice to replace him. After amiable diversions with 'The Battle Of Epping Forest' and the instrumental 'After The Ordeal' the album closes with another jaundiced look at the quaint English character. 'The Cinema Show' describes a suburban lover romancing his demure English rose with a box of chocs and cheap perfume. But it's the endearingly eccentric 'I Know What I Like' which ensures that 'Selling England' retains a special place in the hearts of the fans.

Rating:
Sound ★★★★☆ Content ★★★★☆

Genesis

'THE LAMB LIES DOWN ON BROADWAY'

2 CDs (Virgin) 1974

Track listing: CD 1 – The Lamb Lies Down On Broadway • Fly On A Windshield • Broadway Melody Of 1974 • Cuckoo Cocoon • In The Cage • The Grand Parade Of Lifeless Packaging • Back In NYC • Hairless Heart • Counting Out Time • Carpet Crawlers • The Chamber Of 32 Doors

CD2 – Lilywhite Lilith • The Waiting Room • Anyway • Here Comes The Supernatural Anaesthetist • The Lamia • Silent Sorrow In Empty Boats • The Colony Of Slipperman • Ravine • The Light Dies Down On Broadway • Riding The Scree • In The Rapids • It

The band's magnum opus is a sprawling, intimidatingly ambitious, but almost wholly successful concept album concerning the fortunes of a Puerto Rican street hustler on the search for the meaning of life in Manhattan. As with many similar prog-rock projects it would have benefited from being judiciously pruned down to a single disc, so many of the superfluous tracks being little more than sound effects with ambient trimmings. But fortunately it's only a matter of reprogramming the running order on your CD player to rectify matters. What remains is some of the group's finest work including the majestic title track, the beguiling 'Carpet Crawlers', the uncharacteristically commercial single 'Counting Out Time' and a host of classic rock tracks crammed fit to bursting with good ideas. Who cares what it all means if it makes the inflated rock operas of their peers look like a drop in the Topographic Ocean.

Rating:
Sound ★★★★☆ Content ★★★★★
Also recommended:
'Trespass', 'Nursery Cryme', 'Seconds Out' and 'A Trick Of The Tail' (all on Virgin).
If you like this, why not try:
Peter Gabriel's solo albums, **Yes**, Marillion, **Rush**.

Giant Sand

'GIANT SONGS – THE BEST OF'

(Demon) 1989

Track listing: Down On Town • Valley Of Rain • Thin Line Man • Body Of Water • Moon Over Memphis • Uneven Light Of Day • Big Rock • One Man's Woman, No Man's Land • Mountain Of Love • Curse Of A Thousand Flames • Barrio •

Graveyard • Heartland • Underground Train • Bigger Than That • Wearing The Robes Of Bible Black • Fingernail Moon • Barracuda And Me

Cult Arizona outfit Giant Sand have been corralled with Naked Prey and Green On Red as a 'desert band', which means that their bestial country rock is as prickly as cactus pie and just as nourishing for those stranded in the desert of contemporary corporate rock. Frontman Howie Gelb staked his claim to this particular territory in 1980 with his barbed wire guitar sound and though members have come and gone more frequently than outlaws on their way to Boot Hill, Gelb has stood his ground even when the pickings were lean. Over the course of his 15-year career he roped in country singer Lucinda Williams, members of The Go-Gos and Green On Red as well as a crusty 70-year-old bartender to give his songs that genuine rustic grit.

His wiry western characters inhabit a wild frontier town of the mind in an arid, inhospitable landscape like those featured in a John Ford film. But Gelb adds a dash of Neil Young, Lou Reed and Ennio Moricone to the soundtrack. It makes Springsteen's American dream seem as authentic as a package holiday on a dude ranch.

Rating:
Sound ★★★☆☆ Content ★★★★☆
Also recommended:
'The Best Of…Vol 2' (Demon).
If you like this, why not try:
The Triffids, Green On Red.

Girlschool

'EMERGENCY'

2 CDs (Recall/Snapper Music) 1997

Track listing: CD 1 – Demolition Boys • Not For Sale • Race With The Devil • Take It All Away • Nothing To Lose • Breakdown • Midnight Ride • Emergency • Babydoll • Deadline

Bonus tracks: Furniture Fire • Please Don't Touch • Bomber

CD 2 – C'Mon Let's Go • The Hunter • (I'm Your) Victim • Kick It Down • Following The Crowd • Tush • Hit And Run • Watch The Step • Back To Start • Yeah Right • Future Flash •

Bonus tracks: Tonight • Demolition Boys • Tonight

If you think that all girl groups spend more time under the hair-drier than practising their licks, then lend your lugs to Girlschool who were probably slung out of St Trinian's for taking Motorhead to their music lessons.

No one could accuse these girls of being bimbos. No one dare! There are no so-called 'soft metal' ballads on this 2CD set which repackages the albums 'Demolition' and 'Hit And Run' with half a dozen desirable bonus tracks. This is high-octane biker rock, an unremitting stomp around your ear-holes in size 12 Doc Martens and their axe work is lethal. So don't be surprised if you don't hear them on day-time radio. There was nothing subtle about Girlschool, but if you like your rock loud and sleazy, then these belles from hell could be right up your alley. Do the bad-girl boogie.

Rating:
Sound ★★★★☆ Content ★★★★☆
Also recommended:
'Live' (Communique).
If you like this, why not try:
Motorhead, Joan Jett, Lita Ford.

Robert Gordon

'IS RED HOT!'

(Bear Family) 1991

Track listing: Red Hot • The Fool • I Sure Miss You • Flyin' Saucer Rock And Roll • The Way I Walk • Lonesome Train On A Lonesome Track • I Want To Be Free • Rockabilly Boogie • All By Myself • The Catman • Wheel Of Fortune • Love My Baby • It's Only Make Believe • Crazy Man Crazy • The Worrying Kind • Nervous • Sweet Love On My Mind • Need You • Someday, Someway • Look Who's Blue • Drivin' Wheel • Something's Gonna Happen • Black Slacks • Fire • Red Hot

This is a notoriously difficult beastie to track down, but if you crave red-hot rockabilly that's guaranteed to burn a hole in your brothel creepers then it's well worth hunting down a copy. Gordon is one of those guys who believes that music took a dive when Buddy Holly died and he's been waging a one-man campaign for real rock 'n' boogie since the seventies. This CD compiles the best tracks from the two albums that he made with the legendary Link Wray, whose growling guitar sound has been a major influence on artists as diverse as PJ Harvey and Pete Townsend. If you're a guitarist you'll pick up more licks from these tracks than from a stack of contemporary CDs and if you love lean, mean muscular music that sounds as if it ought to be wearing shades and a black leather jacket, you won't need further persuasion. Imagine what Shakin' Stevens could have recorded if he'd had talent. Or consider what Brian Setzer and the Stray Cats might have made had they met up with Link Wray instead of Dave Edmunds and you'll have some idea of what's on offer here. There are moments when the mask slips and Gordon sounds like a dime-a-dozen Elvis impersonator, but like his guitarist and mentor he knows that simplicity and raw animal passion is the lifeblood of rock and roll. And once you've been bitten by the beast you'll be howling at the moon for more.

Rating:
Sound ★★★★★ Content ★★★★☆
Also recommended:
'Too Fast To Live…Too Young To Die' (Camden/BMG), 'Black Slacks' (Bear Family) and Robert Gordon With Link Wray 'Fresh Fish Special' (Ace).
If you like this, why not try:
The Stray Cats, the various Rockabilly compilations on Sun, **Carl Perkins**, **Elvis**' original Sun recordings.

Gorillaz

'GORILLAZ'

(Parlophone) 2001

Track listing: Re-Hash • 5-4 • Tomorrow Comes Today • New Genious (Brother) • Clint Eastwood • Man Research • Punk • Sound Check • Double Bass • Rock The House • 19-2000 • Latin Simone • Starshine • Slow Country • M1 A1

Bonus Track: Clint Eastwood (Remix)

Blur's Damon Albarn is the brains behind this agreeably chaotic montage of trip hop, Britpop and hip hop soundbites and samples. The cut and paste approach is exemplified by the single 'Clint Eastwood' on which a lazy harmonica introduces a spaghetti western theme before being interrupted by a rapid fire monologue, but there are so many contemporary references in this vibrant collage of sound that its impossible to define it or find a focus. And that is perhaps the point of the exercise. Pop, as exemplified by off-the-wall projects like this, has become so fragmented and incestuous that it can become the expression of an anonymous collective who are content to tinker with technology.

Incidentally, if you were bitten by the fast mix of 'Clint Eastwood' on the 'Now 48' compilation you might find the chill-out tempos of the other tracks a shade too sleep-inducing for comfort. This is an uneven album brimming with interesting ideas, but the participants appear to have been so carried away in experimentation that they haven't developed many of them beyond the initial sketch.

NB: Beware of the 'hidden' bonus track. If you're unprepared for it, it'll make you drop a stitch.

Rating:
Sound ★★★☆☆ Content ★★★☆☆
Also recommended:
n/a.
If you like this, why not try:
Ash, Stereophonics, Portishead, Blur.

The Grateful Dead

'ANTHEM OF THE SUN'

(Warners) 1968

Track listing: That's It For The Other One •
New Potato Caboose • Born Cross-Eyed •
Alligator • Caution (Do Not Step On Tracks)

In the pantheon of rock gods The Grateful Dead are up there with Zeus (aka Elvis), although those born after the acid-saturated sixties may be bored stupid rather than blissed-out by their extended explorations of inner space. 'Anthem Of The Sun' is a largely improvised psychedelic soundtrack to the San Francisco Acid Tests of '68 and of great historical significance. But unless you took the trip first time out, it's bound to sound frenetic and unfocused. However, for Dead Heads this is where their devotion began.

Several tracks are composites of live and studio recordings including 'The Other One', 'Alligator' and 'Caution' which became staples of their live shows for the next 30 years.

Rating:
Sound ★★★☆☆ Content ★★★☆☆

The Grateful Dead

'WORKINGMAN'S DEAD'

(Warners) 1970

Track listing: Uncle John's Band • High Time
• Dire Wolf • New Speedway Boogie •
Cumberland Blues • Black Peter • Easy
Wind • Casey Jones

Taking time out from their epic electric improvisations The Dead went back to their roots with this sparse semi-acoustic collection of close-harmony country-folk tunes. Their vocal harmonies aren't as smooth as Crosby, Stills, Nash and Young, but they sound more authentic. In contrast to the loose, improvised feel of their psychedelic workouts these tracks are condensed and economical; imbued with the rustic hues of the backwoods and the sweet smell of the still.

Rating:
Sound ★★★★☆ Content ★★★☆☆

Also recommended:
'Live Dead', 'American Beauty' (both on Warners), 'Blues For Allah' (Grateful Dead Records/Ace) and 'In The Dark' (Arista) plus all seven volumes of the 'Dick's Picks' official bootleg series (all on Grateful Dead/Ace Records).

If you like this, why not try:
Jefferson Airplane, **The Band**, **Quicksilver Messenger Service**.

David Gray

'WHITE LADDER'

(East West) 2000

Track listing: Please Forgive Me • Babylon •
My Oh My • We're Not Right •
Nightblindness • Silver Lining • White
Ladder • This Year's Love • Sail Away • Say
Hello Wave Goodbye

David Gray has enjoyed a cult following in his native Wales (and Ireland) since the early nineties, but he finally found an international audience with 'White Ladder', having discarded traditional instrumentation and adopted a more contemporary sound. Strip away the fashionable trimmings though and you have an album and an artist that can boast good old-fashioned songwriting values, solid musicianship and a voice that invites comparison with the young Elton John. If he can sustain the quality of the songs on this album and maintain the fine balance that has brought him a broad fan base, then he may well attain a similar level of success – though hopefully without Elton's outrageous taste in clothes.

Rating:
Sound ★★★★★ Content ★★★★☆
Also recommended:
'Lost Songs' (East West).
If you like this, why not try:
Coldplay, Toploader, **Elton John**.

Green Day

'DOOKIE'

(Reprise) 1994

Track listing: Burnout • Having A Blast • Chump • Longview • Welcome To Paradise • Pulling Teeth • Basketcase • She • Sasafras Roots • When I Come Round • Coming Clean • Emenius Sleepus • In The End • FOD

Punk didn't die in 1977, it sold out for a comfortable office in the corporate rock hierarchy and waited for its odious offspring to take up the struggle. Seventeen years later its spotty sprogs dutifully dug out their dads' Stiff Little Fingers T-shirts and learnt the proverbial three-chord thrash before launching the inevitable punk rock revival. Green Day were at the forefront with all the right moves,

a suspiciously refined sound and a singer who sounded uncannily like Billy Bragg's Californian cousin. But they had enough tongue-in-cheek humour to compensate for the high-gloss surface sheen and a fistful of sufficiently strong songs to make up for the feeling that we'd heard it all before.

This time there was no gobbing at the band, precious few profanities and the pogo was choreographed as rigidly as a line-dancing contest. But there's more barely repressed energy and unadulterated fun in a track like 'Basket Case' than in a stadium full of AOR acts. So just be grateful that the band's dads didn't sell their Ramones records.

Rating:
Sound ★★★★☆ Content ★★★★☆
Also recommended:
'Insomniac', 'Warning' and 'Nimrod' (all on Reprise).
If you like this, why not try:
Exploited, **Sex Pistols, Dead Kennedys, The Ramones, Stiff Little Fingers, The Undertones**.

Patty Griffin

'FLAMING RED'

(A&M) 2001

Track listing: Flaming Red • One Big Love • Tony • Change • Goodbye • Carry Me • Christina • Wiggley Fingers • Blue Sky • Big Daddy • Go Now • Mary • Peter Pan

Unlike her 'new country' cousins with their lucrative crossover concessions, Patty refuses to genetically modify her music to appease the pre-teens and the line-dancing contingent. She sides instead with the bad ass guitar slingers on the fringes of rock, riding roughshod over the likes of Shania Twain with this sturdy set of staunchly uncompromising country-rock tunes which bucks like a wild steer with a burr under its saddle. The country element is minimal, meaning that you won't find a fiddle on any of the tracks or stumble over a song about Griffith losing her man, taking to the bottle or shooting her poor little dawgy. Were it not for her indolent Southern drawl you could be mistaken for thinking you were deep in indie territory where they waste no time in getting to the point. In short, this is the sound of the real wild, wild West. So bite the bullet and buy, as albums of this quality don't come around too often, but when they do they make the hairs on your neck stand up and shiver.

Rating:
Sound ★★★★☆ Content ★★★★★
Also recommended: n/a
If you like this, why not try:
Joan Osborne, Emmylou Harris.

Gun Club

'FIRE OF LOVE'

(New Rose) 1981

Track listing: Sex Beat • Preachin' The Blues • Promise Me • She's Like Heroin To Me • For The Love Of Ivy • Fire Spirit • Ghost On The Highway • Jack On Fire • Black Train • Cold Drink Of Water • Goodbye Johnny • Walking With The Beast

Decades after bluesman Robert Johnson sold his solo to the devil in return for immortality his acolytes were making pilgrimages to the crossroads where the deal had been done in the hope of striking up a similar bargain. Jeffrey Lee Pierce and his part-time partner Kid Congo Powers (formerly of The Cramps) were two such disciples with a morbid fascination for the dark side of the delta blues. Whether they made a pact with Old Nick we'll never know, but Pierce evokes the spirit of the haunted bluesman with his keening slide guitar and tremulous voice on a cover of Johnson's 'Preaching The Blues' and a host of mournful originals in the same vein.

Listening to the album with the lights down low and a bottle of hooch will conjure up an image of Pierce pursued by Johnson's ghost along that lonely highway. Chilling stuff.

Rating:
Sound ★★★★☆ Content ★★★★☆

Gun Club

'MOTHER JUNO'

(Solid/Vital) 1987

Track listing: Bill Bailey Won't You Please Come Home • Thunderhead • Lupita Screams • Yellow Eyes • Breaking Hands • Araby • Hearts • My Cousin Kim • Ports Of Souls

In the late eighties Jeffrey Lee Pierce returned from a lengthy sojourn in the desert to begin work on the

'Mother Juno' sessions with Robin Guthrie of the Cocteau Twins. Hardcore fans were dismayed by the lush, layered sound in which Guthrie cocooned the Gun Club's mutant psychobilly sound, but the strength of the songs and Pierce's feral guitar satisfied the critics who were almost unanimous in their praise.

'Thunderhead' and 'Yellow Eyes' sees Pierce exploring his own heart of darkness in the company of a Native American spirit guide who draws him into the charted tributaries of swamp rock before unleashing his troubled spirit on the raging 'My Cousin Kim' and 'Port Of Souls'. Pierce died of a stroke in 1996 having never recaptured the manic energy of his early albums. Few of his recordings are currently available on CD, although even the weakest of them makes most of major label product sound very anemic indeed.

Rating:
Sound ★★★★☆ Content ★★★★☆
Also recommended:
'Las Vegas Story' and the compilation 'Ahmed's Wild Dream' (both on Solid/Vital)
If you like this, why not try:
The Cramps, **Nick Cave**.

Guns 'n' Roses

'APPETITE FOR DESTRUCTION'

(Geffen) 1987

Track listing: Welcome To The Jungle • It's So Easy • Nightrain • Out Ta Get Me • Mr Brownstone • Paradise City • My Michelle • Think About You • Sweet Child O' Mine • You're Crazy • Anything Goes • Rocket Queen

Guns 'N' Roses were one of those rare rock and roll animals who justified the hype that brought them to notoriety. Their image was contrived to appeal to young bucks who had never seen Led Zeppelin or Aerosmith and their sound was similarly styled to ensure a successful hostile takeover of the market. Axl Rose shamelessly affected the mannered vocal histrionics of a horde of heavy metal singers, prompting one critic to describe him as sounding like a man undergoing surgery without the benefit of anaesthetic. Their music too, was a concoction of cliches, but on 'Appetite For Destruction' they served it up steaming and strong. Few albums can boast a track listing as consistently good as this one. They peel off in fourth gear on 'Welcome To The Jungle' then cruise for a couple of tracks that would be considered highlights on anyone else's album before giving it some serious stick on 'Mr Brownstone', 'Paradise City' and 'My Michelle'. They cool things down on the classy anthem 'Sweet Child Of Mine', which one suspects was written just to prove that they could do so.

The group may have acted like a serious case of arrested development, but they made a hell of a kick-ass album.

Rating:
Sound ★★★★☆ Content ★★★★★

Guns 'n' Roses

'USE YOUR ILLUSION VOL I'

(Geffen) 1991

Track listing: Right Next Door To Hell • Dust N' Bones • Live And Let Die • Don't Cry • Perfect Crime • You Ain't The First • Bad Obsession • Back Off Bitch • Double Talkin' Jive • November Rain • The Garden • Garden Of Eden • Don't Damn Me • Bad Apples • Dead Horse • Coma

'USE YOUR ILLUSION VOL II'

(Geffen) 1991

Track listing: Civil War • Fourteen Years • Yesterdays • Knockin' On Heaven's Door • Get In The Ring • Shotgun Blues • Breakdown • Pretty Tied Up • Locomotive • So Fine • Estranged • You Could Be Mine • Don't Cry • My World

There was a time when the only groups who spent months in the studio making a double album were progressive rockers. But in 1991 Guns 'n' Roses surveyed the reels of recording tape that had accumulated over the past four years and couldn't face cutting it down to a double, let alone a single LP. So they ordered the engineers to edit all 30 songs to make two double albums to be released on the same day.

It doesn't take a gifted psychic to foresee that such a strategy would be courting disaster. Sure, the albums sold enough copies to sink a small island, but they were as inconsistent as a politician's promises. There's a slew of boozy bad boy boogie that

would have done the Stones proud and a handful of emotive ballads to satisfy the stadium crowds, but there's a disproportionate amount of so-so material and substandard fillers that their fawning yes men should have said a resounding 'no' to.

'Garden Of Eden' and 'Coma' fall into the former category, 'Don't Cry' into the next and the superfluous covers of 'Live And Let Die' and 'Knockin' On Heaven's Door' into the latter.

Rating:
Sound ★★★★☆
Content ★★☆☆☆/★★★☆☆
Also recommended:
'The Spaghetti Incident' (Geffen).
If you like this, why not try:
Aerosmith, The Black Crowes, **The Rolling Stones**.

Happy Mondays

'PILLS 'N' THRILLS AND BELLYACHES'

(Factory) 1990

Track listing: Kinky Afro • God's Cop • Donovan • Grandbag's Funeral • Loose Fit • Dennis and Louis • Bob's Your Uncle • Step On • Holiday • Harmony

It's alleged that Shaun Ryder and his accomplices managed to graduate from selling E to creating the kind of wiry dance music that would enhance the experience of taking the drug by rigging the result of the talent contest that brought them to the notice of Tony Wilson, boss of the Hacienda and Factory Records.

'Madchester's' finest brought to the mix their authentic sink-estate slang and a jaundiced world view in songs which celebrated their earlier escapades and an excessive intake of their own merchandise. The most addictive tracks are 'God's Cop', which mocks the local chief constable who believed that he had a personal hotline to heaven; 'Grandbag's Funeral' in which Shaun makes his peace with the dear departed, whose funeral he had missed because he was too stoned at the time, and the cover of John Kongos 'Step On' which updates a 'Come Together' type rant for the rave generation.

This is the kind of album that would make even Mark E Smith grin.

Rating:
Sound ★★★★☆ Content ★★★★☆
Also recommended:
'Bummed' and the compilation 'Loads And Loads More' (both on London).
If you like this, why not try:
The Stone Roses, Black Grape, **Talking Heads**.

Geri Halliwell

'SCHIZOPHONIC'

(EMI) 1999

Track listing: Look At Me • Lift Me Up • Walkaway • Mi Chico Latino • Goodnight Kiss • Bag It Up • Sometime • Let Me Love You • Someone's Watching Over Me • You're In A Bubble

Let's face facts, the ex-Spice Girl's first solo outing was never likely to see much dabbling with the formula that had brought her fame and fortune. She was not going to make a radical artistic or political statement when the name of the game had been entertainment for teens. The best one could hope for would be a little more personal insight into the celebrity circus and tracks one could party to.

'Schizophonic' is not as pleasant a surprise, nor as accomplished as Robbie Williams' first solo offering after leaving Take That. While he was revealed to be a larger than life personality with talent to spare, Geri emerges from 'Schizophonic' as a self-possessed celebrity who can sing. This is an agreeable though lightweight pop album with no pretence to be anything else. A handful of tracks work well (the sultry, after-hours jazz pastiche 'Goodnight Kiss', the melding of gospel and breakbeats on 'Sometime' and the two parting shots at her former pop puppets, 'Walkaway' and the more acidic 'You're In A Bubble'). Neither have the artfulness of Lennon's 'How Do You Sleep?', but then The Spice Girls were little more than a female Monkees. This pleased the fans, but it won't give Madonna any worries.

Rating:
Sound ★★★★☆ Content ★★★☆☆
Also recommended: n/a
If you like this, why not try:
The Spice Girls, Destiny's Child.

Steve Harley And Cockney Rebel

'THE CREAM OF STEVE HARLEY AND COCKNEY REBEL'

(EMI) 1999 Budget price

Track listing: Make Me Smile (Come Up And See Me) • Judy Teen • Here Comes The Sun • Love's A Prima Donna • Best Years Of Our Lives • Another Journey • Freedom's Prisoner • Tumbling Down • Mr Raffles • Roll The Dice • Psychomodo • Mr Soft • White White Dove • Sebastian • Love Compared With You • I Can't Even Touch You

Harley's biggest hit, 'Make Me Smile (Come Up And See Me)', is the epitome of lush pop perfection and appears with almost monotonous regularity on seventies compilations, but there are at least half a dozen more that demand space in any self respecting CD collection.

With an image lifted straight from A Clockwork Orange and an extreme sense of camp cabaret Cockney Rebel bridged the gap between glam rock and the more serious rock theatre exemplified by Bowie. The swirling circus organ, violin solo and quirky staccato rhythms of 'Judy Teen' and 'Mr Soft' are redolent of greasepaint and sawdust, while the opulently orchestrated 'Sebastian' is a classic example of the kind of epic pop song that is now sadly out of fashion.

In the absence of a truly representative retrospective, or a reissue of the essential 'Psychomodo' and 'Human Menagerie' albums, this patchy compilation will have to suffice. But be warned, its padded out with a disproportionate amount of flabby post-1975 material.

Rating:
Sound ★★★☆☆ Content ★★★☆☆

Steve Harley And Cockney Rebel

'TIMELESS FLIGHT'

(EMI) 1975

Track listing: Red Is A Mean, Mean Colour • White, White Dove • Understand • All Men Are Hungry • Black Or White • Everything Changes • Nothing Is Sacred • Don't Go, Don't Cry

Bonus tracks: Throw Your Soul Down Here • Mad, Mad Moonlight

Not the most representative title in the group's catalogue, but one of the few original albums that are currently available on CD and as indicative of florid mid-seventies pop as Queen's 'A Night At The Opera'.

By the time they came to record this Harley's name was disconnected from the group as he asserted his status as writer in residence, but at least his boast was offset by some of his best songs. With characteristic modesty he namechecks Baudelaire, Hemingway, Kahlil Gibran and Kipling, but if his own literary ambitions are not fully realized in the obscure lyrics at least the music has a lustrous beauty that beguiles with its melodic strength and sophistication. Audition 'All The Men Are Hungry' or 'Everything Changes' and then you'll know why Harley's repatriation is long overdue.

Rating:
Sound ★★★★☆ Content ★★★★☆
Also recommended:
'The Best Years Of Our Lives' (EMI).
If you like this, why not try:
David Bowie, Suede.

PJ Harvey

'DRY'

(Too Pure) 1992

Track listing: Oh My Lover • O Stella • Dress • Victory • Happy And Bleeding • Sheela-Na-Gig • Hair • Joe • Plants And Rags • Fountain • Water

Like the dress in the song of the same name Polly Jean Harvey wears it well – 'it' being the mantle of the fiercely independent female guitarist with an axe to grind. In fact, the part might have been tailor made for her. PJ clothes her songs in grunge guitar, violin, harmonium and cello like a cross between Nico, Nick Cave and Kurt Cobain to emphasize the relationship between love and pain more keenly than many of her mainstream male contemporaries would dare to do. And she takes her rage and frustration out in music that effectively emasculates the male ego. Just listen to 'Water' a tale of insanity and suicide which builds from a whisper to a full throated primal scream. Just don't listen to it last thing at night.

Harvey gives the impression that she is as angry with herself for needing men as she is with the men who exploit that need and it's this tension that makes 'Dry' one of the

few truly 'adult' rock albums of recent years.

Rating:
Sound ★★★☆☆ Content ★★★★☆
Also recommended:
'Rid Of Me' and 'To Bring You My Love' (Island).
If you like this, why not try:
Bjork, Sheryl Crow, Joan Osborne.

Hawkwind

'DOREMI FASOL LATIDO'

(EMI) 1972

Track listing: Brainstorm • Space Is Deep • One Change • Lord Of Light • Down Through The Night • Time We Left This World Today • Watcher

Bonus tracks: Urban Guerrilla • Brainbox Pollution • Lord Of Light • Ejection

If Pink Floyd were the pioneers of sonic innerspace exploration, Hawkwind were the stoned scrapmetal scavengers who followed in their wake. This, their second outing, finds Captain Brock and his merry crew meandering across the galaxy in a clapped-out old banger, unphased by the sound of serious metal fatigue and unsettling noises in the engine room. To stiffen their resolve they break into a round of ritualistic cosmic chanting accompanied by Second Mate Nik Turner's squawking sax and Captain Brock barking orders from the bridge. 'Doremi Fasol Latido' has them firing on all cylinders as they swiftly approach warp speed and gear themselves up for the greatest light show in the cosmos, pausing only to light another spliff and crank up the volume on the in-flight audio system. Needless to say, nobody has a clue where they're heading, or even why they set off in the first place. All they know is that it's important to enjoy the trip.

In the far distant future extraterrestrial archaeologists will come upon the derelict wreck of the good ship Hawkwind and download this record of their voyage for the listening pleasure of all known lifeforms. And then there will be rejoicing throughout the cosmos.

Rating:
Sound ★★★★☆ Content ★★★★★

Hawkwind

'SPACE RITUAL'

2 CDs (EMI) 1973

Track listing: CD 1 – Earth Calling • Born To Go • Down Through The Night • Awakening • Lord Of Light • Black Corridor • Space Is Deep • Electronic No 1 • Orgone Accumulator • Upside Down • Ten Seconds Of Forever • Brainstorm

CD 2 – Seven By Seven • Sonic Attack • Time We Left This World Today • Masters Of The Universe • Welcome To The Future

Bonus tracks: You Shouldn't Do That • Master Of The Universe • Born To Go

Any normal human being would have to rent a rocket to make a trip into the furthest reaches of outer space, but not the members of Hawkwind. They got out of their heads on more drugs than the average high street chemist would see in a lifetime, and while boldly going where no group had gone before they miraculously managed to play

their instruments in something resembling togetherness. Just imagine a 40-minute long variation on 'Silver Machine' and you have the gist of this gloriously self-indulgent space opera which makes *The Hitchhiker's Guide To The Galaxy* sound like a serious proposition by comparison.

'Space Ritual' sees Captain Brock and his hippie crew forsaking the studio's flight simulator for a live launch before a crowd of fellow space travellers hell bent on riding the riffs to that final frontier. So, light the blue touch paper and retire to a safe distance. It's going to be a thrilling trip.

Rating:
Sound ★★★☆☆ Content ★★★★★
Also recommended:
'Hall Of The Mountain Grill', 'In Search Of Space' and 'Stasis – The UA Years' (all on Fame/EMI).
If you like this, why not try:
Pink Floyd, Spiritualized, **Motorhead, The Orb.**

Jimi Hendrix

'AT WOODSTOCK'

(Polydor) 1994

Track listing: Introduction • Fire • Izabella • Hear My Train A Comin' • Red House • Jam Back At The House • Voodoo Chile • Star Spangled Banner • Purple Haze • Woodstock Improvisation • Villanova Junction • Farewell

When you buy a Hendrix album you're presumably hoping for hard rock riffola, incendiary guitar solos and vivid psychedelic shadings. If so, there's little point in purchasing the first three studio albums as (blasphemous though it might be to say so) they were padded out with more than their fair share of dopey hippy filler. Admittedly, 'Axis: Bold As Love' features 'Little Wing' and 'Castles Made Of Sand'; 'Are You Experienced' has 'Foxy Lady', 'Manic Depression', '3rd Stone From The Sun' and 'Red House' and 'Electric Ladyland' boasts 'Voodoo Chile (Slight Return)', 'Burning Of The Midnight Lamp' and 'All Along The Watchtower'. But all of these and more are now available on competing compilations (see below). The 'real' Hendrix is to be found on live recordings such as this one, where he had the space to stretch out and let his guitar do the talking, articulating what the greatest exponents of rock, soul, jazz, blues and funk had been saying in their own sweet way since the music was born, but putting it into an entirely new perspective.

These versions of 'Voodoo Chile', 'Red House' and 'Hear My Train A'Comin' plus the stunning deconstruction of 'The Star Spangled Banner' are arguably the ultimate demonstration of his total mastery of his instrument, a dazzling display of virtuosity and showmanship. Through the creative use of effects pedals, distortion and screaming feedback Hendrix orchestrates an entirely new spectrum of tonal colours resulting in music unequalled for sheer intensity and invention. It's the ultimate musical 'high'.

Rating:
Sound ★★★☆☆ Content ★★★★★

Jimi Hendrix

'THE ULTIMATE EXPERIENCE'

(Polydor) 1992

Track listing: All Along The Watchtower • Purple Haze • Hey Joe • The Wind Cries Mary • Angel • Voodoo Child (Slight Return) • Foxy Lady • Burning Of The Midnight Lamp • Highway Chile • Crosstown Traffic • Castles Made Of Sand • Long Hot Summer Night • Red House • Manic Depression • Gypsy Eyes • Little Wing • Fire • Wait Until Tomorrow • Star Spangled Banner • Wild Thing

It's not often that a 'best of' compilation really lives up to its name, but this one does, so much so that you might prefer to plump for this choice selection of singles and album cuts and leave the original albums aside. But if you do, you'll still need to sample Hendrix at his most electrifying – in live performance.

In comparison with the live versions these studio recordings might appear somewhat subdued, but the trademark stylings have simply been compressed into three- or four-minute portions of exhilarating pop art. Whether Jimmy was laying back on a standard 12-bar blues such as 'Red House', pausing for reflection on the lyrical 'Little Wing', or riveting repetitive riffs into a prototypical heavy metal anthem such as 'Purple Haze', they were all embellished with his distinctive fluid lead guitar licks. Familiarity has not however, diminished the magic. Sample any track at random and you can appreciate why he is still considered to be one of the most innovative and influential artists of the 20th century.

N.B: The last two tracks on this collection are in-concert recordings.

Rating:
Sound ★★★★☆ Content ★★★★★
Also recommended:
'Are You Experienced', 'Axis: Bold As Love', 'Electric Ladyland', 'Jimi Plays Monterey', 'BBC Sessions', 'Live At The Isle Of Wight', 'Live At Winterland', 'Stages' box set (all on MCA) with highlights distilled on a single CD 'The Jimi Hendrix Concerts'.
If you like this, why not try:
Cream, Led Zeppelin, Prince, Joe Satriani.

Void-Oids

'BLANK GENERATION'

(Sire) 1977

Track listing: Love Comes In Spurts • Liars Between • New Pleasure • Betrayal Takes Two • Down At The Rock And Roll Club • Who Says • Blank Generation • Walking On The Water • The Plan • Another World

When asked why he created the archetypal punk look – all ripped clothes, short spiky hair and wasted appearance – Richard Hell would claim that Rimbaud had looked that way. Whether the tortured French poet would have stuck a safety pin through his flesh we'll never know, but it's quite likely that he would have got off on 'Blank Generation's noise and nihilism, even if its deranged poetry might not have been quite to his taste.

Hell is a hugely significant figure in the New York punk scene (first with Television and then with The Heartbreakers) and he inspired Malcolm McLaren to form the Sex Pistols, but his own record is not as remarkable as the man who made it. It does, however, contain a re-recording of his classic 'Love Comes In Spurts' and the influential title track, but the remainder is uneven and of little interest to those who weren't there at the time. It also proved impossible to follow for various reasons, forcing Hell to follow Rimbaud's example and lose himself in the wilderness until the world finally caught up with him.

Rating:
Sound ★★★☆☆ Content ★★★☆☆
Also recommended:
'Destiny Street' (Danceteria).
If you like this, why not try
Television, The Ramones, Buzzcocks.

Robyn Hitchcock

'BLACK SNAKE DIAMOND ROLE'

(Sequel) 1995

Track listing: The Man Who Invented Himself • Brenda's Iron Sledge • Lizard • Meat • Do Policemen Sing • Acid Bird • I Watch The Cars • Out Of The Picture • City Of Shame • Love • Dancing On God's Thumb

Bonus tracks: Happy The Golden Prince • Kingdom Of Love • It Was The Night

Hitchcock is not exactly a household name and he's never likely to be one, but during the eighties he became a significant and much-loved cult figure after being cited by Peter Buck of REM as one of the guitarist's early influences. Weird, surreal, psychedelic and pleasantly pessimistic are among the words that come most readily to mind when thinking of Hitchcock. But then so do the names Syd Barrett and Reg – the former being his closest musical relative and the latter being an enigmatic character who crops up repeatedly in his songs in the manner of a running gag in Monty Python. Come to think of it, Python is perhaps the closest one comes to Hitchcock's dysfunctional humour. His lyrics go where you least expect them to and the curious thing is that they continue to surprise no matter how many times you've listened to his songs. If Lewis Carrol had written songs instead of writing dubious deranged children's stories he might have come up with some of these.

Rating:
Sound ★★★★☆ Content ★★★★☆

Robyn Hitchcock

'I OFTEN DREAM OF TRAINS'

(Sequel) 1995

Track listing: Nocturne • Sometimes I Wish I Was A Pretty Girl • Cathedral • Uncorrected Personality Traits • Sounds Great When You're Dead • Flavour Of Night • Sleeping Knights Of Jesus • Mellow Together • Winter Love • Bones In The Ground • My Favourite Buildings • I Used To Say I Love You • This Could Be The Day • Trams Of Old London • Furry Green Atom Bowl • Heart Full Of Leaves • Autumn Is Your Last Chance • I Often Dream Of Trains

In a parallel universe Hitchcock would be adding another platinum disc to his collection for selling a million copies of this solo acoustic offering while the Spice Girls would be nursing their egos after being rejected by yet another record company. Aaah, if only.

Robyn has described these tracks as 'Captain Beefheart meets Country Joe And The Fish in Sussex' which is as fair a description as you're likely to get. Other than to add that it's bizarre and very, very beautiful. It's also one of the most original and imaginative albums you're ever likely to hear. As some wise person once remarked, 'If this is your first Hitchcock purchase, mark the date in your diary. You will want to remember it.'

Rating:
Sound ★★★★☆ Content ★★★★★
Also recommended:
'Queen Elvis', 'Fegmania', 'Element Of Light' and 'Eye' (all on Sequel).
If you like this, why not try:
The Soft Boys, Lou Reed, Jonathan Richman, Buzzcocks, The Only Ones, Syd Barrett.

Buddy Holly

'20 GOLDEN GREATS'

(MCA) 1993

Track listing: That'll Be The Day • Peggy Sue • Words Of Love • Everyday • Not Fade Away • Oh Boy • Maybe Baby • Listen To Me • Heartbeat • Think It Over • It Doesn't Matter Anymore • It's So Easy • Well Alright • Rave On • Raining In My Heart • True Love Ways • Peggy Sue Got Married • Bo Diddley • Brown Eyed Handsome Man • Wishing

With his huge horned-rimmed glasses, adenoidal twang and goofy teeth Buddy Holly was the least likely looking rock star of the fifties, but he helped overturn the Tin Pan Alley tradition which cast the singer as the puppet of the record producer by insisting on producing his own records. He was also the first to use multi-tracking to embellish the basic drums, bass and guitar format and the first to feature strings on a pop single. But although Holly didn't rock hard like Elvis, Little Richard or Jerry Lee, his songs endure because he managed to capture the innocent thrill of teenage romance and articulate its cocktail of adolescent emotions with a disarming simplicity.

Rating:
Sound ★★★★☆ Content ★★★★☆
Also recommended:
'Words Of Love – 20 Classic Songs' (Polygram TV).
If you like this, why not try:
Everly Brothers, Eddie Cochran, Dion.

John Lee Hooker

'THE VERY BEST OF JOHN LEE HOOKER'

(MCI) 1991 Budget price

Track listing: I'm In The Mood • Boogie Chillun' • It Serves Me Right To Suffer • This Is Hip • House Rent Boogie • I'm So Excited • I Love You Honey • Hobo Blues • Crawlin' Kingsnake • Maudie • Dimples • Boom Boom • Louise • Ground Hog Blues • Ramblin' By Myself • Walkin' The Boogie • One Bourbon, One Scotch, One Beer • Sugar Mama • Peace Lovin' Man • Leave My Wife Alone • Blues Before Sunrise • Time Is Marching

The late Hooker was the last of the legendary bluesmen. The delta-born son of a sharecropper was the last living link with the rural tradition and the inspiration for several generations of white rock artists who saw him as the connection between rock and its roots. The sheer scale of his recorded output however, is intimidating – over 140 albums at the last count – and the list continues to grow as his recordings are reissued and repackaged by numerous labels. This 22-track compilation is arguably the best of the bunch with a good representative selection of his most significant recordings drawn from the Chess and Veejay catalogue and infinitely superior sound quality.

Every major rock artist from The Rolling Stones, Van Morrison and The Doors in the Sixties to Bruce Springsteen and George Thorogood in the MTV era has covered these songs, but nobody delivers them as powerfully as the man himself.

'Crawlin' Kingsnake' and 'Hobo Blues' exemplify his command of starkly simple country blues, that raw and rhythmic roots music with a loose rural feel around which he wraps that cavernous gravel voice to the accompaniment of a solo electric guitar. In contrast the earthy intensity of the Chicago sessions with a band beefs up the beat, but still wrings out the emotion with all the conviction of a man who didn't just sing the blues, but lived it. As Hooker once told me, 'Ever since Adam and Eve there has been the blues. And as long as there is a man and a woman to love and hurt each other there will be the blues.'

Rating:
Sound ★★★☆☆ Content ★★★★★
Also recommended:
'Boogie Chillun' (Charly).
If you like this, why not try:
Howling Wolf, Elmore James, Muddy Waters.

Horslips

'FROM THE HORSE'S MOUTH'

(Edsel) 2000

Track listing: High Reel • Night Town Boy • Flower Among Them All • Dearg Doom • Faster Than The Hounds • Best Years Of My Life • Man Who Built America • Guests Of The Nation • Daybreak • Everything Will Be Alright • Power And The Glory • Sword Of Light • Warm Sweet Breath Of Love • Speed The Plough • Trouble With A Capital T • Shamrock Shore • King Of The Fairies • High Volume Love • An Bratach Ban • Silver Spear

Horslips were unheralded pioneers of the folk-rock movement who were acclaimed as heroes in their native Ireland. But as soon as they attempted to update their sound and broaden their appeal they lost their sense of identity and with it their musical integrity. 'Flower Among Them All', 'Dearg Doom', 'King Of The Fairies' and 'Trouble' are taken from their earlier albums on which the spirit of the Emerald Isle is invoked through melodic Celtic rock complete with Uillean pipes, bodhrans and penny whistles. But the more commercial tracks are evocative only of compromise.

This compilation has been remastered by the band from the original master tapes, rendering the original poor-quality issues on Outlet obsolete. So make sure it's the Edsel issue that you purchase.

Rating:
Sound ★★★☆☆ Content ★★★☆☆
Also recommended:
'The Book Of Invasions' and 'Guests Of The Nation' (both on Outlet).
If you like this, why not try:
Steeleye Span, Fairport Convention, Wishbone Ash.

Hot Chocolate

'GREATEST HITS'

(EMI) 1993

Track listing: You Sexy Thing • It Started With A Kiss • Brother Louie • Girl Crazy • So You Win Again • Put Your Love In Me • Love Is Life • I'll Put You Together Again • No Doubt About It • Every 1's A Winner • Emma • I Gave You My Heart • You Could've Been A Lady • Don't Stop It Now • Child's Prayer • What Kinda Boy You Looking For • I Believe • Are You Getting Enough Happiness

Hot Chocolate merit little more than a footnote in serious rock books, but they racked up an impressive 25 hits in a lengthy and lucrative career which ran from 1970 to the mid-eighties. Shaven-headed singer-songwriter Errol Brown chose their name wisely to reflect the blending of his rich and creamy voice with a sweet soul confection that became a staple diet of daytime radio and the dancefloors. Even more remarkable than their release-to-hit ratio is the fact that several of these songs charted again when reissued, some of them reaching a higher position than when originally released. Everyone a winner, indeed.

Rating:
Sound ★★★★☆ Content ★★★☆☆
Also recommended:
'Rest Of The Best' (EMI).
If you like this, why not try:
Chic, Smokey Robinson, Marvin
Gaye.

Whitney Houston

'WHITNEY HOUSTON'

(Arista/BMG) 1986

*Track listing: How Will I Know • Take Good
Care Of My Heart • Greatest Love Of All •
Hold Me • You Give Good Love • Thinking
About You • Someone For Me • Saving All
My Love For You • Nobody Loves Me Like
You Do • All At Once*

It is safe to assume that this album will
never be rated as a classic, although it
entered the US charts at number one,
remained in the higher reaches for over
four years and went on to sell a
staggering 15 million copies. It is,
however, historically significant for the
fact that it introduced a new brand of
glassy smooth and rather insubstantial
soul music to the MTV generation who
appropriated the term R&B, although it
had nothing to do with the bump 'n'
grind variety of an early era.

Whitney is the niece of Aretha
Franklin and shares a innate feeling
for gospel which she has since
demonstrated to stunning effect on
the soundtrack to 'The Preacher's
Wife', but on her debut album she
settles for a set of sophisticated,
melodramatic ballads which she
begins on a crescendo and builds to a
climax. Every copy should come
with a free box of Kleenex.

Rating:
Sound ★★★★☆ Content ★★★☆☆
Also recommended:
'The Bodyguard', 'Whitney', 'The
Preacher's Wife' and 'I'm Your Baby
Tonight' (all on Arista/BMG).
If you like this, why not try:
Janet Jackson, Celine Dion, Mariah
Carey.

Howlin' Wolf

'THE LONDON SESSIONS'

(Chess/Charly) 1970

*Track listing: Rockin' Daddy • I Ain't
Superstitious • Sittin' On Top Of The World •
Worried About My Baby • What A Woman!
• Poor Boy • Built For Comfort • Who's
Been Talking • Little Red Rooster • Do The
Do • Highway • Wang Dang Doodle*

Howlin' Wolf had one of the most
distinctive and intimidating voices in
popular music, a huge grisly bear of a
voice that reaches out of the speakers
and threatens to hug you to death.
Everything is subordinate to that
awesome growl; the instrumentation,
even the songs. When Wolf is
confessing to his voracious appetite
for food, booze and women it
expresses a hunger for life and when
he bemoans the injustices of the world
it is the sound of souls in suffering.
Yes, it's that powerful. The voice of
Howlin' Wolf is the voice of the blues.

To hear the real Howlin' Wolf in
the raw, so to speak, you have to
search out his Sun, Chess and RPM
sides from the fifties and sixties, but
this all-star session from 1970 is
reasonably successful in capturing
his incomparable combination of

rural ruggedness and urban intensity in a sterile studio environment. Wolf revisits some of his best-known songs in the company of Eric Clapton, Steve Winwood, Bill Wyman and Charlie Watts, who are more than capable of recreating an authentic Chicago sound and there are a few snatches of between-takes chat that reveals the high regard the British bluesmen held for their hero.

Rating:
Sound ★★★★☆ Content ★★★★☆
Also recommended:
Although it entails a major investment, the 7CD box set 'The Complete Recordings' (Charly) will pay dividends for decades to come.
If you like this, why not try:
Sonny Boy Williamson, Elmore James, **John Lee Hooker**, Muddy Waters.

The Human League

'GREATEST HITS'

(Virgin) 1995

Track listing: Don't You Want Me • Love Action • Mirror Man • Tell Me When • Stay With Me Tonight • Open Your Heart • Fascination • Sound Of The Crowd • Being Boiled • Lebanon • Love Is All That Matters • Louise • Life On Your Own • Together In Electric Dreams • Human

Bonus track: Don't You Want Me (Remix)

During a decade dominated by machine manufactured dance music the Human League were initially seen as state-of-the-art sophisticates. Their self-confessed limitations as musicians were glossed over by Martin Rushent's clever

production techniques, but even he couldn't hide the fact that the emotional content of their music was as transparently synthetic as their instruments. After failing to fulfil the expectations set by their most consistent album, 'Dare', they settled for following fashion and were swiftly superceded by their more talented contempories, The Pet Shop Boys, Depeche Mode and Erasure. However, their early hits 'Don't You Want Me', 'Love Action' and 'Mirror Man' gleam with the sophisticated sheen and irresistible hooks of the best commercial pop music. And, most important of all, you can dance to them.
Rating:
Sound ★★★★☆ Content ★★★☆☆
Also recommended:
'Dare' (Virgin).
If you like this, why not try:
The Thompson Twins, Ultravox, Heaven 17.

Husker Dü

'CANDY APPLE GREY'

(Warner Bros) 1986

Track listing: Crystal • Don't Want To Know If You Are Lonely • I Don't Know For Sure • Sorry Somehow • Too Far Down • Hardly Getting Over It • Dead Set On Destruction • Eiffel Tower High • No Promise Have I Made • All This I've Done For You

While acts such as the Human League and Depeche Mode were using electronics to make lightweight, programmable pop Minneapolis trio Husker Dü harnessed technology to serve a hardcore psychpunk soundtrack. 'Candy Apple Grey' was their first major label release after years paying their dues as cult indie artists, but it's as uncompromising, intense and claustrophobic as any of their earlier albums. It's group therapy for bruised psyches presented as a sequence of perversely pleasurable tunes, none of which are artificially sweetened for mass consumption. These guys are bitter and slightly twisted by the tricks life has played on them and they won't let up until we've heard them out. The unrelenting tension is however, occasionally relieved by moments of intimacy and reflection as on the acoustic 'Hardly Getting Over It' and 'Too Far Down'.

Rating:
Sound ★★★★☆ Content ★★★☆☆
Also recommended:
'New Day Rising', 'Flip Your Wig' and 'Warehouse: Songs And Stories' (all on Warners).
If you like this, why not try:
Sugar, **Sonic Youth, The Jesus And Mary Chain**.

Ice-T

'O.G. ORIGINAL GANGSTER'

(Sire) 1991

Track listing: Home Of The Bodybag • First Impressions • Ziplock • Mic Contract • Mind Over Matter • New Jack Hustler • Ed • Bitches 2 • Straight Up Nigger • O.G. Original Gangster • The House • Evil E – What About Sex? • Fly By • Midnight Fried Chicken • MVP's • Lifestyles Of The Rich And Famous • Body Count • Prepared To Die • Escape From The Killing Fields • Street Killer • Pulse Of The Rhyme • The Tower • You Should Killed Me Last

Ice-T drew on his own criminal past to create an uncompromising West Coast gangsta brand that would rival the New York crews. But he fell foul of the Moral Majority with his deliberately provocative 'Cop Killer' and never really recovered his initial impetus.

'Original Gangster' is the musical equivalent of a Martin Scorsese movie – sour, cynical and unflinching in its depiction of the sordid underbelly of inner city life. But his conviction makes it also utterly compelling.

Rating:
Sound ★★★★☆ Content ★★★★☆
Also recommended:
'Return Of The Real' (Rhyme Syndicate/EMI).
If you like this, why not try:
Public Enemy, Cypress Hill.

Billy Idol

'IDOL SONGS'

(Chrysalis) 1988

Track listing: Rebel Yell • Hot In The City • White Wedding • Eyes Without A Face • Catch My Fall • Mony Mony • To Be A Lover • Sweet Sixteen • Flesh For Fantasy • Don't Need A Gun • Dancing With Myself

Idol followed fashion with variable success during the late seventies as a member of punk pretenders Generation X. But when he relocated to the USA his diluted, disco-friendly productions and Presleyesque pose proved a huge hit with the MTV generation, who had been too young to perforate their anatomy with safety pins when punk was fashionable the first time around.

'Rebel Yell', 'White Wedding' and 'Sweet Sixteen' bristle with the sneering defiance of shockabilly at its very best, although the rest pale into a plastic imitation of the real thing as Billy sells his rock and roll soul for synthetic sounds and the adulation of screaming teens.

Rating:
Sound ★★★★★ Content ★★★☆☆
Also recommended:
'Charmed Life' (Chrysalis).
If you like this, why not try:
Generation X, **Elvis Presley, Robert Gordon.**

Iggy And The Stooges

'RAW POWER'

(CBS) 1973

Track listing: Search And Destroy • Gimme Danger • Your Pretty Face Is Going To Hell (aka Hard To Beat) • Penetration • Raw Power • I Need Somebody • Shake Appeal • Death Trip

In the days before punk they called this visceral sound garage rock. But 'Raw Power' is far uglier, hungrier and meaner than that. This is the sound of Iggy's inner demons straining at the leash like a rabid dog as he struggles with the effects of serious chemical abuse. From the opening thrash of 'Search And Destroy' to the grating chords which brings 'Death Trip' to its knees, Iggy, the original wild child, howls at the moon while James Williamson

wrings the neck of his guitar until it screams for mercy. Intense? You won't know the meaning of the word until you've allowed this record to scramble your brain cells.

The album was originally mixed by Iggy and David Bowie, both of whom must have been dazed and confused at the time as they submerged Iggy's vocal beneath the grinding guitars until it was almost inaudible. Iggy always feared that if he remixed 'Raw Power' he might exorcize his 'angels' along with the 'devils', but it's as violent as before, with the meters stubbornly in the red, but more beef in the bottom end.

The booklet contains a lengthy interview with Iggy about the making and remixing of the album illustrated with previously unpublished photos.

Rating:
Sound ★★★☆☆ Content ★★★★★

Iggy Pop

'NUDE & RUDE – THE BEST OF'

(Virgin) 1996

Track listing: I Wanna Be Your Dog • No Fun • Search And Destroy • Gimme Danger • I'm Sick Of You • Funtime • Nightclubbing • China Girl • Lust For Life • The Passenger • Kill City • Real Wild Child • Cry For Love • Cold Metal • Candy • Home • Wild America

Iggy, the self-destructive protopunk and 'vainglorious junkie' was ahead of his time, at least 20 years too early judging by the number of recent films that have featured some of these songs on their soundtrack. The fact is that his songs of self-abuse, urban disintegration and mindless violence were too strong even for the safety pin heads of '77 to swallow whole.

This useful compilation draws on the paranoid psychotic rock of the Stooges era and the pick of the Bowie-produced albums. The trio of tracks drawn from 'The Idiot' – Iggy's description of life on a diet of downers, dark dreams and general excess – reveal that even when he was wired to an electronic life support machine, in an effort to wean him off his addiction to barbed wire guitars, he was still plagued by visions that would have put less balanced souls in a straitjacket. But then again, Iggy sounds as if he was simply too numb to register the pain. In contrast, those drawn from 'Lust For Life' see him high on a sensual overdose, riding through the city's 'ripped back side' after shooting up on a cocktail of cocaine and alcohol. Narcotic rock – chilling and exhilarating at the same time.

Rating:
Sound ★★★★☆ Content ★★★★★
Also recommended:
'Fun House' (Elektra), 'Kill City' (Bomp), 'The Idiot' (Virgin), 'Lust For Life' (Virgin), 'Studio Sessions' (Burning Airlines).
If you like this, why not try:
The Velvet Underground, David Bowie, MC5, Lou Reed.

INXS

'KICK'

(Mercury) 1987

Track listing: Guns In The Sky • New Sensation • Devil Inside • Need You Tonight • Mediate • The Loved One • Wild Life • Never Tear Us Apart • Mystify • Kick • Calling All Nations • Tiny Daggers

The sixth album by Australia's answer to Bon Jovi was a global multi-million seller and, for a time, an almost permanent fixture on the MTV playlist. It's a perfect example of the group's designer rock-by-numbers approach, entirely predictable but effective on its own terms. It spawned a trio of hits in the funky dancefloor favourites 'Devil Inside', 'New Sensation' and 'Need You Tonight' which reinforced the image of the late Michael Hutchence as yet another Jagger clone, albeit one without the belligerent dynamic and panache of the original.

Rating:
Sound ★★★★☆ Content ★★★☆☆
Also recommended:
'Greatest Hits' (Mercury).
If you like this, why not try:
Bon Jovi, Bryan Adams.

Iron Maiden

'THE NUMBER OF THE BEAST'

(EMI) 1982

Track listing: Invaders • Children Of The Damned • The Prisoner • 22 Acacia Avenue • The Number Of The Beast • Run To The Hills • Gangland • Hallowed Be Thy Name

Had it not been for Derek Riggs' grotesque album cover artwork Iron Maiden might not have been singled out for success, as their music was largely indistinguishable from the hordes of heavy metal revivalists who surfaced in the early eighties. But unlike their rivals Maiden had a knack of penning radio-friendly singles ('Run To The Hills' being a prime example) and didn't take themselves too seriously. Their sound may be as medieval as their name implies, but there are traces of punk in their impatience with plodding, Neanderthal riffs. Tracks change pace more frequently than Sabbath changed their singer, while for sheer naked aggression they bludgeon the opposition into submission. 'Beast' may be a half-baked offering of left-overs from grander feasts, but it is sufficiently satisfying to appease those who dine with the dark gods.

Rating:
Sound ★★★☆☆ Content ★★★☆☆
Also recommended:
The albums 'No Prayer For The Dying', 'Live After Death', 'Fear Of The Dark' and 'Best Of The Beast' (EMI). The latter is available as both a single and double CD set.
If you like this, why not try:
Metallica, Motorhead, Def Leppard.

Michael Jackson

'OFF THE WALL'

(Epic) 1979

Track listing: Don't Stop Til You Get Enough • Rock With You • Working Day And Night • Get Off The Floor • Off The Wall •

Girlfriend • She's Out Of My Life • I Can't Help It • It's The Falling In Love • Burn This Disco Down

Michael Jackson's miraculous transformation from Motown child star to global pop phenomenon can be credited to the musical makeover given to him by mentor and producer Quincy Jones. Jones supplied most of the material (including four multi-million selling singles) and the cutting edge contemporary pop/soul/dance/funk ambience that made disco passé overnight. His production tricks are as slick as Michael's carefully choreographed dance routines, but the songs are strong enough to retain their spark and the quality control is remarkably consistent (unlike 'Thriller'). But most important of all perhaps is the fact that it sounds like Jackson is having fun and that excitement is conveyed through the music. Although it has sold only 20 million copies in comparison to the 50 million racked up by 'Thriller', it's the better album and is vastly more enjoyable.

Rating:
Sound ★★★★★ Content ★★★★★

Michael Jackson

'THRILLER'

(Epic) 1982

Track listing: Wanna Be Startin' Somethin' • Baby Be Mine • The Girl Is Mine • Thriller • Beat It • Billie Jean • Human Nature • P.Y.T. (Pretty Young Thing) • The Lady In My Life

Although universally panned by the critics on its release, 'Thriller' spawned seven top ten US hit singles and went on to sell over 50 million copies. It was more than a record, it was a cultural phenomenon. And it proved how all-pervading pop had become. More significantly, the seamless mix of pop, soul, dance and funk was universally popular and helped to demolish the former cultural and racial market boundaries at a stroke. Having axe god Eddie Van Halen play the frantic guitar solo on 'Beat It' was a masterstroke, and was a significant factor in creating the new universal dance music market.

Rating:
Sound ★★★★★ Content ★★★★☆

Michael Jackson

'HISTORY PAST, PRESENT AND FUTURE VOL 1

2 CDs (MJJ/Sony) 1995

Track listing: Billie Jean • Way You Make Me Feel • Black Or White • Rock With You • She's Out Of My Life • Bad • I Just Can't Stop Loving You • Man In The Mirror • Thriller • Beat It • The Girl Is Mine • Remember The Time • Don't Stop Till You Get Enough • Wanna Be Starting Something • Heal The World • Scream • They Don't Care About Us • Stranger In Moscow • This Time Around • Earth Song • DS • Money • Come Together • You Are Not Alone • Childhood • Tabloid Junkie • 2 Bad • History • Little Susie • Smile

After his image was tarnished by a succession of allegations and scandals, Jacko attempted to regain lost ground with this double CD comprising a disc of greatest hits and another of new material. 'History' is

an ideal introduction for those who don't want to wade through the inconsistent follow ups to 'Thriller' and it also serves to highlight some of his less celebrated songs such as 'Stranger In Moscow' and the uncharacteristically cutting 'They Don't Care About Us'.

Rating:
Sound ★★★★★ Content ★★★★☆
Also recommended:
'Bad' (Epic) and 'The Best Of Michael Jackson And The Jackson Five'(Polygram).
If you like this, why not try:
The Jackson Five, Diana Ross, **Stevie Wonder**.

Janet Jackson

'DESIGN OF A DECADE'

(A&M) 1995

Track listing: What Have You Done For Me Lately • Best Things In Life Are Free • Nasty • Control • When I Think Of You • Pleasure Principle • Escapade • Black Cat • Miss You Much • Rhythm Nation • Whoops Now • That's The Way Love Goes • Love Will Never Do • Come Back To Me • Alright • Let's Wait Awhile • Runaway • Twenty Foreplay

The Jackson family franchise has something nearing a monopoly on sleek, chic soul as well as an unfortunate tendency to preach Walt Disney's 'one world' philosophy to listeners who should know a lot better than to believe in such tosh. Fortunately, there is a little less of the sermonizing on this outing than on 'Rhythm Nation' and a fair share of slinky funk and swingbeat for close contact dancing. But don't expect any surprises. With a multi-million dollar marketing budget and mega sales to play for no one was going to take risks with the 'product'.

Rating:
Sound ★★★★☆ Content ★★★☆☆
Also recommended:
'Janet' and 'Janet Remixed' (both on Virgin).
If you like this, why not try:
Whitney Houston, **Michael Jackson**, Destiny's Child.

The Jam

'SETTING SONS'

(Polydor) 1979

Track listing: Girl On The Phone • Thick As Thieves • Private Hell • Little Boy Soldiers • Wasteland • Burning Sky • Smithers-Jones • Saturday's Kids • Eton Rifles • Heat Wave

The Jam fashioned a sound as sharp as their suits with acerbic lyrics tailored to match. By the time they came to record 'Setting Sons' the initial influence of The Who, The Kinks and The Small Faces had waned and Weller's love-hate relationship with England was being expressed with equal passion but less fury. A seething resentment saturates 'Eton Rifles', 'Little Boy Soldiers', 'Private Hell' and 'Burning Sky', but there is also a certain nostalgia in 'Thick As Thieves' and 'Saturday's Kids' which reveals a new depth to Weller's writing.

Foxton gets his sixpence worth in

with 'Smithers-Jones' and if 'Girl On The Phone' and the pedestrian cover of 'Heatwave' aren't in the same class, it's forgivable under the circumstances. Who but Townsend or Ray Davies could top them?

Rating:
Sound ★★★★☆ Content ★★★★☆

The Jam

'SOUND AFFECTS'

(Polydor) 1980

Track listing: Pretty Green • Monday • But I'm Different Now • Set The House Ablaze • Start! • That's Entertainment • Dreamtime • Man In The Corner Shop • Music For The Last Couple • Boy About Town • Scrape Away

The Jam's strongest set to date finds Weller at the peak of his creative powers articulating the frustrations of a generation who felt that they had been shafted by the system in Thatcher's self-serving Britain.

'That's Entertainment' describes a dispiriting scene of inner-city decay in a way that suggests that Weller is resigned to the fact that Britain is destined to become a third-world country, crippled by class division, rising crime, high unemployment and wanton neglect. The characters in the more social songs fear that they had sold their ideals short and with them their ability to influence their own lives.

This theme of increasing alienation and disorientation is echoed in the music which forsakes the rigid structures and powerchords of the past for Beatlesque psych-pop, specifically

on 'Start!' and 'But I'm Different
Now', the former filching the riff from
'Taxman' and the latter nodding in the
direction of 'Dr Robert'.

The comparisons with 'Revolver'
are, for once, fully justified.

Rating:
Sound ★★★★☆ Content ★★★★☆
Also recommended:
'Snap' a comprehensive 2CD
retrospective, or for hardcore fans the
5CD box set ''Direction, Reaction,
Creation' (both on Polydor). Of the
original albums other essential items
include 'All Mod Cons', In The City'
and 'This Is The Modern World'.
If you like this, why not try:
Paul Weller's solo albums, **The Who**,
The Creation, Small Faces.

James

'GOLD MOTHER'

(Fontana) 1990

Track listing: Come Home • Lose Control •
Government Walls • God Only Knows • You
Can't Tell How Much Suffering • How Was It
For You • Sit Down • Walking The Ghost •
Gold Mother • Top Of The World

Manchester has produced a resourceful
and tenacious breed of young men, none
more so than Tim Booth and his mates
who funded their band on a £34-a-week
state-funded small business allowance.
Their loose-limbed indie dance hit 'Sit
Down', had been part of their set for
almost ten years before a deal with
Fontana offered the chance to re-record
it and put some promo muscle behind it.
Booth's impeccable English diction and
the band's sense of the bizarre make for

a thrilling experience and offered a good
return on the state's investment.

Rating:
Sound ★★★★☆ Content ★★★★☆
Also recommended:
'Strip Mine' and 'Stutter' (both on
Sire).
If you like this, why not try:
Inspiral Carpets, **Brian Eno**, **Happy
Mondays**.

James

'PLEASED TO MEET YOU'

(Mercury) 2001

Track listing: Space • Falling Down • English
Beefcake • Junkie • Pleased To Meet You •
The Shining • Senorita • Gaudi • What Is It
Good For • Give It Away • Fine • Getting
Away With It • Alaskan Pipeline

Twenty years on and James draw on
their collective strengths and
experience for an album that looks
back with a certain skewed nostalgia to
their quirky beginnings and to the
future with characteristic cynicism.
The songs are a summation of all that
the band have exemplified in the past –
frequently surreal, occasionally sinister
but always strikingly beautiful songs
that Bowie might have written had he
done a Dorian Gray and let his portrait
take the can for everything that came
after 'Scary Monsters'. 'Gaudi'
recreates the 80s obsession with
synths, 'Junkie' delivers an anti-
capitalist tirade and 'Space' betrays the
guiding hand of Brian Eno at the helm.

Though polished and frighteningly
self-assured, there is a spontaneity to
the tracks similar to that which made

'Laid' so invigorating, a spontaneity that belies the fact that they were all given the acid test of a live performance before being committed to tape. If you haven't made the acquaintance of James by now, 'Pleased To Meet You' will serve as the perfect introduction.

Rating:
Sound ★★★★☆ Content ★★★★☆
Also recommended:
'Gold Mother', 'Best Of' (both on Fontana).
If you like this, why not try:
The Divine Comedy, Ocean Colour Scene, **Manic Street Preachers**.

Jamiroquai

'EMERGENCY ON PLANET EARTH'

(Sony) 1993

Track listing: When You Gonna Learn • Too Young To Die • Hooked Up • If I Like It,I Do It • Music Of The Mind • Emergency On Planet Earth • Whatever It Is,I Just Can't Stop • Blow Your Mind • Revolution 1993 • Didgin' Out

The 'Mad-hatter' of acid jazz, Jason Kay, attempted to cast off the inevitable comparisons with Stevie Wonder by losing himself in extended improvisational jams and dragging on a didgeridoo, but the analogy remains. The music may be derivative, but it doesn't spoil the enjoyment of this seriously funky debut which is as smart-mouthed and eminently entertaining as the man himself. Good vibes guaranteed.

Rating:
Sound ★★★★☆ Content ★★★★☆
Also recommended:
'Return Of The Space Cowboy' and 'Travelling Without Moving' (both on Sony).
If you like this, why not try:
Stevie Wonder, **Sly Stone**, Gil Scott-Heron.

Japan

'TIN DRUM'

(Virgin) 1988

Track listing: Visions Of China • Art Of Parties • Talking Drum • Cantonese Boy • Canton • Ghosts • Still Life In Mobile Homes • Sons Of Pioneers

Although often painfully pretentious and burdened with a singer who sounded uncomfortably close to Bryan Ferry, Japan were capable of moments of exquisite beauty. Such a moment was 'Ghosts' where the Erik Satie-styled minimalist approach attains the sublime simplicity of a Japanese hai-ku or rice paper watercolour. It's only when the group's artistic aspirations become subservient to their image that their music becomes distinctly mannered and is revealed to be a mere shadowplay, studied and at worst, a sham.

Rating:
Sound ★★★★☆ Content ★★★☆☆
Also recommended:
'Oil On Canvas', 'Gentlemen Take Polaroids' and 'Exorcizing Ghosts' (all on Virgin).
If you like this, why not try:
Dali's Car, **David Bowie**, **Brian Eno**.

Janis Joplin

'THE ULTIMATE COLLECTION'

2 CDs (Columbia) 1998

Track listing: CD 1 – Me And Bobby McGee • Move Over • Kozmic Blues • Piece Of My Heart • Down On Me • Try Just A Little Bit Harder • My Baby • Ball And Chain • I'll Drown In My Own Tears • Maybe • To Love Somebody • A Woman Left Lonely • Raise Your Hand • Magic Of Love • Bye Bye Baby • Buried Alive In The Blues

CD 2 – Cry Baby • Get It While You Can • Mercedes Benz • Little Girl Blue • Work Me Lord • Summertime • Half Moon • Silver Threads And Golden Needles • San Francisco Bay Blues • Trust Me • Misery 'N' • One Good Man • Tell Mama • Medley: Amazing Grace, Hi Heel Sneakers • One Night Stand • Farewell Song

Janis didn't just sing the blues, she lived them. Even in her more unguarded moments you can tell that she hasn't finished paying her dues. Her vulnerability, sincerity and emotional range recalls the great Bessie Smith in her prime as she wraps her husky voice around songs of lost love and loneliness. The smouldering intensity of her performance on 'Ball And Chain', 'Piece Of My Heart' and 'Cry Baby' in particular, proves that she poured every ounce of her being into her performance in the belief that only by baring her soul would she invest the song with the necessary degree of integrity. On 'Try Just A Little Bit Harder' one can imagine her gripping the microphone as she would the neck of a bottle of bourbon and belting out the blues with sufficient strength to floor any of the middle-weight rock

singers of the era. But 'To Love Somebody' and 'A Woman Left Lonely' reveal that she was equally adept at the intimate barfly confession where her sincerity demands that you hear her out. Thirty years on these recordings still pack a wallop.

Rating:
Sound ★★★☆☆ Content ★★★★☆
Also recommended:
'18 Essential Songs' and the 3CD box set 'Janis' (both on Columbia).
If you like this, why not try:
Bessie Smith, Maggie Bell, Stone The Crows.

Jethro Tull

'BENEFIT'

(Chrysalis) 1970

Track listing: With You There To Help Me • Nothing To Say • Inside • Son • For Michael Collins, Jeffrey And Me • To Cry You A Song • A Time For Everything • Teacher • Play In Time • Sossity, You're A Woman

In 1970 it was perfectly acceptable for a young man of the prog-rock persuasion to grow a bird's nest of a beard, perch himself precariously on one leg and trill on a flute. But curiously, only one man was brave enough to do so. Ian Anderson of Jethro Tull not only attempted such a feat in full view of the paying public and sceptical critics, he even made a damn good living at it.

'Benefit' is one of the great under-rated albums of the era, bursting with good ideas, whistle-worthy tunes and clever wordplay all wrapped in an agreeable mix of rustic folk, hard-bitten blues and flute filigree. It was presumably deprived of its 'classic' stamp posthumously, in the light of the band's subsequent terminally unfashionable status. And for that punk has a lot to answer for.

Rating:
Sound ★★★★☆ Content ★★★★★

Jethro Tull

'AQUALUNG'

(Chrysalis) 1971

Track listing: Aqualung • Cross-Eyed Mary • Cheap Day Return • Mother Goose • Wond'ring Aloud • Up To Me • My God • Hymn 43 • Slipstream • Locomotive Breath • Wind Up

Bonus Tracks: Lick Your Fingers Clean • Wind-Up • Ian Anderson Interview • Songs For Jeffrey • Fat Man • Bouree

In the mid-seventies, during the wholesale slaughter of rock's 'dinosaurs', Tull provided an easy target. Everything they stood for was passé – extended solos, complex time signatures, jazz-styled improvisations, long hair, beards and of course, that ubiquitous flute. The quality of their music was conveniently overlooked and they were airbrushed out of history.

'Aqualung' is an accomplished, intelligent, skillfully structured and eloquent collection of tunes as you're ever likely to hear. Its theme is hypocrisy and the fate of social outcasts as embodied in the bronchial tramp who gives the album its title. This 25th anniversary edition boasts several extra tracks and an extract from an interview with Anderson on the making of the album. But it doesn't offer a significant improvement in sound quality over the original CD issue. After all, the album wasn't an audiophile's audition piece in the first place. Its rustic charm, however, remains intact.

Rating:
Sound ★★★★☆ Content ★★★★★

Jethro Tull

'ORIGINAL MASTERS'

(Chrysalis) 1985

Track listing: Living In The Past • Aqualung • Too Old To Rock 'n' Roll • Locomotive Breath • Skating Away On The Thin Ice Of A New Day • Bungle In The Jungle • Sweet Dream • Songs From The Wood • Witches Promise • Thick As A Brick • Minstrel In The Gallery • Life's A Long Song

Tull subscribed to that curious sixties custom which discouraged artists from including singles on their albums. So, the only way you're going to acquire such essential one-legged pogo dancing items as 'Witches Promise', 'Sweet Dreams', 'Living In The Past' and 'Life's A Long Song' is to put this on your Christmas list and be very, very polite to little old ladies until Santa comes a-calling.

If you've ever wondered why such a shamelessly retro folk-rock group could claim to play 'progressive rock', this will answer the big question and let you sleep at night with a clear conscience.

Rating:
Sound ★★★★☆ Content ★★★★★

Also recommended:
For a good introduction try the double
disc retrospective 'Best Of' or single
CD 'The Very Best Of'. Completists
should track down the '25th
Anniversary' and the '20th
Anniversary' box sets, plus the
original albums 'Minstrel In The
Gallery' and 'Stand Up'. If you're
really hooked you could try the
Grammy Award-winning 'Crest Of A
Knave' if you don't mind hearing Ian
Anderson sounding uncannily like
Mark Knopfler of Dire Straits! (all on
Chrysalis.)
If you like this, why not try:
Steeleye Span, **Free**, **Rory Gallagher**.

Bon Jovi

'SLIPPERY WHEN WET'

(Vertigo) 1990

*Track listing: Let It Rock • You Give Love A
Bad Name • Livin' On A Prayer • Social
Disease • Wanted Dead Or Alive • Raise
Your Hands • Without Love • I'd Die For You
• Never Say Goodbye • Wild In The Streets*

To paraphrase the second track on this
mega-seller, Bon Jovi gave metal a
bad name. And they did it by
emasculating the music until it seemed
to consist of little more than contrived,
overwrought ballads dressed up in
tight leather trousers and impossible
hairdos that made Prince look butch.
They've been credited with bringing
melody to metal, but it had plenty
before they muscled in, thank you.
What they did was to gut it, leaving it
dead from the waist up. It looks the
part, but it's dumb and derivative
serving up a catalogue of metal cliches

for those too young to know better.
Their hairdressers must be laughing all
the way to the bank.

Seventeen million record buyers
can't be wrong? Don't bet on it.

Rating:
Sound ★★★★☆ Content ★★★☆☆
Also recommended:
'These Days' a 2CD Tour Pack
souvenir set (Jambco).
If you like this, why not try:
**Aerosmith, Bryan Adams, Def
Leppard**.

The Jesus And Mary Chain

'PSYCHOCANDY'

(Blanco Y Negro) 1986

*Track listing: Just Like Honey • Living End •
Taste The Floor • Hardest Walk • Cut Dead
• In A Hole • Taste Of Cindy • Never
Understand • It's So Hard • Inside Me •
Sowing Seeds • My Little Underground • You
Trip Me Up • Something's Wrong*

'They were either the best or the
worst band I'd ever seen' declared
Creation Records supremo Alan
McGee on hearing one of the Reid
brothers' legendary 15-minute sets of
feedback-saturated songs. One critic
described their music as a 'great
searing citadel of beauty' whose wall
of noise had to be scaled if the
listener was to enjoy the 'endless
vistas of melody and emotion' on the
other side. But those who were less
enthralled heard The Velvet
Underground grappling with The
Ramones in a swirling dust cloud of
fuzz guitar, clinically detached vocals

and ragged, echoing percussion which appeared to have been recorded from the other side of the studio wall. Not only are the band on a bum trip, the engineer appears to be too. But beneath the deliberately inverted mix, the cynically contrived publicity stunts and the heavy-handed hype, lurk classic pop values and traditional tunes cleverly contrasted in what appears to be a chaotic free-for-all.

Rating:
Sound ★★★☆☆ Content ★★★★☆

The Jesus And Mary Chain

'DARKLANDS'

(Blanco Y Negro) 1987

Track listing: Darklands • Deep One Perfect Morning • Happy When It Rains • Down On Me • Nine Million Rainy Days • April Skies • Fall • Cherry Came Too • On The Wall • About You

By '87 the group had mutated from a cult indie act into that rarest of creations (sic), a hit-making machine with street cred. Both 'April Skies' and 'Happy When It Rains' were on heavy rotation on poptastic daytime radio which helped give the album a leg up into the top five. Percussionist/vocalist Bobby Gillespie had by this time returned to his day job with Primal Scream and had been replaced by guitarist John Moore who invested the tracks with a sombre, moody ambience that nagged at the nerves more mercilessly than the howling feedback had done.

Rating:
Sound ★★★☆☆ Content ★★★☆☆
Also recommended:
'Barbed Wire Kisses' (Blanco Y Negro)
If you like this, why not try:
The Velvet Underground, Husker Dü, Sonic Youth.

Joan Jett

'BAD REPUTATION'

(Epic) 1981

Track listing: Bad Reputation • Make Believe • You Don't Know What You've Got • You Don't Own Me • Too Bad On Your Birthday • Do You Wanna Touch Me • Shout • Let Me Go • Doin' All Right With The Boys • Jezebel • Don't Abuse Me • Wooly Bully

Had this been recorded in the early seventies the title track would have been preceded by the sound of revving motorbike engines and the choruses punctuated by yells of 'Heh!' from a muscular male chorus. However, by the eighties both rock and Joan Jett (a fugitive from the all-girl glam band The Runaways) had grown up and those kitsch cliches were out with the likes of Gary Glitter and The Village People. Anyway, Jett didn't need to labour the point, her records were redolent with the smell of engine oil and leather. 'Bad Reputation' sounds like the kind of album girls play when they're tattooing their Barbie dolls. It's bad-girl boogie with a sticky bubblegum base, in the same mould as those heavily compressed glam rock singles of the early Seventies, but with the contemptuous attitude of punk. Jett plays tough and tender on brassy remakes of the Gary Glitter classics 'Do You Wanna Touch' and 'Doing Alright With The Bones' and selected Sixties girl group and garage anthems. The perfect antidote to the girl-power puppets.

Rating:
Sound ★★★★☆ Content ★★★★☆
Also recommended:
'I Love Rock And Roll' and 'Up Your Alley' (both on Epic).
If you like this, why not try:
The Runaways, **Girlschool**, Lita Ford.

Elton John

'DON'T SHOOT ME, I'M ONLY THE PIANO PLAYER'

(Rocket/Polygram) 1972

Track listing: Daniel • Teacher I Need You • Elderberry Wine • Blues For My Baby And Me • Midnight Creeper • Have Mercy On The Criminal • I'm Gonna Be A Teenage Idol • Texan Love Song • Crocodile Rock • High Flying Bird

Bonus tracks: Screw You • Jack Rabbit • Whenever You're Ready • Skyline Pigeon

Elton's showmanship and outrageous lack of taste in clothes gave the impression that he didn't take himself too seriously. Consequently, the critics didn't take him very seriously either, despite the fact that he racked up a staggering six consecutive number one albums and a further 18 top 40 albums over the course of three decades.

His early albums were in the earnest singer-songwriter mould, whereas 'Don't Shoot Me' celebrated pop and popular culture with a misty-eyed nostalgia that gave the songs an almost mythic quality.

'Daniel' was one of the few downbeat tunes, voicing a young brother's unspoken admiration for his elder brother who had been blinded in Vietnam. Elton and lyric partner Bernie Taupin were particularly adept at turning on the waterworks in the corny Tin Pan Alley tradition, but during this period they were just the right side of mawkish sentimentality. More typical of the album are the upbeat 'Elderberry Wine', 'Teenage Idol' (a song for Elton's friend Marc Bolan) and the fifties rock pastiche 'Crocodile Rock' complete with 'Speedy Gonzales' style falsetto.

All of EJ's albums have been remastered and boast extra tracks, the four on offer here being among his strongest B-sides.

Rating:
Sound ★★★★☆ Content ★★★★☆

Elton John

'GOODBYE YELLOW BRICK ROAD'

(Rocket/Polygram) 1973

Track listing: Funeral For A Friend – Love Lies Bleeding • Candle In The Wind • Bennie And The Jets • Goodbye Yellow Brick Road • This Song Has No Title • Grey Seal • Jamaican Jerk-Off • I've Seen That Movie Too • Sweet Painted Lady • The Ballad Of Danny Bailey • Dirty Little Girl • All The Girls Love Alice • Your Sister Can't Twist • Saturday Night's Alright For Fighting • Roy Rogers • Social Disease • Harmony

Elton evidently had melodies to spare when it came to recording the follow up to 'Don't Shoot Me', a set which originally filled four sides of a double LP and which has now been squeezed onto a single CD. Few were obvious fillers ('Jamaican Jerk-Off' and 'Your Sister Can't Twist' being the obvious exceptions), while there was more than a fair share of certified classics including the perennially popular 'Candle In The Wind', the gorgeous 'Grey Seal', the raunch 'n' rock of 'Saturday Night's Alright', 'Dirty Little Girl' and 'All The Young Girls Love Alice', a choice selection of wistful ballads plus the tastefully understated title track.

Elton's music has shown irrefutable evidence of middle-aged spread in recent years, but this veritable feast for the ears justifies his place in pop history.

Rating:
Sound ★★★★☆ Content ★★★★★

Elton John

'CAPTAIN FANTASTIC AND THE BROWN DIRT COWBOY'

(Rocket/Polygram) 1975

Track listing: *Captain Fantastic And The Brown Dirt Cowboy • Tower Of Babel • Bitter Fingers • Tell Me When The Whistle Blows • Someone Saved My Life Tonight • Meal Ticket • Better Off Dead • Writing • We All Fall In Love Sometimes • Curtains*

Bonus tracks: *Lucy In The Sky With Diamonds • One Day At A Time • Philadelphia Freedom*

By the mid-seventies, balding, bespectacled Reg Dwight of Pinner,

Middlesex had become one of the biggest stars on the planet and the unreality of his own life had made him more interesting to his fans than those of the characters in his songs. In the autobiographical 'Captain Fantastic', Elton and partner Bernie Taupin became the subject of their own songs; cartoon strip characters whose early struggles and disappointments were romanticized in almost mythic terms. Fortunately, 'Bitter Fingers', 'Better Off Dead' and the genuinely moving 'Someone Saved My Life Tonight' were strong enough to sustain the Tin Pan Alley plot. Honesty and insight triumphing over self-indulgence.

Rating:
Sound ★★★★☆ Content ★★★★☆
Also recommended:
'Tumbleweed Connection', 'Honky Chateau', 'Greatest Hits Vol 1 & Vol 2' or 'The Very Best Of' (all on DJM).
If you like this, why not try:
David Gray, Billy Joel, The Band.

Joy Division

'UNKNOWN PLEASURES'

(Factory) 1980

Track listing: *Disorder • Day Of The Lords • Candidate • Insight • New Dawn Fades • She's Lost Control • Shadowplay • Wilderness • Interzone • I Remember Nothing*

Joy Division's austere soundscapes made the nihilistic philosophy of the punks seem almost comforting by comparison. At least there were human beings behind those grinding guitars and they were angry, no doubt about that. But Joy Division's metal machine music is driven by an unrelenting pneumatic percussion and augmented by a wall of industrial noise which is nothing short of numbing. The funereal voice of the ill-fated Ian Curtis struggles to articulate what the mystics called 'the dark night of the soul', made more hellish by drug-induced depression, a compulsive need for self-destruction and the nagging accusations of personal demons whispering from the wings.

'Unknown Pleasures' is a deeply disturbing record, even if one wasn't aware of the tragic circumstances of Curtis' death, but it is one which is also utterly addictive.

Rating:
Sound ★★★★☆ Content ★★★★★

Joy Division

'CLOSER'

(Factory) 1980

Track listing: Heart And Soul • 24 Hours • The Eternal • Decades • Atrocity • Exhibition • Isolation • Passover • Colony • Means To An End

'Closer' was completed shortly before Curtis committed suicide and is pervaded by a sense of eerie beauty, like the still before the storm. If it wasn't for the piano fills in 'The Eternal', occasional flashes of overdriven guitar and the momentum secured by Hook's melodic bass lines, the tracks would be in danger of grinding to a complete standstill, enthralled by their own spectral

grandeur. There is a chilling detachment in Curtis' vocals which seems to haunt the stark, minimalist backdrop like a troubled earth-bound spirit, pleading for release. There is nothing of its like in rock.

Rating:
Sound ★★★★☆ Content ★★★★★
Also recommended:
'Heart And Soul' a 4CD retrospective.
If you like this, why not try:
New Order or the Various Artists tribute album 'Means To An End' (Hut).

King Crimson

'IN THE COURT OF THE CRIMSON KING'

(EG/Virgin) 1969

Track listing: 21st Century Schizoid Man • I Talk To The Wind • Epitaph (including March For No Reason & Tomorrow And Tomorrow) • Moonchild (including The Dream & The Illusion) • The Court Of The Crimson King (including Return Of The Fire Witch & The Dance Of The Puppets)

With conspicuous instrumental expertise, a preference for symphonic dynamics and lyrics which tottered between the poetic and pretentious, King Crimson were expected to fulfil progressive rock's untapped potential. But shortly after the release of this impressive debut Greg Lake left to form 'supergroup' ELP and Crimson turned inward to experiment with jazz-rock fusion. 'In The Court Of The Crimson King' however remains to suggest the infinite possibilities that might have been.

It opens in melodramatic style with '21st Century Schizoid Man', a manic hymn to a world descending into madness whose paranoia is expressed through a distorted vocal pursued by rasping saxophones. In the calm that follows a flute introduces the melancholic beauty of 'I Talk To The Wind' which continues the theme of fateful resignation but in a pastoral setting. 'Epitaph' leads us further into a dark fairy-tale world of decaying mock-Gothic grandeur before the wistful 'Moonchild' loses itself in a protracted and formless instrumental passage pretentiously entitled 'The Dream'. Ah well, it was the sixties. But then comes the majestic closing track, 'The Court Of The Crimson King' with its soaring ethereal strings, grotesque minuet for marionettes and lyrical allusions to jugglers, jesters, witches and a whole gallery of grotesques that inhabit this crumbling kingdom.

In retrospect the album may appear to be a pretentious folly on the musical landscape, but in spite of all its faults it's an imposing and impressive edifice, a fitting monument to the promise that was progressive rock.

Rating:
Sound ★★★★☆ Content ★★★★★
Also recommended:
'Starless And Bible Black' and the 4CD set 'Frame By Frame' (both on Virgin).
If you like this, why not try:
Emerson, Lake And Palmer, **Yes**.

The Kinks

'THE DEFINITIVE COLLECTION'

(Polygram) 1997

Track listing: You Really Got Me • All Day And All Of The Night • Stop Your Sobbing • Tired Of Waiting For You • Everybody's Gonna Be Happy • Set Me Free • See My Friends • Till The End Of The Day • Where Have All The Good Times Gone • Well Respected Man • Dedicated Follower Of Fashion • Sunny Afternoon • Dead End Street • Waterloo Sunset • Death Of A Clown • Autumn Almanac • Suzannah's Still Alive • David Watts • Wonder Boy • Days • Plastic Man • Victoria • Lola • Apeman • Come Dancing • Don't Forget To Dance

Ray Davies' astute observations of his fellow Englishmen's eccentricities, and specifically his portraits of mundane middle-class suburbia, ensured that The Kinks became the quintessential English group of the sixties. Although their albums were often erratic, their choice of singles was impeccable. This compilation scores by simply collecting their singles, from the impeccably tailored sketches of the mods' mores and manners to the garishly coloured snapshots of Carnaby Street culture. Ray's ambivalence towards his countrymen embellishes tracks such as 'Waterloo Sunset' and 'Where Have All The Good Times Gone' with a hint of bitter-sweet nostalgia.

Twenty-six tracks of sixties pop at its most articulate and collectively a perfect snapshot of the period.

Rating:
Sound ★★★☆☆ Content ★★★★★

Also recommended:
'The EP Collection' (See For Miles) and 'Fab Forty – The Singles Collection', a double CD set (Decal/Koch).
If you like this, why not try:
The Jam, The Pretenders, Blur, Pulp.

Kraftwerk

'THE MAN MACHINE'

(Capitol) 1978

Track listing: Robots • Spacelab • Metropolis • The Model • Neon Lights • The Man Machine

If it had not been for these German electro-pop pioneers, bands such as the Human League, Ultravox, Depeche Mode and the entire Eurodisco fad would probably never have come into being. For that they have a lot to answer for, but Kraftwerk's own work is immeasurably more listenable to than that of their imitators because they created an entirely artificial ambience with their machinery, rather than attempting to program it with a synthetic soul. The Germans were limited by the synthesizer technology of the time, but they employed their rigid, robotic minimalism and a monotonous vocal to suggest a sinister side to man's fascination with machines, and of more importance, our apparent willingness to designate responsibility to computers. But it was their bleak ambient soundscapes rather than their subject-matter which encouraged David Bowie, Brian Eno and Joy Division to use electronics to express the emotional nihilism of our times.

Rating:
Sound ★★★☆☆ Content ★★★☆☆
Also recommended:
'Autobahn', 'Trans Europe Express' and 'Showroom Dummies'.
If you like this, why not try:
Joy Division, New Order, Ultravox, Human League, and the Brian Eno/David Bowie albums 'Low' and 'Heroes'.

Lenny Kravitz

'LET LOVE RULE'

(Label) 1989

Track listing: Sittin' On Top Of The World • Let Love Rule • Freedom Train • My Precious Love • I Build This Garden For Us • Fear • Does Anybody Out There Even Care • Mr Cabdriver • Rosemary • Be • Blues For Sister Someone • Empty Hands • Flower Child

Quite why Kravitz, a child of the seventies, became infatuated with the music of the previous decade is hard to understand, but he invoked the spirit of the late sixties to perfection, had the Hendrix riffs down note for note and looked every inch the part of the born-again flower child in feather boa and flares. He may be unashamedly retro, inviting comparison with John Lennon, Curtis Mayfield and Sly Stone as well as Hendrix, but he's got funky licks that make Prince sound like the kid that's auditioning a new guitar in the back of the shop, while his insistence on recording using analogue equipment ensures that his albums have a warmth and depth that digital processing just can't recreate.

Rating:
Sound ★★★★☆ Content ★★★★☆
Also recommended:
'Circus', 'Mama Said' and 'Greatest Hits' (all on Virgin).
If you like this, why not try:
Jimi Hendrix, **Prince**, **Sly And The Family Stone**.

kd lang

'INGENUE'

(Sire) 1992

Track listing: Save Me • The Mind Of Love • Miss Chatelaine • Wash Me Clean • So It Shall Be • So Thrives This Love • Season Of Hollow Soul • Outside Myself • Tears Of Loves Recall • Constant Craving

After being blacklisted by country music radio in the States for taking part in an animal rights TV advert, lang abandoned country for articulate, adult-orientated rock and an image described as 'lesbian chic'. For 'Igenue' she retained the services of long-time collaborator and producer Ben Mink whose pop sensibilities sugared her often embittered reflections about love, but she didn't lose her affection for the music of Patsy Cline, nor her taste for sobering love songs with a bitter-sweet aftertaste, as exemplified by the single 'Constant Craving'.

Madonna paid lang the greatest compliment when she said, 'Elvis is alive – and she's beautiful'. She sounds pretty good too.

Rating:
Sound ★★★★★ Content ★★★★☆
Also recommended:
'All You Can Eat' (Sire).

If you like this, why not try:
Patsy Cline, **Patty Griffin**, **Suzanne Vega**.

Led Zeppelin

'I'

(Atlantic) 1969

Track listing: Good Times Bad Times • Babe I'm Gonna Leave You • You Shook Me • Dazed And Confused • Your Time Is Gonna Come • Black Mountain Side • Communication Breakdown • I Can't Quit You Baby • How Many More Times

Zeppelin's first offering was recorded live in the studio after a gruelling American tour during which they honed these songs to the nth degree, the experience investing the performances with an authority and emotional charge which few rock groups have been able to match.

'Good Times, Bad Times' opens their account with an insistent riff and a typical frenetic solo from Jimmy Page. In contrast, 'Babe, I'm Gonna Leave You' begins deceptively in olde English folk mode with a pleading vocal from Robert Plant before being pulverized by powerchords that gives the traditional melody a good hammering. Other highlights include 'Communication Breakdown', which jerks like a mad dog snagged on a short lead; a reworking of Howling Wolf's walking blues 'How Many More Years', which is frog marched to the fade under the new title 'How Many More Times' and two slow, smouldering blues, 'You Shook Me' and 'I Can't Quit You Baby'. The first is distinguished by a fine organ solo and the second features a guitar-vocal duel of the kind that was to become a staple feature of their stage act. But the tour de force is without doubt 'Dazed And Confused'. It opens with an insidious, stalking bass line doubled by an unearthly piercing guitar and is soon joined by a tortured vocal and lashings of feedback, not to mention a violin bow shredded across the steel strings. Awesome.

Rating:
Sound ★★★★☆ Content ★★★★★

Led Zeppelin

'II'

(Atlantic) 1971

Track listing: Whole Lotta Love • What Is And What Should Never Be • The Lemon Song • Thank You • Heartbreaker • Living Loving Maid • Ramble On • Moby Dick • Bring It On Home

The second (untitled) Zeppelin album is generally regarded as their finest hour, if only because it features the best-known riff in the repertoire, a sledgehammer staccato guitar figure that sums up everything you need to know about heavy rock. 'Whole Lotta Love' is typical of the more muscular music on offer, in contrast to the leaner, meaner beast unleashed on their first record. While that first session produced what was essentially a heavy blues set, this second instalment demonstrates their diversity and fast maturing songwriting skills from Tolkien-themed folk-rock and locomotive blues to hot-bloodied boogie that made the earth move for a generation of air guitar stars.

A monolithic milestone in the history of rock.

Rating:
Sound ★★★★☆ Content ★★★★★

Led Zeppelin

'PHYSICAL GRAFFITI'

2 CDs (Atlantic) 1975

Track listing: CD 1 – Custard Pie • The Rover • In My Time Of Dying • Houses Of The Holy • Trampled Under Foot • Kashmir

CD 2 – In The Light • Bron-Yr-Aur • Down By The Seaside • Ten Years Gone • Night Flight • The Wanton Song • Boogie With Stu • Black Country Woman • Sick Again

After the uncharacteristically subdued third album and the uneven fourth (how often have you actually played the four songs after 'Stairway To Heaven'?), Zeppelin made their grandest statement so far with this impressive double. Having found themselves with a surfeit of songs and a few choice items in the cupboard left over from earlier albums, they decided to go for the big one. The whole of the first disc is classic Zep. The inexorable grinding riff and swirling Arabic strings on 'Kashmir', the radical revision of Leadbelly's emotive bottleneck blues 'In My Time of Dying', that would get any sinner into heaven and the swaggering funk that drives 'Trampled Underfoot' are among the very best that the band had to offer.

Some of the out-takes such as 'Down By The Seaside', 'Black Country Woman' and 'Boogie With Stu' suggest that they had been suffering from an identity crisis which encouraged them to dabble with disparate styles in an effort to shrug off their 'monsters of metal' tag. But other previously unreleased items, namely 'Night Flight' and 'The Rover', revealed that what they had considered to be substandard would have been a highpoint of anyone else's album.

'Physical Graffiti' offers irrefutable proof that Zeppelin's music was built on much more than the brute force, full-throated vocals and interminable guitar solos of their less talented contemporaries.

Rating:
Sound ★★★★☆ Content ★★★★★

Led Zeppelin

'REMASTERS'

2 CDs (Atlantic) 1990

Track listing: CD 1 – Communication Breakdown • Babe I'm Gonna Leave You • Good Times Bad Times • Dazed And Confused • Whole Lotta Love • Heartbreaker • Ramble On • Immigrant Song • Celebration Day • Since I've Been Loving You • Black Dog • Rock And Roll • The Battle Of Evermore • Misty Mountain Hop • Stairway To Heaven

CD 2 – The Song Remains The Same • The Rain Song • D'Yer Mak'er • No Quarter • Houses Of The Holy • Kashmir • Trampled Under Foot • Nobody's Fault But Mine • Achilles Last Stand • All My Love • In The Evening

On the sixth day The Lord created Led Zeppelin. And on the seventh he wrote 'Stairway To Heaven'.

Zep alternated the raw, virile intensity of the blues with the fanciful romanticism of folk to create an uncommonly diverse repertoire

with fanciful acoustic folk on the one hand, steamhammer riffing on the other and intense, smouldering blues somewhere in between.

'Remasters' gathers all the gems and none of the fillers from their eight studio albums affording the opportunity to have such essential tracks as 'The Immigrant Song', 'Since I've Been Loving You', 'No Quarter', 'Achilles Last Stand' and 'In The Evening' without having to buy the comparatively substandard albums from which they were taken. It also eliminates the distortion that marred 'Stairway To Heaven' on the original CD issue and wipes the grime from the remainder to give them considerably more clarity, impact and bite. Here endeth the first lesson.

Rating:
Sound ★★★★☆ Content ★★★★★

Led Zeppelin

'BOXED SET 2'

2 CDs (Atlantic) 1993

Track listing: CD 1 – Good Times Bad Times • We're Gonna Groove • Night Flight • That's The Way • Baby Come On Home • The Lemon Song • You Shook Me • Boogie With Stu • Bron-Yr-Aur • Down By The Seaside • Out On The Tiles • Black Mountain Side • Moby Dick • Sick Again • Hot Dog • Carouselambra

CD 2 – South Bound Saurez • Walter's Walk • Darlene • Black Country Woman • How Many More Times • The Rover • Four Sticks • Hats Off To (Roy) Harper • I Can't Quit You Baby • Hots On For Nowhere • Living Loving Maid • Royal Orleans • Bonzo's Montreux • The Crunge • Bring It On Home • Tea For Home

The final essential item in the Zeppelin catalogue is this attractively packaged 2CD set which comes complete with a 54-page full-colour booklet featuring rare photos and extensive liner notes.

Unlike the 'Remasters' compilation these tracks are not in chronological order, which makes it a rather disorientating experience for those who own the original albums, while the tight editing between tracks emphasizes the impression that we're on a rushed tour of the Zep repertoire. But as with the earlier collection, remastering has opened up the soundstage giving an improved sense of space plus greater depth and detail than on the earlier CD issues.

Again, it gives the opportunity to acquire some of the more interesting items from the patchy later albums plus a couple of tracks from the barrel-scraping out-takes collection, 'Coda'. But the chief item of interest is the previously unreleased 'Baby Come On Home', an emotive Memphis soul cover from the '69 sessions which incredibly didn't make the shortlist for their first album.

'Boxed Set 2' should be seen as compiling the rest of the best, rather than the best of the rest.

Rating:
Sound ★★★★★ Content ★★★★★
Also recommended:
Their third and fourth numerically titled albums plus their fifth 'Houses Of The Holy', 'BBC Sessions' and the erratic soundtrack to 'The Song Remains The Same' which was recorded live at the peak of their popularity (all on Atlantic).

If you like this, why not try:
Kingdom Come, Robert Plant's solo albums, **Bad Company**, **Deep Purple**, **Black Sabbath**, **Howlin' Wolf.**

John Lennon

'JOHN LENNON/PLASTIC ONO BAND'

(Parlophone) 1970

Track listing: Mother • Hold On • I Found Out • Working Class Hero • Isolation • Remember • Love • Well Well Well • Look At Me • God • My Mummy's Dead

Bonus tracks: Power To The People • Do The Oz

McCartney had the greater gift for melody, but he settled for schmaltz while Lennon went on to make the more engaging, enduring and personal solo albums. John's first solo offering is an often painful soul-baring musical therapy session beginning with the primal scream of 'Mother' and progressing through bitter self-loathing in 'Working Class Hero', before culminating in the liberating self-awareness of 'God'. 'I don't believe in Beatles. I just believe in Yoko and me and that's reality'. Amen.

For once, producer Phil Spector resists the temptation to swamp the songs in saccharine-sweet strings and ethereal choirs, opting instead for a sparse, intimate sound which kept

John's emotionally draining confessional sharply in focus.

This 'millennial edition' of the album was remixed under the personal supervision of Yoko Ono. In addition to infinitely superior sound, it offers two additional tracks and is packaged in a 12-page booklet with new photographs and copies of the original handwritten lyrics.

Rating:
Sound ★★★★☆ Content ★★★★★

John Lennon

'IMAGINE'

(Parlophone) 1971

Track listing: Imagine • Crippled Inside • Jealous Guy • It's So Hard • I Don't Want To Be A Soldier • Gimme Some Truth • Oh My Love • How Do You Sleep • How • Oh Yoko

Once Lennon had exorcized his personal demons he felt free to rant against the wrongs of the world and make a vain plea for tolerance. Both went unheeded, but the quality of the songs on this second solo session are undiminished by his naïve idealism, and the saccharine sweetness of the title track ensures that the sentiment gets a regular airing on national TV and radio at least.

'Imagine' also finds this most paradoxical of personalities indulging the romantic side of his nature, though he couldn't resist a parting shot at his ex-partner in the acidic 'How Do You Sleep'. Lennon may have been 'a dreamer', but he wasn't forgiving of those whom he felt had betrayed him.

Rating:
Sound ★★★★★ Content ★★★★★
Also recommended:
The compilation 'Shaved Fish', the covers album 'Rock n Roll' and the 4CD box set 'Lennon' (all on Parlophone).
If you like this, why not try:
The Beatles, Oasis, Paul Weller.

Annie Lennox

'DIVA'

(RCA) 1992

Track listing: Why • Walking On Broken Glass • Precious • Legend In My Living Room • Cold • Money Can't Buy It • Little Bird • Primitive • Stay By Me • The Gift • Keep Young And Beautiful

There is little to distinguish this solo outing from Annie's work with the Eurythmics, other than the conspicuous absence of ex-partner Dave Stewart and a certain world-weary cynicism that he brought to the mix. Motherhood has evidently mellowed her, but she remains as enigmatic as ever, revealing precious little of her emotions or private personality whilst putting her characters through the highs and lows of modern love. The setting is again an alluring fusion of designer dance chic and noveau classical with a lush orchestral wash of synths melting the edges of one of the few voices that can form a frosting on the sultriest of tunes.

Rating:
Sound ★★★★☆ Content ★★★★☆
Also recommended:
If you like this, why not try:
Eurythmics, Aretha Franklin.

Level 42

'RUNNING IN THE FAMILY/ STARING AT THE SUN'

2 CDs (Polydor) 2000

Track listing: Lessons In Love • Children Say • Running In The Family • It's Over • To Be With You Again • Two Solitudes • Fashion Fever • The Sleepwalkers • Freedom Someday • Heaven In My Hands • I Don't Know Why • Take A Look • Over There • Silence • Tracie • Staring At The Sun • Two Hearts Collide • Man • Gresham Blues

Bonus tracks: Lessons In Love • Children Say • To Be With You Again • Running In The Family • Three Words • Take A Look • Tracie • Take Care Of Yourself

Level 42 appealed to two distinct types of people: the largely undiscriminating and other musicians. The former found the group's mild, radio-friendly funk easy on the ear and an ideal background for cruising, smooching or simply getting mellow whenever the mood took them, while the latter admired the band's polished professionalism and the subtle production touches that only other musicians would appreciate. The group's seemingly anonymous music came a distant third, although the singles 'Lessons In Love' and 'Running In The Family' were aired so often that they became part of the fabric of the affluent eighties – especially for those who frequented wine bars or trendy clubs.

This reissue is a good value package offering two of their best albums on two CDs bolstered by a total of eight extra tracks (mostly remixes, but a couple of extended versions and the previously unreleased 'Three Words').

Rating:
Sound ★★★★☆ Content ★★☆☆☆
Also recommended:
'Level Best' (Polydor).
If you like this, why not try:
ABC, Wham, INXS.

Jerry Lee Lewis

'FERRIDAY FIREBALL'

(Charly) 1986

Track listing: Lewis Boogie • It'll Be Me • High School Confidential • Whole Lotta Shakin' Goin' On • Good Rockin' Tonight • Big Legged Woman • Great Balls Of Fire • Drinkin' Wine Spo-dee-O-dee • Matchbox • You Win Again • Will The Circle Be Unbroken • That Lucky Old Sun • Crazy Arms • Break Up • Memory Of You • Johnny B Goode • Little Queenie • Milkshake Mademoiselle • Big Blon' Baby • Breathless • Mean Woman Blues • Down The Line • When The Saints Go Marching In • End Of The Road • What'd I Say

'My name is Jerry Lee Lewis from Louisiana, I'm gonna play a little boogie on this piano,' sings 'The Killer' with a wry suggestive smile on his self-celebratory 'Lewis Boogie'. It's a classic understatement by the man who was once seen as the satanic spirit of rock incarnate.

Jerry Lee was the original 'wild man of rock', a flamboyant exhibitionist on and off stage who would incite his audience by kicking back his piano stool, swinging the microphone stand over his head and hammering the keys with his heels whilst hollering like a revivalist preacher. These performances from the Sun years once put the fear of God into eveybody over 30, although Jerry was himself a God-fearing country boy whose conscience continuously nagged him for playing the 'devil's music'. But it was this contradiction which fired these early records with an intensity which his teenage audience, in the turmoil of adolescence, could relate to, but were unable to express themselves. Whether he's drawling a country ballad, belting out an earthy blues, making his peace with the Lord on a gospel tune or getting down with the devil, Jerry Lee holds nothing back. They didn't call him 'The Killer' for nothing.

Rating:
Sound ★★★★☆ Content ★★★★★
Also recommended:
'Great Balls Of Fire' (Polydor) original soundtrack album featuring red-hot remakes of the Killer's greatest fifties hits plus the 4CD collection 'Sun Classics' which offers selected highlights from the definitive 8CD box set 'The Sun Years' (both on Charly).
If you like this, why not try:
Robert Gordon, **Little Richard**, Professor Longhair.

Limp Bizkit

'CHOCOLATE STARFISH AND THE HOT DOG FLAVOURED WATER'

2 CDs (Interscope) 2000

Track listing: Intro • Hot Dog • My Generation • Full Nelson • My Way • Rollin' • Livin' It Up • One • Getcha Groove On • Boiler • Hold On • Rollin' • Outro • Crushed • Faith • Counterfeit • Faith (Video) • Take A Look Around • I'll Be OK • Nookie (Video) • Rearranged (Video) • N2gether Now (Video)

Sooner or later someone had to do it – merge nu-metal, electro-funk, grunge and rap into a new fighting style which can hold its own in the ring with the heavyweights and soon have them on the ropes. Bizkit were contenders from the moment they supplied The Undertaker with his WWF theme, but with 'Rollin' they got an arm lock on the charts and they won't let up until the boy bands and girl-power puppets are chewing the canvas.

Pop has gone flabby around the waist in recent years and needs someone to get it back on its feet and working off those excess pounds. Some of Fred Durst's rants hit below the belt, but damn it, this is war.

Rating:
Sound ★★★★☆ Content ★★★★☆
Also recommended:
'Significant Other' (Interscope).
If you like this, why not try:
Nirvana, Stone Temple Pilots, **Cypress Hill**.

Loop Guru

'DUNIYA'

(Nation Records) 1994

Track listing: Hymn • Sussan 11 • Jungle A • Through Cinemas • Bangdad • The Fine Line Between Passion And Fear • Senseless • Freedom From The Known • Aphrodite's Shoe • Under Influence • Tchengo • The Third Chamber

Hitch your camel to Salman and Jamud's caravan, for without these nomadic global gurus you pink Westerners will never find the hidden treasures of world fusion, that exotic mix of world music and techno-trance with cross-cultural appeal.

The duo's music lies dormant like a coiled snake at the waterhole, waiting to strike and send its victims into delirium with droning guitars, mantric chants and exquisitely tortured samples; the latter culled from a vast archive of field recordings taped in a forbidden quarter of Marrakesh where even the souvenir sellers fall silent at the very mention of its name. Most tracks are atmospheric mid-tempo chill-out classics, revolving around a central axis of entrancing tribal beats and exotic ethnic instruments that weave a richly textured magic-carpet ride in sound. So let the genie out of the bottle and rock the casbah!

Rating:
Sound ★★★★☆ Content ★★★★☆

Also recommended:
'Amrita' (North–South).
If you like this, why not try:
Trans-Global Underground, The Orb, Orbital, Dead Can Dance.

Love

'DA CAPO'

(Elektra) 1967

Track listing: Stephanie Knows Who • Orange Skies • Que Vida • Seven And Seven Is • She Comes In Colours • Revelation • Castle

If Arthur Lee had split his group in the Summer of Love after making 'Da Capo' it's doubtful that they would have become the cult band that they are today. This, their second album, crystallizes the naïve idealism of the California counter culture, but doesn't embrace it. Lee is clearly fascinated by the freak show and you get the impression that he suspects it will end in disillusionment – which it did with the Manson 'family' murders and Altamont.

After a surreal first side of psychpop, garage and languid acid rock it stumbles and collapses in an unsightly heap half way to greatness, the other half of the original vinyl album being taken over by 'Revelation', a tediously self-indulgent blues jam. But half a masterpiece is better than nothing. And then there was...

Rating:
Sound ★★★★☆ Content ★★★☆☆

Love

'FOREVER CHANGES'

(Elektra) 1968

Track listing: Alone Again Or • A House Is Not A Motel • Andmoreagain • The Daily Planet • Old Man • The Red Telephone • Maybe The People Would Be The Times Or Between Clark And Hilldale • Live And Let Live • The Good Humour Man He Sees Everything Like This • Bummer In The Summer • You Set The Scene

'Forever Changes' ranks high in many critics' lists of 'all-time classic albums', although it has never been more than a steady, respectable seller. At the time the group were living in a gloomy Hollywood mansion that had served as a horror film set, which might account for the pervading atmosphere of grandeur and decay. The mix is much as before; elegant melodies swathed in ornate orchestral arrangements, exotic instrumentation (woodwind, trumpets and Spanish guitars) and venomous guitar solos. But occasionally psychedelia gives way to the psychotic, revealing the dark side of the California dream, as on 'A House Is Not A Motel' and 'Live And Let Live'.

Love were the Stone Roses of their day, a band whose belligerent attitude contrasted with the stoned euphoria of their music and the free love philosophy of the hippies. And it is this which gives their tracks a sense that the drug-induced ecstasy might at any moment dissolve into the nightmare of a bad trip.

Rating:
Sound ★★★☆☆ Content ★★★☆☆
Also recommended:
'Love' and 'Four Sail' (both on Elektra).
If you like this, why not try:
Beau Brummels, Chocolate Watch Band, **Thirteenth Floor Elevators**.

Lynyrd Skynyrd

'ONE MORE FOR THE ROAD'

(MCA) 1992

Track listing: Workin' For MCA • I Ain't The One • Searching • Tuesdays Gone • Saturday Night Special • Travellin' Man • Whiskey Rock n Roller • Sweet Home Alabama • Gimme Three Steps • Call Me The Breeze • T For Texas • Needle And Spoon • Crossroads • Freebird

Lynyrd Skynyrd penned the air guitar anthem 'Free Bird' in 1973 as a tribute to the late Duane Allman, but four years later the track became their epitaph after the key members were killed in an aircrash. The group had taken the laid-back Allman Brothers southern boogie and doused it in bourbon to add a more authentic flavour, but they were longhairs and had no truck with rednecks, as the tounge-in-cheek reposte to Neil Young, 'Sweet Home Alabama', testifies. Skynyrd were essentially a hard-working, crowd-pleasing live act and are best served by this double live album recorded on home territory where 'Free Bird' and a dozen similarly styled Dixie-fried rockers get a rigorous reworking.

Rating:
Sound ★★★★☆ Content ★★★★☆
Also recommended:
'The Very Best Of' and the aptly titled 'The Definitive Lynyrd Skynyrd', a 3CD set (both on MCA).
If you like this, why not try:
The Allman Brothers, ZZ Top.

Madness

'DIVINE MADNESS'

(Virgin) 1992

Track listing: The Prince • One Step Beyond • My Girl • Nightboat To Cairo • Baggy Trousers • Embarrassment • Return Of The Los Palmas 7 • Grey Day • Shut Up • It Must Be Love • Cardiac Arrest • House Of Fun • Driving In My Car • Our House • Tomorrow's Just Another Day • Wings Of A Dove • Sun And The Rain • Michael Caine • One Better Day • Yesterday's Men • Uncle Sam • Waiting For The Ghost Train

To paraphrase those North London 'nutty' boys, 'don't listen to that, listen to this.' It's the heavy, heavy monster sound of Madness who brought the quirky, jerky offbeat of ska and comic strip humour to a decade dominated by self-conscious synth acts and New Romantic style disasters. Even without their clever videos these songs promise more laughs than *The Beano* and you don't have to strain your mince pies reading it by torchlight under the bedclothes.

'Divine Madness' compiles the pick of their 21 skanking hit singles including the more serious 'Grey Day' and 'Cardiac Arrest', but ignores some of their finest album tracks such as 'Benny Bullfrog' and 'Bed And Breakfast Man'. So make

sure you add the albums 'One Step Beyond' and 'Seven' to your basket on the way to the checkout... and don't forget to demand a free fez.

Rating:
Sound ★★★★☆ Content ★★★★☆
Also recommended:
Their first album 'One Step Beyond' and the definitive singles collection 'The Business' on 3 CDs (both on Virgin).
If you like this, why not try:
The Specials, Prince Buster, Augustus Pablo, U-Roy.

Madonna

'IMMACULATE COLLECTION'

(Sire) 1990

Track listing: Holiday • Lucky Star • Borderline • Like A Virgin • Material Girl • Crazy For You • Into The Groove • Live To Tell • Papa Don't Preach • Open Your Heart • La Isla Bonita • Like A Prayer • Express Yourself • Cherish • Vogue • Justify My Love • Rescue Me

'Immaculate' may be pushing it, but this is certainly a fair summary of La Ciccone's career as a prototypical girl-power icon, a cultural phenomenon and a guaranteed party pleaser. The first four hits are pretty standard Euro disco fodder, but from 'Material Girl' onwards the breathless girlish voice gives way to a smoky-toned, worldy-wise young woman, enlivening even the most mundane material with a playful sensuality.

This collection also serves to chart her change of image from an icon of sexual freedom to that of a sexual fantasy figure, coming to a premature end with the explicit 'Justify My Love', and thereby leaving the option open for a second instalment to feature her more mature material.

Rating:
Sound ★★★★☆ Content ★★★★☆

Madonna

'BEDTIME STORIES'

(Maverick/Warners) 1994

Track listing: Survival • Secret • I'd Rather Be Your Lover • Don't Stop • Inside Of Me • Human Nature • Forbidden Love • Love Tried To Welcome Me • Sanctuary • Bedtime Story • Take A Bow

If the fans were expecting more frothy orgasmic pop in the wake of the provocative 'Erotica' they would have been disappointed by this subdued offering which was suggestive rather than explicit, coyly romantic rather than raunchy. 'Bedtime Stories' marks the point at which Madonna attempted to recast herself as a serious artist after the trash chic narcissism of the previous decade. Its theme is summed up in 'Human Nature' on which she turns on the hypocrisy of the media machine in the guise of a two-faced lover, 'You punished me for telling you my fantasies, I'm breakin' all the rules I didn't make… Did I say something true, Oops, I didn't know I couldn't talk about sex.'

The only disappointment is her collaboration with Björk on the title track which is as overdressed and as synthetically sexy as one of those filthy rich, elderly Hollywood madams with a soft spot for pink poodles and annual facelifts.

Otherwise, 'Bedtime Stories' presses all the right buttons, seducing the soft centres with some seriously sinewy grooves. It may be laid-back, but it suggests that the girl who was once described as sounding like 'Minnie Mouse on helium' has finally grown up.

Rating:
Sound ★★★★☆ Content ★★★★☆

Madonna

'RAY OF LIGHT'

(Maverick/Warners) 1998

Track listing: Drowned World – Substitute For Love • Swim • Ray Of Light • Candy Perfume Girl • Skin • Nothing Really Matters • Sky Fits Heaven • Shanti–Ashtangi • Frozen • The Power Of Goodbye • To Have And Not To Hold • Little Star • Mer Girl

'Everything has changed, I'll never be the same,' sings Madonna and how right she is. A second marriage and motherhood has obviously mellowed her and there is evidence too of some serious soul-searching in the lyrics which question the superficial nature of fame. Musically, we're in 'Beautiful Stranger' mode, thanks to collaborations with 'electronica' maestro William Orbit, but the sixties cartoon-strip humour of that hit is discarded for contemporary obsessions and the kaleidoscopic psychpop colours are more muted.

Highlights to show off your midi system include 'Candy Perfume Girl', 'The Power Of Goodbye' and the title track.

Rating:
Sound ★★★★☆ Content ★★★★☆
Also recommended:
'Music' (Maverick/Warners)
If you like this, why not try:
Destiny's Child, Sheryl Crow.

Manic Street Preachers

'GENERATION TERRORISTS'

(Columbia) 1992

Track listing: Slash N' Burn • Nat West – Barclays – Midlands – Lloyds • Born To End • Motorcycle Emptiness • You Love Us • Love's Sweet Exile • Little Baby Nothing • Repeat (Stars And Stripes) • Tennessee • Another Invented Disease • Stay Beautiful • So Dead • Repeat (UK) • Spectators Of Suicide • Damn Dog • Crucifix Kiss • Methadone Pretty • Condemned To Rock 'N' Roll

It's the end of the eighties and The Manics are suffering an identity crisis. They've got a serious Clash fixation and enough sixth-form angst to fill a double album before they carry out their threat to split in a grand empty gesture of defiance. However, they're also struggling with an overwhelming desire to dress up and party like the New York Dolls. So what do they do? They dress up like The Dolls and thrash around like early Clash on a double album that was intended to be a significant statement, but which turns out to be the first big seller in a conventional mainstream pop career. Their passion, however remains.

Stand out tracks include the single 'You Love Us' which rages at the fickle music press and 'Methadone Pretty' which pays their dues to The Dolls with interest.

Rating:
Sound ★★★★☆ Content ★★★☆☆

Manic Street Preachers

'EVERYTHING MUST GO'

(Epic) 1996

Track listing: Elvis Impersonator • Blackpool Pier • Design For Life • Kevin Carter • Enola Alone • Everything Must Go • Small Black Flowers That Glow In The Sky • Girl Who Wanted To Be God • Removeables • Australia • Interiors • Further Away • No Surface All Feeling

'Generation Terrorists' was intended to be the band's big statement before they split in the belief that it would deliver them from the temptation of selling out. As it turned out they made a second, 'The Holy Bible', before their guitarist Richey James did a Lord Lucan and disappeared, his whereabouts still a mystery. And then came a third on which they attempted to exorcize his restless spirit and settle down to the serious business of selling records. Somehow they managed to reconcile their pseudo-punk politics with a lush, everything-but-the-kitchen-sink production, though each track is permeated by the Pagliacci factor – a sense of loss behind the fixed smiles, as exeplified by opera's classic tragi-comic hero.

Highlights include their biggest hit to date, 'Design For Life' and 'Elvis Impersonator', one of James' last completed songs before his disappearance.

Rating:
Sound ★★★★☆ Content ★★★★☆

Also recommended:
'Gold Against The Soul' and 'The Holy Bible' (both on Columbia).
If you like this, why not try:
Hanoi Rocks, **The New York Dolls**, **The Clash**.

Bob Marley

'NATTY DREAD'

(Tuff Gong/Island) 1974

Track listing: Lively Up Yourself • No Woman, No Cry • Them Belly Full (But We Hungry) • Rebel Music • So Yah Say • Natty Dread • Bend Down Low • Talkin' Blues • Revolution

Bob Marley was the first Third World superstar, an artist of uncommon integrity and compassion who spoke more eloquently than most for the underclass in Jamaica and elsewhere through music that has proven universally popular, enduring and pervasively influential. 'Natty Dread' took rootsy Trenchtown rock upmarket and it encapsulated his spiritual aspirations, his sensual love of life and also his 'radical' political ideology.

It is the authentic voice of Jamaica and a crucial addition to a serious CD collection.

Rating:
Sound ★★★★☆ Content ★★★★☆

Bob Marley

'EXODUS'

(Tuff Gong/Island) 1977

Track listing: Natural Mystic • So Much Things To Say • Guiltiness • Heathen • Exodus • Jamming • Waiting In Vain • Turn Your Lights

Down Low • Three Little Birds • One Love – People Get Ready

Marley brought a quiet dignity and sincerity to his music that was an expression of his Rasta beliefs, but after the staggering success of 'No Woman, No Cry' the pressure was on him to produce more commercial music with a less prominent political component. Increasing sales encouraged him to write comparatively lightweight fare such as 'Three Little Birds' and the title track (which became his first top 20 hit), and yet he managed to keep faith with his personal spiritual and political philosophy without having to compromise or sell-out.

Three songs describe the failed assassination attempt that had recently sent him into temporary exile and several feature the militant four-to-the-bar 'rockers' style drumming, but they are sweetened by the customary lilting, off-beat skank and Marley's expressive, heartening vocal. He had evidently mellowed, but his unerring gift for melody and the joy of making music had not deserted him.

Rating:
Sound ★★★★☆ Content ★★★★☆

Bob Marley

'LEGEND'

(Tuff Gong/Island) 1990

Track listing: Is This Love • Jamming • No Woman, No Cry • Stir It Up • Get Up Stand Up • Satisfy My Soul • I Shot The Sheriff • One Love • Buffalo Soldier • Exodus • Redemption Song • Could You Be Loved • Want More

With Marley's death from cancer in 1981 the spirit seemed to go out of Jamaican music and it's unlikely that we'll hear an artist of his stature again. There is a wealth of fine reggae to be heard, but for many Marley embodied the music to the exclusion of all other artists. This is a serviceable singles collection, but the crucial cuts are to be found on the original albums.

Rating:
Sound ★★★★☆ Content ★★★★★
Also recommended:
'Live!' and the comprehensive 'Songs Of Freedom' 4CD box set (both on Tuff Gong/Island).
If you like this, why not try:
Peter Tosh, Toots And The Maytals, Jimmy Cliff, Black Uhuru, Burning Spear.

Massive Attack

'BLUE LINES'

(Wild Bunch/EMI) 1991

Track listing: Safe From Harm • One Love • Blue Lines • Be Thankful For What You've Got • Five Man Army • Unfinished Sympathy • Daydreaming • Lately • Hymn Of The Big Wheel

The sweet-scented, spaced-out vibes of trip-hop were brewed in Bristol by a cooperative of system DJs known as The Wild Bunch as an alternative to the frenetic intensity of rave and jungle. Wild Bunch founders Daddy G, 3D and Mushroom raided their record collections for samples to create the perfect soundtrack for cruising and chilling out then brought in a host of respected guests including

Tricky and soul diva Shara Nelson to add vocals. 'Unfinished Sympathy' was the big dancefloor hit, a dazzling mosaic of narcotic beats and cryptic lyrics iced with Nelson's mellifluous lines.

The epitome of cool and an instant classic.

Rating:
Sound ★★★★☆ Content ★★★★★
Also recommended:
'Protection' and the dub version 'No Protection' (both on Wild Bunch Records).
If you like this, why not try:
Tricky, Soul ll Soul, Neneh Cherry, Portishead, De La Soul.

Paul And Linda McCartney

'RAM'

(Parlophone) 1971

Track listing: Too Many People • 3 Legs • Ram On • Dear Boy • Uncle Albert-Admiral Halsey • Smile Away • Heart Of The Country • Monkberry Moon Delight • Eat At Home • Long Haired Lady • Ram On • The Back Seat Of My Car

Bonus tracks: Another Day • Oh Woman, Oh Why

There was a rumour being circulated at the time of 'Abbey Road' which claimed that Paul had died and that his place had been taken by a look-alike. Listening to the ex-Beatle's second solo album one can almost believe it. McCartney bubbles over with delicious melodies, but he's out to lunch when it comes to developing them and his lyrics betray both a lack of inspiration and the inclination to say anything substantial. No offence Mac, but 'the lovely Linda' was no substitute for your previous writing partner.

Rating:
Sound ★★★★☆ Content ★★★☆☆

Paul McCartney And Wings

'RED ROSE SPEEDWAY'

(Parlophone) 1973

Track listing: Big Barn Bed • My Love • Get On The Right Thing • One More Kiss • Little Lamb Dragonfly • Single Pigeon • When The Night • Loup • Medley: Hold Me Tight, Lazy Dynamite, Hands Of Love, Power Cut

Bonus tracks: C Moon • Hi Hi Hi • The Mess • I Lie Around

Lennon famously described McCartney's solo material as sounding like muzak to his ears and after trawling through these half-baked home demos it's difficult to disagree. Most of the tracks sound like fragments of unfinished songs stitched together in a similar manner to the medley on 'Abbey Road', but with considerably less success. The comparison with The Beatles' final studio album is made all the more poignant by Mac's attempt to replicate the sound of that album, but the material is strictly second rate. The best tracks are the two single sides, 'C Moon' and 'Hi Hi Hi' which have been added as bonus tracks. Without them this would be very meagre fare. This is the blueprint for a far better record than the one that we actually get.

Rating:
Sound ★★★★☆ Content ★★★☆☆

Paul McCartney

'BAND ON THE RUN'

2 CD Special Edition (Apple) 1973

Track listing: Band On The Run • Jet • Bluebird • Mrs Vanderbelt • Let Me Roll It • Mamunia • No Words • Helen Wheels • Picasso's Last Words • Nineteen Hundred And Eighty Five

After a series of lucklustre solo outings 'Band On The Run' re-established McCartney's artistic credentials and earned him the coveted 'Album Of The Year' award from *Rolling Stone*. He had been galvanized by the departure of two band members who had left shortly before the sessions were scheduled to begin and he was evidently determined to show them and a sceptical music press that he was back in business.

The customary McCartney whimsy is in evidence on only three tracks, 'Picasso's Last Words', the banal 'Bluebird' and the novelty sing-along 'Mamunia'. The remainder are largely upbeat, richly melodic rockers benefiting from biting brass and dusky orchestral colours. There are even echoes of past glories in the Beatlesque 'No Words' and 'Let Me Roll It' with its Lennon-styled vocal and guitar, but the overall impression is one of McCartney finally finding his feet as a bona fide solo artist.

The 25th anniversary edition comes with an additional CD of previously unreleased tracks (rehearsals, rough mixes and alternate versions) plus a fascinating commentary by McCartney and those involved telling the story of the recording and the celebrity sleeve photo shoot. It's a pity that more classic albums aren't repackaged with this degree of care.

Rating:
Sound ★★★★★ Content ★★★★☆
Also recommended:
'Wingspan' (EMI).
If you like this, why not try:
The Beatles, Steve Miller, Paul Weller, Oasis.

Metallica

'LOAD'

(Vertigo) 1996

Track listing: Ain't My Bitch • 2X4 • The House Jack Built • Until It Sleeps • King Nothing • Hero Of The Day • Bleeding Me • Cure • Poor Twisted Me • Wasting My Hate • Mama Said • Thorn Within • Ronnie • The Outlaw Torn

There are unholy hordes of heavy metal bands stalking the planet, but only one Metallica. While many are content to bludgeon their way to notoriety with the subtlety of an inebriated Neanderthal, this Californian quartet boast a consummate mastery of technique and a shrewd sense of melody. In harnessing this heady mix of precision and primeval power to Lovecraftian lyrics they conjure up a nightmare world of eldritch horrors delivered in a demonic snarl. Play loud, or perish!

Rating:
Sound ★★★★☆ Content ★★★★☆

Metallica

'RELOAD'

(Vertigo) 1997

Track listing: Fuel • The Memory Remains • Devil's Dance • The Unforgiven II • Better Than You • Slither • Carpe Diem Baby • Bad Seed • Where The Wild Things Are • Prince Charming • Low Man's Lyric • Attitude • Fixxxer

Metallica reopen the book of shadows and unleash the demons that will haunt your dreams for decades to come. Demented, but highly disciplined riffing alternates with refined melodic ballads evoking images of California's uncrowned lords of chaos striding the land and putting all soft rockers to the sword.

Had Attila The Hun banged a few heads to 'Bad Seed' or the almighty 'Fuel' he might have got all his aggression out at home and not been such a naughty boy. 'Load' was awesome, but 'Reload' has surely earned the group their place in the hallowed halls of Valhalla.

If this doesn't move you, you're already dead.

Rating:
Sound ★★★★☆ Content ★★★★☆

Metallica

'S&M'

2 CDs (Vertigo) 1999

Track listing: The Ecstasy Of Gold • The Call Of The Ktulu • Master Of Puppets • Of Wolf And Man • The Thing That Should Not Be • Fuel • The Memory Remains • No

Leaf Clover • Hero Of The Day • Devil's Dance • Bleeding Me • Nothing Else Matters • Until It Sleeps • For Whom The Bell Tolls • - Human • Wherever I May Roam • Outlaw Torn • Sad But True • One • Enter Sandman • Battery

The title of this epic double live album refers not to dubious sexual practices, but to the in-concert collaboration between the San Francisco Symphony Orchestra and Metallica, the Californian thrash metal merchants whose speed, strength and stamina makes Black Sabbath sound like the senior citizens of rock. You would be forgiven for thinking that this unholy alliance between the dark hordes of heavy metal and the conventional forces of classical music would degenerate into a diabolical mess, but no. The fusion of vivid orchestral colour and Metallica's awesome wall of sound is a revelation. Something must have taken possession of their souls for this is the very definition of precious metal and an exhilarating aural experience. Exorcize your memories of the ill-conceived orchestra-meets-rock-group concept albums of the seventies and surrender to the lords of chaos!

Rating:
Sound ★★★★★ Content ★★★★★
Also recommended:
'And Justice For All' and 'Ride The Lightning' (both on Vertigo).
If you like this, why not try:
Napalm Death, **Motorhead**, Pantera, Megadeth, Mercyful Fate.

Meatloaf

'BAT OUT OF HELL'

(Epic) 1977

Track listing: Bat Out Of Hell • You Took The Words Right Out Of My Mouth • Heaven Can Wait • All Revved Up With No Place To Go • Two Out Of Three Ain't Bad • Paradise By The Dashboard Light • For Crying Out Loud

If Wagner had been reborn as an overweight rock singer with far less taste and talent than he had the first time around, he might have made 'Bat Out Of Hell', a record so overwrought and melodramatic that its songs suffocate under the weight of its own pretensions.

It's the sound of the American dream slipping into a coma as images of drive-in movies, teenage sexual fantasies and motorbike mythology flash before its eyes. It's rock as soap opera with Meatloaf, the corpulent rock star in question, cast as a grotesque caricature of Bruce Springsteen and suffering so much that one feels compelled to put him out of his misery. But it's also a parody of pop and its tendency to take itself far too seriously which 12 million record buyers took at face value. It's a safe bet that they still haven't seen the joke.

Rating:
Sound ★★★★☆ Content ★★★☆☆
Also recommended:
'Bat Out Of Hell II' (Epic).
If you like this, why not try:
Bruce Springsteen, Todd Rundgren.

George Michael

'FAITH'

(Epic) 1987

Track listing: Faith • Father Figure • I Want Your Sex • One More Try • Hard Day • Hand To Mouth • Look At Your Hands • Monkey • Kissing A Fool

After serving time as an impeccably coiffeured, sun-tanned teen idol in Wham! George Michael celebrated his new found solo status by growing a beard as a mark of his maturity and duetting with Aretha Franklin. Her endorsement led credibility to his stated ambition to be accepted as an authentic soul singer and a serious songwriter, but 'Faith' is no more 'authentic' than the music of George's childhood hero, Elton John.

The title of this first solo outing was presumably chosen to reflect his unshakable belief in himself, but it revealed little of substance beneath the thick veneer of sophistication.

Of the four successful singles taken from the album the title track is the funkiest, clearly designed to awaken the first stirrings of womanhood in George's pubescent female fans. 'I Want Your Sex' is a more cynical attempt to court controversy and secure rabid tabloid coverage, while the remainder suggests that Michael can carry a tune with some style but he is too often concerned with showmanship than soul.

Rating:
Sound ★★★★★ Content ★★★☆☆

George Michael

'OLDER'

(Virgin) 1996

Track listing: Jesus To A Child • Fast Love • Older • Spinning The Wheel • It Doesn't Really Matter • The Strangest Thing • To Be Forgiven • Move On • Star People • You Have Been Loved • Free

George may be older, but it's questionable whether he's any wiser. He has endured the glare of public scandal and a bruising legal battle with Sony, but his music doesn't demonstrate a greater depth or perception. He remains a master of the Sade school of chic, designer disco and a blue chip investment opportunity for those record companies who can handle his demanding personality. However, this brand of blue-eyed soul is as wholesome and insubstantial as white bread. The beatbox percussion patterns and South American samples suggest that George has his finger on the pulse of contemporary pop, but there are little signs of life.

Those who like Phil Collins, Elton John, Steve Winwood and Peter Gabriel may find that this is a grower, but those who want music that will move them should pass.

Rating:
Sound ★★★★☆ Content ★★★☆☆
Also recommended:
'Listen Without Prejudice' (Epic).
If you like this, why not try:
Wham!, **Steve Winwood, Peter Gabriel**, **Sting**.

Steve Miller Band

'GREATEST HITS'

(Polygram) 1998

Track listing: The Joker • Space Intro • Fly Like An Eagle • Jet Airliner • Dance Dance Dance • Give It Up • Keeps Me Wondering Why • Abracadabra • Swingtown • Jungle Love • Take The Money And Run • Rock N Me • The Stake • Heart Like A Wheel • Wide River • True Fine Love • Cry Cry Cry • Serenade • Winter Time • Wild Mountain Honey

Miller was a great blues guitarist who paid his dues and then proceeded to accumulate mountains of capital in hard cash with the royalties from these simple, mainstream pop singles. At a little over three minutes each with smart hooks, succinct solos and a sound that was as smooth as peaches and cream they became every radio producer's dream. Twenty years on, they still sound as easy on the ear as they did when first released and provide the perfect antidote whenever pop threatens to take itself too seriously.

Rating:
Sound ★★★★☆ Content ★★★☆☆
Also recommended:
'Fly Like An Eagle', 'Book Of Dreams', 'Born 2B Blue', 'Circle Of Love' and 'Abracadabra' (all on Mercury).
If you like this, why not try:
Tom Petty, The Cars, Paul McCartney.

The Mission

'SUM AND SUBSTANCE'

(Vertigo) 1994

Track listing: Wasteland • Severina • Stay With Me • Tower Of Strength • Beyond The Pale • Butterfly On A Wheel • Deliverance • Into The Blue • Amelia • Hands Across The Ocean • Never Again • Shades Of Green • Like A Child Again • Sour Puss • Afterglow

Wayne Hussey's Goth-rockers are frequently dismissed as a mere footnote to The Sisters Of Mercy saga, but the family resemblance is entirely superficial. The Mission's everything-but-the-kitchen-sink productions are on an epic scale and endowed with more passion than their cold-blooded sibling rivals could ever muster. Through the swirling dry ice the band ride a richly woven magic carpet of sound out of the Goth graveyard, soaring over the seas to more exotic lands where they find inspiration in fairy tales and among the forbidden books of magical lore. They may not be subtle or original, but their melodies are presented as precious stones in a sumptuous setting, ideal for whiling away the hours while clearing the cobwebs from your castle.

Rating:
Sound ★★★★☆ Content ★★★★☆
Also recommended:
'Carved In Sand' and 'Children' (Vertigo).
If you like this, why not try:
Fields Of The Nephilim, **The Sisters Of Mercy, Siouxsie And The Banshees**.

Joni Mitchell

'BLUE'

(Reprise) 1971

Track listing: All I Want • My Old Man • Little Green • Carey • Blue • California • This Flight Tonight • River • A Case Of You • The Last Time I Saw Richard

With 'Blue' Joni Mitchell confirmed her status as one of the most significant and influential singer-songwriters of the late sixties and early seventies. Like Dylan, she had shed the restricting 'folk singer' image early on, emerging as a poet with a highly distinctive 'voice'. But unlike Dylan she demonstrated an ability to take a tune in unexpected directions, just like the best jazz singers.

In contrast to the intensity and introspection of its predecessor, 'Ladies Of The Canyon', the prevailing mood of this album is relaxed and conversational; enriched with candid recollections of friends and lovers, but tinged with a bitter-sweet regret. It is essentially a solo set with minimal accompaniment, recreating a floor spot in one of the 'dark cafes' to which she alludes in the poignantly personal 'The Last Time I Saw Richard'. Original songs such as 'Carey', 'The River' and 'A Case Of You' affirmed that she was no longer the spokesperson for her idealistic generation, but rather an eloquent and perceptive commentator on the complex subject of personal relationships.

The album also serves as the blueprint for her subsequent work in its fusion of jazz and folk, the intimate narrative style and the focus placed on her idiosyncratic vocal which has more peaks and troughs than a politician's lie detector test.

Rating:
Sound ★★★★☆ Content ★★★★☆

Joni Mitchell

'COURT AND SPARK'

(Asylum) 1974

Track listing: Court And Spark • Help Me • Free Man In Paris • People's Parties • The Same Situation • Car On A Hill • Down To You • Just Like This Train • Raised On Robbery • Trouble Child • Twisted

With 'Court And Spark' Joni traded the pastel sketches of 'Blue' for the vivid hues and broad strokes of an impressionist. An enlarged ensemble gave her a more varied palette and a larger canvas to work with resulting in a richer and warmer sounding record. Her performance too, reveals an increasing self-confidence and an innate talent for writing sophisticated 'pop' songs while retaining a healthy disregard for commercial interests. Three of the tracks became hits, 'Freeman In Paris', 'Raised On Robbery' and 'Help Me' (her only top ten single) making this one of her most accessible albums to date.

Rating:
Sound ★★★★☆ Content ★★★★★

Joni Mitchell

'THE HISSING OF SUMMER LAWNS'

(Asylum) 1975

Track listing: In France They Kiss On Main Street • The Jungle Line • Edith And The Kingpin • Don't Interrupt The Sorrow • Shades of Scarlett Conquering • The Hissing Of Summer Lawns • The Boho Dance • Harry's House – Centerpiece • Sweet Bird • Shadows And Light

Musically speaking 'Summer Lawns' marks a move uptown from the jazz clubs and cafes of Greenwich Village to the penthouses of Manhattan, although once there Joni questions the values of its affluent inhabitants. Two years in the making, it is an intricate and densely layered jazz-rock collage through which her inimitable vocal lines weave with the flexibility of a virtuoso instrumentalist.

   Whilst the songs aren't as immediately appealing as those on 'Court And Spark' they reveal their subtle charms with repeated listening. If there is a weakness, it is the infatuation with wordplay which tends to get entangled in the tunes. But although it's an album which demands much from its listener repeated listening will pay significant dividends.

Rating:
Sound ★★★★☆ Content ★★★★☆
Also recommended:
'Ladies Of The Canyon' and Hejira' (Warners).
If you like this, why not try:
Dido, **Suzanne Vega**, Judy Collins, **The Byrds**, **Leonard Cohen**.

Moby

'EVERYTHING IS WRONG'

(Mute) 1995

Track listing: Hymn • Feeling So Real • All That I Need Is To be Loved • Let's Go Free • Everytime You Touch Me • Bring Back My Happiness • What Love • First Cool Hive • Into The Blue • Anthem • Everything Is Wrong • God Moving Over The Face Of The Waters • When It's Cold I'd Like To Die

There can't be many artists who give thanks to Jesus on their albums as if he was a member of their management team. Moby does. Moreover, the American remix maestro and devout Christian shows his devotion by moving in very mysterious ways. One moment he's chilling out with the ambient 'Hymn', next he's invoking the Holy Ghost to the satanic speed metal of 'All That I Need Is To Be Loved'.

   The title of this eclectic collection refers to Moby's belief that our survival and the survival of the Earth is threatened by our rapacious appetite for self-destruction, an idea that he explains at length in the sleeve notes, alongside his advocacy of vegetarianism. Fortunately, his New Age philosophy doesn't prevent him from worshipping a very broad church that embraces acid-house, hip-hop, jungle and techno. Here he offers salvation through sound. The gospel according to Moby is dance!

Rating:
Sound ★★★★☆ Content ★★★☆☆

Moby

'PLAY'

(Mute) 1999

Track listing: Honey • Find My Baby • Porcelain • Why Does My Heart Feel So Bad • Southside • Rushing • Bodyrock • Natural Blues • Machete • 7 • Run On • Down Slow • If Things Were Perfect • Ever Loving • Inside • Guitar Flute And String • Sky Is Broken • My Weakness

After succumbing to temptation with the retro-techno album 'Animal Rights', God's favourite DJ redeemed himself with this superb soul food sampler and earned 'Play' a place in many critics' lists of top albums of the nineties.

'Play' finds Moby back on the side of the angels, fighting the good fight, bible in one hand, beatbox in the other, mixing gospel and blues samples with devilishly danceable breakbeats that spells salvation in sound. 'Bodyrock' will have his devout disciples moving in mysterious ways and 'Natural Blues' has the power to convert even the most conservative of highbrows to the redemptive power of dance.

Rating:
Sound ★★★★☆ Content ★★★★☆
Also recommended:
'Animal Rights' (Mute).
If you like this, why not try:
Brian Eno, Orbital, **Pet Shop Boys**.

The Monkees

'GREATEST HITS'

(East West) 1996

Track listing: Monkees Theme • Last Train To Clarksville • Wanna Be Free • I'm A Believer • I'm Not Your Steppin' Stone • Mary Mary • Little Bit Me A Little Bit You • Girl I Knew Somewhere • Randy Scouse Git • Pleasant Valley Sunday • Words • Daydream Believer • Going Down • Valleri • DW Washburn • It's Nice To Be With You • Porpoise Song • Listen To The Band • That Was Then This Is Now • Heart And Soul

If any group personified what became known as bubblegum pop, it was The Monkees. Mickey, Mike, Peter and Davey were manufactured by a Californian corporation to cash-in on The Beatles' success. They were groomed in the image of an American Fab Four, given their own weekly national TV series and spoon-fed hit records which they hadn't actually played on. But what no one had reckoned on was the fact that the boys might actually possess talent and come together as a group. Before long they were demanding a share of the songwriting and the right to perform their own music.

If you didn't live through the sixties these songs will effortlessly evoke the endless summer of that era and if you did, nostalgia comes neatly formatted and prepackaged, just like the group. They may have been manufactured, but kitsch pop culture doesn't come more enjoyable than this.

Rating:
Sound ★★★☆☆ Content ★★★★☆
Also recommended:
'Instant Replay' (Rhino).
If you like this, why not try:
The Lovin' Spoonful, The Mamas And Papas.

Moody Blues

'THIS IS'

2 CDs (Deram) 1974

Track Listing: Question • The Actor • The Word • Eyes Of A Child • Dear Diary • Legend Of A Mind • In The Beginning • Lovely To See You • Never Comes The Day • Isn't Life Strange • The Dream • Have You Heard? Pt 1 • The Voyage • Have You Heard? Pt 2 • Ride My See-Saw • Tuesday Afternoon • And The Tide Rushes In • New Horizons • Simple Game • I'm Just A Singer (In A Rock And Roll Band) • Watching And Waiting • For My Lady • The Story In Your Eyes • Melancholy Man • Nights In White Satin • Late Lament

'That Was,' might be a more appropriate title for a disc by a group who have been consigned to the bargain bin of rock history, but who enjoy a periodic return to the racks whenever their perennially popular single 'Nights In White Satin' has a revival. In less sophisticated times the Moodys enjoyed superstar status, but by 1972 their fans stirred from their stoned reverie and discovered that their pomp-rock gurus had as little grasp of Eastern philosophy as the average sixth former. Their pseudo-symphonic albums are patchy to say the least with only two or three good tracks amid the dross of twee tunes and pretentious psychobabble, so this double album of highlights will save you cash and a lot of frustration.

Turn off your critical faculties, relax and float down the black hole of time to a parallel universe where the Moodys had meaning... and, to be fair, a good tune or two.

Rating:
Sound ★★★☆☆ Content ★★★☆☆

Also recommended:
'To Our Children's Children' (London).
If you like this, why not try:
Barclay James Harvest, **Jeff Wayne**'s 'War Of The Worlds'.

Alanis Morissette

'JAGGED LITTLE PILL'

(Maverick) 1995

Track listing: All I Really Want • You Oughta Know • Perfect • Hand In My Pocket • Right Through You • Forgiven • You Learn • Head Over Feet • Mary Jane • Ironic • Not The Doctor • Wake Up

Many of the songs on this critically acclaimed, multi-million seller reveal Alanis' preoccupation with the sexual repression that comes from a strict religious upbringing. It's something that she shares with her label boss, Madonna, although Alanis doesn't celebrate her hard-won independence as flamboyantly as Madonna does. Songs such as 'All I Really Want' and 'Forgiven' fester with a barely suppressed rage against institutionalized hypocrisy and what she sees as the emotional dishonesty of the male species. This anger is articulated by a ferocious, sub-grunge sound (courtesy of Flea and Dave Navarro of the Red Hot Chili Peppers), focused around her histrionic vocal which chews up and spits out the lyrics in a style reminiscent of Tori Amos at her most melodramatic. This combination of unsophisticated, low-fi sound and sexually explicit lyrics caught the mood of the moment and inspired a generation of soundalikes to bare their souls on record.

Rating:
Sound ★★★★☆ Content ★★★★☆
Also recommended:
'Supposed Former Infatuation Junkie'
(Maverick).
If you like this, why not try:
Tori Amos, Patty Griffin, Sheryl
Crow, Red Hot Chili Peppers.

Morrissey

'YOUR ARSENAL'

(EMI) 1992

Track listing: You're Gonna Need Someone On Your Side • Glamorous Glue • We'll Let You Know • The National Front Disco • Certain People I Know • We Hate It When Our Friends Become Successful • You're The One For Me, Fatty • Seasick, Yet Still Docked • I Know It's Gonna Happen Someday • Tomorrow

Morrissey's penchant for maudlin self-pity got a well-needed kick up the jacksie when rockabilly guitarist Alan Whyte plugged in his Strat and cranked up the intensity. Mozza had been whingeing about how miserable he was for far too long and Whyte's wired guitar together with Mick Ronson's production was just what the shrink ordered to get these songs on their feet. After years of dithering, he finally said where he stood on racism with 'The National Front Disco' and he also came up with the goods tune-wise, laying to rest Elvis Costello's accusation that Morrissey 'comes up with the best greatest song titles in the world, only somewhere along the line he forgets to write the song'.

Rating:
Sound ★★★★★ Content ★★★★★

Morrissey

'VAUXHALL AND I'

(Parlophone) 1994

Track listing: Now My Heart Is Full • Spring Heeled Jimmy • Billy Budd • Hold Onto Your Friends • The More You Ignore Me, The Closer I Get • Why Don't You Find Out For Yourself • I Am Hated For Loving • Lifeguard Sleeping, Girl Drowning • Used To Be A Sweet Boy • The Lazy Sunbathers • Speedway

'Vauxhall And I' marked the belated appearance of the mature Morrissey, more subdued and serious than the neurotic, artful youth of yore. Perhaps it was the recent death of several close friends, including Mick Ronson, which encouraged him to drop the pretence and return to his favourite haunt to observe the working class characters and outcasts who had provided a rich source of inspiration in the past.

Self-obsession and scathing self-analysis are evident in equal measures on what must be his most self-assured and personal statement to date.

His honesty and keener eye on quality control was rewarded with the second chart-topping album of his career.

Rating:
Sound ★★★★☆ Content ★★★★☆
Also recommended:
'The World Of Morrissey' (HMV) serves as a good sampler but doesn't include all of the essential items.
If you like this, why not try:
The Smiths, Suede, REM.

Van Morrison

'ASTRAL WEEKS'

(Warner Brothers) 1968

*Track listing: Astral Weeks • Beside You •
Sweet Thing • Cyprus Avenue • The Way
Young Lovers Do • Madame George •
Ballerina • Slim Slow Slider*

Morrison is a notoriously 'difficult'
character whose prickly personality is
in complete contrast to his music,
which is warm, lyrical, laid-back and
ruggedly romantic.

His first serious solo album was
recorded in just two days after the
sudden death of his manager had left
him stranded in New York with no
return ticket. With nothing to lose he
recorded the album that he wanted to
make, a largely improvisational
acoustic set with jazz musicians that
he had never worked with before and
featuring unusual instrumentation
that included vibes, horns, flute,
harpsichord and double bass.

On the record's sublime central
pieces, 'Cyprus Avenue', 'Madame
George' and the title track, his
urgent, blues-tinged vocal and fluid
phrasing is matched by the
musicians' technical agility and
graceful, lucid playing; summoning
up bitter-sweet memories of lost
lovers and the colourful Joycean
characters of his youth.

Needless to say, your CD
collection will be incomplete
without it.

Rating:
Sound ★★★★☆ Content ★★★★★

Van Morrison

'MOONDANCE'

(Warner Brothers) 1970

*Track listing: And It Stoned Me • Moondance
• Crazy Love • Caravan • Into The Mystic •
Come Running • These Dreams Of You •
Brand New Day • Everyone • Glad Tidings*

'Moondance' is more firmly focused
and 'commercial', but no less essential
than its somewhat rambling
predecessor. It is a product of Van's
residency in Woodstock and betrays
the influence of his neighbours, The
Band, particularly on the opening cut.

Its tasteful blend of Celtic folk,
blues, jazz and soul underscores one
of the most expressive voices in
modern music and enriches a strong
set of songs that are pervaded by
compassion and optimism.

Rating:
Sound ★★★★☆ Content ★★★★★

Van Morrison

'ST DOMINIC'S PREVIEW'

(Warner Brothers) 1972

*Track listing: Jackie Wilson Said • Gypsy • I
Will Be There • Listen To The Lion • Saint
Dominic's Preview • Redwood Tree • Almost
Independence Day*

Morrison's moods are legendary, but
his music has an easy grace and an
innate elegance that speaks direct to
the human spirit. On 'St Dominic's
Preview' he is backed by a rhythm
section of rare refinement who prove
equally adept at belting out blue-eyed

Celtic soul on 'Jackie Wilson Said' (later to be revived by Dexy's Midnight Runners) and musing on the mystical in 'Listen To The Lion' and 'Almost Independence Day'.

On the latter two Van deconstructs the songs into their constituent parts, then reassembles them on the hoof to reveal an unconventional beauty.

Thirty years after the original release of these albums the indomitable spirit of Morrison's music is as strong, vibrant and moving as ever.

Rating:
Sound ★★★★☆ Content ★★★★★
Also recommended:
'It's Too Late To Stop Now', an excellent live performance with Van backed by strings and a brass section, 'Hard Nose The Highway' and of course the inevitable 'Best of' compilations available in two complimentary volumes (all on Warners).
If you like this, why not try:
Them, **Joni Mitchell**, **Dexy's Midnight Runners**, Stax Soul.

Motorhead

'NO REMORSE'

(Castle Classics) 1988

Track listing: Ace Of Spades • Motorhead • Jailbait • Stay Clean • Too Late, Too Late • Killed By Death • Bomber • Iron Fist • Shine • Dancing On Your Grave • Metropolis • Snaggletooth • Overkill • Please Don't Touch • Stone Dead Forever • Like A Nightmare • Emergency • Steal Your Face • No Class • Iron Horse • We Are The Roadcrew • Locomotive

This one goes all the way up to 11! Yeh, we're talking 'Spinal Tap' territory, though to be fair Lemmy and crew never took themselves as seriously as some who followed their flight path. The titles tell the tale – 'Iron Fist', 'Bomber', 'Overkill' and the self-mocking 'Killed By Death'. And those are only the ballads. No, just kidding. This is a full-frontal assault on the senses, a blitz on the brain, carpet bombing of the little grey cells. Over 70 minutes of sledgehammer riffing, drumming that sounds like a panzer beating the stuffing out of your speakers and Lemmy the loon gargling gravel for breakfast. Heavy metal heaven.

This headbanger's bible is a double album reissued on one CD and contains all you'll ever need. Prime meat and no surplus fat.

Rating:
Sound ★★★★☆ Content ★★★★★
Also recommended:
If you crave the hair of the dog that bit you then you'll have to have the live albums 'No Sleep Till Hammersmith' and 'No Sleep At All' (both on Castle).
If you like this, why not try:
Girlschool, **Hawkwind**, Megadeth.

Mott The Hoople

'GREATEST HITS'

(CBS) 1989

Track listing: All The Way From Memphis • Honoloochie Boogie • Hymn For The Dudes • Born Late '58 • All The Young Dudes • Ro...

Away The Stone • Ballad Of Mott The
Hoople • Golden Age Of Rock N Roll • Foxy
Foxy • Saturday Gigs

In 1972 Mott were an anonymous
hardworking rock band on the verge of
calling it a day when they were saved
from obscurity by David Bowie.
Bowie offered to supply them with a
tailor-made hit, 'All The Young
Dudes', which concentrated the
group's working-class bravado into a
classic three-minute sing-along single
and trimmed off the excesses that had
made them unpalatable for mass
consumption.

Despite the title of this
compilation Mott made little
impact on the charts after that
initial success and have had a
negligible influence on the
evolution of pop, but they livened
things up with laddish, good-time
pub and party music when the
festivities were beginning to flag.
Those who remember them do so
largely because of their Bowie-
penned hit, but the Roxy-styled
'Honoloochie Boogie', the
Spectorish 'Roll Away The Stone'
and the camp rocker 'All The Way
From Memphis' are among glam
rock's finest moments.

Rating:
Sound ★★★☆☆ Content ★★★☆☆
Also recommended:
'Ballad Of Mott' a 2CD retrospective
(Columbia).
If you like this, why not try:
Ian Hunter's solo albums, **Bad
Company**, **David Bowie**, **Cockney
Rebel**.

New Order

'SUBSTANCE'

2 CDs (Factory) 1993

Track listing: Ceremony • Everythings Gone
Green • Temptation • Blue Monday •
Confusion • Thieves Like Us • Perfect Kiss •
Subculture • Shellshock • State Of The
Nation • Bizarre Love Triangle • True Faith •
Procession • Mesh • Hurt • In A Lonely
Place • Beach • Confused • Murder •
Lonesome Tonight • Kiss Of Death • Shame
Of The Nation • 1963

Substantial might have been a more
appropriate title for this heavy duty
compilation which collects all of the
band's extended 12 inch mixes that
were issued between 1981–87, many
of which are not available elsewhere
on CD.

Sumner's thin, arid vocal, their
melancholic melodies and the
mechanical metronomic beat tends to
grate after a while, but given the
right atmosphere, a crowded
dancefloor and liberal amounts of
alcohol their melodious brand of
techno-pop can have a mantra-like
effect. 'Substance' also serves as a
reminder that they maintained a
consistently high quality as a singles
band and that their B-sides were
frequently of a similar standard.
Altogether, an essential supplement
to their official albums.

Rating:
Sound ★★★★☆ Content ★★★★☆
Also recommended:
'Electronic', the compilations 'The
Best Of', 'The Rest Of' and their best
studio album 'Low Life'(all on
Factory).

If you like this, why not try:
Joy Division, **Kraftwerk**, Can,
Tangerine Dream.

The New York Dolls

'ROCK 'N' ROLL'

(Mercury) 1994

Track listing: Courageous Cat Theme • Trash • Personality Crisis • Babylon • Looking For A Kiss • Lone Star Queen • Vietnamese Baby • Lonely Planet Boy • Frankenstein • Private World • Chatterbox • Bad Girl • Don't Mess With Cupid • Subway Train • Who Are The Mystery Girls? • Stranded In The Jungle • It's Too Late • Puss 'n' Boots • Jet Boy • Human Being

Without the New York Dolls there would have been no Sex Pistols, or Guns 'N' Roses. The Dolls dressed as drag queens and affected both the Stones' cocksure swagger and the Stooges' appetite for self-destruction. But as protopunks they were a few years too early for that bash, while their high-camp image labelled them as faded glam queens who had gatecrashed the party long after the guests had gone. Their endearing amateurishness was seen as simply shambolic in the days before punk and the Stones were still young enough to strut and see off all pretenders to their throne.

The Dolls never stopped bitching about the fact that none of their albums accurately captured them in the raw, but if nothing else this compilation at least preserves their insatiable appetite for an excess of absolutely everything. You also get three previously unreleased tracks and a dozen or more of the most rabid, mongrelized raunch 'n' roll

you are likely to find on record. Get yer mits on it before it's quarantined.

Rating:
Sound ★★★☆☆ Content ★★★★☆
Also recommended:
'Rock 'N' Roll' the definitive compilation (Mercury).
If you like this, why not try:
Johnny Thunders, **Sex Pistols**, **Lou Reed**, **The Rolling Stones**.

Nico

'CHELSEA GIRL'

(Polydor) 1966

Track listing: The Fairest Of The Seasons • These Days • Little Sister • Winter Song • It Was A Pleasure Then • Chelsea Girls • I'll Keep It With Mine • Somewhere There's A Feather • Wrap Your Troubles In Dreams • Eulogy To Lenny Bruce

Nico's romantic liaisons with Alain Delon and Jim Morrison made her an 'underground' celebrity, but it was her contribution to the first Velvet Underground album that ensured the dark-voiced German model and chanteuse legendary status.

'Chelsea Girl', her first solo album, features contributions by Lou Reed and John Cale and is bolstered by songs penned by Bob Dylan and Jackson Browne. Nico intones in the dusky Marianne Faithfull manner accompanied by a small string ensemble and wistful woodwinds; its delicate, coffee-bar ambience is at times pervaded by an air of Gothic gloom that owes more to Grimm's fairy tales than Warhol's surreal dream factory.

Her subsequent albums were far gloomier affairs in which Nico cast herself as a forsaken Miss Haversham figure rooted to her harmonium and shrouded in cobwebs. But 'Chelsea Girl' reveals a fleeting glimpse of the doomed beauty beneath the mask.

Rating:
Sound ★★★★☆ Content ★★★★☆
Also recommended:
'The Marble Index' (WEA), 'Camera Obscura' (Beggars Banquet).
If you like this, why not try:
The Velvet Underground, John Cale, **Leonard Cohen.**

Nirvana

'NEVERMIND'

(DGC) 1991

Track listing: Smells Like Teen Spirit • In Bloom • Come As You Are • Breed • Lithium • Polly • Territorial Pissings • Drain You • Lounge Act • Stay Away • On A Plain • Something In The Way

Nirvana threatened the anonymous dance-dominated music scene of the early nineties with the primal power of grunge, which promised 'real music' for 'real people'. The smouldering intensity of 'Smells Like Teen Spirit' fused a bloody-minded heavy rock riff to the in-your-face rage of hardcore punk. For those over 30 who'd lost their faith in the redemptive power of rock it was musical Viagra and for the MTV generation it offered salvation from girl-power pop puppets and identikit boy bands. Cobain's snarling vocals don't ride on a riff as in a conventional rock

song, but are wedged between a wall of overdriven guitars that surge forward on the chorus then fall back for a subdued verse reflecting the violent mood swings of the proverbial alienated and angry adolescent.

With one full-throated primal scream of an album Nirvana laid waste the previous ten years of synthesized sludge and rendered a roster of stadium rock dinosaurs extinct at a stroke.

Rating:
Sound ★★★★☆ Content ★★★★★

Nirvana

'UNPLUGGED IN NEW YORK'

(Geffen) 1994

Track listing: About A Girl • Come As You Are • Jesus Doesn't Want Me For A Sunbeam • Man Who Sold The World • Pennyroyal Tea • Dumb • Polly • On A Plain • Something In The Way • Plateau • Oh Me • Lake Of Fire • All Apologies • Where Did You Sleep Last Night

'Unplugged' proved that Seattle's finest didn't need wads of volume to convey the rage of a soul in torment. 'Polly', a story of kidnapping and torture, is far more disturbing in this stark acoustic setting where the dispassionate narrative comes across in shock cuts like an episode from the psychic serial killer TV series 'Millennium'. Cobain's gift for melody and unpredictable chord changes are also revealed in a recording that periodically offers the flip side to the numbing pain of

'Nevermind' and offers a glimpse of what might have been had he been able to exorcize his demons.

Rating:
Sound ★★★★☆ Content ★★★★☆
Also recommended:
'In Utero', 'Bleach' and 'The Singles' box set (all on Geffen).
If you like this, why not try:
Stone Temple Pilots, Soundgarden, Alice In Chains, **Smashing Pumpkins**, Foo Fighters.

Oasis

'DEFINITELY MAYBE'

(Creation) 1994

Track listing: Rock N Roll Star • Shakermaker • Live Forever • Up In The Sky • Columbia • Supersonic • Bring It On Down • Cigarettes And Alcohol • Digsy's Dinner • Slide Away • Married With Children

In the early nineties, when the dance-dominated chart was dumbing down with a vengeance, the Gallagher brothers gave a two-fingered salute to synthetic pop and went back to basics. Their brazen self-confidence and commitment made this album's mosaic of sixties and seventies soundbites one of the most profusely melodic and fully realized debut albums for decades. The fact that they had apparently filched every riff, hook and chord progression they fancied from the Lennon and McCartney songbook didn't detract from the quality of the songs which were delivered with the sneering insolence of five 'mad Mancs' who knew that their time had come.

Rating:
Sound ★★★★☆ Content ★★★★★

Oasis

'(WHAT'S THE STORY) MORNING GLORY'

(Creation) 1995

Track listing: Hello • Roll With It • Wonderwall • Don't Look Back In Anger • Hey Now • Some Might Say • Cast No Shadow • She's Electric • Morning Glory • Champagne Supernova

In the summer of '95 Britain was obsessed with a battle royal that for once had nothing to do with the scandals surrounding the House of Windsor, but of the relative merits of the so-called Britpop bands Blur and Oasis. For those over a certain age it revived memories of the Stones and the Beatles, only this time round Oasis sounded like an amalgam of both bands whereas their rivals had more in common with the Kinks.

'Morning Glory' settled the argument in the Gallaghers' favour with four hit singles that attested to the strength and consistent high quality of the material. Again, The Beatles' influence is blatant to the point of plagarism, but the nagging familiarity of the material and the group's stroppy self-confidence made criticism redundant. If this doesn't hit the spot you must be Damon Albarn.

Rating:
Sound ★★★★☆ Content ★★★★★

Oasis

'BE HERE NOW'

(Creation) 1997

Track listing: D'You Know What I Mean? • My Big Mouth • Magic Pie • Stand By Me • I Hope, I Think, I know • The Girl In The Dirty Shirt • Fade In-Out • Don't Go Away • Be Here Now • All Around The World • It's Getting Better (Man) • All Around The World (Reprise)

The disappointment that greeted the group's eagerly awaited third album was almost audible as thousands of gobsmacked punters wondered if they had been sold one of their earlier albums by mistake. No mistake. Oasis now appeared to be pinching ideas from themselves. The feeling of déjà vu is particularly strong on 'All Around The World' with its 'Penny Lane' inspired trumpets and Noel's cameo spot on 'Magic Pie', their token Ringo track this time around. It wouldn't have been so bad if the songs had been up to scratch, but they're tired, threadbare retreads of past (morning) glories.

Rating:
Sound ★★★★☆ Content ★★★☆☆

Oasis

'STANDING ON THE SHOULDER OF GIANTS'

(Big Brother) 2000

Track listing: Fuckin' In The Bushes • Go Let It Out • Who Feels Love? • Put Yer Money Where Yer Mouth Is • Little James • Gas Panic! • Where Did It All Go Wrong? • Sunday Morning Call • I Can See A Liar • Roll It Over

By the time the group came to record 'Giants' their swaggering self-confidence had given way to arrogance and the hunger to be famous that had put fire in their guts had all but been extinguished. The endless recycling of riffs was beginning to give diminishing returns and the stroppy rock star attitude was merely boorish and worse, a bore.

They were no longer cool, merely contrived. In fact, they had become everything that they had once despised.

'Where Did It All Go Wrong?' Indeed.

Rating:
Sound ★★★★☆ Content ★★★☆☆
Also recommended:
'Familiar To Millions' (Creation).
If you like this, why not try:
Ride, **The Rolling Stones, The Beatles, Stereophonics**.

Sinead O'Connor

'I DO NOT WANT WHAT I HAVEN'T GOT'

(Ensign/EMI) 1990

Track Listing: Feel So Different • I Am Stretched On Your Grave • Three Babies • Emperor's New Clothes • Black Boys On Mopeds • Nothing Compares 2 U • Jump In The River • You Cause As Much Sorrow • Last Day Of Our Acquaintance • I Do Not Want What I Haven't Got

A run in with U2 over royalties and a bárrage of tabloid flack for being a single mother, swearing on a Christmas carol, shaving her head and ripping up a photo of the Pope on TV was not enough to faze the fiercely independent Dublin-born songstress who flexed her artistic muscle with this multi-million selling album. The subject of her songs ranges from universal themes such as child abuse, religious hypocrisy, Irish politics and feminist issues in a manner that reflected her provocative, uncompromising nature to intimate personal confessions. But no matter how tiresome her publicity-seeking antics became no one could deny that she possessed a gorgeous voice, one which graces a stunning cover of Prince's 'Nothing Compares 2 U' and ensured that it outsold every hit that its writer had.

Rating:
Sound ★★★★☆ Content ★★★★☆
Also recommended:
'Lion And The Cobra' (Ensign/EMI).
If you like this, why not try:
Dido, Joan Osborne, The Cranberries.

Joan Osborne

'RELISH'

(Blue Gorilla/Mercury) 1995

Track listing: St Teresa • Man In The Long Black Coat • Right Hand Man • Pensacola • Dracula Moon • One Of Us • Ladder • Spider Web • Lets Just Get Naked • Help Me • Crazy Baby • Lumina

If Janis Joplin had come up through the indie 'underground' circuit in the eighties with a taste for off-beat songs would she have made a record like 'Relish'? Such hypothetical questions appear to regularly occupy the mind of Joan Osborne, whose songs consider the question of what Ray Charles would do if he recovered his sight and

what a pickle the Almighty might find himself in if he manifested on earth as a ordinary working Joe. But her unusual subject matter is only half the appeal of the smoky-voiced singer whose songs benefit from a kick-ass backing band and highly imaginative production ideas.

This is an album that just grows better and better with repeated plays.

Rating:
Sound ★★★★☆ Content ★★★★☆
Also recommended:
'Early Recordings' (Mercury).
If you like this, why not try:
Patty Griffin, Janis Joplin, Sheryl Crow, Alanis Morrisette.

Mike Oldfield

'TUBULAR BELLS'

(Virgin) 1973

Track listing: Tubular Bells Pts 1 & 2

Oldfield's multi-layered minimalist soundscape involved 1,000 individual overdubs and took the 20 year-old multi-instrumentalist six months of studio time to complete. The two sections are developed in architectural fashion as additional parts are added to a simple repeated theme. But the themes are never developed beyond a riff and variations and for that reason it lacks the depth and dynamics of music by such contemporary composers as Michael Nyman and Philip Glass. However, at the time it was distinctly different, appealing to those who liked both rock and classical music, or to those who had simply been entranced by its hypnotic quality. It provided the financial foundation of Richard Branson's business empire and established the formula for the whole New Age genre which provides soothing instrumental music for meditation. But it was significant for another reason – the appearance of Viv Stanshall as the eccentric master of ceremonies in the final section, which proved that hippies really do have a sense of humour.

Rating:
Sound ★★★★☆ Content ★★★★☆

Mike Oldfield

'HERGEST RIDGE'

(Virgin) 1974

Track listing: Hergest Ridge Pts 1 & 2

Oldfield's romanticism was clearly unsullied by reality, but then he could afford to be optimistic. 'Tubular Bells' had bought him his own 24-track studio and the home in the hills where this second album was recorded. But it isn't merely 'Tubular Bells Pt 2', although many of the elements from that first album feature here. This is one musician's attempt to distil the spirit of those innocent days of the late sixties into a verdant pastorale. Even Oldfield's aimless ambient offerings of later years wouldn't diminish this achievement.

Rating:
Sound ★★★☆☆ Content ★★★★☆

Also recommended:
'Ommadawn' and 'The Complete Mike Oldfield' 2CD set (both on Virgin).
If you like this, why not try:
Michael Nyman, Philip Glass, The Orb.

Orchestral Manoeuvres In The Dark

'DAZZLE SHIPS'

(Virgin) 1983

Track listing: Radio Prague • Genetic Engineering • ABC Auto Industry • Telegraph • This Is Helena • International • Romance Of The Telescope • Silent Running • Dazzle Ships • Radio Waves • Time Zones • Of All The Things We've Made

With their knack for writing catchy pop singles and their preference for analogue synthesizers OMD brought a warm neon glow to the austere inner-city soundscape that was associated with electro-pop. Their initial influence had been Kraftwerk, but unlike the Germans, the duo looked to the past for inspiration rather than the future and it was this, plus a certain epic quality, that offset the clinical sterility of their electronic instrumentation.

'Dazzle Ships' presents another immaculate collection of tunes that was once summed up as 'the human interface between electronics and pop'.

Rating:
Sound ★★★★☆ Content ★★★★☆
Also recommended:
'Architecture And Morality', 'Junk Culture' and 'Sugar Tax' (all on Virgin).
If you like this, why not try:
Kraftwerk, The Human League, Tangerine Dream.

The Only Ones

'THE ONLY ONES'

(CBS) 1978

Track listing: Whole Of The Law • Another Girl, Another Planet • Breaking Down • City Of Fun • Beast • Creature Of Doom • It's The Truth • Language Problem • No Peace For The Wicked • Immortal Story

The Only Ones had a lot going for them – Peter Perrett's precious, heavily enunciated drawl, a set of too-good-to-be-true tunes and Columbia's marketing muscle. But what they didn't have was luck, or at least enough of it to see them through the internal wrangling and chemical abuse that led to their premature demise in '81. 'Another Girl, Another Planet' was one of the era's most stimulating singles, but it wasn't the hit that it deserved to be until 15 years later.

Perrett's world-weary cynicism and the group's ragged glam chic put them somewhere between The New York Dolls and the *Rocky Horror Picture Show* while his heroin habit consigned them to the 'if only...' file.

Rating:
Sound ★★★☆☆ Content ★★★★★
Also recommended:
'Even Serpents Shine' (CBS), the compilation 'Special View' (Epic) and Perrett's solo outing 'Wake Up Sticky' (Demon).
If you like this, why not try:
The Soft Boys, Lou Reed, Knox, Vibrators, Buzzcocks.

The Orb

'THE ORB'S ADVENTURES BEYOND THE ULTRAWORLD'

2 CDs (Big World/Island) 1991

Track listing: Little Fluffy Clouds • Earth • Supernova At The End Of The Universe • Back Side Of The Moon • Spanish Castles In Space • Perpetual Dream • Into The Fourth Dimension • Outlands • Star 6 & 7 8 9 • A Huge Ever Growing Pulsating Brain That Rules From The Centre Of The Ultraworld

If anyone had suggested that Pink Floyd would become fashionable again in the nineties they would have been strapped into a straitjacket and given a one-way ticket to the funny farm. But that is effectively what happened when remix DJ Alex Paterson formed an ambient house collective with his mates, KLF's Jimmy Cauty, Killing Joke bassist Youth and Glastonbury relic Steve Hillage, to create aural Prozac for clubland's chill-out rooms. Of course, The Orb are much more than cosmic rock revivalists, as the healthy dose of self-effacing humour on 'Back Side Of The Moon' attests. Dance, dub reggae and funky grooves provide a departure point for aural excursions into another dimension where hippies, punks and clubbers share a spliff and discuss the significance of the symbolism in *2001: A Space Odyssey*.

Rating:
Sound ★★★★☆ Content ★★★★☆

The Orb

'UFORB'

(Island) 1996

Track listing: OOBE • UFOrb • Blue Room • Towers Of Dub • Close Encounters • Majestic • Sticky End

When you're chilling out, time has no meaning. It certainly didn't concern The Orb who let the grooves run their course to make 'UFOrb' a sprawling triple album and earning the 40-minute 'Blue Room', its place as the longest single in recording history. On the latter Jah Wobble provides a sinewy reggae bass line for the heavily textured keyboards and soundbites to surf. Otherwise, the structure is non-existent, the samples coming in and out of focus at random and the pulse simulating that of a comatose clubber whose dancing days are done, but the light show inside his or her head is, to borrow a phrase, 'something else'. Quite what that something might be only those on a higher plane of consciousness could tell us. Listen to this while waiting for them to land.

Rating:
Sound ★★★★☆ Content ★★★★☆
Also recommended:
'Pomme Fritz' (Island).
If you like this, why not try:
Tangerine Dream, **Pink Floyd**, Spiritualized, **Orbital**.

Orbital

'IN SIDES'

(Internal) 1996

Track listing: Girl With The Sun In Her Hair • Petrol • Box • Dwr Budr • Adnans • Out There Somewhere • Saint

Each and every weekend during the summer of '88 brothers Paul and Phil Hartnoll set out from their home in Kent in search of the ultimate rave, cruising the London bypass from which they would later take the name of their 'band'. Their first two self-titled albums are archetypal techno – with loops created from hardcore punk, Hi-NRG dance grooves and industrial strength electro-pop overlays. But by the time they came to record 'Snivilisation' sonic experimentation was less a case of cut-and-paste, more an organic process with the tracks growing from the seed of an idea or sample. The process culminated with 'In Sides', arguably their most fully realised album to date, which offered aural explorations into the unknown regions of acid-house at a less frantic and intense pace than on previous excursions and even boasted a unifying theme. On 'Out There Somewhere' they send the audience into a state bordering on suspended animation before bringing them back to consciousness with a jolt to view the brave new world that they have created. Also included is an edit of 'The Box', their 28-minute 'single' featuring a harpsichord figure that might have been lifted from a sixties spy spoof supplemented with a montage of kitsch horror movie effects.

If you want a leisurely psychedelic trip into the unconscious, then you might be better off with The Orb because the Hartnoll brothers are offering an alternate view of reality and want you to be fully conscious to appreciate the scenery.

Rating:
Sound ★★★★☆ Content ★★★★☆

Orbital

'THE MIDDLE OF NOWHERE'

(FFRR) 2000

Track listing: Way Out • Spare Parts Express • Know Where To Run • I Don't Know You People • Otono • Nothing Left • Nothing Left 2 • Style

The Hartnoll Brothers turn their backs on the searing arid heat of ambient desert landscapes and the solitude of deep space for the primitive rhythms of the urban jungle on an album that has been aptly described as 'a soundtrack in search of a movie'. If it ever finds the film in question it's likely to be a big, mean monster movie for the brother's music still has bite and the beast's hunger is far from satiated. To tell the truth, it's a bit of a mongrel – elements of

Kraftwerk creep into 'Spare Parts Express', strands of Tangerine Dream are evident on 'Style' and there are echoes of the duo's earlier albums scattered like bait to lure us into its jaws. Hell, there are even strings and irreverent soundbites from kitsch acts like Dollar and Erasure to persuade us that the beast has been tamed. But the beats still hammer down harder than Godzilla and if you don't treat this disc with respect it's likely to slobber all over you.

Rating:
Sound ★★★☆☆ Content ★★★☆☆
Also recommended:
'In Sides', 'Snivilisation' and 'Orbital ll'.
If you like this, why not try:
The Orb, Leftfield, Future Sound Of London.

Ozzy Osbourne

'BLIZZARD OF OZ'

(Epic) 1980

Track listing: I Don't Know • Crazy Train • Goodbye To Romance • Dee • Suicide Solution • Mr Crowley • No Bone Movies • Revelation • Steal Away

All aboard the ghost train for a white knuckle ride with Ozzy (late of his Satanic Majesty's favourite band, Black Sabbath), but hold on tight as 'the madman' is going off the rails and we're going with him. Oz has a bad reputation for biting the heads off bats and urinating on national monuments, acts that have not endeared him to America's moral majority. But he's really quite a cuddly old devil and his albums are more schlock-horror than satanic.

He's not averse to sending himself up something rotten, as he does on the opener. 'What's the future of mankind. How do I know, I got left behind... Don't look at me for answers. Don't ask me – I don't know.' But if he has got his tongue wedged firmly in his cheek his band certainly play it straight, hewing monumental slabs of hard rock till you can almost smell the sweat. The late Randy Rhoads (who was killed in a plane crash two years after recording this album) was a graduate of the Van Halen school of guitar soloing, which means that he managed to squeeze more notes out of the guitar than it's physically possible to hear.

And as for Ozzy, he sings as if he was trying to summon up old Beelzebub himself. So brace yourself, it's going to be a bumpy ride.

Rating:
Sound ★★★☆☆ Content ★★★☆☆
Also recommended:
'Bark At The Moon', 'Diary Of A Madman' and the live all Sabbath set 'Speak Of The Devil' (all on Epic/CBS).
If you like this, why not try:
Black Sabbath, Motorhead, Metallica.

Carl Perkins

'THE SUN YEARS'

3 CDs (Charly) 1989

Track listing: Honky Tonk Babe • Honky Tonk Gal • Movie Magg • Turn Around • Gone Gone Gone (2 takes) • You Can't Make Love To Somebody • Dixie Bop • Perkins Wiggle • Let The Jukebox Keep On Playing • What You Doin' When You're Crying • You Can't Make Love To Somebody • Everybody's Trying To Be My Baby • Right String Baby • Only You • Sure To Fall • Tennessee • Blue Suede Shoes (2 takes) • Honey Don't • Boppin' The Blues • All Mama's Children • Everybody's Trying To Be My Baby • Put Your Cat Clothes On • Dixie Fried • Put Your Cat Clothes On • That Don't Move Me • I Sorry I'm Not Sorry • Put Your Cat Clothes On • Matchbox • Your True Love • Put Your Cat Clothes On • Million Dollar Session (extracts) • Lonely Street • Keeper Of The Key • Sweethearts Or Strangers • Be Honest With Me • Calodonia • Her Love Rubbed Off • Roll Over Beethoven • You Can Do No Wrong • Pink Pedal Pushers • That's Right • Forever Yours • I Care • Y.O.U. • Try My Heart Out • Look At That Moon • Lend Me Your Comb • Glad All Over • Movie Magg • Turn Around • Let The Jukebox Keep On Playing • Gone Gone Gone • Blue Suede Shoes • Honey Don't • Sure To Fall • Tennessee • Boppin' The Blues • All Mama's Children • Dixie Fried • I'm Sorry I'm Not Sorry • Matchbox • Your True Love • That's Right • Forever Yours • Lend Me Your Comb • Glad All Over • Everybody's Trying To Be My Baby • Only You • Right String Baby • Radio Advert • Pink Pedal Pushers • Breakin' My Heart • Take Back My Love • Instrumental Medley • Down By The Riverside • Drink Up And Go Home • Somebody Tell Me

Forget the glut of budget-priced compilations which promise to summarize Carl's career on a single CD and instead invest in this comprehensive and competitively priced 3CD set which contains every song that he recorded for Sun between 1954–57.

Carl was playing country rock at honky tonks and hoe downs years before Elvis entered the recording studio, but it wasn't until Elvis had a nationwide hit with a cover of 'Blue Suede Shoes' that Carl's career began to gather momentum. Tragically, he was invalided out of the race for fame by a horrific car crash in 1956 and had to be content with cult status as the original rockabilly rebel for the rest of his days. However, his place in rock's Hall Of Fame is assured thanks to half a dozen self-penned standards and an economic guitar style which has influenced successive generations of would-be guitar stars.

On these tracks Carl and his band re-create a Saturday night barn dance atmosphere live in the studio with the only concession to technical sophistication being the distinctive 'slap-back' split-second tape delay that became a trademark for all the Sun recordings. So, put your cat clothes on, dust off your brothel creepers and get Dixie fried.

Rating:
Sound ★★★☆☆ Content ★★★★☆
Also recommended:
'Boppin' Blue Suede Shoes' (Charly).
If you like this, why not try:
Eddie Cochran, Chuck Berry, Billy Lee Riley, Johnny Burnette.

Pearl Jam

'10'

(Epic) 1992

Track listing: Once • Even Flow • Alive • Why Go • Black • Jeremy • Oceans • Porch • Garden • Deep • Release

Seattle's finest were first falsely accused of being retro-retentives by Kurt Cobain and were then slagged off for jumping aboard the grunge bandwagon in the wake of Cobain's death. In truth, they are simply the latest manifestation of the primeval power that galvanizes rock whenever it gets complacent or too serious for its own good. '10' harnesses that power in a ferocious synthesis of hard rock and punk to articulate the pain and frustration of a generation disenfranchised by MTV and the major labels' mass marketing of music. However, the most affecting tracks are those inspired by Eddie Vedder's own childhood traumas, 'Jeremy' and 'Alive', on which Vedder vents his rage to Mike McCready's mournful Hendrix-styled guitar lines.

Rating:
Sound ★★★★☆ Content ★★★☆☆

Pearl Jam

'VS'

(Epic) 1993

Track listing: Go • Animal • Daughter • Glorified G • Dissident • W.M.A. • Blood • Rearview Mirror • Rats • Elderly Woman Behind The Counter In A Small Town • Leash • Indifference

If anyone expected Vedder to have mellowed following the success of 'Ten' they were soon set straight. Token ballads such as 'Daughter' offer only temporary respite from the savage battering dealt out by the likes of 'Go', 'Animal' and 'Blood' as the group justify their name and their unshakable status as the prime exponents of the Seattle sound.

This is the kind of album that prowls around inside its cover like a hungry predator. Be careful where you let it loose.

Rating:
Sound ★★★★☆ Content ★★★★☆
Also recommended:
'Live' and their collaboration with Neil Young 'Mirrorball' (Warners).
If you like this, why not try:
Alice In Chains, Soundgarden, Stone Temple Pilots.

Pet Shop Boys

'VERY'

(Parlophone) 1995

Track listing: Can You Forgive Her • I Wouldn't Normally Do This Kind Of Thing • Liberation • Different Point Of View • Dreaming Of The Queen • Yesterday When I Was Mad • Theatre • One And One Make Five • To Speak Is A Sin • Young Offender • One In A Million • Go West

With their fifth album Neil Tennant and Chris Lowe dispelled the myth that synth groups have no soul. 'Very' is the epitome of pop-synth sophistication, but it's also an album of uncommon emotional depth. The sounds may be manufactured, but they

are orchestrated to convey compassion for the cast of characters who are experiencing the highs and lows of modern love. These include a married man struggling to come to terms with his own homosexual nature in 'Can You Forgive Her?' and the homeless outcasts of 'Theatre' who are forced to sleep rough in the streets. The sense of life as a pageant of tragic-comic episodes gives the album its humanity that is enhanced by both the detailed descriptions and the ornate symphonic arrangements. But for all their artistic aspirations and nouvelle baroque music Neil and Lowe never forget that their audience also wants to dance.

Rating:
Sound ★★★★☆ Content ★★★★☆

Pet Shop Boys

'DISCOGRAPHY'

(EMI) 1991

Track listing: West End Girls • Love Comes Quickly • Opportunities • Suburbia • It's A Sin • What Have I Done To Deserve This • Rent • Always On My Mind • Heart • Domino Dancing • Left To My Own Devices • It's Alright • So Hard • Being Boring • Where The Streets Have No Name • Jealousy • DJ Culture • Was It Worth It?

On their early hits Tennant and Lowe serve up a frothy, synth-pop confection with a sprinkling of irony, but the lush orchestrated electronics and infectious dance beats can't conceal the fact that they are, in essence, two songsmiths in the Tin Pan Alley tradition. Whereas 'West End Girls', 'Opportunities' and 'Suburbia' exhibit an ironic detachment, the somewhat camp theatrical quality of their later material clearly owes as much to the Broadway musical as it does to disco. Their elaborate stage shows also reflect this infatuation with pop as a performance art, but their lyrics don't flinch from examining 'uncomfortable' subjects such as homelessness and obsessive homosexual love with the emotional astuteness of a Jacques Brel or Stephen Sondheim. This 18-track compilation concentrates almost exclusively on their impeccably tasteful three-minute singles, so you'll need to supplement it with at least one of their other albums to appreciate what lies beneath the surface sheen.

Rating:
Sound ★★★★☆ Content ★★★★☆
Also recommended:
'Behaviour' and 'Very' (both on Parlophone).
If you like this, why not try:
Depeche Mode, OMD, Erasure.

Tom Petty

'GREATEST HITS'

(MCA) 1993

Track listing: American Girl • Breakdown • Anything That's Rock 'n' Roll • Listen To Her Heart • I Need To Know • Refugee • Don't Do Me Like That • Even The Losers • Here Comes My Girl • Waiting • You Got Lucky • Don't Come Around Here No More • I Won't Back Down • Runnin' Down A Dream • Free Fallin' • Learning To Fly • Into The Great Wide Open • Mary Jane's Last Dance • Something In The Air

Petty's unassuming songs rarely use more than four chords, but they can catch you unawares with their sharp

little hooks and nag at the back of your mind. Petty updated The Byrds' 12-string chiming guitar sound and shares both McGuinn's nasal drawl and also his habit of bolstering every song with a killer middle-eight, which another artist might have kept as the chorus to a new song. McGuinn returned the compliment by covering 'American Girl', which sounds more like The Byrds than The Byrds did in their latter years. But although there were occasional attempts to restyle Petty's laidback, blue collar music for the MTV generation, (with the Dave Stewart-produced 'Mary Jane's Last Dance' and Jeff Lynne's contribution to 'Into The Great Wide Open'), he remains firmly entrenched in the sixties. Reliable, if uninspiring.

Rating:
Sound ★★★★☆ Content ★★★★☆
Also recommended:
'Damn The Torpedos' (MCA).
If you like this, why not try:
The Steve Miller Band, The Cars, The Byrds.

Wilson Pickett

'THE VERY BEST OF...'

(Atlantic) 1993

Track listing: In The Midnight Hour • 634 5789 • Land Of A Thousand Dances • Mustang Sally • Funky Broadway • I'm In Love • She's Looking Good • Hey Jude • Sugar Sugar • Engine No 9 • Don't Let The Green Grass Fool You • Don't Knock My Love • Fire And Water • I'm A Midnight Mover • I Found A Love • Everybody Needs Somebody To Love

When 'The Wicked Pickett', as they called him, saw Sam Cooke and Aretha

Franklin crossing the tracks into the musical mainstream of the 'Hot 100' in the early sixties he promptly left the gospel group that he had formed and invited the nation's nubile young ladies to party. From that first secular session when Pickett emitted his distinctive feral growl it was obvious that he wouldn't be satisfied just holding their hands. His vocal wasn't merely raw, it crowed of passion incarnate. He was aided and abetted in his attempted seduction by Memphis' ace session men who oiled the wheels and stoked the furnaces for the Stax soul factory. Together they worked up some of the steamiest soul sides to make it to wax.

If some of the selections on this CD, such as the covers of 'Hey Jude', the Archies' bubblegum hit 'Sugar Sugar' and Free's 'Fire And Water', seem incongruous fear not, 'The Wicked Pickett' could make even 'Jack And Jill' sound like a salacious tale of sexual misadventure. However, the inclusion of the rare early Doo Wop single 'I Found A Love' was a mistake as it's been transferred from a (very) well-worn disc.

Rating:
Sound ★★★☆☆ Content ★★★☆☆
Also recommended:
'Man And A Half' a double CD set and 'The Best Of...' a single CD with a slightly different track listing to the issue described above (both on Atlantic).
If you like this, why not try:
Otis Redding, Sam And Dave, *The Commitments* original soundtrack.

Pink Floyd

'RELICS'

(EMI) 1995

Track listing: Arnold Layne • Interstellar Overdrive • See Emily Play • Remember A Day • Paint Box • Julia Dream • Careful With That Axe, Eugene • Cirrus Minor • The Nile Song • Biding My Time • Bike

Psychedelia flowered in California during the late sixties, but its seeds were swiftly scattered across Europe with England proving particularly fertile ground, no doubt because of the tradition for opium-induced inspiration among the literati.

Syd Barrett, a prodigously imaginative eccentric came down from Cambridge to the capital in the winter of '65 with the idea of combining Alice In Wonderland whimsy with mind-expanding music and formed Pink Floyd for the purpose.

'Relics' is a collection of antiques and curiosities from Floyd's formative years before their sonic experimentations became excessively self-indulgent. Included are the two classic psychpop singles, 'Arnold Layne' and 'See Emily Play' from the brief period with Barrett, a couple of choice cuts from the film soundtrack 'More', 'Careful With That Axe, Eugene' from the patchy 'Ummagumma' and the languid pastoral psychedelia of 'Julia Dream', which was the flip side of an obscure early single. In all, an essential supplement to the albums.

Rating:
Sound ★★★☆☆ Content ★★★★☆

Pink Floyd

'PIPER AT THE GATES OF DAWN'

(EMI) 1967

Track listing: Astronomy Domine • Lucifer Sam • Matilda Mother • Flaming • Pow R. Toc H • Take Up Thy Stethoscope And Walk • Interstellar Overdrive • The Gnome • Chapter 24 • Scarecrow • Bike

Syd titled the band's first album after a chapter in Kenneth Grahame's perennially popular children's story, *The Wind in the Willows*, and took further inspiration from nursery rhymes, music hall novelties and the surreal imagery fuelled by his acid-induced visions. His shorter songs, 'Matilda Mother', 'The Gnome', 'Scarecrow' and 'Bike', exhibit a child-like wonder which has lost little of its charm over the years, while 'Interstellar Overdrive', an extended, freeform instrumental freakout, featured his uniquely fractured guitar style and hinted at the direction the group's later sonic excursions would take.

Rating:
Sound ★★★★☆ Content ★★★★☆

Pink Floyd

'DARK SIDE OF THE MOON'

(EMI) 1972

Track listing: Speak To Me • Breathe • On The Run • Time • The Great Gig In The Sky • Money • Us And Them • Any Colour You Like • Brain Damage • Eclipse

In the 30 years since its initial release, 26 million copies of 'Dark Side Of The Moon' have been sold worldwide, with an estimated one in five British homes owning either the LP or the CD. In the early seventies it was the album for serious rock fans to be seen with – the LP that defined album-orientated rock — and in the late eighties it was the top selling CD, being an obvious choice for putting a new CD player through its paces. For 11 consecutive years it remained lodged in the American album charts, which is a staggering achievement for a record whose theme is the apparent futility of life, madness, disillusionment, decay and death.

One of its most distinctive features is the collage of sound effects and soundbites including heartbeats, manic laughter, ticking clocks and even an aircrash which help the tracks melt seamlessly into one another, encouraging the listener to experience the album as a whole rather than dipping in and out to sample a favourite track. But although it has a cohesion several titles stand out; 'The Great Gig In The Sky' with its soaring soprano and elegant piano, the instantly identifiable cash register motif on 'Money' and the cathartic climax 'Brain Damage' and 'Eclipse'.

Roger Waters' songs of 'quiet desperation' and Dave Gilmour's precision guitar solos are cushioned by lush keyboards and arresting sound effects to create an album for those who have outgrown pop, but who have little taste for the demands of classical music.

Rating:
Sound ★★★★☆ Content ★★★★★

Pink Floyd

'WISH YOU WERE HERE'

(EMI) 1975

Track listing: Shine On You Crazy Diamond (Pt 1) • Welcome To The Machine • Have A Cigar • Wish You Were Here • Shine On You Crazy Diamond (Pt 2)

It took two years for Floyd to produce the follow up to 'Dark Side Of The Moon', during which they nearly split under the strain. When 'Wish You Were Here' was finally released it inevitably suffered from comparisons with its predecessor, but can now be seen as an assured, mature work featuring some of Gilmour's most fluent solos and even a rare moment of humour in 'Have A Cigar'. The key track is, however, 'Shine On You Crazy Diamond', an affectionate two-part tribute to the group's lamented leader Syd Barrett which was inspired by his unexpected visit to the studio when he is said to have announced that he was ready to do his bit.

Rating:
Sound ★★★★☆ Content ★★★★☆

Pink Floyd

'THE WALL'

2 CDs (EMI) 1979

Track listing: In The Flesh • Thin Ice • Another Brick In The Wall Pt 1 • Happiest Days Of Our Lives • Another Brick In The Wall Pt 2 • Mother • Goodbye Blue Sky • Empty Spaces • Young Lust • One Of My Turns • Don't Leave Me Now • Another Brick In The Wall Pt 3 • Goodbye Cruel World • Hey You • Is There Anybody Out There • Nobody Home • Vera • Bring The Boys Back Home • Comfortably Numb • Show Must Go On • In The Flesh • Run Like Hell • Waiting For The Worms • Trial • Outside The Wall

By the late seventies Floyd were designated for extinction with the rest of rock's dinosaurs, but returned like Godzilla to stomp all over the spiky-haired upstarts who had rejoiced in their (premature) demise. Against all the odds this weighty double album topped the American album charts for four months and spawned the group's only post-Barrett hit single, 'Another Brick In The Wall'. The songs were cut from the same cloth as 'Dark Side' and 'Wish You Were Here' ('Comfortably Numb' and 'Run Like Hell' being particularly powerful) and the musicianship was impeccable, but the subject matter was unremittingly bleak and being spread over two CDs it made for particularly heavy going.

The resulting film directed by Alan Parker and starring Bob Geldof as the demented rock star was only partly successful, but the subsequent all-star stage production at the site of the Berlin Wall in 1990 was one conceit too many and almost buried the band for good.

Rating:
Sound ★★★★★ Content ★★★★☆
Also recommended:
'A Saucerful Of Secrets', 'Animals' and 'The Delicate Sound Of Thunder', a live 2CD set (all on EMI).
If you like this, why not try:
The Orb, Syd Barrett's solo albums, Spiritualized.

The Pixies

'BOSSANOVA'

(4AD) 1990

Track listing: Cecilia Ann • Velouria • Is She Weird • All Over The World • Down To The Well • Blown Away • Stormy Weather • Rock Music • Alison • Ana • Dig For Fire • Happening • Hang Wire • Havalina

Boston garage band the Pixies made hardcore for the intellect with a sound composed of rib-rattling bass, a guitar as penetrating as a dentist's drill and oblique references to extraterrestrials. But although it's a relatively painless process to identify the individual elements that made them the most popular indie outfit since the Smiths, they remain stubbornly indefinable. It's like trying to describe *The X-Files* to your granny. Their music is as unpredictable as their frontman, Black Francis, whose whisper-to-a-scream approach to the art of singing will ensure that these 14 songs will burrow into your brain and nag at the nerves like an alien implant.

Rating:
Sound ★★★★☆ Content ★★★★☆
Also recommended:
'Surfer Rosa', 'Doolittle' and 'Trompe Le Monde' (all on 4AD).
If you like this, why not try:
Husker Dü, **The Smiths**, The Breeders.

The Pogues

'RUM, SODOMY AND THE LASH'

(WEA) 1985

Track listing: Sick Bed Of Cuchulainn • The Old Main Drag • Wild Cats Of Kilkenny • I'm A Man You Don't Meet Everyday • A Pair Of Brown Eyes • Sally Mac Lenanne • A Pistol For Paddy Garcia • Dirty Old Town • Jesse James • Navigator • Billie's Bones • The Gentleman Soldier • And The Band Played Waltzing Matilda

The title of the album is taken from Winston Churchill's pithy description of navy life and the band's name from the Gaelic word for a universal insult. Both were well chosen and evocative of the beating meted out to traditional Irish music by MacGowan and his mates in the name of punk. Once they'd kicked the shit out of smug, pipe-smoking folk they got it back on its feet, dusted it down and taught it a few new tricks, tempering their drunken revelry with sober, barfly ballads which are unvarnished by sentiment. Their covers of Ewan MacColl's 'Dirty Old Town' and Eric Bogle's 'Waltzing Matilda' make both relevant for a new generation and MacGowan's contributions hint at a potential that was later drowned in booze. But it's Kate O'Riordon's moving 'Man You Don't Meet Everyday' which still gets grown men gurning into their Guinness.

If ever rock gives up the ghost and needs a good send off The Pogues will surely play at its wake.

Rating:
Sound ★★★★☆ Content ★★★★★

Also recommended:
'If I Should Fall From Grace With God' (WEA).
If you like this, why not try:
The Clash, **Van Morrison**, **Billy Bragg**.

The Police

'REGATTA DE BLANC'

(A&M) 1978

Track listing: Message In A Bottle • Regatta de Blanc • It's All Right For You • Bring On The Night • Deathwish • Walking On The Moon • On Any Other Day • Bed's Too Big Without You • Contact • Does Everyone Stare • No Time This Time

Sting, Summers and Copeland followed their audacious debut, 'Outlandos d'Amour', with a more accomplished sequel, although they couldn't disguise the haste with which it had been assembled. Copeland contributed three songs that were strictly second division while another track had been lifted from the B-side of an earlier single. But in mitigation there is a quartet of certified classics culled from their directory of 'white reggae' riddims and played with their usual surgical precision, if little passion. 'The Bed's Too Big Without You', 'Bring On The Night', 'Message In A Bottle' and 'Walking On The Moon' are cleverly crafted from a mosaic of fractured chords and shimmering guitar harmonics which are allied to some of the most infectious melodies in the pop repertoire. Add a ream of unusually erudite lyrics delivered in Sting's chilly, translucent falsetto and all accusations of sterility can be dropped.

Rating:
Sound ★★★★☆ Content ★★★★☆
Also recommended:
'Outlandos d'Amour', 'Synchronicity', 'Ghost In The Machine' and 'Greatest Hits' (all on A&M).
If you like this, why not try:
Sly and Robbie, **Bob Marley**, **The Clash**, Sting's solo albums.

Portishead

'DUMMY'

(Go Discs) 1994

Track listing: Mysterons • Sour Times • Strangers • It Could Be Sweet • Wandering Star • Numb • Roads • Pedestal • Biscuit • Glory Box

Portishead emerged from the same Bristol club scene that spawned Tricky and Massive Attack with a sultry, melancholic mosaic of sound evocative of sixties cold war spy thrillers. Geoff Barrow supplied the ambient, atmospheric soundtrack comprised of reedy Hammond organs, guitars drenched in reverb and soundbites sampled from SF movies and soul records, which is embellished by Beth Gibbons' bewitching siren song. The tracks merge into one another to form a contemporary classical soundtrack to urban paranoia that is as distant from 'traditional' rock as it is possible to be. The very definition, in fact, of the kind of record that will haunt both your waking hours and your dreams.

Rating:
Sound ★★★★☆ Content ★★★★☆

Also recommended:
'Portishead' (Go Discs).
If you like this, why not try:
Massive Attack, Neneh Cherry.

Elvis Presley

'THE SUN SESSIONS'

(RCA) 1987

Track listing: That's All Right • Blue Moon Of Kentucky • Good Rockin' Tonight • I Don't Care If The Sun Don't Shine • Milkcow Blues Boogie • You're A Heartbreaker • Baby Let's Play House • I'm Left, You're Right, She's Gone • Mystery Train • I Forgot To Remember To Forget • I Love You Because • Blue Moon • Tomorrow Night • I'll Never Let You Go • Just Because • Trying To Get To You

Bonus tracks: Harbor Lights • I Love You Because • That's All Right • Blue Moon Of Kentucky • I Don't Care If The Sun Don't Shine • I'm Left, Your Right, She's Gone • I'll Never Let You Go • When It Rains It Really Pours • I Love You Because (2 alternate takes) • I'm Left, You're Right, She's Gone (2 alternate takes)

'The Sun Sessions' records the birth pangs of rock and roll one sultry summer night in July 1954. While the tapes are rolling 19-year-old Memphis truck driver Elvis Aaron Presley and his hillbilly friends can be heard horsing around, boogie-ing up some country tunes and accidentally stumbling upon that elusive sound that studio owner Sam Philips once boasted would make him a million dollars. It's the inarticulate holler of the illegitimate offspring of white country music and black urban blues which they later christened rockabilly and it's aching to rock the house.

At one point between takes of 'That's All Right Mama' Sam can be heard asking the group what it is that they're doing. 'We don't know,' admits Scotty with obvious embarrassment. 'Well, back up,' says Sam in a state of excitement, 'and do it again.'

Rockabilly was dynamite, a spontaneous combustion of sound that could barely be contained, but if the rednecks heard a white boy singing 'nigga' music and corrupting white folks Sam feared they might lynch the lot of them. So he underwrote the risk by asking Elvis, Scotty and Bill to record a country tune for the flip side of every single. These brought out Elvis' rustic, mom's-apple-pie southern boyish charm, but there's also a hint of yearning from his God-fearin' gospel Baptist background and a barely suppressed sexuality smouldering beneath the shy exterior. It was this volatile combination that made Elvis and these recordings unique. This is where it all began.

Rating:
Sound ★★★☆☆ Content ★★★★★

Elvis Presley

'ALL TIME GREATEST HITS'

2 CDs (RCA) 1987

Track listing: Heartbreak Hotel • Blue Suede Shoes • Hound Dog • Love Me Tender • Too Much • All Shook Up • Teddy Bear • Paralysed • Party • Jailhouse Rock • Don't • Wear My Ring Around Your Neck • Hard Headed Woman • King Creole • One Night • A Fool Such As I • A Big Hunk O' Love • Stuck On You • The Girl Of My Best Friend • It's Now Or Never • Are You Lonesome Tonight • Wooden Heart •

Surrender • His Latest Flame • Can't Help Falling In Love • Good Luck Charm • She's Not You • Return To Sender • Devil In Disguise • Crying In The Chapel • Love Letters • If I Can Dream • In The Ghetto • Suspicious Minds • Don't Cry Daddy • The Wonder Of You • I Just Can't Help Believin' • An American Trilogy • Burning Love • Always On My Mind • My Boy • Suspicion • Moody Blue • Way Down • It's Only Love

Elvis' influence on popular music is incalculable, despite the fact that he didn't write a single one of these perennially popular hits, nor did he develop the music that he helped to create much beyond the initial prototype. But the dozens of sides that he cut for Sun and RCA before he was conscripted into the army in 1958 define rock and roll. When he returned he made some fine pop singles, but they lacked the raw excitement of the early records. After his last truly great single, 'Return To Sender', the King effectively abdicated in favour of the next generation and passed the sixties in second-rate movies and the seventies in Las Vegas before moving on to the great gig in the sky. Meanwhile the music moved on under its own momentum, but it was Elvis who first shook 'em up.

You may think that you're familiar with these tracks – perhaps overly familiar – but you haven't really heard them until you've wrapped your ears around these pristine, remastered sides.

This is rock and roll heaven. Don't wait until you die to enjoy it.

Rating:
Sound ★★★★☆ Content ★★★★★

Also recommended:
'The Fifties Masters' a 4CD box set including previously unreleased tracks or selected highlights on the single CD 'Elvis 56' (both on RCA).
If you like this, why not try:
Robert Gordon, **Jerry Lee Lewis**, **Carl Perkins**, Billy Lee Riley, Warren Smith.

The Pretenders

'THE SINGLES'

(WEA) 1987

Track listing: Stop Your Sobbing • Kid • Brass In Pocket • Talk Of The Town • Go To Sleep • Day After Day • Message Of Love • Back On The Chain Gang • Middle Of The Road • 2000 Miles • Show Me • The Thin Line Between Love And Hate • Don't Get Me Wrong • Hymn To Her • My Baby • I Got You Babe • What You Gonna Do About It

Former *NME* journalist Chrissie Hynde formed The Pretenders in '78 to subvert the traditional macho rock star image with her contemptuous independent attitude and with the intention of processing punk into pop.

She possessed a voice that would have got a rise out of a celibate monk and she wrote a string of classic songs that transposed sixties pop sensibilities into the post-punk vernacular. Her choice of covers revealed an infatuation with The Kinks which eventually evolved into a personal relationship with Ray Davies with whom she shared a talent for writing sharp-tongued and concise 'commercial' songs. But she was also fortunate to have recruited one of the best backlines in the business with Honeyman-Scott's sparse and subtle lead providing the perfect complement to her fluid rhythm guitar.

'The Singles' is a 17-part lesson in crafting perfect pop, although you'll need the original albums to get crucial cuts such as 'Precious', 'Tattooed Love Boys' and 'The Adulteress.'

Rating:
Sound ★★★★☆ Content ★★★★☆
Also recommended:
'The Pretenders' and 'The Pretenders II' (both on WEA).
If you like this, why not try:
Texas, Blondie, Elvis Costello, Garbage.

The Pretty Things

'SINGLES 1967–1971'

(See For Miles) 1996

Track listing: Defecting Grey • Mr Evasion • Talkin' Bout The Good Times • Walking Through My Dreams • Private Sorrow • Balloon Burning • Good Mr Square • Blue Serge Blues • October 26 • Cold Stone • Summertime • Circus Mind • Stone Hearted Mama

If your idea of musical nirvana is Stones-styled sixties R&B at 45 revolutions per minute then look no further. Ecstasy is now available in the crackle-free digital format. The Pretty Things were formed by Dick Taylor, who had been the Stones' original bass player, but when he chose to stay on at art school they gave the gig to Bill Wyman. When Taylor finally formed his own band they set out to out-sleaze the Stones,

but they'd left it too late. A brace of collectable singles is all that remains from that period, two of which were covered by Bowie on 'Pin Ups'. A belated move to psychedelia produced the early Floyd-styled 'Defecting Grey' and the first real rock opera, 'S.F Sorrow', which predated 'Tommy'. It reputedly gave Pete Townshend the idea to write his inflated opus and once again, the Pretty Things were consigned to the second division. They remain, however, a cult among collectors.

Rating:
Sound ★★★☆☆ Content ★★★☆☆
Also recommended:
'SF Sorrow' and 'The EP Collection' (both on See For Miles).
If you like this, why not try:
The Rolling Stones, The Small Faces, The Who.

Primal Scream

'SCREAMADELICA'

(Creation) 1991

Track listing: Movin' On Up • Slip Inside This House • Don't Fight It, Feel It • Higher Than The Sun • Come Together • Damaged • Loaded • Shine Like Stars • Inner Flight • I'm Coming Down

'Powders and pills won't cure my ills, but they make me feel better for a while.' These lines from 'I'm Coming Down' sum up the hedonistic philosophy of Primal Scream, a band who ingested the more potent influences from the psychedelic era and processed it through the rave scene in order to give their generation a weekend trip to the twilight zone. 'Screamadelica' takes over where the Stones' 'Beggars Banquet' left off adding tape loops, samples, dub deconstructions and house-style piano over both ambient and dancefloor grooves to generate a highly effective dance/rock synthesis. The all-pervading influence of the Stooges and the Stones on the group's earlier and subsequent offerings (with the exception of 'Vanishing Point') suggested that much of the credit for the success of 'Screamadelica' could be attributed to the imaginative input of remix gurus Andy Weatherall and The Orb, but 20 years from now this record will still be up there in the all-time classics listings. As the man says, 'don't fight it, feel it'.

Rating:
Sound ★★★★☆ Content ★★★★★

Primal Scream

'GIVE OUT BUT DON'T GIVE UP'

(Creation) 1994

Track listing: Jailbird • Rocks • (I'm Gonna) Cry Myself Blind • Funky Jam • Big Jet Plane • Free • Call On Me • Stuttin' • Sad And Blue • Give Out But Don't Give Up • I'll Be There

In '93 the group took a trip down south to Memphis to record an album that was intended to be as different from its predecessor as possible. With the legendary Tom Dowd at the controls club culture became subservient to soulful R&B as the Stones' influence was intensified and input was solicited from Dr Funkenstein himself, George Clinton. The result lost the group much of its cutting-edge credibility and put them firmly back in the racks marked 'rock'. But their commitment to recreating 'real music' is evident in every track.

Rating:
Sound ★★★★☆ Content ★★★★☆
Also recommended:
'Sonic Flower Groove', 'Vanishing Point', 'Echo Dek' (all on Creation.)
If you like this, why not try:
The Black Crowes, **The Rolling Stones, The Stone Roses**.

Prince

'SIGN O' THE TIMES'

2 CDs (Paisley Park/WEA) 1987

Track listing: Play In The Sunshine • Housequake • Ballad Of Dorothy Parker • It • Starfish And Coffee • Slow Love • Hot Thing • Forever In My Life • U Got The Look • If I Was Your Girlfriend • Strange Relationship • I Could Never Take The Place Of Your Man • Cross • It's Gonna Be A Beautiful Night • Adore • Sign O' The Times

When Prince recorded 'Sign O' The Times' he was Pan personified, a mischievous Pied Piper who promised eternal good times and a party that would last for a thousand years. Now his impish optimism is passé and all we have are the records and the memory of a more affluent era that was pregnant with possibilities. Prince appeared to embody those possibilities. He was prodigiously talented; a multi-instrumentalist and one-man hit factory who churned out so many songs that he had to give them away to others so that he wouldn't clog up the charts all by himself. But perhaps of greater significance is the fact that he distilled various elements from rock's past to brew the musical equivalent of the alcopop, a luridly coloured cocktail of soul, funk and fizzy pop that guaranteed to make every party rock like it was 1999.

He's at his most seductive on 'Slow Love' and 'I Could Never Take The Place Of Your Man', but he also takes time out to preach another kind of soul power on 'The Cross', which mirrors Madonna's preoccupation with carnality and Catholicism. There's social comment too, on the title track with its anti-drug diatribe, but it's the stripped-down, muscular-funk tracks, 'Hot Thing', 'Housequake' and 'It's Gonna Be A Beautiful Night', that promise all manner of earthy pleasures for the true party animals.

Rating:
Sound ★★★★☆ Content ★★★★☆

Prince

'THE HITS VOL I'

(Paisley Park/WEA) 1993

Track listing: When Doves Cry • Pop Life • Soft And Wet • I Feel For You • Why You Wanna Treat Me So Bad • When You Were Mine • Uptown • Let's Go Crazy • 1999 • I Could Never Take The Place Of Your Man • Nothing Compares 2 U • Adore • Pink Cashmere • Alphabet Street • Sign O'The Times • Thieves In The Temple • Diamonds And Pearls • 7

'THE HITS VOL 2'

(Paisley Park/WEA) 1993

Track listing: Controversy • Dirty Mind • I Wanna Be Your Lover • Head • Do Me Baby • Delirious • Little Red Corvette • I Would Die 4 U • Raspberry Beret • If I Was Your Girlfriend • Kiss • Peach • U Got The Look • Sexy M.F. • Gett Off • Cream • Pope • Purple Rain

Before Prince became a squiggly symbol and sank under the weight of his own artistic pretensions, he had personified the affluent eighties and its passion for partying like it was 1999. And being *the* party animal he had more energy than he could satisfy on the dancefloor. Although it's evident that he had his hang-ups with organized religion, the artist formerly known as 'the saviour of pop' was clearly obsessed with the liberating power of sex and was a fervent believer in the rhythm method. Every track is designed for dancing or sex, or preferably both. But if the lyrics are explicit, the music is an ambiguous but potent mix of plastic pop, sultry funk and synthetic soul with the occasional splash of psychedelia. Prince wanted to be Jimi Hendrix, Sly Stone and James Brown simultaneously and almost managed to fulfil his ambition. The tracks from 'Purple Rain' showcase his fluid guitar style while those from 'Diamonds And Pearls' are as fat 'n' funky as anything James Brown came up with. Prince even equals Sly on 'Raspberry Beret' and 'Pop Life' from the paisley patterned 'Around The World In A Day'.

Having all the hits on two single

CDs is the perfect way to get the best and leave the rest and should satisfy even his most loyal and devoted subjects. But for those who crave the complete experience any of the albums from the eighties will confirm what a prodigious and prolific talent he once was.

Rating:
Sound ★★★★☆ Content ★★★★☆
Also recommended:
The albums '1999', 'Diamonds And Pearls' and 'Parade' (all on Paisley Park).
If you like this, why not try:
James Brown, Sly And The Family Stone, Jimi Hendrix's Band Of Gypsies.

Public Enemy

'FEAR OF A BLACK PLANET'

(Def Jam) 1990

Track listing: Contract On The World Love Jam • Brothers Gonna Work It Out • 911 Is A Joke • Incident At 666 FM • Welcome To The Terrordome • Meet The G That Killed Me • Pollywanacraka • Anti-nigger Machine • Burn Hollywood Burn • Power To The People • Who Stole The Soul • Fear Of A Black Planet • Revolutionary Generation • Can't Do Nuttin' For Ya Man • Reggie Jax • Leave This Off Your Fuckin' Charts • B Side Wins Again • War At 331 • 3 • Final Count Of The Collision Between Us And Them • Fight The Power

This is powerful, provocative music with an unmistakable undercurrent of anger and paranoia. Both the title and the polemics were designed to arouse anxiety and play on the fears of the complacent using the beatbox as a bazooka to deliver their fiercely militant message. The group 'diss' those that they believe don't have the stomach for the coming confrontation and threaten those who they claim are involved in 'a worldwide conspiracy to destroy the black race'. Their paranoia is as illogical as that of their white racist enemies, but they know how to wind up and manipulate their audience as effectively as a professional politician. After a couple of tracks underscored by the sound of urban riots you'll be checking your locks and windows and wishing you'd bought a manual on urban survival tactics.

Rating:
Sound ★★★★☆ Content ★★★☆☆
Also recommended:
'It Takes A Nation Of Millions' and 'Apocalypse 91' (Def Jam).
If you like this, why not try:
Cypress Hill, Ice-T, NWA.

Pulp

'DIFFERENT CLASS'

(Island) 1995

Track listing: Mis-Shapes • Pencil Skirt • Common People • I Spy • Disco 2000 • Live Bed Show • Something Changed • Sorted For E's And Whizz • Feeling Called Love • Underwear • Monday Morning • Bar Italia

Jarvis Cocker's satiric sketches of the British working class plays like a cross between an animated Sunday supplement and a saucy seaside postcard with a soundtrack supplied by the Small Faces. But what makes such songs as 'Underwear', 'Live Bed Show' and 'I Spy' much more than just another nudge and a wink exposé of sexual obsession in suburbia is Cocker's insight into his characters and the class system. His wit is as sharp as a political cartoonist and he has the ability to cut his victims down to size with a few well-chosen words. But his melancholic love songs are equally affecting.

The perfect marriage of poetry and pop for the nineties.

Rating:
Sound ★★★★☆ Content ★★★★☆
Also recommended:
'This Is Hardcore' (Island).
If you like this, why not try:
The Kinks, Blur, The Smiths.

Queen

'QUEEN II'

(Label) 1974

Track listing: Procession • Father To Son • White Queen • Some Day One Day • The Loser In The End • Ogre Battle • The Fairy Feller's Master-Stroke • Nevermore • The March Of The Black Queen • Funny How Love Is • Seven Seas Of Rhye

Freddie Mercury conceived every Queen album as a combination of grand opera and pantomime, with himself in the dual role of tragic heroine and principal boy. Even when corseted in the constraints of a three-minute rock song Freddie was living out his fantasy, turning every song into a comic or tragic aria with a touch of melodrama and high camp.

If Queen's debut album was the audition piece, their second was the dress rehearsal for a series of larger-than-life productions. It's a mock-baroque fantasy whose cast includes a snow-white heroine, a wicked rival and enough fairy folk to repopulate Tolkien's Middle Earth. The big production numbers are pure prog-rock without the superfluous solos. Instead, Brian May provides orchestral interludes with layer upon layer of warm-toned guitars, while Freddie conducts a choir of multi-tracked voices to soften the harder edges. His own, of course, takes centre stage, not as imperious and commanding as on later productions, but clearly possessing that regal quality that made every performance a showstopper.

Rating:
Sound ★★★★☆ Content ★★★★☆

Queen

'SHEER HEART ATTACK'

(EMI) 1974

Track listing: Brighton Rock • Killer Queen • Tenement Funster • Flick Of The Wrist • Lily Of The Valley • Now I'm Here • In The Lap Of The Gods • Stone Cold Crazy • Dear Friends • Missfire • Bring Back That Leroy Brown • She Makes Me • In The Lap Of The Gods...Revisited

Queen cast off their pomp-rock frippery and played it fairly straight for their breakthrough album, although the production remains characteristically OTT. Even the rockers 'Killer Queen', 'Now I'm Here' and 'Stone Cold Crazy' are overdressed for the occasion, with Freddie's penchant for mock-operatic vocals threatening to overwhelm the swathe of distorted guitars and smother the rhythm section. But the ostentatious production and occasional bouts of bad taste are partly redeemed by the group's staggering self-confidence, energy and panache.

'Brighton Rock' raises the curtain on a briskly paced end-of-the-pier show with sketches and songs to please all tastes. Queen were always good at the period pastiche and here we are treated to a sentimental Victorian parlour piece ('Dear Friends'), a breathless burlesque ('Leroy Brown') and even a full-blooded Wagnerian climax with 'In The Lap Of The Gods'. Their prog-rock pretentions may have been discarded, but their love of pomp and musical exhibitionism remained. Fortunately, the meticulously crafted tunes stubbornly refuse to be stifled under the weight of the excessive ornamentation.

Rating:
Sound ★★★☆☆ Content ★★★★☆

Queen

'A NIGHT AT THE OPERA'

(EMI) 1975

Track listing: Death On Two Legs • Lazing On A Sunday Afternoon • I'm In Love With My Car • You're My Best Friend • '39 • Sweet Lady • Seaside Rendevous • The Prophet's Song • Love Of My Life • Good Company • Bohemian Rhapsody • God Save The Queen

'A Night At The Opera' marks the pinnacle of Queen's ambitions to reign supreme over every principality in pop. Whether it's their crowning achievement, or merely an extravagant indulgence that proves that nothing succeeds like excess, will depend on whether you're a loyalist or not. It was certainly the most expensive album made at that time and took months to record, with various elements being worked on at six different studios simultaneously. It was conceived as a showcase for the diverse talents of the four individual members who each contributed songs and it contained the group's usual mixture of hard rock, wistful ballads, music hall pastiche and perfectly crafted pop with classical trimmings. In the case of their *tour de force*, 'Bohemian Rhapsody', all these elements were combined in one grandiose statement.

Wolfing down this overblown wedding cake of an album at one sitting can only result in severe musical indigestion, but if taken a slice or two between more substantial and nourishing courses it could prove rather moreish.

Rating:
Sound ★★★★☆ Content ★★★★☆

Queen

'GREATEST HITS VOL I'

(Parlophone/EMI) 1991

Track listing: Bohemian Rhapsody • Another One Bites The Dust • Killer Queen • Fat Bottomed Girls • Bicycle Race • You're My Best Friend • Don't Stop Me Now • Save Me • Crazy Little Thing Called Love • Somebody To Love • Now I'm Here • Good Old Fashioned Lover Boy • Play The Game • Flash • Seven Seas Of Rhye • We Will Rock You • We Are The Champions

'GREATEST HITS VOL 2'

(Parlophone/EMI) 1994

Track listing: A Kind Of Magic • Under Pressure • Radio Gaga • I Want It All • I Want To Break Free • Innuendo • It's A Hard Life • Breakthru' • Who Wants To Live Forever • Headlong • Miracle • I'm Going Slightly Mad • Invisible Man • Hammer To Fall • Friends Will Be Friends • Show Must Go On • One Vision

Queen were primarily a singles band who gave the impression that they conceived every release as further proof of their divine right to rule. Whereas mere mortals released singles, Queen issued edicts in musical form asserting their supremacy. Of course, they played the part of the royal family of rock as a high camp pantomime, but as each single topped the last in terms of artistic achievement or commercial success it was hard to dispute their sovereignty over all that they surveyed.

They mastered hard rock with the early singles 'Seven Seas Of Rhye', 'Killer Queen' and 'Now I'm Here', proved experts at period pastiche with 'Crazy Little Thing Called Love' and 'Good Old Fashioned Lover Boy', dabbled with disco and conquered stadiums and terraces alike with the rousing anthems 'We Are The Champions' and 'We Will Rock You'. Then just when it looked like they ought to abdicate they found favour again with the self-mocking show business schmaltz of 'The Show Must Go On' and 'Who Wants To Live Forever' before Freddie bowed out for real.

Each of these tracks was produced with the intention of sounding as different from its predecessors as was possible, although it was this eclecticism which ultimately led to the band being seen by some as too clever for their own good. In their eagerness to play every part and please all their subjects they risked becoming masters of none. But as a national institution Queen are now, arguably, beyond criticism.

Rating:
Sound ★★★★☆ Content ★★★★☆
Also recommended:
'Queen 1', 'News Of The World', 'Live Killers' a double CD set (all on Parlophone).
If you like this, why not try:
David Bowie, Rush, Mott The Hoople, Cockney Rebel.

Quicksilver Messenger Service

'HAPPY TRAILS'

(Beat Goes On) 1992

Track listing: Who Do You Love Pt 1 • When You Love • Where You Love • How Do You Love • Which Do You Love • Who Do You Love Pt 2 • Mona • Maiden Of The Cancer Moon • Calvary • Happy Trails

Like their Bay Area brothers, The Grateful Dead, Frisco's Quicksilver drew on extended in-concert instrumental workouts and studio sessions for this, their second album. One side of the original vinyl version was taken up with a suite based loosely around Bo Diddley's' 'Who Do You Love?' on which the twin guitars of John Cipollina and Gary

Duncan trade lines across shifting time signatures until the intensity becomes almost incandescent. Another highlight is the Spanish-styled 'Calvary', which took the crucifixion as its inspiration, but was primarily concerned with the redeeming power of the guitar solo. Of course it sounds more enlightening if you're stoned, but the tracks are so heavily saturated with the heady scent of incense that you only have to turn it on to take the trip.

Rating:
Sound ★★★☆☆ Content ★★★☆☆
Also recommended:
'Anthology' (Beat Goes On).
If you like this, why not try:
The Grateful Dead, Wishbone Ash.

Radiohead

'THE BENDS'

(Parlophone) 1995

Track listing: Planet Telex • The Bends • High And Dry • Fake Plastic Trees • Bones • Nice Dream • Just • My Iron Lung • Bullet Proof...I Wish I Was • Black Star • Sulk • Street Spirit (Fade Out)

Radiohead were among a new generation of British bands who claimed to owe no debt to the past and had no desire to recycle the customary rock cliches. They strived for a more expansive sound that set them apart from the sixties-inspired Britpop brigade and after several false starts constructed it around Thom Yorke's morose vocal and a surge of insidiously malevolent guitars.

'The Bends' is the result of a gruelling tour as support to REM

during which Yorke's despair and contempt for the rapacious consumer society reached new depths. Sapped of energy, but not indignation, he bemoans the apparent purposelessness of life on 'Bullet Proof' and 'Fake Plastic Trees' with a chilling intensity that finally gives way to fateful resignation on 'Street Spirit'. One suspects that if he didn't believe his message had a chance of getting through he might do something desperate. Fortunately, he channelled his anger into music.

Rating:
Sound ★★★★☆ Content ★★★★☆

Radiohead

'OK COMPUTER'

(Parlophone) 1997

Track listing: Airbag • Paranoid Android • Subterranean Homesick Alien • Exit Music (For A Film) • Let Down • Karma Police • Fitter Happier • Electioneering • Climbing Up The Walls • No Surprises • Lucky • The Tourist

One can imagine Thom Yorke foraging through his father's record collection in the early 90s for the foundation stones with which to build an imposing new edifice to the doomed romantics of his generation and coming across 'The Wall', Roger Waters' monument to disillusionment and despair. Although contemporary in sound and subject matter Radiohead's portentious, claustrophobic, cerebral art rock owes as much to Pink Floyd as it does to U2, REM and the Seattle sound.

Comparisons have also been made between the eight-minute epic 'Paranoid Android' and Queen's 'Bohemian Rhapsody', although the only things that the two songs share are a perverse pleasure in dynamic contrasts, stylistic shocks and an unnerving sense of their own significance. Among the other delights on offer are the luscious harmonies on 'Let Down', the toy guitar and vocals on 'No Surprises', the spectral beauty of 'Climbing Up The Walls' and the genuinely moving 'Lucky', which is said to have reduced Yorke to tears when he first heard it.

Radiohead's erudite anthems to self-pity were the antithesis of chirpy sixties styled Britpop, the very definition of 'classic rock' and proof that an English public school education is never wasted.

Rating:
Sound ★★★★☆ Content ★★★★★
Also recommended:
'Pablo Honey' and 'OK Computer' (Parlophone).
If you like this, why not try:
James, Portishead, The Smiths.

Rainbow

'RICHIE BLACKMORE'S RAINBOW'

(Polydor) 1975

Track listing: Man On The Silver Mountain • Self Portrait • Black Sheep Of The Family • Catch The Rainbow • Snake Charmer • The Temple Of The King • If You Don't Like Rock 'N' Roll • Sixteenth Century Greensleeves • Still I'm Sad

Ex-Deep Purple axeman Richie Blackmore proved himself a master of the black art of the successful 'come back' by brewing a stew of ingredients that would appeal to the more fancifully minded hard-rock fans for whom 'Dungeons & Dragons' was more than a role-playing game – more a way of life. In place of the necromancer's traditional recipe of bat's wings and lizard's entrails Richie assembled a group of like-minded acolytes including the diminutive Ronnie James Dio who could deliver the verbal medieval mumbo jumbo with conviction.

Expectations were high for the group's first foray into the dark realms of the imagination, but in truth not all of the material is as strong as it might have been, with second-rate rockers 'If You Don't Like Rock And Roll' and 'Black Sheep of the Family' sounding stodgy by comparison with the more imaginative 'sword and sorcery' inspired songs. Curiously, one of the more awesome items is the instrumental reworking of The Yardbirds' 'Still I'm Sad' on which Richie gives a devilishly fine demonstration of how to make your guitar sound like it wants to possess its player. The gods have, however, cursed this 'remastered' reissue with a diabolically ill-defined sound which leaves the drums sounding as if Gary Driscoll is hammering soggy cardboard boxes.

Rating:
Sound ★★★☆☆ Content ★★★★☆

Rainbow

'RAINBOW RISING'

(Polydor) 1976

Track listing: Tarot Woman • Run With The Wolf • Starstruck • Do You Close Your Eyes • Stargazer • A Light In The Black

Rainbow's second album saw the replacement of the entire backline and the addition to powerhouse percussionist Cozy Powell whose presence served to stoke Blackmore's boiler. Again, the strongest songs are those which remain faithful to the fantasy ('Tarot Woman' and the exhilarating 'Stargazer'), while the run-of-the-mill rockers are undistinguished. 'Rainbow Rising' gives Blackmore more opportunity to show off his mastery of the screaming guitar, while Dio wails waistdeep in dry ice about a kingdom inhabited by helpless fair maidens and wicked wizards. Even the keyboards don't sound incongruous once we're past the cheesy intro to 'Tarot Woman'.

Rating:
Sound ★★★☆☆ Content ★★★★☆

Rainbow

'LONG LIVE ROCK 'N' ROLL'

(Polydor) 1978

Track listing: Long Live Rock 'n' Roll • Lady of The Lake • LA Connection • Gates Of Babylon • Kill The King • The Shed • Sensitive To Light • Rainbow Eyes

This was the last album on the fantasy theme before the group went into pub-pleasing AOR, scoring hits with 'Since You've Been Gone', 'All Night Long' and 'I Surrender' under their new vocalist Graham Bonnet. Here the mix of material is much as before; hard-riffing, show-off solos, demonstrative vocals and comic book occultism with a sprinkling of exotic Arabian Knights style imagery for good measure. Even the cod-rock cliches of 'LA Connection', 'The Shed' and the superfluous 'Sensitive To Light' can't break the spell for those who believe in a kingdom somewhere over the rainbow where hard rock is king.

Rating:
Sound ★★★★☆ Content ★★★★☆
Also recommended:
'Long Live Rock And Roll' and 'The Best Of' (both on Polydor).
If you like this, why not try:
Deep Purple, Whitesnake, The Mission.

The Ramones

'ALL THE STUFF AND MORE VOL 1'

(Sire/Warner Brothers) 1990

Track listing: Blitzkrieg Bop • Beat On The Brat • Judy Is A Punk • I Wanna Be Your Boyfriend • Chain Saw • Now I Wanna Sniff Some Glue • I Don't Wanna Go Down To The Basement • Loudmouth • Havana Affair • Listen To My Heart • 53rd & 3rd • Let's Dance • I Don't Wanna Walk Around With You • Today Your Love, Tomorrow The World • I Don't Wanna Be Learned • I Don't Wanna Be Tamed • I Can't Be • Glad To See You Go • Gimme Gimme Shock Treatment • I Remember You • Oh Oh I Love Her So • Sheena Is A Punk Rocker •

Suzy Is A Headbanger • Pinhead • Now I Wanna Be A Good Boy • Swallow Your Pride • What's Your Game • California Sun • Commando • You're Gonna Kill That Girl • You Should Never Have Opened That Door • Babysitter • California Sun • I Don't Wanna Walk Around With You

Bop Til You Drop • We're A Happy Family • Bonzo Goes To Bitburg • Outsider • Psycho Therapy • Wart Hog • Animal Boy • Needles And Pins • Howling At The Moon • Somebody Put Something In My Drink • We Want The Airwaves • Chinese Rock • I Just Wanna Have Something To Do • The KKK Took My Baby Away • Indian Giver • Rock 'n' Roll High School

'Gabba gabba, hey!' There aren't many bands who could claim to have crammed the cream of a dozen albums on a single CD, but the Ramones rarely wrote a song that lasted more than two minutes and they detested the idea of padding them out with superfluous guitar solos. Moreover, they managed to squeeze everything worth saying on the subject in question (from the pleasures of pogoing to DIY lobotomy) into those frantic few minutes with no surplus fat or filler. They looked like a bunch of hoodlums with a bad attitude and their three-chord songs sounded like a parody of punk, but the joke was such a good one that everyone with a sense of humour wanted in on it. Even the titles can make you smile.

This is the one for hardcore fans as it includes some previously unreleased demos.

Rating:
Sound ★★★★☆ Content ★★★★★

The Ramones

'RAMONESMANIA'

(Sire/Warner Brothers) 1988

Track listing: I Wanna Be Sedated • Teenage Lobotomy • Do You Remember Rock 'n' Roll Radio? • Gimme Gimme Shock Treatment • Beat On The Brat • Sheena Is A Punk Rocker • I Wanna Live • Pinhead • Blitzkrieg Bop • Cretin Hop • Rockaway Beach • Commando • I Wanna Be Your Boyfriend • Mama's Boy •

An alternative collection offering more or less the same mix, but with some of the later Spector-produced tracks plus the essential Reagan parody 'Bonzo Goes To Bitburg' and some hardcore thrash in the mutant form of 'Warthog' and 'Animal Boy'.

The Ramones exemplify the short, sharp shock that was punk and epitomize its credo, 'don't bore us, get to the chorus'. This is bubblegum with balls and it hasn't lost its flavour. 'Hey, ho, let's go!'

Rating:
Sound ★★★★☆ Content ★★★★★
Also recommended: 'Rocket To Russia' (Sire).
If you like this, why not try:
Green Day, The Stranglers, Dead Kennedys, Patti Smith.

Otis Redding

'DOCK OF THE BAY' (THE DEFINITIVE COLLECTION)

(Atlantic) 1992

Track listing: Shake • Mr Pitiful • Respect • Lover Man • Satisfaction • I Can't Turn You Loose • Hard To Handle • Fa Fa Fa Fa Fa (Sad Song) • My Girl • I've Been Loving You Too Long • Try A Little Tenderness • My Lover's Prayer • That's How Strong My Love Is • Pain In My Heart • Change Is Gonna Come • (Sittin' On The) Dock Of The Bay • Cigarettes And Coffee • These Arms Of Mine • Tramp

On stage Otis was ripe ham, stalking the stage on his heels, waving his arms in the air and mimicking James Brown's carefully choreographed routines, but on record he was the Southern soul man personified. He was blessed with a rich, dark voice and a resonance to match his six-foot frame. He had a way of wringing every last drop of emotion from a song that would leave the listener enervated and begging for release and an inimitable, faltering phrasing that gave the impression that he had stepped up to the microphone to get something serious off his chest. With the Stax house band Booker T And The MGs stoking the furnace Otis ranged across the emotional range, alternately pleading, boasting and begging for a little understanding and a heap of good lovin' from womankind in a voice that was baptized in the blues and marinated in grief. Nobody could spin a sob story with quite the degree of sincerity that Otis could. But this collection shows that there was more, much more to the man than playing the part of 'Mr Pitiful'.

Rating:
Sound ★★★★☆ Content ★★★★★
Also recommended:
'Otis Blue' and 'The Soul Album' from which many of the above tracks were taken and 'The Very Best Of Otis Redding' a superlative 40-track 2CD set (all on Atlantic).
If you like this, why not try:
Booker T And The MGs, James Brown, Solomon Burke, Percy Sledge.

Lou Reed

'TRANSFORMER'

(RCA) 1972

Track listing: Vicious • Andy's Chest • Perfect Day • Hangin' Around • Walk On The Wildside • Makeup • Satellite Of Love • Wagon Wheel • New York Telephone Conversation • I'm So Free • Goodnight Ladies

With his second solo album Lou came out of the closet in the company of soul mate and producer David Bowie to introduce a cast of characters that could have stepped straight out of a Scorsese movie; a parade of friends and freaks from New York's twilight world. His incisive descriptions of the pushers and the pimps, the addicts, the hustlers and the hangers-on who haunt the neon-lit alleys and sidewalks around Times Square are set to his best set of tunes since 'Loaded'. And as the parade passes by Lou bitches about them all, yet finds them strangely alluring.

'Transformer' marked his transformation from street poet to pop star, a change confirmed by the sales of the insidiously commercial 'Walk On The Wild Side', which boasted one of the best bass lines ever recorded. It also had the dubious honour of managing to slip a description of several sexual practices past the censors under the guise of an innocuous pop song. And in a bizarre irony the track 'Perfect Day', which concerned an addict's experience of a blissful fix, became a second hit 25 years later when it was recorded by an all-star line-up to raise funds for a children's charity!

Rating:
Sound ★★★★☆ Content ★★★★☆

Lou Reed

'BERLIN'

(RCA) 1973

Track listing: Berlin • Lady Day • Men Of Good Fortune • Caroline Says I • How Do You Think It Feels • Oh Jim • Caroline Says II • The Kids • The Bed • Sad Song

Lou has frequently taken a perverse pleasure in thwarting expectations. A psychiatrist might conclude that it has something to do with him wanting revenge on authority figures following his parents' decision to subject their wayward son to electric-shock therapy. Or perhaps he just hates being predictable. Whatever the reason, Lou caused confusion among the critics, frustration among his fans and apoplexy among the RCA executives by releasing this deeply depressing record about doomed romance and drug addiction in place of a similarly styled sequel to 'Transformer'. That album and its accompanying hit single, 'Walk On The Wild Side', had subverted the moral minority by cleverly sugar coating its sordid stories as fashionably decadent glam rock. But 'Berlin' doesn't boast the type of tune needed to leaven its cinematic scenes of sexual betrayal, self-deception and suicide. Its narrator is a man who has been numbed by his experiences and tormented by dark dreams.

It is only now in the post-punk/post-grunge era when we are less reliant on happy endings that

'Berlin' is revealed as being beautifully bleak, chilling and curiously compelling.

Rating:
Sound ★★★★☆ Content ★★★☆☆

Lou Reed

'NEW YORK'

(Sire) 1989

Track listing: Romeo Had Juliette • Halloween Parade • Dirty Boulevard • Endless Cycle • There Is No Time • Last Great American Whale • Beginning Of A Great Adventure • Busload Of Faith • Sick Of You • Hold On • Good Evening Mr Waldheim • Xmas In February • Strawman • Dime Store Mystery

The subtext of this late offering from Reed can be summed up in a line from 'Dirty Boulevard' in which he paraphrases the sign which greeted immigrants at New York's Ellis Island, 'Give me your tired, your poor... and I'll piss on 'em.' Lou's wit is as acidic as ever and his critical faculties acute as he explores the seamier side of the American dream, turning over the paving stones and observing the personal tragedies that crawl from underneath.

Bleeding-heart liberals and political fascists are both targets for his attacks, but he doesn't forget to rock with simple street stories of the lost souls and low-lifes who inhabit the Dirty Boulevards of the city he loves to hate.

Rating:
Sound ★★★★☆ Content ★★★☆☆

'Berlin', 'Coney Island Baby', 'The Blue Mask', 'Rock And Roll Animal' and 'Walk On The Wild Side (The Best Of)' (all on RCA).
If you like this, why not try:
The Velvet Underground, Iggy Pop, David Bowie.

Red Hot Chili Peppers

'BLOOD SUGAR SEX MAGIK'

(Warner Brothers) 1991

Track listing: The Power of Equality • If You have To Ask • Breaking The Girl • Funky Monks • Suck My Kiss • I Could Have Lied • Mellowship Clinky In B Major • The Righteous And The Wicked • Give It Away • Blood Sugar Sex Magik • Under The Bridge • Naked In The Rain • Apache Rose Peacock • The Greeting Song • My Lovely Man • Sir Psycho Sexy • They're Red Hot

The Peppers at the pinnacle of their career benefited from the guiding hand of Rick Rubin, whose experience with heavy metal acts brought a tighter, more sharply focused sound.

After a few false starts the band had finally distilled a potent mix of punk and funk with a sprinkling of psychedelia and a liberal dose of sex plus a side order of more sex and er… still more sex. It was brewed to hook the hard-rock crowd, gratify the bump 'n' grind brigade and intoxicate everyone else who got a taste via the radio-friendly club favourite 'Under The Bridge'. And it satisfies on all counts.

Are they red hot? To quote the band, 'If you have to ask, you'll never know.'

Rating:
Sound ★★★★★ Content ★★★★☆
Also recommended:
'One Hot Minute' (Warners)
If you like this, why not try:
Limp Bizkit, Aerosmith, The Beastie Boys, Gang Of Four.

REM

'OUT OF TIME'

(Warner Brothers) 1991

Track listing: Radio Song • Losing My Religion • Low • Near Wild Heaven • Endgame • Shiny Happy People • Belong • Half A World Away • Texarkana • Country Feedback • Me In Honey

In the eighties REM were just another melodic indie guitar group from Smallsville, USA, working away quietly to develop their songwriting skills and building a following with the support of college radio. When they finally broke into the big time, almost a decade after the release of their debut LP, they hadn't changed nor compromised their integrity. For once, the mountain, or rather the market, had come to the prophet.

Their music stands out from the crass commercial and commonplace because it is subtle, simple and understated. Michael Stipe's vocal is equally undemonstrative and the instrumentation almost translucent. There are strong echoes of The Byrds, The Flaming Groovies and the West Coast close harmony outfits of the late sixties in 'Losing My Religion' and 'Shiny Happy People' which lead critics to complain that there was little on this record that couldn't have been created back then. But REM never claimed to be innovative. Their qualities lay elsewhere and are conspicuous on every track of this CD.

Rating:
Sound ★★★★☆ Content ★★★★☆

REM

'AUTOMATIC FOR THE PEOPLE'

(Warner Brothers) 1992

Track listing: Drive • Try Not To Breathe • The Sidewinder Sleeps Tonight • Everybody Knows • New Orleans Instrumental No.1 • Sweetness Follows • Monty Got A Raw Deal • Ignoreland • Star Me Kitten • Man On The Moon • Nightswimming • Find The River

The most unconventional rock band in the business built their reputation on a secure and solid foundation of consistently high-quality albums, any one of which could qualify as a classic. But this was the album that focused all the elements that had made them one of the most popular groups of the nineties; Stipes' broody musings on the state of the nation and the environment, Buck's chiming guitar, the obligatory mandolins and seamless sixties harmonies. 'Automatic' is generally considered to be their finest hour, a superior set of exquisitely crafted and intimate songs unadulterated by sophisticated production trickery. It's an album that delights in being at odds with fashion. Stipe described it as 'a punk record – just a very quiet one'.

Rating:
Sound ★★★★☆ Content ★★★★★

Also recommended:
'Murmur', 'Adventures In Hi-Fi' and 'Green' (WEA).
If you like this, why not try:
Green On Red, **The Soft Boys**, **Robyn Hitchcock**, **The Byrds**, the dbs.

Cliff Richard

'THE WHOLE STORY'

2 CDs (EMI) 2000

Track listing: Move It • Living Doll • Travellin' Light • Please Don't Tease • I Love You • The Young Ones • It'll Be Me • Do You Wanna Dance • The Next Time • Bachelor Boy • Summer Holiday • It's All In The Game • Don't Talk To Him • Constantly • On The Beach • I Could Easily Fall • The Minute You're Gone • Visions • In The Country • The Day I Met Marie • Power To All Our Friends • Miss You Nights • Devil Woman • My Kinda Life • We Don't Talk Anymore • Carrie • Dreamin' • Wired For Sound • Daddy's Home • The Only Way Out • True Love Ways • Please Don't Fall In Love • She's So Beautiful • My Pretty One • Some People • Mistletoe And Wine • The Best Of Me • I Just Don't Have The Heart • Silhouettes • From A Distance • Saviour's Day • I Still Believe In You • Peace In Our Time • Be With Me Always • Can't Keep This Feeling In • The Millennium Prayer

Before succumbing to the bland MOR repertoire of the variety hall circuit Sir Cliff was a credible pop performer with a fair share of half-decent hits to his credit. Beginning with 'Move It' from 1959, when Cliff's quivering lip had more life in it than most of Britain's Tin Pan Alley talent, though the snappy early seventies hits ('Devil Woman', 'Carrie' et al) to the banal ballads of the eighties and nineties this double CD set celebrates his four decades in showbusiness and ably demonstrates why he is now a national institution, if not a national treasure.

Rating:
Sound ★★★★☆ Content ★★★☆☆
Also recommended:
'Nearly Famous' (EMI).
If you like this, why not try:
The Shadows.

Little Richard

'20 CLASSIC CUTS'

(Ace) 1990

Track listing: Long Tall Sally • Ready Teddy • Girl Can't Help It • Rip It Up • Miss Ann • She's Got It • Lucille • Keep A' Knockin' • Good Golly Miss Molly • Send Me Some Lovin' • Tutti Frutti • Hey Hey Hey • Slippin' And Slidin' • Heebie Jeebies • Baby Face • Jenny Jenny • By The Light Of The Silvery Moon • Ooh My Soul • True Fine Mama • Bama Lama Bama Loo • I'll Never Let You Go • Can't Believe You Wanna Leave

'Awopbopaloobopalopbamboom!' To anyone over 30 in the fifties 'Tutti Frutti' and the other 19 raw slices of Americana on this compilation must have sounded like their worst nightmare was on the loose. Little Richard, 'the Georgia Peach', may have looked like a black cherub with a monstrous brilliantined quiff, but he was blessed with the voice of a bordello queen and the fiery conviction of a Holy Roller. His irrepressible energy and outrageous self-confidence injected enough adrenaline into these songs to revive the dead, defying you to remain still while he pumps that piano till it screams for mercy. Ooh mah soul!

Rating:
Sound ★★★★☆ Content ★★★★★

Also recommended:
'The Speciality Sessions' the complete recordings on six CDs including alternate takes, false starts and previously unreleased versions of these classic cuts.
If you like this, why not try:
Jerry Lee Lewis, Smiley Lewis, **Fats Domino, James Brown, Prince**.

Jonathan Richman And The Modern Lovers

'MODERN LOVERS'

(Rev-Ola) 1976

Track listing: Roadrunner • Astral Plane • Old World • Pablo Picasso • I'm Straight • She Cracked • Hospital • Some I Care About • Girlfriend • Modern World • Dignified And Old • Government Center

It was said that Jonathan Richman went to more Velvet Underground performances than the band themselves. His fixation with the VU remained throughout his career, during which he sounded like Lou Reed's adenoidal younger brother and looked the part of the eternal gawky teenager, even into his late 40s.

This debut album was actually a collection of demos produced by John Cale in 1971. It was shelved for five years after Richman and his tapes were shown the door by every A&R exec in town. Had it been released at the time it is possible that it might have altered the course of popular music. Instead, the group split. Drummer David Robinson joined The Cars and keyboard player Jerry Harrison offered his services to Talking Heads while Jonathan went on to indulge his passion for whimsical novelty numbers and became a cult figure on the college circuit. 'The Modern Lovers' could be said to provide the missing link between The Velvets and punk, but its historical significance comes second to its endearing charm and tremulous energy.

Rating:
Sound ★★★☆☆ Content ★★★★★
Also recommended:
'Rock 'n' Roll With The Modern Lovers' and 'Jonathan Richman And The Modern Lovers'.
If you like this, why not try:
The Velvet Underground, Lou Reed, Talking Heads, Robyn Hitchcock.

Smokey Robinson

'GREATEST HITS'

(Motown) 1996

Track listing: Being With You • Tracks Of My Tears • I Second That Emotion • I'm The One You Need • Mickey's Monkey • Going To A Go Go • I Don't Blame You At All • If You Can Want • Just To See Her • More Love • Just My Soul Responding • Tears Of A Clown • Abraham, Martin And John • You've Really Got A Hold On Me • Shop Around • What's So Good About Goodbye • Ooo Baby Baby • The Love I Saw In You Was Just A Mirage • Quiet Storm • One Heartbeat • Baby, Baby Don't Cry • Cruisin'

Smokey was Berry Gordy's secret weapon. He turned out hit after hit for Motown with the precision of Detroit's car-plant production lines, but his smooth, controlled falsetto, the quality of his songs and the sophisticated nature of his productions ensured that his own

singles were class A luxury models. The early records serve up both slick, foot-tappin' soul that is designed for dancing and softly sighing ten-cent romantic sob stories. But when he developed a social conscience in the late sixties with 'Abraham, Martin and John' it wasn't only teenage girls who were moved.

This compilation is the only Smokey Robinson CD currently available in the UK.

Rating:
Sound ★★★★☆ Content ★★★★★
Also recommended:
'Whatever Makes You Happy' a compilation of lesser hits from 1961–71, the double disc set 'Anthology' and the exhaustive 4CD box set '35th Anniversary' (all available on import).
If you like this, why not try:
'Smokey's Songbook' an album of cover versions ((Motor City Records), early **Stevie Wonder, Marvin Gaye,** Diana Ross And The Supremes.

Paul Rodgers

'A TRIBUTE TO MUDDY WATERS'

2 CDs (Victory Records/London) 1993

Track listing: Muddy Water Blues (Acoustic Blues) • Louisiana Blues • I Can't Be Satisfied • Rollin' Stone • Good Morning Little Schoolgirl Pt 1 • I'm Your Hoochie Man • She's Alright • Standing Around Crying • The Hunter • She Moves Me • I'm Ready • I Just Wanna Make Love To You • Born Under A Bad Sign • Good Morning Little Schoolgirl Pt 2 • Muddy Water Blues (electric version) • All Right Now • Wishing Well • Fire And Water • Bad Company • Feel Like Making Love • Can't Get Enough

The title tells all that you need to know about this criminally under-rated album from the former frontman of Free and Bad Company. In his tribute to the undisputed heavyweight champ of the blues Rodgers is aided and abetted by such luminaries as Jeff Beck, David Gilmour, Brian May, Gary Moore, Buddy Guy and Slash. Normally these all-star celebrity bouts turn out to be awkward blind dates contrived by the record companies in the mistaken belief that more stars mean substantially more sales, but this collaboration is the exception. Big-name guitarists of this calibre are inclined to throw their weight about to score points off their rivals, but all pay their dues in a manner that would have made the big man grin from ear to ear. Rodgers' band spars sportingly with each to leave the listener in no doubt that the blues may be down, but it's by no means out for the count.

As a bonus a second CD offers superior re-recordings of highlights from Rodgers' back catalogue.

Rating:
Sound ★★★★☆ Content ★★★★☆
Also recommended:
'Now' (London).
If you like this, why not try:
Free, **Bad Company**, **Rory Gallagher**, the original Muddy Waters recordings.

The Rolling Stones

'SINGLES COLLECTION. THE LONDON YEARS'

3 CDs (Abkco/London) 1986

Track listing: Come On • I Want To Be Loved • I Wanna Be Your Man • Stoned • Not Fade Away • Little By Little • It's All Over Now • Good Times, Bad Times • Tell Me • I Just Wanna Make Love To You • Time Is On My Side • Congratulatuions • Little Red Rooster • Off The Hook • Heart Of Stone • What A Shame • The Last Time • Play With Fire • (I Can't Get No) Satisfaction • The Under Assistant West Coast Promotion Man • The Spider And The Fly • Get Off My Cloud • I'm Free • The Singer Not The Song • As Tears Go By • Gotta Get Away • 19th Nervous Breakdown • Sad Day • Paint It Black • Stupid Girl • Long Long While • Mother's Little Helper • Lady Jane • Have You Seen Your Mother, Baby, Standing In The Shadow? • Who's Driving Your Plane? • Let's Spend The Night Together • Ruby Tuesday • We Love You • Dandelion • She's A Rainbow • 2000 Light Years From Home • In Another Land • The Lantern • Jumpin' Jack Flash • Child Of The Moon • Street Fighting Man • No Expectations • Surprise, Surprise • Honky Tonk Women • You Can't Always Get What You Want • Memo From Turner • Brown Sugar • Wild Horses • I Don't Know Why • Try A Little Harder • Out Of Time • Jiving Sister Fanny

The Stones were the lecherous, sullen bad boys of sixties Britpop. With their early singles they attempted to recreate the authentic sound of black R&B, although they hadn't been further south than Surrey at the time. But by the time they wrote and recorded 'Brown Sugar' at the end of the decade they could claim to have been prime movers in pop's assimilation of black music. In the process Jagger had created the archetype for the decadent androgynous rock star and Keith had provided rock with a repertoire of greasy thumb guitar riffs that could be recycled *ad nauseam* by any group that wanted to adopt a stroppy, snotty nose image.

But while the Stones posed as his Satanic Majesty's altar boys and spent much of the sixties elegantly wasted, they remained acutely aware of the need to write good songs. Here are over 50 of them, including all 14 hit singles from 1963–69 with their B-sides, eight of which hit number one.

Rating:
Sound ★★★★☆ Content ★★★★★

The Rolling Stones

'BEGGAR'S BANQUET'

(London) 1968

Track listing: Sympathy For The Devil • No Expectations • Dear Doctor • Parachute Woman • Jig-Saw Puzzle • Street Fighting Man • Prodigal Son • Stray Cat Blues • Factory Girl • Salt Of The Earth

With 'Beggar's Banquet' the Stones earned the right to sit at the high table of his Satanic Majesty and indulge themselves to excess. 'Sympathy For The Devil' was calculated to reinforce their image as acolytes of the antichrist, at least in the eyes of the nation's outraged parents; 'Street Fighting Man' was their two-fingered salute to the hippies and a call to arms for all counter-culture revolutionaries at the time of the anti-Vietnam riots and 'Stray Cat Blues' restated their desire to satiate their carnal appetites on any young female that took their fancy. After the ill-conceived psychedelic shambles, 'Their Satanic Majesties

Request', this was the album that confirmed that Jagger and Richard were back in business. Even their dishevelled attempts at authentic delta blues and country rock were more than creditable.

Rating:
Sound ★★★★☆ Content ★★★★★

The Rolling Stones

'STICKY FINGERS'

(CBS) 1971

Track listing: Brown Sugar • Sway • Wild Horses • Can't You Hear Me Knocking • You Gotta Move • Bitch • I Got The Blues • Sister Morphine • Dead Flowers • Moonlight Mile

Nobody, but nobody, did the debauched rock and roll decadence routine quite as convincingly as the Stones and on 'Sticky Fingers' they surpassed themselves with the lascivious 'Brown Sugar', sleazy 'Bitch' and chilling 'Sister Morphine', the latter supplied by Marianne Faithfull. Only the perfunctory 'I Got The Blues' and ragged 'Can't You Hear Me Knockin'' betrayed the fact that the album had been assembled from left-overs culled from sessions recorded over the past two years.

The one drawback of having the album on CD is that we don't get Andy Warhol's original zip cover which opened to reveal the Jagger tongue cartoon that has since become the logo of Stones Inc.

Rating:
Sound ★★★★☆ Content ★★★★☆

The Rolling Stones

'EXILE ON MAIN STREET'

(CBS) 1972

Track listing: Rocks Off • Rip This Joint • Shake Your Hips • Casino Boogie • Tumbling Dice • Sweet Virginia • Torn And Frayed • Sweet Black Angel • Loving Cup • Happy • Turd On The Run • Ventilator Blues • I Just Want To See His Face • Let It Loose • All Down The Line • Stop Breaking Down • Shine A Light • Soul Survivor

Recorded in the basement of Richards' villa in the south of France, 'Exile' is an album shrouded in stale cigarette smoke and stained with the dregs of empty bourbon bottles.

It was criticized at the time for being a sprawling self-indulgent mess, but that is the core of its appeal; the off-the-cuff attitude, Jagger's lazy drawl, Keith's tanked-up riffing and the rhythm section which lays back in the groove and grins with smug satisfaction.

Besides, few albums kick off with a sequence of songs as strong as these. And although there are longueurs ('I Just Want To See His Face', 'Let It Loose' and 'Shine A Light'), there are unexpected surprises such as Keith's party piece, the uncharacteristically upbeat 'Happy' and the gospel-tinged closer 'Soul Survivor' which sees the group staggering blindly into the sunshine at the end of the sessions.

'Exile On Main Street' became a template for a generation of copyists including Guns 'N' Roses, Counting Crows, Aerosmith and The New York Dolls who took their riffs, their 'heroin chic' image and their affected sullen attitude from the Stones. The original however, remains unsurpassed.

Rating:
Sound ★★★★☆ Content ★★★★★

The Rolling Stones

'GOAT'S HEAD SOUP'

(CBS) 1973

Track listing: Dancing With Mr D • 100 Years Ago • Coming Down Again • Doo Doo Doo Doo Doo (Heartbreaker) • Angie • Silver Train • Hide Your Love • Winter • Can You Hear The Music • Star Star

Long before the release of this unfairly neglected album The Stones had justified their claim to be 'the greatest rock and roll band in the world'. So this can be regarded as a delightful bonus delivered on borrowed time. Although it doesn't rate highly in most critics' lists of classic Stones albums, the inclusion of butt shakers 'Heartbreaker' and 'Star Star' plus the seductive 'Angie' ensures it has the requisite amount of puissance and polish to warrant space in your CD collection.

Rating:
Sound ★★★★☆ Content ★★★★☆
Also recommended:
'Let It Bleed' and 'It's Only Rock And Roll' (CBS).
If you like this, why not try:
The Pretty Things, The Black Crowes, **Guns 'n' Roses**.

Roxy Music

'FOR YOUR PLEASURE'

(EG/Virgin) 1973

Track listing: Do The Strand • Beauty Queen • Strictly Confidential • Editions Of You • In Every Dream Home A Heartache • The Bogus Man • Grey Lagoons • For Your Pleasure

'All styles served here,' promises Bryan Ferry in that distinctive exaggerated vibrato of his on the opening track of Roxy's second genre-defying album and that is precisely what the group deliver over the next 42 minutes. Roxy's mutant hybrid of fifties rock revivalism, old-style Hollywood glamour and futurist kitsch wilfully defied categorization by embracing a multitude of apparently contradictory styles and carrying them off with conviction. The music on the first four albums is alternately spikey, sensual, savage, sophisticated, decadent, danceable, quirky, complex, camp, nostalgic, avant-garde, icily aloof and romantic. And occasionally, all at once.

Kicking off this second album in fine style, the quirky 'Do The Strand', offers 'a danceable solution to teenage revolution', before 'Beauty Queen' slows the pace, changing the mood to one of 'hopefully yearning', as the lyric would have it. Its theme was one that Ferry was to return to repeatedly – the transient nature of beauty and the fickle nature of fashion. Then 'Strictly Confidential' attempts to integrate both styles as Ferry assumes his languid, lounge-lizard persona for a romantic ballad which

mutates into something distinctly alien with overdriven guitar and electric piano. This was the kind of style shock tactic that made early Roxy so exciting and reduced their glam-rock rivals to the status of bemused onlookers.

An honourable mention too for 'The Bogus Man' on which Andy Mackay's warped sax lines and Brian Eno's electronic creations stalk each other through the neon glare of rainswept streets to a lean, mean dance beat. But the real high point is the two-part tour de force 'In Every Dream Home A Heartache', a disquieting peek through the curtains of sleepy suburbia. The first section is all brooding menace as Ferry agonizes over his character's obsession with an inflatable sex toy before the tension is released in an orgasmic surge of sound which builds in intensity to the fade.

This is one instance where remastering is unnecessary as they got it spot on the first time. Its only failing is the absence of the contemporaneous single 'Pyjamarama' which really ought to have been added as a bonus track.

Rating:
Sound ★★★★★ Content ★★★★★

Roxy Music

'STRANDED'

(EG/Virgin) 1973

Track listing: Street Life • Just Like You • Amazona • Psalm • Serenade • A Song For Europe • Mother Of Pearl • Sunset

As the group's chaotic visual contrasts of lamé, leathers, leopard skin, PVC and platform boots was toned down to present a more unified image so too was their sound. 'Stranded' marks a distinct move towards the mainstream and Ferry's adoption of what he called 'the Casablanca look' for which he affected a world-weary fatalism, as exemplified by the grandiose 'Song For Europe'. Other highpoints are the single 'Street Life' which struts as self-consciously as a catwalk model replete with finger clicks, brassy backing and nagging guitar riff; 'Psalm' and 'Mother of Pearl', the former a hymn to religious hypocrisy and the latter the confession of an listless party-going sophisticate.

With Brian Eno replaced by electric violinst Eddie Jobson, Roxy became little more than a backing band for Bryan Ferry who now allayed their art-school exhibitionism with his shrewd pop sensibility and a sound as instantly identifiable as his highly mannered vocals. But although one misses the 'insanity' which Eno brought to the band, the interplay between Mackay's oboe and sax with the Jobson's violin and keyboard colourings ensured that the band remained infinitely more interesting than anything else in the charts at the time.

Rating:
Sound ★★★★☆ Content ★★★★☆

Roxy Music

'COUNTRY LIFE'

(EG/Virgin) 1974

Track listing: The Thrill Of It All • Three And Nine • All I Want Is You • Out Of The Blue • If It Takes All Night • Bitter-Sweet • Triptych • Casanova • A Really Good Time • Prairie Rose

The choice of title confirmed Ferry's burning ambition to airbrush out his working-class origins and join the smart set. 'Country Life' was an obvious allusion to the select magazine of the same title, though it substituted two scantily clad models for the magazine's prim country-house covers.

It was evident from the first track that the thrill had indeed all but gone, that art-school innovation had sold out to vested commercial interests so that Roxy could become a part of the musical establishment. But there are still enough good tracks to justify a regular spin on your CD player – the exhilarating single 'All I Want Is You', the mock medieval 'Triptych', the swirling rush of 'Out Of The Blue' with its haunting oboe line and of course, the rousing closer, 'Prairie Rose'.

Rating:
Sound ★★★★☆ Content ★★★★☆

Roxy Music

'VIVA!'

(EG) 1976

Track listing: Out Of The Blue • Pyjamarama • The Bogus Man • Chance Meeting • Both Ends Burning • If There Is Something • In Every Dream Home A Heartache • Do The Strand

It's rare for a live album to add anything significant to the original recordings other than extended solos, but 'Viva!' thaws the studied cool of the studio versions to reveal the romantic beneath the group's urbane exterior. 'Out Of The Blue' and 'If There Is Something' take on an almost epic quality with their languid oboe, violin and sax lines, while the intensity of a live show allows the band to turn the screw even tighter during the malevolent 'In Every Dream Home A Heartache'. The 'straight' songs also benefit immeasurably from the immediacy of a live performance. 'Both Ends Burning' has rarely sounded so ardent as it does here and there can be few introductions that are guaranteed to stimulate anticipation more than the opening chords of 'Pyjamarama'.

So, at the risk of recommending more Roxy albums than the average buyer might require, may I strongly urge you to visit your friendly neighbourhood record store one more time and add 'Viva' to your collection.

Rating:
Sound ★★★☆☆ Content ★★★★★
Also recommended:
'Roxy Music', 'Siren' and the 4CD set 'The Thrill Of It All' (all on Virgin).
If you like this, why not try:
Brian Eno, Bryan Ferry's solo albums, **Japan**.

Run DMC

'RAISING HELL'

(London) 1986

Track listing: Peter Piper • It's Tricky • My Adidas • Walk This Way • Is It Live • Perfection • Hit It And Run • Raising Hell • You Be Illin' • Dumb Girl • Son Of Byford • Proud To Be Black

'Raising Hell' was rap's first million seller and the album that broke MTV's alleged ban on this illegitimate offspring of hip hop and street funk. Jam Master Jay's turntable skills shred the original backstreet beats as Run and D trade verbals. It's kicking and its cool, but it's also a lesson in how you need to use your head to get ahead in the music business. The crew's shrewd use of hard-rock samples, specifically Aerosmith's 'Walk This Way', secured the lucrative white middle-class market and brought rap into the mainstream.

Rating:
Sound ★★★★☆ Content ★★★★☆
Also recommended:
'Run DMC Together Forever' (Greatest Hits), 'Run DMC' and 'Back From Hell' (all on London).
If you like this, why not try:
Public Enemy, The Beastie Boys.

Rush

'2112'

(Mercury) 1976

Track listing: Lessons • Passage To Bangkok • Something For Nothing • Tears • Twilight Zone • 2112 Overture • The Temples Of Syrinx • Discover • Presentation • Oracle: The Dream • Soliloquy • Grand Finale

'I lie awake starring out at the bleakness of Megadon...' So begins the opening to this mid-seventies' SF epic by a band who defied fashion and good taste to become one of the biggest live acts on the planet. Their success still confounds the critics and most of the record-buying public who can't bring themselves to embrace a metal-lite sound which has the most unlikely male falsetto as its focus, nor tracks which bear titles such as 'The Temples Of Syrinx', 'Oracle: The Dream' and 'Soliloquy'. If you're going to buy into the mythology this is a good place to start, but be warned – they make Yes sound like Motorhead!

Rating:
Sound ★★★★☆ Content ★★☆☆☆
Also recommended:
'All The World's A Stage', 'Caress Of Steel', 'A Farewell To Kings' and 'Rush Retrospective 1974–1980' (all on Mercury).
If you like this, why not try:
Led Zeppelin, Yes, Genesis, ELP.

Santana

'THE VERY BEST OF'

(Columbia) 1997

Track listing: Europa • Black Magic Woman • Oye Coma Va • Samba Pa Ti • Carnival • She's Not There • Soul Sacrifice • Let The Children Play • Jugando • No One To Depend On • Evil Ways • Dance Sister Dance • Jingo-Lo-Ba • Everybody's Everything • Hold On • One Chain • Lightning In The Sky • Aqua Marine • Chill Out (Things Gonna Change)

Long before the advent of so-called 'world music' Carlos Santana brought

steaming Latin rhythms to the street parties of San Francsico and the searing heat of the African savannas to the mud-bound festivals at the height of the hippie era. Thirty years on his music has lost none of its passion or power to possess, the sacred and the secular fusing in the iridescent flame of his guitar solos. From the fervid invocation of 'Soul Sacrifice' to the devotional groove of 'Chill Out' these tracks overflow with an ardent love of life that is guaranteed to stir the soul and move the body.

Rating:
Sound ★★★☆☆ Content ★★★★☆
Also recommended:
'Abraxas', 'The Ultimate Collection' and the live set 'Viva Santana' (all on Columbia.)
If you like this, why not try:
Buddy Miles, Sly Stone, Jan Hammer, early Fleetwood Mac.

The Sensational Alex Harvey Band

'THE SENSATIONAL ALEX HARVEY BAND'

(Carlton Sounds) 1992 Budget price

Track listing: Faith Healer • Delilah • Framed • Tomahawk Kid • School's Out • Vambo • Boston Tea Party • Gang Bang • Gamblin' Bar Room Blues • Tomorrow Belongs To Me • Mrs Blackhouse • Dogs Of War • Anthem • To Be Continued

In 1975 veteran Scots rocker Alex Harvey enjoyed a long overdue hit with a cruelly mocking cover of the Tom Jones ballad 'Delilah' for which guitarist Zal Cleminson donned full clown makeup and minced across the 'Top Of The Pops' stage in melodramatic fashion, led by Alex as a lunatic circus ringmaster. From that moment on the record-buying public associated the group with comic novelty numbers and Harvey was never able to capitalize on his hard-earned break. For the rest of his life he remained a strong live draw and a much-loved cult figure for those with a taste for cod-rock theatre, songs about comic book heroes and idiosyncratic cover versions (The Osmonds, Irving Berlin and the musical 'Cabaret' were all mercilessly lampooned).

This well-chosen collection gathers all the singles and the cream from their five albums (with the exception of the title track from 'Next', written by Jacques Brel).

Not many bands would have the nerve to describe themselves so immodestly, but this collection proves that their boast was justified.

Rating:
Sound ★★★★☆ Content ★★★★★
Also recommended:
With all of the original albums having been deleted the only alternative is another compilation 'All Sensations' (Vertigo) which features several essential items missing from the above collection.
If you like this, why not try:
Steve Harley and Cockney Rebel, Jacques Brel, **Sparks**, Captain Beefheart, **Tom Waits**.

The Sex Pistols

'NEVER MIND THE BOLLOCKS'

(Virgin) 1977

Track listing: Holidays In The Sun • Bodies • No Feelings • Liar • God Save The Queen • Problems • Seventeen • Anarchy In The UK • Submission • Pretty Vacant • New York • EMI

The Sex Pistols dealt the complacent, incestuous music industry a short sharp shock that sent it reeling. It wasn't simply Johnny Rotten's vicious snarl and vomiting stream of obscenities, or the raw power of the music that outraged the moral minority and sent the media into a feeding frenzy. It was the way these snotty, odious oiks ripped the smug grin from the face of not-so-Great Britain in The Queen's jubilee year and exposed the festering mess beneath. 'Never Mind...' gobs all over the establishment's cherished institutions and picks the scabs from the seamier side of society that disturbed the Brits' sensibilities.

But for all its rude, righteous fury 'Never Mind The Bollocks' is still eminently listenable because producer Chris Thomas knew that if the group were to be more than just a provocative noise he couldn't afford to lose sight of the songs. Moreover, the garage rehearsal atmosphere couldn't disguise the fact that these guys could play.

McLaren claimed that he created The Pistols as Dickensian caricatures to test the gullibility of the music business and contrived their singles to provoke a reaction and to titillate the tabloids. But the group became more than puppets in his 'Great Rock and Roll Swindle', they participated willingly in the wanton destruction of the establishment until they themselves self-destructed. And in the 18 months or so that they held together they recorded one of the ten greatest albums ever made.

Rating:
Sound ★★★★☆ Content ★★★★★

Sex Pistols

'THERE IS NO FUTURE'

(Castle/Essential) 1999

Track listing: Pretty Vacant • Seventeen • Dolls (New York) • Satellite • No Feelings • I Wanna Be Me • Submission • Anarchy In The UK • Anarchy In The UK (Alternative Version) • No Fun • God Save The Queen • Problems • Pretty Vacant • Liar • EMI • Substitute

This is, in essence, a legitimate version of the legendary 'spunk' bootleg which captured the Pistols in their initial shameless scramble for notoriety. It's a mixture of rough early demos and even rougher live tracks with the Glen Matlock lineup. The demos make them sound like a bunch of amateur Pistol impersonators who haven't yet got their act together and the live tracks must have been taped on a cheap cassette recorder in the club's toilet. But what these tracks lack in sound quality and sophistication they more than make up for in vitriol and sheer bloody rage. Even nostalgic middle-aged punks might not play this when

they're sober, but you've got to own it – it's a putrid but significant slice of this nation's history and that's the most ironic aspect of the whole punk phenomenon.

Rating:
Sound ★★☆☆☆ Content ★★★☆☆
Also recommended:
'This Is Crap' (Virgin), a 2CD set comprising 'Never Mind' and teh early Chris Spedding-produced demos.
If you like this, why not try:
The Clash, UK Subs, Public Image Ltd.

Paul Simon

'GRACELAND'

(WEA) 1986

Track listing: Boy In The Bubble • Graceland • I Know What I Know • Gumboots • Diamonds On The Soles Of Her Shoes • You Can Call Me Al • Under African Skies • Homeless • Crazy Love Vol 2 • All Around The World Or The Myth Of Fingerprints

Paul Simon had proven himself a consummate craftsman and an astute observer of human frailties long before he embarked on this collaboration with South African musicians, but on 'Graceland' he excelled himself. His preoccupation with alienation and injustice found a new focus in the South African setting, although the bitterness was softened, as always on a Paul Simon song, by fatalism and a pained resignation. Indigenous rhythms rather than lyrics provided the inspiration for some of his strongest songs since splitting with Art

Garfunkel, while his infamous perfectionism, which had blunted the edge of his seventies solo offerings, gave way to a more spontaneous vibe. The contribution of Ladysmith Black Mambazo, The Soweto Rhythm Section and Youssou N'Dour on 'The Boy In The Bubble', 'Diamonds On The Soles Of Her Shoes', 'You Can Call Me Al' and the sublime 'Homeless' ensured that each are imbued by an air of celebration and an earthy spirituality.

Impeccably produced and polished as smooth as a cut diamond 'Graceland' is one of the most mature and fully realized albums of the eighties, but it is also historically significant in that it helped to introduce what became known as 'world music' to the West.

Rating:
Sound ★★★★★ Content ★★★★★
Also recommended:
'Still Crazy After All These Years', 'There Goes Rhymin' Simon' and 'Rhythm Of The Saints' (all on WEA).
If you like this, why not try:
David Gray, Jackson Browne, Nick Drake, Jeff Buckley.

Simon And Garfunkel

'BRIDGE OVER TROUBLED WATER'

(Columbia) 1970

Track listing: Bridge Over Troubled Water • El Condor Pasa • Cecilia • Keep The Customer Satisfied • So Long, Frank Lloyd Wright • Boxer • Baby Driver • Only Living Boy In New York • Why Don't You Write Me • Bye Bye Love • Song For The Asking

One of the biggest-selling and best-loved albums of all time was many months in the making as Paul Simon honed his gentle, pensive folk songs to perfection. But his meticulous attention to detail paid off handsomely with sales in excess of 12 million, a six-year residency in the UK album charts and numerous nominations for 'All Time Greatest Album' decades after he and partner Art Garfunkel had gone their separate ways.

Art's contribution is limited to providing angelic harmonies to Paul's melodies, but this was an essential element of their appeal. The title track has an elegiac, classical quality that still moves many soft-centred romantics, but there are also lively, upbeat numbers such as 'Cecilia' and 'Keep The Customers Satisfied' to compliment the quiet, understated sketches 'The Only Living Boy In New York' and 'The Boxer' that helped widen pop's appeal to the 30-somethings and even beyond.

Rating:
Sound ★★★★☆ Content ★★★★★

Simon And Garfunkel

'TALES FROM NEW YORK'

2 CDs (Columbia) 1999

Track listing: CD 1 – The Sound Of Silence • Wednesday Morning 3am • The Sun Is Burning • Peggy-O • Benedictus • He Was My Brother • We've Got A Groovy Thing Goin' • Homeward Bound • I Am A Rock • Kathy's Song • April Come She Will • Leaves That Are Green • Flowers Never Bend With The Rainfall • The Dangling Conversation • Scarborough Fair-Canticle • Patterns • Cloudy • For Emily, Wherever I May Find Her • Save The Life Of My Child • 7 O'Clock News-Silent Night

CD 2 – A Hazy Shade Of Winter • The 59th Street Bridge Song (Feelin' Groovy) • At The Zoo • Fakin' It • Punky's Dilemma • You Don't Know Where You Interest Lies • Mrs Robinson • Old Friends-Bookends • The Boxer • Baby Driver • Keep The Customer Satisfied • So Long, Frank Lloyd Wright • Bridge Over Troubled Water • Cecilia • The Only Living Boy In New York • Bye Bye Love • Song For The Asking • El Condor Pasa • America • My Little Town

With their seamless blend of gossamer-light close-harmony pop and semi-acoustic folk-rock Simon And Garfunkel seemed to sum up the innocent aspirations of the sixties' generation and presage the restless soul-searching of the self-conscious seventies.

After all these years their music retains the power to transport the listener to the time and place where they first heard it; when they were struck by its poetry and purity of tone. Paul Simon's literate and acute observations on the themes of fatalism and fulfilment gave real hope that pop music might become the most expressive art form of the 20th century. Although such aims may have been unrealistic, these songs went a considerable way towards fulfilling that aspiration.

Rating:
Sound ★★★★☆ Content ★★★★★
Also recommended:
'Bookends' and 'Live In Central Park' (Columbia).
If you like this, why not try:
The Everly Brothers, Crosby Stills Nash and Young, **The Byrds**, **Jeff Buckley**.

Simple Minds

'NEW GOLD DREAM'

(Virgin) 1992

Track Listing: Someone, Somewhere In Summertime • Colours Fly And Catherine Wheel • Promised You A Miracle • Big Sleep • Somebody Up There Likes You • New Gold Dream • Glittering Prize • Hunter And The Hunted • King Is White And In The Crowd

Simple Minds personified the kind of bombastic, overwrought, ostentatious pop that gadget-obsessed blokes would consider ideal for showing off the wall-shaking power of their new stereo. Even their ballads are of epic proportions. As if to labour the point it's the drums that dominate with a thick wad of keyboards enveloping the vocals like a boa constrictor and squeezing the life out of the song until Jim Kerr utters his last heroic gasp. They offer an inversion of the traditional rock line-up with songs taking a back seat to the big beat and the sparse guitar fills relegated to a supporting role. At times they sound more like U2 than U2 did at that time prompting one reviewer to remark that they had become 'a legend in their own minds'. But it spawned three hit singles and broke the band big time in America.

Rating:
Sound ★★★★☆ Content ★★★☆☆
Also recommended:
'Glittering Prize 1981–1992' offers a fair summary of their career (Virgin).
If you like this, why not try:
INXS, U2.

Simply Red

'HOLDING BACK THE YEARS'

(East West) 1996

Track listing: Holding Back The Years • Money's Too Tight To Mention • Right Thing • It's Only Love • New Flame • You've Got It • If You Don't Know Me By Now • Stars • Something Got Me Started • Thrill Me • Your Mirror • For Your Babies • So Beautiful • Angel • Fairground

Mick Hucknall has been somewhat unfairly described as 'pop's most successful cabaret singer' because of his preference for smoochy old standards from the seventies, a time when soul had gone soft and sticky around the middle. But his albums are always good value with a fair proportion of original material in the classic Motown mould, immaculate musicianship and first-class production. 'Holding Back The Years' collects the pick of the hits including a sympathetic cover of Harold Melvin's 'If You Don't Know Me By Now' which showcases one of the most expressive voices in pop.

Rating:
Sound ★★★★★ Content ★★★★☆
Also recommended:
'Stars' and 'Picture Book' (both on East West).
If you like this, why not try:
Marvin Gaye, Smokey Robinson, Al Green, Percy Sledge.

Siouxsie And The Banshees

'ONCE UPON A TIME – THE SINGLES'

(Polydor) 1981

Track listing: Hong Kong Garden • Mirage • The Staircase (Mystery) • Playground Twist • Love In A Void • Happy House • Christine • Israel • Spellbound • Arabian Knights

'TWICE UPON A TIME – THE SINGLES'

(Polydor) 1992

Track listing: Fireworks • Slowdive • Melt • Dear Prudence • Swimming Horses • Dazzle • Overground • Cities In Dust • Candyman • This Wheel's On Fire • The Passenger • Peek-A-Boo • The Killing Jar • The Last Beat Of My Heart • Kiss Them For Me • Shadowtime • Fear • Face To Face

An all-pervasive melancholia and an incandescent beauty irradiates the music of the Banshees, a group who cast off the ripped T-shirts and safety pins, along with their punk origins and took shelter in the decaying mansion of Goth-rock.

'Hong Kong Garden' and 'Love In A Void' are the remnants of their punk roots, onto which were grafted the darker seeds of psychedelia. The resulting hybrid blooms like an exotic but deadly orchid saturating the air with the sickly-sweet scent of poisonous perfume, all the while wrapping its tendrils around the unsuspecting to the accompaniment of an insistent, ominous drone, a swarm of strings and a smattering of ethnic percussion. And gilding this fatal flower is Siouxsie's spectral, keening vocal swamped in reverb and sounding like a fairground barker announcing the macabre attractions in her freak show.

Despite the title of these two CDs there are no happy endings or major key modulations to bring the nightmare to an end. Sweet dreams.

Rating:
Sound ★★★★☆ Content ★★★★★
Also recommended:
'Kaleidoscope', 'A Kiss In The Dreamhouse' and the covers album 'Through The Looking Glass' (all on Polydor).
If you like this, why not try:
The Cure, The Sisters of Mercy, The Mission, The Cult.

The Sisters Of Mercy

'VISION THING'

(Merciful Release/East West) 1990

Track listing: Vision Thing • Ribbons • Detonation Boulevard • Something Fast • When You Don't See Me • Doctor Jeep • More • I Was Wrong

There is a scene in the cult comic book horror film *Blade* in which modern-day vampire hunter Wesley Snipes slaughters the bloodsucking dancers at a disco for the undead. Had our hero been less trigger-happy he might have stayed and got his rocks off to The Sisters Of Mercy, which as every good Goth knows is the music most commonly favoured by the undead in their leisure hours.

Against a chorus of ominous droning voices, tribal drums and

slabs of bible-black guitars Andrew Eldritch invokes unseen horrors from the abyss.

Fortunately, you don't have to wait until you're six feet under to enjoy it.

Rating:
Sound ★★★★☆ Content ★★★★☆
Also recommended:
'A Slight Case Of Overbombing – Greatest Hits Vol:1' and 'First, Last And Always' (both on Merciful Release).
If you like this, why not try:
The Mission, Siouxsie And The Banshees, Fields Of The Nephilim.

Slade

'SLAYED'

(Polydor) 1972

Track listing: How D'You Ride? • The Whole World's Goin' Crazee • Look At Last Nite • I Won't Let It 'Appen Agen • Move Over • Gudbuy T'Jane • Gudbuy Gudbuy • Mama Weer All Crazee Now • I Don' Mind • Let The Good Times Roll • Feel So Fine

Slade rarely feature in the heavyweight histories of rock, or in lists of classic albums, and yet they were one of the most successful and best-loved bands in Britain for almost 20 years. If your party is flagging, Slade can be guaranteed to get the bodies back on the dancefloor and if your team is trailing 2–1 at half-time Noddy and the lads have a rousing chant for the terraces to galvanize them into getting that winning goal.

'Slayed' marks the group's transition from boozy, working-class rabble-rousers to noisy chart champions with a sound that stomped all over the opposition and titles that exasperated the nation's English teachers. So crank up the volume and immerse yourself in a ravishingly raucous noise fortified by Noddy's foghorn vocal. Crazee.

Rating:
Sound ★★★★☆ Content ★★★★☆

Slade

'GREATEST HITS'

(Polydor) 1999

Track listing: Get Down And Get With It • Coz I Luv You • Look Wot You Dun • Take Me Bak 'Ome • Mama Weer All Crazee Now • Gudbuy T' Jane • Cum On Feel The Noize • Skweeze Me Pleeze Me • My Friend Stan • Everyday • Bangin' Man • Far Far Away • How Does It Feel • In For A Penny • We'll Bring The House Down • Lock Up Your Daughters • My Oh My • Run Run Away • All Join Hands • Radio Wall Of Sound • Merry Xmas Everybody

Few compilations can boast the inclusion of 17 consecutive top 20 singles, (six of which were number ones) by a band whose career spans two decades as unrivalled hit makers and then top it off with the most fun festive Christmas single ever recorded.

'Hits' charts Slade's career from the pub pleaser 'Get Down And Get With It' to their brief tenure as teen heroes in the early seventies, through to the weaker work of the eighties when they enjoyed a second run as festival favourites.

Remastering has opened out the heavily compressed sound of previous issues so there has never been a better time to replace those worn-out 45s or to discover why your dad goes all misty-eyed when he hears 'Merry Christmas Everybody' every year. It isn't the booze, you know.

Rating:
Sound ★★★★☆ Content ★★★★☆
Also recommended:
'Sladest' and 'Slade In Flame' (both Polydor).
If you like this, why not try:
Gary Glitter, Mud, **Mott The Hoople**, **Sweet**.

Sly And The Family Stone

'BEST OF'

(Epic) 1992

Track listing: Dance To The Music • I Want To Take You Higher • Family Affair • Thank You • I Get High On You • Stand • M'Lady • Skin I'm In • Everyday People • Sing A Simple Song • Hot Fun In The Summertime • Don't Call Me Nigger, Whitey • Brave And Strong • Life • Everybody Is A Star • If You Want Me To Stay • (You Caught Me) Smilin' • Whatever Will Be Will Be • Running Away • Family Affair (Remix)

'I want to take you higher,' declares Sly on the song of the same name – and he more than fulfils his desire on 20 of the funkiest tracks ever committed to tape. At a time when flower power and black power were empowering a generation, Sly provided the music for them all to party to – an intoxicating synthesis of soul and psychedelia spiked with a smattering of social comment and some seriously stoned sounds. James Brown may be the undisputed

'Godfather Of Soul', but it was Sly who prescribed the formula for all future experiments by Funkadelic, Prince, Michael Jackson and a host of rap and hip-hop artists. Samplers, too, continue to find these tracks a rich source of inspiration. But here are the originals in all their digital glory. If these tracks don't have you groovin' till you wear a whole in the carpet, then you must be comatose!

Rating:
Sound ★★★★☆ Content ★★★★☆
Also recommended:
'Stand!' (Epic).
If you like this, why not try:
Funkadelic, Parliament, **Prince**.

Smashing Pumpkins

'SIAMESE DREAM'

(Hut/Virgin) 1993

Track listing: Cherub Rock • Quiet • Today • Hummer • Rocket • Disarm • Soma • Geek USA • Mayonaise • Spaceboy • Silverfuck • Sweet Sweet • Luna

Chicago's Smashing Pumpkins ring the changes on grunge with an album that adds cellos, Mellotron and strings to Sub Pop's customary slabs of sound. The Pumpkins are more melodic than their contemporaries Soundgarden, Alice In Chains and The Stone Temple Pilots; their material ranging from manic metal riffing to delicate acoustic introspection with an 'alternative' ambience.

The band are the brainchild of Billy Corgan whose embittered confessions reveal a contempt for

middle-class values which is equaled only by his loathing for those bands who leapt aboard the grunge bandwagon as it careered towards the corporate rock cash machine.

To paraphrase Forest Gump, if music was a box of chocolates 'Siamese Dream' would be the nut cluster with the soft caramel centre – a bitter-sweet assortment with a decidedly moreish aftertaste. A confection to be savoured.

Rating:
Sound ★★★★☆ Content ★★★☆☆

Smashing Pumpkins

'MELLON COLLIE AND THE INFINITE SADNESS'

2 CDs (Hut/Virgin) 1995

Track listing: Mellon Collie And The Infinite Sadness • Tonight Tonight • Jellybelly • Zero • Here Is No Why • Bullet With Butterfly Wings • To Forgive • Fuck You • Love • Cupid De Locke • Galapogos • Muzzle • Porcelina Of The Vast Oceans • Take Me Down • Where Boys Fear To Tread • Bodies • Thirty Three • In The Arms Of Sleep • 1979 • Tales Of A Scorched Earth • Thru The Eyes Of Ruby • Stumbleine • XYU • We Only Come Out At Night • Beautiful • Lily • By Starlight • Farewell And Goodnight

After the success of 'Siamese Dream' Billy Corgan set himself a seemingly impossible mission – to boldly go where few 'alternative rock' artists have gone before – the black hole of infinite possibilities and potential disaster known as the double album. For a grunge act this was a perilous expedition into uncharted territory, but The Pumpkins are no ordinary navigators. Their dark melodies are welded to a penetrating power that sees them through the storms of uncertainty to the dark matter at the heart of their own peculiar universe. Imagine *Alice In Wonderland* with a soundtrack by Black Sabbath and you have some idea what you're in for. A singular experience.

Rating:
Sound ★★★★☆ Content ★★★☆☆
Also recommended: 'Adore' (Hut).
If you like this, why not try:
Soundgarden, The Stone Temple Pilots, Alice In Chains.

Patti Smith

'HORSES'

(Arista/BMG) 1975

Track listing: Gloria • Redondo Beach • Birdland • Free Money • Kimberly • Break It Up • Land • Horses • Land Of A Thousand Dances • La Mer • Elegie • My Generation

Had Patti Smith been born in another time she might have been hanging out with the romantic poets Rimbaud and Baudelaire and getting elegantly wasted. Fortunately for us she was instead born in time to hang out with Tom Verlaine and John Cale at CBGBs.

In using punk and poetry to exorcize a festering hatred for her strict religious upbringing and its intolerance of her homosexuality, she made one of the most eloquent and powerful statements of the period. The unholy alliance of rock and Catholic iconography is most striking

on the opener, 'Gloria in excelsis deo' in which she juxtaposes a vitriolic diatribe against the church with the explicit erotic hunger for another woman expressed in the old Van Morrison song of the same name.

As one critic remarked, her poetry was 'too raw, uninhibited and spontaneous to shine in print', but it made a glorious sound when messing with the riffs and rhythms of rock.

Rating:
Sound ★★★★☆ Content ★★★★★
Also recommended:
'Easter' (BMG).
If you like this, why not try:
Television, The Doors, MC5, Iggy And The Stooges.

The Smiths

'THE QUEEN IS DEAD'

(WEA) 1986

Track listing: The Queen Is Dead • Frankly Mr Shankly • I Know It's Over • Never Had No One Ever • Cemetery Gates • Bigmouth Strikes Again • The Boy With The Thorn In His Side • Vicar In A Tutu • There Is A Light That Never Goes Out • Some Girls Are Bigger Than Others

In a decade characterized by compromise and conformity The Smiths stood for integrity, independence and a healthy dose of sarcasm. Their choice of moniker was intended to convey their unglamorous image, their Britishness and their contempt for pop's preoccupation with pretentious names. Morrissey even wore a hearing aid as a homage to another unlikely icon, crooner Johnny Ray. But when added together their entire output (four albums and 18 singles) occupied less than a month in the charts, although their influence was considerably greater than is suggested by the statistics.

On their third studio album Morrissey's self-pitying monologues are offset by waspish observations on the British obsession with social propriety and its appetite for juicy scandal.

The songs point accusing fingers at a society that jealously guards its privacy, but doesn't see any harm in poking its collective nose in the affairs of others, while Marr's shimmering guitar assuages the stinging sarcasm and even manages to sweeten Morrissey's excesses of winsomeness and whingeing. Ten years after The Sex Pistols incited revolt against Her Majesty's 'fascist regime' The Smiths recast her as a tragicomic figure, a poor old dear beseiged by a demented royalist who offers her his thoughts on the state of the nation.

The Smiths made it possible for future independent acts such as Oasis and The Stones Roses to break into the mainstream and they also created some of the most sardonic and significant songs of the period. And for that Morrissey surely earned the right to wring his hands and moan about how miserable he is.

Rating:
Sound ★★★★☆ Content ★★★★★

The Smiths

'STRANGEWAYS HERE WE COME'

(WEA) 1987

Track listing: A Rush And A Push And The Land Is Ours • I Started Something I Couldn't Finish • Death Of A Disco Dancer • Girlfriend In A Coma • Stop Me If You Think You've Heard This One Before • Last Night I Dreamt That Somebody Loved Me • Unhappy Birthday • Paint A Vulgar Picture • Death At One's Elbow • I Won't Share You

Completed just before they split, 'Strangeways' has the air of a band who knew they had come as far as they could before the law of diminishing returns set in. It's not their best album by far – there are too many half-hearted throwaways for that to be the case – and it plays safer than 'Meat Is Murder'(which tackles the subjects of child abuse, sadistic school teachers and the systematic slaughter of animals for mass consumption), but it boasts a confidence and defiance that the earlier albums lacked. It also happens to be the album that begs to be played loud and annoy the neighbours.

Rating:
Sound ★★★★☆ Content ★★★★☆
Also recommended:
'The Smiths', 'Meat Is Murder', 'Hatful Of Hollow', 'Louder Than Bombs' (a collection of B-sides and rarities) and 'Rank' the live album (all on WEA).
If you like this, why not try:
Morrisey's solo albums, **Pulp**, **The Stone Roses**, **Happy Mondays**.

Soft Cell

'NON-STOP EROTIC CABARET'

(Some Bizarre/Mercury) 1996

Track listing: Frustration • Tainted Love • Seedy Films • Youth • Sex Dwarf • Entertain Me • Chips On My Shoulder • Bedsitter • Secret Life • Say Hello, Wave Goodbye

Bonus tracks: Where Did Our Love Go? • Memorabilia • Facility Girls • Fun City • Torch • Insecure Me • What? • ...So

Soft Cell were the prototypical synth-pop duo for the eighties, although their salacious stories of seedy Soho nightlife were the antithesis of the New Romantics' fancy-dress-party fantasies. While Dave Ball tinkered on rinky-dink keyboards Marc Almond played the gay torch singer to the hilt, sighing seductively in heavy mascara and inviting the listener to enjoy the peep show. Almond described their music as a 'Eurodisco, melancholic, introspective electro-cabaret thing', and it proved incredibly popular in the clubs and in the charts. 'Tainted Love' became one of the ten biggest-selling singles in America ever and provided the springboard for Almond's subsequent solo career.

This reissue of their first album adds eight extra tracks including the singles 'Torch' and 'What?' together with their B-sides.

Rating:
Sound ★★★★★ Content ★★★★☆
Also recommended:
'The Art Of Falling Apart' and 'This Last Night Of Sodom' (Mercury).

If you like this, why not try:
Marc Almond's solo albums, The Grid, Orchestral Maneouvres in the Dark.

The Soft Boys

'UNDERWATER MOONLIGHT'

(Rykodisc) 1980

Track listing: I Wanna Destroy You • Kingdom Of Love • Positive Vibrations • I Got The Hots • Insanely Jealous • Tonight • You'll Have To Go Sideways • Old Pervert • Queen Of Eyes • Underwater Moonlight

Bonus tracks: Vegetable Man • Strange • Only The Stones Remain • Where Are The Prawns? • Dreams • Black Snake Diamond Rock • There's Nobody Like You • Song No 4

In 1981 The Television Personalities declared that they knew where Syd Barrett lived. They may have tracked down the man, but his restless spirit went roaming the streets until it took possession of Robyn Hitchcock, leader of the Soft Boys. It has inspired Robyn to write some of the most skewed psych-pop songs since Syd went off the rails and in return its host continues to keep the old boy in work to this day. Robyn has gone on to produce more commercially successful records than this early offering, especially since he found a mentor in Peter Buck of REM, but this has an unrefined charm and honesty that he rarely recaptured. Oddball lyrics, a quintessentially English psych sound and some deliriously warped guitars. If you like Barrett, The Byrds and The Velvet Underground find a space on your shelf for this criminally under-rated record and make an old ghost very happy.

Rating:
Sound ★★★★☆ Content ★★★★☆
Also recommended:
'The Soft Boys 1976–1981' a 2CD set of rarities and previously unreleased items (Rykodisc).
If you like this, why not try:
Robyn Hitchcock's solo albums, Syd Barrett, **The Only Ones**.

Soft Machine

'SOFT MACHINE VOL 1'

(Big Beat) 1989

Track listing: Hope For Happiness • Joy Of A Toy • Hope For Happiness (Reprise) • Why Am I So Short • So Boot If At All • Certain Kind • Save Yourself • Priscilla • Lullaby Letter • We Did It Again • Plus Belle Qu'une Poubelle • Why Are We Sleeping • Box 25-4 Lid

'SOFT MACHINE VOL 2'

(Big Beat) 1989

Track listing: Pataphysical Introduction Pt 1 • Concise British Alphabet Pt 1 • Hibou, Anenome And Bear • Concise British Alphabet Pt 2 • Hulloder • Dada Was Here • Thank You Pierrot Lunaire • Have You Ever Bean Green • Pataphysical Introduction Pt 2 • Out Of Tunes • As Long As He Lies Perfectly Still • Dedicated To You But You Weren't Listening • Fire Engine Passing With Bells Clanging • Pig • Orange Skin Food • Door Opens And Closes • 10.30 Returns To The Bedroom

Soft Machine's first two albums are often combined as a two-for-the-price-of-one package, which may prove too tempting to resist if you're into free-form improvisational jazz-rock fusion, or will serve to confirm that the Softs are well past their sell-by date, if you're not.

The band's first and only single 'Love Makes Sweet Music', which bore superficial similarities to Traffic and early Floyd, was their only concession to commercialism after which they abandoned psychedelia for a form of musical existentialism. The focus on the first album oscillates between Robert Wyatt's fragile, wistful vocal and Kevin Ayer's deep ominous singing, while keyboard player Mike Ratledge responds with avant-garde lines that would have confounded Thelonious Monk. By the second set Ayers has been ousted in favour of bassist Hugh Hopper, but the atmosphere of amiable anarchy and experimentation remains.

Rating:
Sound ★★★☆☆ Content ★★★☆☆
Also recommended:
'The Harvest Years – The Best Of Soft Machine' (See For Miles).
If you like this, why not try:
Caravan, Gong, Matching Mole, Kevin Ayers and Robert Wyatt solo albums.

Sonic Youth

'DAYDREAM NATION'

(Blast First) 1988

Track listing: Teenage Riot • Silver Rocket • The Sprawl • Cross The Breeze • Eric's Trip • Total Trash • Hey Joni • Providence • Candle • Rain King • Kissability • Trilogy: The Wonder Hyperstation Eliminator

On 'Daydream Nation' Thurston Moore and Lee Ranaldo erect a granite monolith between themselves and the rest of the rock world as some form of significant statement and then proceed to demolish it with the sonic drill of their twin guitars. When it finally crumbles what is revealed is a teeming urban sprawl of graffiti-scrawled alleyways lit by spluttering neon signs where the trash is looked on as art. This is the musical equivalent of Tracy Emin's notorious 'Bed' exhibit or Damien Hirst's cows in formaldehyde. The only 'traditional' rock songs are to be found in the sated rapture of 'Teen Age Riot' and 'Silver Rocket', although 'Rain King' usurps a nifty riff from ZZ Top and 'The Sprawl' recalls The Velvet Underground's morbid obsession with sex, insanity and death. Yes, this is Sonic Youth at their most optimistic and accessible. Major label cheque books could already be heard unfolding in the wail of fading feedback.

Rating:
Sound ★★★☆☆ Content ★★★★☆

Sonic Youth

'GOO'

(Geffen) 1990

Track listing: Dirty Boots • Tunic (Song For Karen) • Mary Christ • Kool Thing • Mote • My Friend Goo • Disapearer • Mildred Pierce • Cinderella's Big Score • Scooter And Jinx • Titanium Expose

Sonic Youth took atonal avant-garde cacophony to subterranean levels where even The Jesus And Mary Chain feared to tread. In the days before Nirvana, the Big Apple's guitar anarchists dominated the indie underground, evoking urban degeneration through unrelenting guitar noise and intervals of ominous cinematic mood music that might have come from a cyberpunk soundtrack.

If you suffer from claustrophobia, steer clear of this album which will make you feel like you've been smothered by a collapsing skyscraper. Or, alternatively, invest in their more accessible offering 'Daydream Nation' which fuses garage and grunge to melodies that Neil Young would have died for. But whichever option you choose, don't ignore this band.

Rating:
Sound ★★★☆☆ Content ★★★★☆
Also recommended:
'Daydream Nation' and 'Sister' (both on Blast First).
If you like this, why not try:
Husker Dü, The Pixies, The Jesus And Mary Chain.

Spandau Ballet

'GOLD – THE BEST OF'

(EMI) 2000

Track listing: Gold • True • Only When You Leave • Lifeline • Communication • Instinction • Chant No 1 (I Don't Need This Pressure On) • To Cut A Long Story Short • The Freeze • Musclebound • Paint Me Down • She Loved Like Diamond • Round And Round • Highly Strung • Fight For Ourselves • I'll Fly For You • Through The Barricades

Back in the eighties, when sampling was a word used only by those carrying out market research,

Spandau Ballet were raiding the dressing-up box to gatecrash the trendiest parties at chic clubs such as Billy's and Blitz. But they were only nominal New Romantics. Blessed with one of the best names in the business, but questionable dress sense, they attempted to cultivate an image of Eastern European decadence. Their earliest hits, 'To Cut A Long Story Short', 'The Freeze' and 'Musclebound' are partially successful in blending electropop with black American dance music, but their later tracks are outrageously overdressed with a sound as slick and soporific as Roxy Music during their Euro-pop period. One for the nostalgia crowd.

Rating:
Sound ★★★★☆ Content ★★★☆☆
Also recommended:
'Journeys To Glory' (Chrysalis).
If you like this, why not try:
Duran Duran, Heaven 17, **The Human League**.

Sparks

'MAEL INTUITION – THE BEST OF SPARKS 1974–76'

(Island) 1990

Track listing: This Town Ain't Big Enough For Both Of Us • Amateur Hour • Here In Heaven • Thank God It's Not Christmas • Hasta Manana Monsieur • Complaints • Never Turn Your Back On Mother Earth • Something For The Girl With Everything • Achoo • Propaganda • At Home, At Work, At Play • Reinforcements • B.C. • Hospitality On Parade • Happy Hunting Ground • Without Using Hands • Get In The Swing • It Ain't 1918 • In The Future • Looks, Looks, Looks

Commercial pop acts don't come much more eccentric than Sparks whose frontmen, Ron and Russell Mael, presented their idiosyncratic songs as if they were the soundtrack to an animated Marx Brothers movie. In '74 they caught the public imagination with the quirky curiosity 'This Town Ain't Big Enough For Both Of Us', for what many thought would be their 15 minutes of fame. But with their subsequent singles the duo continued to dazzle the sensibilities with an eclectic and frenetic mix of styles that distilled elements of Judy Garland, Betty Boop and Frank Zappa. Russell's unintelligible falsetto and Ron's manic stare had them classified as a novelty act, but here are 20 good reasons why they shouldn't be dismissed as simply another seventies curiosity.

Unfortunately they couldn't sustain the joke beyond the first act. But they returned after the interval in the role of an electropop duo with a string of hits produced by Euro-disco Svengali Giorgio Moroder. None of which, sadly, are included on this compilation. Needless to say, their sense of irony and the absurd remained as sharp as ever.

Rating:
Sound ★★★★☆ Content ★★★★☆
Also recommended:
'Gratuitous Sax And Senseless Violins' (Arista/BMG).
If you like this, why not try:
XTC, The Sensational Alex Harvey Band, Julian Cope, Syd Barrett.

The Spice Girls

'SPICE'

(Virgin) 1996

Track listing: Wannabe • Say You'll Be There • 2 Become 1 • Love Thing • Last Time Lover • Mama • Who Do You Think You Are • Something Kinda Funny • Naked • If U Can't Dance

The Spice Girls were manufactured and marketed as the embodiment of girl power, the impudent answer to the boy band phenomena, but they proved to be no more provocative than a live action version of Minnie The Minx. Girl power was the flavour of the mid-nineties and Simon Fuller, the Svengali behind the Spice Girls, ensured that his creations served up the most easily digestible fare on the menu. Their music is as brightly coloured as a bag of dolly mixtures and of equally questionable nutritional value, having been concocted by a small army of producers and session musicians from a catalogue of techno, house and club cliches. But the ingenious element that ensured brand loyalty was to use the girls' distinctive personalities as an essential ingredient in the mix, rather than merely as decorative trimmings.

'Spice' provides a sampling of skilfully crafted pop that preserves the sound of the times as perfectly as anything else in the singles chart at the time. By the time it had passed its sell-by date the girls were multi-millionaires and immune to criticism.

Rating:
Sound ★★★★☆ Content ★★★☆☆

Also recommended:
'Spiceworld – Original Soundtrack' (Virgin).
If you like this, why not try:
All Saints, **Geri Halliwell**, The Sugar Babes.

Bruce Springsteen

'DARKNESS ON THE EDGE OF TOWN'

(Columbia) 1978

Track listing: Badlands • Adam Raised A Cain • Something In The Night • Candy's Room • Racing In The Street • The Promised Land • Factory • Streets Of Fire • Prove It All Night • Darkness On The Edge Of Town

Springsteen had a lot to live up to after being hailed as 'the future of rock and roll' and a lot to live down after producing the overwrought, Spector-styled 'Born To Run'. He managed both with this more modest companion piece which many regard as his finest album. The melodrama and heart-on-the-sleeve romanticism of its predecessor has been replaced by fatalism and a keener sense of character, particularly in the melancholy which pervades 'Candy's Room' and the desperation evoked in 'Racing In The Street'.

Other songs such as 'Badlands' and 'Adam Raised A Cain' enhance Springsteen's image as the hoarse voice of the honest, hard-working small town guy who is nostalgic for a past that never existed and is disillusioned with the broken promises made in the name of the American Dream. In Springsteen's songs the system grinds the good men down, but so long as he has a guitar, a girl and a gleaming automobile there is always hope at the end of the highway.

Rating:
Sound ★★★★☆ Content ★★★★☆

Bruce Springsteen

'THE RIVER'

2 CDs (Columbia) 1980

Track listing: The Ties That Bind • Sherry Darling • Jackson Cage • Two Hearts • Independence Day • Hungry Heart • Out In The Street • Crush On You • You Can Look (But You Better Not Touch) • I Wanna Marry You • The River • Point Blank • Cadillac Ranch • I'm A Rocker • Fade Away • Stolen Car • Ramrod • The Price You Pay • Drive All Night • Wreck On The Highway

Opinions are sharply divided over the merits of this erratic double album. 'Cadillac Ranch', 'Stolen Car', 'Drive All Night' and 'Wreck On The Highway' suggest that Springsteen's favourite themes had already become a cliche and that he had put commercial interests above his hard-won credibility as a social commentator. But the title track reveals an uncommon talent for narrative and an empathy for the anonymous individuals whose dreams have been overwhelmed by reality. The record-buying public don't seem to care too much for social realism and were happy to swallow this whole, giving Bruce his first number one American album and his first top ten single with 'Hungry Heart'.

If this had been released by any other artist it would have been welcomed as one for the jukebox with songs for the working stiffs to dance to, or to drown their sorrows at the bar. But coming from 'The Boss' it smacks of treading water when he should be walking on it. Perhaps all that was needed was for Springsteen to assess his own work with the same acutely critical eye as he did American society and its self-serving system.

If you want social realism or the serious side of relationships seek out 'Darkness On The Edge Of Town' or 'Tunnel Of Love'. And if you want something for the car stereo buy 'Greatest Hits'. But give this a miss.

Rating:
Sound ★★★★☆ Content ★★★☆☆

Bruce Springsteen

'NEBRASKA'

(Columbia) 1982

Track Listing: Nebraska • Atlantic City • Mansion On The Hill • Johnny 99 • Highway Patrolman • State Trooper • Used Cars • Open All Night • My Father's House • Reason To Believe

Legend has it that Springsteen decided to issue this solo acoustic 'demo', which he had recorded at home on cassette, after dismissing the full band versions as being overproduced. It's a pity he hadn't done the same after recording 'Born To Run', though subsequent solo performances of the title track suggest that he wished he had.

'Nebraska' sketches a portrait of small-town America in stark monochromatic images that might have come from a forties *film noir*, or a low-budget exploitation shocker. There is little colour either in the lives of the characters who are mainly modern-day outlaws, or flawed tough guys with a soft centre who can't seem to escape their fate.

The comparisons with Johnny Cash are not entirely gratuitous. Cash recorded 'Johnny 99' and 'Highway Patrolman' with a voice that might have been sculpted in sound.

Ideal late night listening and a much under-rated album.

Rating:
Sound ★★★☆☆ Content ★★★★★

Bruce Springsteen

'LIVE 1975–1985'

3 CDs (Columbia) 1986

Track listing: Thunder Road • Adam Raised A Cain • Spirit In The Night • 4th July, Ashbury Park • Paradise By The 'C' • Fire • Growing Up • It's Hard To Be A Saint In The City • Backstreets • Rosalita • Raise Your Hand • Hungry Heart • Two Hearts • Cadillac Ranch • You Can Look (But You'd Better Not Touch) • Independence Day • Badlands • Because The Night • Candy's Room • Darkness On The Edge Of Town • Racing In The Street • This Land Is Your Land • Nebraska • Johnny 99 • Reason To Believe • Born In The USA • Seeds • The River • Darlington County • Working On The Highway • Promised Land • Cover Me • I'm On Fire • Bobby Jean • My Home Town • Born To Run • No Surrender • 10th Avenue Freeze Out • Jersey Girl

Bruce didn't do anything by halves. His live shows were legendary for running over four hours and this compilation of essential 'in-concert' performances delivers the same more-bangs-for-your-bucks philosophy. For the hardcore fan this is the business – 'The Boss' in his preferred setting, working up a sweat with the E Street Band in front of ecstatic audiences and performing a set's worth of rarities, such as 'Fire' and 'Because The Night' as well as covers of Woody Guthrie's 'This Land Is Your Land' and Edwyn Starr's 'War'. The former were recorded by other artists during the period when Springsteen was forbidden from entering a recording studio for legal reasons.

He may not be as fashionable now as he was back in the eighties, but after three hours of virile, chest-beating, blue-collar anthems and smoky bar room ballads you'll know why they called him 'The Boss'.

Rating:
Sound ★★★★☆ Content ★★★★☆

Bruce Springsteen

'GHOST OF TOM JOAD'

(Columbia) 1995

Track listing: The Ghost Of Tom Joad • Straight Time • Highway 28 • Youngstown • Sinola Cowboys • The Line • Balboa Park • Dry Lightning • The New Timer • Across The Border • Galveston Bay • My Best Was Never Good Enough

After the grossly disappointing 'Lucky Town' and 'Human Touch' (which had been released simultaneously) critics and fans alike began to despair of hearing the authentic voice of 'The Boss' again. But then Bruce returned to his roots for a semi-acoustic album inspired by John Steinbeck's social parable 'The Grapes Of Wrath'. The flag-waving populism of 'Born In The USA' was replaced by songs in the manner of Woody Guthrie which articulated the frustration felt by the impoverished farmers of the mid-west and those who despaired of sharing in the American dream. 'The Boss' had found his voice again and it was a voice that was at times earnest, sincere, sombre, subdued and philosophical. 'Tom Joad' was a mature and fitting coda to a career which owed more to Steinbeck than it had done to Dylan.

Rating:
Sound ★★★★☆ Content ★★★★☆

Bruce Springsteen

'GREATEST HITS'

(Columbia) 1995

Track listing: Born To Run • Thunder Road • Badlands • River • Hungry Heart • Atlantic City • Dancing In The USA • Born In The USA • My Home Town • Glory Days • Brilliant Disguise • Human Touch • Better Days • Streets Of Philadelphia • Secret Garden • Murder Incorporated • Blood Brothers • This Hard Land

By the time you've been through this useful collection of big hits it's evident that Bruce's music hasn't changed that much over the years. He mellowed in the nineties on such songs as 'Streets Of Philadelphia' and 'Secret Garden' with their soft synth backing, revealed his introspective side on the intimate 'Atlantic City' and bared his soul on 'Brilliant Disguise' which analysed his disintegrating marriage. More recently he revisited his roots with the Woody

Guthrie and Bob Dylan styled dust-bowl saga 'The Ghost Of Tom Joad', but beneath his well-worn chequered shirt he's still the blue-collar rocker.

He may be one of rock's most articulate spokesmen, but he never shrugged off his obsession with cars, girls and that endless rolling highway.

Rating:
Sound ★★★★☆ Content ★★★★★
Also recommended:
'Tunnel Of Love' (Columbia).
If you like this, why not try:
Bob Dylan, Bryan Adams.

Lisa Stansfield

'LISA STANSFIELD'

(Arista) 1997

Track listing: Never Gonna Fall • Real Thing • I'm Leavin' • Suzanne • Never, Never Gonna Give You Up • Don't Cry For Me • Line • Very Thought Of You • You Know How To Love Me • I Cried My Last Tear Last Night • Honest • Somewhere In Time • Got Me Missing You • Footsteps • Real Thing • People Hold On

Stansfield, 'the Rochdale diva', is blessed with the mellifluous voice of a black soul singer that she cultivated during a childhood spent in front of the radio singing along to Diana Ross. Her self-titled album was produced by the same team who worked with Michael Jackson; their brief being to coat her brand of sinewy dance music in a smooth sugar coating that would make it irresistible to those with a taste for bitter-sweet soul with a soft centre. If you like your ear candy poured on thick, this is for you.

Rating:
Sound ★★★★☆ Content ★★★☆☆
Also recommended:
'Affection' and 'Real Love' (both on Arista).
If you like this, why not try:
Diana Ross, **Mariah Carey**, Soul ll Soul.

Status Quo

'12 GOLD BARS'

(Phonogram) 1980

Track listing: Rockin' All Over The World • Down Down • Caroline • Paper Plane • Break The Rules • Again And Again • Mystery Song • Roll Over Lay Down • Rain • Wild Side Of Life • Whatever You Want • Living On An Island

Back in the early seventies, before they deteriorated into a wrinkly bunch of old rockers on the cabaret and holiday camp circuit, Quo were the personification of heads-down-no nonsense-mindless 12-bar boogie. 25 years later they're still wringing the variations on a very familiar theme, but this party-friendly retrospective has enough genuine rockers from their youthful years to satisfy the air guitar brigade, provided of course that they have the stamina to stay the course.

Rating:
Sound ★★★☆☆ Content ★★★☆☆
Also recommended:
'Hello' and 'Piledriver' (both on Vertigo) plus 'Dog Of Two Heads' (Castle).
If you like this, why not try:
George Thorogood, ZZ Top.

Stereophonics

'JUST ENOUGH EDUCATION TO PERFORM'

(V2) 2001

Track listing: Vegas Two Times • Lying In The Sun • Mr Writer • Step On My Old Size Nines • Have A Nice Day • Nice To Be Out • Watch Them Fly Sundays • Everyday I Think Of Money • Maybe • Caravan Holiday • Rooftop

The third album by the chill-out rockers divided their fans into those who were disappointed by the increased emphasis on acoustic numbers and those who persevered and found that it was a grower. Kelly Jones' wistful semi-acoustic, countrified ballads are in the classic mould and his crowing vocal recalls the young Rod Stewart, but like a fine wine the combination requires a little time to settle and mature.

Although the album marks a promising development, it's not entirely successful. The single, 'Mr Writer', was a wild swing at the music press which missed its target, but the remainder should appeal to those with more subtle tastes.

Rating:
Sound ★★★★☆ Content ★★★★☆
Also recommended:
'Word Gets Around' and 'Performance And Cocktails' (V2).
If you like this, why not try:
Soul Asylum, **Manic Street Preachers**, Oceon Colour Scene.

Al Stewart

'CHRONICLES'

(EMI) 1991

Track listing: Year Of The Cat • On The Border • If It Doesn't Come Naturally, Leave It • Time Passages • Almost Lucy • Song On The Radio • Running Man • Merlin's Time • In Brooklyn • Soho • Small Fruit Song • Manuscript • Roads To Moscow • Nostradamus Pt 1 World Goes To Riyadh – Nostradamus Pt 2

Al's fanciful folk tales and precious Scottish brogue endeared him to sensitive romantic girls the world over who, one imagines, passed their teenage years brooding in their bedsits to the beguiling sound of his understated melodies. But there was also much to set the male imagination afire – the richly detailed descriptions of the ancient warrior bard in 'Merlin's Time' and the bitter winter battle scene in 'Roads Of Moscow', to name but two.

As with the similarly sounding Donovan, Al is another neglected artist overdue for reassessment, but this casually assembled collection won't do him any favours. Better to track down those listed below and give this one a miss.

Rating:
Sound ★★★★☆ Content ★★★☆☆
Also recommended:
'To Whom It May Concern – Al Stewart 1966–70' and 'Best Of –The Centenary Collection' (both EMI) and 'Past, Present And Future' (Beat Goes On).
If you like this, why not try:
Donovan, Nick Drake, Leonard Cohen, Jeff Buckley, Cat Stevens.

Rod Stewart

'HANDBAGS AND GLADRAGS'

2 CDs (Mercury) 1995

Track listing: CD 1 – Every Picture Tells A Story • Interludings • You Wear It Well • You Put Something Better Inside Of Me • Only A Hobo • Reason To Believe • It's All Over Now • Cut Across Shorty • Lost Paraguayos • Mandolin Wind • Crying, Laughing, Loving, Lying • Street Fighting Man • Man Of Constant Sorrow • I'm Losing You • Lady Day • So Tired • Oh No Not My Baby • What Made Milwaukee Famous • Handbags And Gladrags

CD 2 – Henry • Maggie May • Gasoline Alley • Dixie Toot • Every Time We Say Goodbye • Twistin' The Night Away • True Blue • Lochinvar • Farewell • Italian Girls • Mama You've Been On My Mind • Country Comfort • I Wouldn't Change A Thing • Sweet Little Rock And Roller • I'd Rather Go Blind • Angel • Missed You • Dirty Old Town

Long before the excesses of a celebrity lifestyle ravaged his voice and diminished his talent, Rod was held in high regard as one of the great rock vocalists and a songwriter of considerable sensitivity. He had an ear for a good tune and the rare ability of making them his own. Although he didn't consider himself a serious songwriter 'Mandolin Wind', 'You Wear It Well', 'Maggie May' and 'Handbags and Gladrags' stand with the very best work that any singer-songwriter of any era has produced. On the latter the old rascal wears his heart on his sleeve, but his soulful, brandy-saturated vocal brings a virile power to a tender ballad that would have turned to sentimental mush in a lesser artist's hands.

This thoughtfully compiled retrospective of his early seventies recordings includes five previously unreleased tracks which rank with his most impassioned performances and goes some way towards making amends for the countless scrappy compilations that still clutter up the racks. Rod may well have proved that blondes have more fun, but being unfaithful to his muse evidently cost him dear.

Rating:
Sound ★★★★☆ Content ★★★★★
Also recommended:
'Gasoline Alley' and 'The Rod Stewart Album' (both on Mercury).
If you like this, why not try:
The Faces, **The Jeff Beck Group,**
Sam Cooke, Al Green.

Stiff Little Fingers

'ALL THE BEST'

2 CDs (EMI) 1991

Track listing: Suspect Device • Wasted Life • Alternative Ulster • 78rpm • Gotta Get Away • Bloody Sunday • Straw Dogs • You Can't Say Crap On The Radio • At The Edge • Running Bear • White Christmas • Nobody's Hero • Tin Soldiers • Back To Front • Mr Fire Coal Man • Just Fade Away • Go For It • Doesn't Make It Alright • Silver Lining • Safe As Houses • Sad Eyed People • Two Guitars Clash • Listen • That's When You're Blood Bumps • Good For Nothing • Talkback • Stands To Reason • Bits Of Kids • Touch And Go • Price Of Admission

The title of a rare EP track, 'Two Guitars Clash', describes the adrenaline rush of hearing punk for the first time and it also aptly describes the abrasive sound of

Belfast's best punk band whose collective singles are compiled on this essential double CD set. But scouring guitars was only one element of their sound. The most distinctive feature was Jake Burns' irate roar which, when allied to astringent lyrics, catchy hooks and rapid-fire drumming produced some of the most durable artefacts of the era. But many will remember SLF for the fire and fury of their anthem 'Alternative Ulster' and a fistful of frenetic singles such as 'Straw Dogs' and 'Tin Soldiers' which belittled bull-headed macho posturing, political expediency and prejudice.

This inflammable material has lost little of its incendiary power.

Rating:
Sound ★★★★☆ Content ★★★★☆
Also recommended:
'Inflammable Material' (EMI).
If you like this, why not try:
The Undertones, The Clash, UK Subs.

Sting

'TEN SUMMONER'S TALES'

(A&M) 1993

Track listing: Prologue (If I Ever Lose My Faith In You) • Love Is Stronger Than Justice • Fields Of Gold • Heavy Cloud, No Rain • She's Too Good For Me • Seven Days • Saint Augustine In Hell • It's Probably Me • Everybody Laughed But You • Shape Of My Heart • Something The Boy Said • Epilogue (Nothing 'Bout Me)

After the ill-conceived forays into 'jazz-rock fusion' and sombre self-indulgence which marred his first solo albums, Sting fought his way out of a creative cul-de-sac and the Brazilian rainforest to record this modest, more traditional set of tunes. The opener, 'Fields Of Gold' and 'Shape Of My Heart' demonstrate what he does best – McCartneyesque melodic pop without the winsome wordplay – and are set to become modern standards, assuming that anyone has the good sense and taste to cover them.

Rating:
Sound ★★★★★ Content ★★★★☆
Also recommended:
'The Dream Of The Blue Turtles', 'Nothing Like The Sun' and 'Fields Of Gold – The Best Of Sting' (both on A&M).
If you like this, why not try:
The Police, Peter Gabriel

Stone Roses

'THE COMPLETE STONE ROSES'

(Silvertone) 1996

Track listing: So Young • Tell Me • Sally Cinnamon • All Across The Sands • Here It Comes • Elephant Stone • Full Fathom Five • Hardest Thing In The World • Made Of Stone • Going Down • She Bangs The Drum • Mersey Paradise • Standing Here • I Wanna Be Adored • Waterfall • I Am The Resurrection • Where Angel's Play • Fool's Gold • What The World Is Waiting For • Something Burning • One Love

It's hard to imagine that there is anyone who doesn't already own this testament to the power of 'Madchester' rock-dance fusion, but if not suffice to say that the Roses

brought sixties psych-pop sensibilities, incandescent melody and glistening guitars back to an anaemic music scene when it was most in need of a transfusion of fresh blood. Of course, it was all too good to last. Their arrogance ensured that a promising career went pear-shaped long before the belated second album saw the light of day, after which the inevitable press backlash seem to have buried them for good.

Rating:
Sound ★★★★★ Content ★★★★☆
Also recommended:
'The Stone Roses' (Silvertone).
If you like this, why not try:
Love, The Byrds, Happy Mondays.

The Stranglers

'THE HITMEN'

2 CDs (Fame/EMI) 1996

Track listing: CD 1 – Grip '89 • London Lady • Peaches • Go Buddy Go • Hanging Around • Choosey Susie • Something Better Change • Straighten Out • No More Heroes • English Towns • 5 Minutes • Nice 'N' Sleazy • Toiler On The Sea • Mean To Me • Walk On By • Duchess • Nuclear Device • Don't Bring Harry • The Raven • Bear Cage • Who Wants The World

CD 2 – Waltzinblack • Thrown Away • Just Like Nothing On Earth • Let Me Introduce You To The Family • Golden Brown • La Folie • Tramp • Strange Little Girl • European Female • Midnight Summer Dream • Paradise • Skin Deep • No Mercy • Let Me Down Easy • Nice In Nice • Always The Sun • Big In America • Shakin' Like A Leaf • Was It You? • All Day And All Of The Night • 96 Tears • Sweet Smell Of Success

The Stranglers might have languished in the no-man's land of the pub-rock circuit had not punk thrown them a lifeline. But once aboard they were in no mood to be gobbed at by spotty little Herberts with spiky hair and a safety pin through their fleshy parts. The group looked like they could give punk a thorough going over and promptly set about it on a series of ominously aggressive singles beginning with the luridly suggestive 'Peaches'. They may have been old enough to have been Johnny Rotten's uncles, but they summed up punk's fighting spirit better than many of the younger groups. Burnel's rumbling bass and Greenfield's swirling organ circle Cornwell's glowering vocal on these early cuts like opportunist thieves round an unlocked jag. But just when they look like they're going down with the rest of the young lags, they went straight with the gentle, hallucinatory 'Golden Brown' and its upmarket companions 'European Female', 'Always The Sun' and 'Strange Little Girl.'

The CD in question rounds up the usual suspects from the sweaty summer of '77 to the clinical polish of 'Sweet Smell Of Success' in '91.

Rating:
Sound ★★★★☆ Content ★★★★☆
Also recommended:
'The Collection 1977–82' and the original albums 'No More Heroes' and 'Rattus Norvegicus' (all on EMI).
If you like this, why not try:
The Clash, Patti Smith, The Ramones.

Suede

'COMING UP'

(Nude) 1996

Track listing: Trash • Filmstar • Lazy • By The Sea • She • Beautiful Ones • Star Crazy • Picnic By The Motorway • The Chemistry Between Us • Saturday Night

Suede were at the vanguard of the Britpop brat pack, but they clearly owed more to the seventies glam stars than the Beatles or the Kinks who had inspired Blur and Oasis. Suede inhabited a darker, more desolate urban landscape than their rivals, a landscape inhabited by bored youths who stalked the streets looking for casual sex, chemicals and rock and roll suicide in a sequel to 'Ziggy Stardust'. Brett Anderson's studied Bowie impersonation and bruised romanticism irked some, but delighted those who had feared that all the good tunes had been written. Suede proved them wrong.

Rating:
Sound ★★★★☆ Content ★★★★★
Also recommended:
'Dog Man Star' and 'Head Music'.
If you like this, why not try:
David Bowie, Marc Bolan, Roxy Music.

Sweet

'BALLROOM BLITZ – THE VERY BEST OF'

(Polygram TV) 1996

Track listing: Ballroom Blitz • Blockbuster! • Teenage Rampage • Wig Wam Bam • Funny Funny • Action • Fox On The Run •

Hell Raiser • The Six Teens • Alexander Graham Bell • Call Me • Stairway To The Stars • Love Is Like Oxygen • The Lies In Your Eyes • Lost Angels • Turn It Down • Burning • Fever Of Love • Sixties Man • Poppa Joe • Co-Co • Little Willy

Sweet were a heavy-rock act who felt constrained by their ludicrously tight costumes and were embarrassed by their camp glam image. When they tired of playing the big, bouncy bubblegum hits that Chinn and Chapman had been knocking out for them with almost monotonous regularity, they ended the profitable partnership but found that they couldn't replicate the formula. The strength of their pre-teen fan base ensured that their first 'solo' singles, 'Action', 'Fox On The Run' and 'Love Is Like Oxygen', sold in reasonable quantities, but thereafter they suffered the law of diminishing returns. They may have felt that these playground chants were beneath them, but it is for these that they'll be remembered.

Rating:
Sound ★★★★☆ Content ★★★★★
Also recommended:
'Sweet Fanny Adams' and 'Desolation Boulevard' (Castle).
If you like this, why not try:
Gary Glitter, Mud, **Slade**, **Mott the Hoople**.

T Rex

'ELECTRIC WARRIOR'

(Essential/Castle) 1971

Track listing: Mambo Sun • Cosmic Dancer • Jeepster • Monolith • Lean Woman Blues • Get It On • Planet Queen • Girl • The Motivator • Life's A Gas • Rip Off

When Marc Bolan, the elfin emissary of the 'underground', climbed down from his toadstool, cast off his kaftan and plugged in his electric guitar there was no denying his boast that he was 'born to boogie'.

Many of these tracks were recorded live in the studio with a minimum of overdubs which lends them an earthy ambience similar to that of the early Sun records. Several songs suggest that Marc had been digging through his record collection prior to the sessions in search of inspiration. 'Jeepster' is a blatant rip off of 'You'll Be Mine' by Howling Wolf, 'Get It On' acknowledges 'Little Queenie' by Chuck Berry in the fade out and 'Monolith' steals from Gene Chandler's 'Duke Of Earl' (as Marc freely admitted on an early take which featured on the posthumously released 'Electric Warrior Sessions'). But he recycles the riffs with such audacity and charm that few could fail to fall under his spell.

This was the first roar of T-Rextasy, a teasing amalgam of self-made mythology, wistful wordplay and gender-bending bump 'n' grind. Bolan didn't become a cult figure merely because he looked great; he was great.

Rating:
Sound ★★★★☆ Content ★★★★☆

T Rex

'THE SLIDER'

(Edsel) 1972

Track listing: Metal Guru • Mystic Lady • Rock On • The Slider • Baby Boomerang • Spaceball Richochett • Buick Mackane • Telegram Sam • Rabbit Fighter • Baby Strange • Ballrooms Of Mars • Chariot Choogle • Main Man

Bonus tracks: Cadillac • Thunderwing • Lady

From the minimalist mantra that is 'Metal Guru', through the electric boogie of 'Telegram Sam' to the title track with its slow, shuffle rhythm, sinewy strings and melancholic refrain 'The Slider' is Marc at his most charismatic, alternately childlike and seductive. Only 'Chariot Choogle' and 'Buick Mackane' betray his burning obsession with Hendrix and his determination to prove himself a serious musician in the face of those who cruelly wrote him off as a pre-teen phenomenon.

The tracks were evidently laid down in one or two takes in an attempt to recreate the spontaneous feel of the early rock records, leaving producer Tony Visconti to paper over the cracks with strings, backing harmonies and a wall of multi-tracked guitars. For that reason the sound of 'The Slider' owes more to Phil Spector than to Sun.

Unfortunately, the casual, off-hand attitude extends to some of the lyrics which are not surreal, as Bolan later claimed, but merely superficial. Though the sound of the words was always more important to Marc than their meaning. Here is irrefutable evidence that Bolan could work magic with three simple chords and an inspired turn of phrase.

Rating:
Sound ★★★★☆ Content ★★★★☆

T Rex

'TANX'

(Edsel) 1973

Track listing: Tenement Lady • Rapids • Mister Mister • Broken Hearted Blues • Shock Rock • Country Honey • Electric Slim And The Factory Hen • Mad Donna • Born To Boogie • Life Is Strange • The Street And Babe Shadow • Highway Knees • Left Hand Luke And The Beggar Boys

Bonus tracks: Children Of The Revolution • Jitterbug Love • Sunken Rags • Solid Gold Easy Action • Xmas Message • 20th Century Boy • Free Angel

With its mellow mix of laid-back boogie and a sardonic look at Americana, 'Tanx' was the album that Marc had hoped would satisfy the teenyboppers and also win over a more mature audience. But it proved too mellow to appease the fickle, pre-pubescent punters and too insubstantial to attract an older audience. Instead of getting it on, Marc seemed to be leaning back with a self-satisfied smirk on his face and taking it easy as he viewed the world through the window of his limousine. Could it be that he was taking his fans for granted? It certainly sounds like it. 'Mister Mister', 'Shock Rock' and 'The Street And Babe Shadow' sound only half finished, while 'Mad Donna' and 'Born To Boogie' are little more than riffs matched to an easy slogan.

Sandwiched between two hard-rock singles, '20th Century Boy' and 'The Groover' (neither of which were included on the original LP), 'Tanx' was considered lacklustre in comparison with the proud, strutting monster of the T-Rextasy era and the old dinosaur was deemed extinct. However, the presence of a Mellotron and the predominance of languid sax solos suggests that Marc was making a serious effort to find new sounds. It's just that he was too busy being a star to pay enough attention to his music.

Rating:
Sound ★★★★☆ Content ★★★☆☆

T Rex

'GREAT HITS – THE A-SIDES 1972–77

(Demon) 1994

Track listing: Telegram Sam • Metal Guru • Children Of The Revolution • Solid Gold Easy Action • 20th Century Boy • The Groover • Tuck On (Tyke) • Teenage Dream • Light Of Love • Zip Gun Boogie • New York City • Dreamy Lady • London Boys • I Love To Boogie • Laser Love • To Know You Is To Love You • The Soul Of My Suit • Dandy In The Underworld • Celebrate Summer

'GREAT HITS – THE B-SIDES 1972–77'

(Demon) 1994

Track listing: Cadillac • Baby Strange • Thunderwing • Lady • Jitterbug Love • Sunken Rags • Xmas Riff • Born To Boogie • Free Angel • Midnight • Sitting Here • Satisfaction Pony • Explosive Mouth • Space Boss • Chrome Sitar • Do You Wanna Dance? • Dock Of The Bay • Solid Baby • Baby Boomerang • Life's An Elevator • City Port • All Alone • Groove A Little • Tame My Tiger • Ride My Wheels

A little glitter dust under the eyes, a rack of satin jackets and a wardrobe full of hand-made girls shoes completed the transformation from 'bopping elf' to teen idol as Bolan brought an audacious sense of style to the gloom of post-Beatles Britain. For these singles he shamelessly recycled riffs from the golden age of rock, drawing inspiration from Chuck Berry, Eddie Cochran and Howling Wolf to ensure that he dominated the singles charts for three consecutive years before he ditched the successful formula for funk, or 'space age soul', as he preferred to call it.

The collection of B sides is every bit as essential as its companion hits CD because Bolan was a shrewd operator who knew that to maximise the chance of a single entering the chart he had to put strong songs on the flip and not just throwaways or filler. Fifteen of the tracks on the B side collection and nine of those on the A side compilation (including some of his biggest hits) were exclusive single sides and unavailable on CD, until Edsel's reissue campaign added them to the appropriate albums. But as the post '73 albums are patchy, to say the least, it would be wise to grab a copy of these two plus the three recommended studio albums to ensure you don't miss any of the indispensable items.

Rating:
Sound ★★★★☆ Content ★★★★★

Also recommended:
'T Rex' (Essential/Castle), 'Marc – Words And Music' (A&M), 'The Electric Warrior Sessions' (Burning Airlines) and 'Rabbit Fighter – The Alternate Slider' (Edsel).

If you like this, why not try:
Tyrannosaurus Rex, Marc Bolan's solo albums, **Donovan**, **The Cars**.

Talking Heads

'MORE SONGS ABOUT BUILDINGS AND FOOD'

(Sire) 1978

Track listing: Thank You For Sending Me An Angel • With Our Love • The Good Thing • Warning Sign • The Girls Want To Be With The Girls • Found A Job • Artists Only • I'm Not In Love • Stay Hungry • Take Me To The River • The Big Country

In the summer of '76 the 'blank generation' were expressing themselves by gobbing at the bands at CBGBs and pogoing until they puked. No wonder the punks considered Talking Heads too clever by half. Three of them were graduates of the Rhode Island School of Design and the fourth a product of Harvard with a degree in architecture. Their music appealed particularly to college students and young professionals who thought that safety pins were for diapers, not for piercing your body parts. These were people who were looking for music that would stimulate their minds and animate their bodies, music that they could discuss with their friends. Even the covers were a conversation piece.

The group's first album and its single 'Psycho Killer' exemplified the literate New Wave, but 'More Songs…' revealed the band's ambitions to be an art form in their own right.

It was the album to be seen with in '78 and it has never gone out of fashion.

'More Songs…' was produced by Brian Eno who proved to be the perfect choice for synthesizing the group's fusion of funk, punk and pop art and for helping to articulate David Byrne's urban neuroticism which brought a sense of ironic detachment to a scene singularly lacking in humour.

Rating:
Sound ★★★★☆ Content ★★★★☆

Talking Heads

'FEAR OF MUSIC'

(Sire) 1979

Track listing: I Zimbra • Mind • Cities • Paper • Life During Wartime • Memories Can't Wait • Air • Heaven • Animals • Electric Guitar • Drugs

Talking Heads exemplified the Zen ethic – in the white heat of punk they kept a cool head while all around them were losing theirs. Their near-perfect fusion of quirky dance rhythms, pop-art aspirations and intellectual concerns appealed to the head, heart and feet at a time when most teenagers were preoccupied with deciding which part of their anatomy they should perforate with a safety pin.

To those who had sniffed too much glue the album's monochromatic cover suggested that this might be another set of bleak, urban industrial synth-pop, but in fact it combined unfashionably cool white funk with Afrocentric polyrhythms that anticipated world music by more than a decade. 'I Zimbra' features two African drummers, Robert Fripp on guitar and 'nonsense' lyrics taken from a poem by Dadaist Hugo Ball. The other obvious highlight being the single 'Life During Wartime' in which Byrne's paranoia makes you want to check that you've got enough groceries in the basement just in case the bomb drops before the fade.

Their music was becoming increasingly complex, but Brian Eno's participation as producer brought a clarity that helped offset the band's studied sophistication and kept the increasingly elaborate song structures from becoming entangled.

For once, the British music press were unanimous in their praise and voted 'Fear of Music' Album of the Year.

Rating:
Sound ★★★★☆ Content ★★★★☆

Talking Heads

'REMAIN IN LIGHT'

(Sire) 1980

Track listing: Great Curve • Cross-Eyed And Painless • Born Under Punches • Houses In Motion • Once In A Lifetime • Listening Wind • Seen And Not Seen • Overload

'Remain In Light' offers further evidence of David Byrne's growing fascination with world music, electronics and polyrhythms which was to have a significant impact on the sound of pop throughout the eighties.

On 'The Great Curve' Byrne casts himself in the role of an evangelist who has succumbed to temptation and seeks redemption through the ecstasy of sex and dance. If anyone could be said to move in mysterious ways it's David Byrne who took the theme to its extreme in the video for 'Once In A Lifetime' in which he appeared to be possessed by a whirling dervish. But again, the lyrics offer little hope of escape from the insidious influences of the modern world. Only the redemptive power of music can cast out the corporate devil, according to Byrne. The theme is continued on the fragmented and funky 'Born Under Punches' and the gospel-styled 'Houses In Motion' on which Byrne works himself up into a trance in the hope of losing himself and his fear of the modern world.

The album furnishes another superior set of edgy and ironic songs bringing art and the intellect to twitchy dancefloor grooves. Rolling Stone named it as the fourth best album of the eighties and you'd be hard pressed to find someone that would dispute that assessment.

Rating:
Sound ★★★★★ Content ★★★★★
Also recommended:
'Once In A Lifetime – The Best Of', 'Little Creatures', 'Talking Heads '77' and 'Speaking In Tongues' (all on Sire).
If you like this, why not try:
Tom Tom Club, **Television**, **Jonathon Richman**.

Television

'MARQUEE MOON'

(WEA) 1977

Track listing: See No Evil • Venus • Friction • Marquee Moon • Elevation • Guiding Light • Prove It • Torn Curtain

Fred 'Sonic' Smith must have kicked himself black and blue for leaving Blondie on the eve of their breakthrough to join Verlaine in the belief that Television would become the more commercially successful band, but presumably he has since consoled himself with the fact that Television proved infinitely more influential.

As purveyors of austere, cryptic ice-cool rock Television were ahead of their time. Verlaine's elliptical songs and extended, fragmented guitar solos were out of key with the curt, three-minute thrash of his CBGB contemporaries, though they were to prove immensely influential with the post-punk guitar bands and particularly early Talking Heads.

The CD features the full-length version of the enigmatic title track in place of the prematurely faded eight-minute mix on the original vinyl LP.

Rating:
Sound ★★★★☆ Content ★★★★★
Also recommended:
'Adventure' and 'Television'.
If you like this, why not try:
Talking Heads, The Soft Boys.

Television Personalities

'YES DARLING, BUT IS IT ART?'

(Fire) 1995

Track listing: 14th Floor • Oxford St W1 • Part Time Punks • Where's Bill Grundy Now • Happy Families • Posing At The Roundhouse • Smashing Time • King And Country • I Know Where Syd Barrett Lives • Arthur The Gardener • The Prettiest Girl In The World • That's What Love Is • Three Wishes • And Don't The Kids Just Love It • A Sense Of Belonging • How I Learned To Love The Bomb • A Girl Called Charity • She's Only The Grocer's Daughter • Now You're Just Being Ridiculous • God Snaps His Fingers • The Dream Inspires • Favourite Films • Me And My Desire • Miracles Take Longer

The TVP's total record sales can be counted in thousands and they can't claim to have been a major influence on any other groups, but in the mid-eighties they were one of the most popular acts on the indie circuit and they remain adored by their fans.

Singer-songwriter Dan Treacy claimed to have had an intimate acquaintance with the Sex Pistols – his mum ran the dry cleaners where the band had the spittle scrubbed from their strides – but he also admired 'loopy' Syd Barrett and particularly the former Floyd frontman's fascination with Alice In Wonderland whimsy. So having learnt the obligatory three chords Treacy combined low-fi punk and childlike psych-pop to charm the likes of John Peel and, through his patronage, ensure the group cult status.

'Yes Darling…' gathers most of their essential offerings including

Treacy's taunts at the weekend poseurs in 'Part Time Punks' and a scathing swipe at smug small-screen celebrities in 'Where's Bill Grundy Now?'. Toy-town psychedelia colours 'I Know Where Syd Barrett Lives' and 'Arthur The Gardener' and there are half a dozen more to delight those with an ear for the mordant and gently mocking art that is peculiar to the English. A point has been deducted for the exclusion of 'The Boy With The Paisley Shirt' and 'Salvador Dali's Garden Party', but otherwise this is an excellent primer.

Rating:
Sound ★★★☆☆ Content ★★★★☆
Also recommended:
'And Don't The Kids Just Love It', 'Mummy, You're Not Watching Me', 'They Could Have Been Bigger Than The Beatles' and 'The Painted Word' (all on Fire).
If you like this, why not try:
The Soft Boys, Syd Barrett, **Julian Cope**, **The Fall**.

Texas

'WHITE ON BLONDE'

(Mercury) 1997

Track listing: 0.30 • Say What You Want • Drawing Crazy Patterns • Halo • Put Your Arms Around Me • Insane • Black- Eyed Boy • Polo Mint City • White On Blonde • Postcard • 0.25 • Ticket To Lie • Good Advice • Breathless

Texas mine their raw material from a rich vein in rock's past and refine it until it shines like a precious metal of their own making. This, their third

album, blends blue-eyed soul with the big beat of Motown and sixties sensibilities in a lushly orchestrated wall of sound that seems to distil the very essence of pop's 'prima materia'. Whether it's fool's gold, or the genuine article will depend on whether you're the right side of 30, but there's no denying that 'Say What You Want' is uncomfortably close to Marvin Gaye's 'Sexual Healing' and 'Black-Eyed Boy' invites comparison with Smokey Robinson's 'Tears Of A Clown'. Of course, all that becomes academic once Sharleen Spiteri takes to the mike and transmutes those base elements into that which is beyond price.

Rating:
Sound ★★★★☆ Content ★★★★☆
Also recommended:
'Greatest Hits' and 'The Hush' (all on Mercury).
If you like this, why not try:
Smokey Robinson, **The Pretenders**, The Cranberries, **The Cardigans**.

Thin Lizzy

'JAILBREAK'

(Vertigo) 1976

Track listing: Jailbreak • Angel From The Coast • Running Back • Romeo And The Lonely Girl • Warriors • The Boys Are Back In Town • Fight Or Fall • Cowboy Song • Emerald

Those who had dismissed the Irish rockers as one-hit wonders after their 1973 reworking of the traditional 'Whisky In The Jar' must have spluttered in their Guinness when the band broke through big time with this, their sixth and strongest album. But there were plenty in the know who had waited patiently for Lynott and the lads to fulfil their long promised potential. They were not disappointed. 'Jailbreak' preserves the trademark Lizzy sound spearheaded by the twin lead guitars of Brian Robertson and Scott Gorham which frame Lynott's wry, double-tracked vocals. The combination of hard rock, melody and romanticism ensured the group a fair slice of pop singles success as well as a loyal live following and this album supplied their live set with several guaranteed crowd pleasers including 'The Boys Are Back In Town', 'Warriors', 'Emerald', 'The Cowboy Song' and the title track.

Remastering has added much needed punch and sparkle, although the dull sounding 'Angel From The Coast' sounds as if it has been spliced in from an entirely different session.

Rating:
Sound ★★★★☆ Content ★★★★☆

Thin Lizzy

'LIVE AND DANGEROUS'

(Vertigo) 1978

Track listing: Jailbreak • Emerald • Southbound • Rosalie • Cowgirl's Song • Dancing In The Moonlight • Massacre • Still In Love With You • Johnny The Fox Meets Jimmy The Weed • Cowboy Song • The Boys Are Back In Town • Don't Believe A Word • Warrior • Are You Ready • Suicide • Sha La La • Baby Drives Me Crazy • The Rocker

Lizzy's live album is more than the standard in-concert recording which

many acts sanction in order to fulfil their contractual obligations it's an experience. Lizzy were a wild act who burned bright in front of an audience. On their 1977 tour of the States they upstaged headliners Queen and returned determined to capture the excitement of their live shows on record.

Originally released on a double album, 'Live And Dangerous' has been squeezed onto a single CD with no loss of sound quality, nor power. A smattering of hit singles has been supplemented with less-familiar material, but the standout track is without doubt the elegiac romantic ballad 'Still In Love With You'.

Rating:
Sound ★★★★☆ Content ★★★★☆
Also recommended:
'Johnny The Fox' and 'Wild One – The Very Best Of' (both on Mercury).
If you like this, why not try:
Wishbone Ash, Gary Moore, Horslips.

The Thirteenth Floor Elevators

'ALL TIME HIGHS'

(Music Club) 1995 Budget price

Track listing: You're Gonna Miss Me • Rollercoaster • Splash • Reverberation • Fire Engine • Kingdom Of Heaven • Monkey Island • Tried To Hide • Slip Inside This House • Slide Machine • She Lives (In A Time Of Her Own) • Nobody To Love • Baby Blue • Earthquake • Levitation • Pictures • Till Then • Never Another • Street Song • May The Circle Remain Unbroken

Acid-rock is traditionally associated with the bohemian Bay Area of San

Francisco, but its roots spread as far south as Austin, Texas. There Rocky Erickson coupled the primal energy of garage rock to the delirium of the psychedelic experience to produce three classic albums which teetered on the very edge of sanity. Exotic Eastern-styled melodies struggled for breath through a heavily distorted sound pervaded by the sickly sweet scent of incense and the eerie oscillating whine from an electric jug tuned according to the amount of marijuana that was stored in it.

This compilation cherry picks 20 of the choicest tracks from those three LPs and invites you to turn on, tune in and seek enlightenment through sound.

Rating:
Sound ★★★☆☆ Content ★★★★☆
Also recommended:
'The Psychedelic Sounds Of…' (Decal/Charly).
If you like this, why not try:
Roky Erickson solo albums, **Captain Beefheart**, The Seeds.

George Thorogood

'THE BADDEST OF'

(EMI) 1992

Track listing: Bad To The Bone • Move It On Over • I'm A Steady Rollin' Man • You Talk Too Much • Who Do You Love • Gear Jammer • I Drink Alone • One Bourbon, One Scotch, One Beer, If You Don't Start Drinkin' • Treat Her Right • Long Gone • Louie To Frisco

Ready to rock? Ready or not, George Thorogood and his barfly band are straining at the leash to lay some bad-boy boogie on ya. With rhythms like rivets and some of the meanest guitar licks to crawl out of the Mississippi swamp lands Thorogood and his Delaware-born Destroyers have been barnstorming their way across the States since the seventies. Unfortunately, only 'Bad To The Bone' crossed the tracks due to its use in the soundtrack to the Stephen King chiller 'Christine'.

Well, if you got shaken up by that there are 11 more where it came from, all built like a Buick with riffs borrowed from the Chicago chapter of Blues Inc. This is a band that believes that music isn't worth a damn unless you're working up a sweat. And if you think The Destroyers are baaad mothers, wait till you hear George let rip, shredding his tonsils on hymns to hard drinkin' and hot lovin'. He sounds like he gargles with neat bourbon and wrestles alligators for fun.

So if you're having a 'real' party don't forget to invite George and his friends Bud Weiser, Jimmy Beam and Jack Daniels, but make sure you nail down your speakers, or risk 'em lifting off the floor.

Rating:
Sound ★★★★☆ Content ★★★★★
Also recommended:
'Move It On Over' and 'Live' (EMI).
If you like this, why not try:
Bo Diddley, **John Lee Hooker**, **Howlin' Wolf**, Elmore James, **Chuck Berry**, **The Rolling Stones**.

Traffic

'BEST OF TRAFFIC'

(Island) 1993

Track listing: Paper Sun • Heaven Is In Your Mind • No Face, No Name, No Number • Coloured Rain • Smiling Phases • Hole In My Shoe • Medicated Goo • Forty Thousand Headmen • Feeling Alright • Shanghai Noodle Factory • Dear Mr Fantasy

Traffic aspired to create a new form of eclectic rock music that was quintessentially English, but the synthesis of folk, psychedelia, prog-rock and white soul with lengthy free jazz-style improvisations proved an incompatible mix. Part of the problem was that they had an embarrassment of talent and didn't know what to do with it. Winwood's keyboard dexterity and soulful vocals sat well with Chris Wood's flute and saxaphone, but the other members were pulling in different directions and the lack of a permanent bass player made for an unstable foundation.

Much of their music asks to be admired rather than enjoyed, but the early psych singles 'Paper Sun' and 'Hole In My Shoe' (which were excluded from the original albums) are superior artefacts of the era and the inclusion of 'No Face, No Name, No Number' and 'Forty Thousand Headmen' demonstrated that when they exercised a degree of self-discipline they could be formidable.

Rating:
Sound ★★★★☆ Content ★★★★☆

Also recommended:
'John Barleycorn Must Die' (Island).
If you like this, why not try:
Stevie Winwood's solo albums, Blind Faith, Family.

Transglobal Underground

'DREAM OF 100 NATIONS'

(Nation) 1993

Track listing: Temple Head • Shimmer • Slowfinger • I, Voyager • La Voix Du Sang • El Hedudd • This Is The Army Of Forgotten Souls • Sirius B • Earth Tribe • Zombie'ites • Tutto Grande Discordia • Hymn To Us

After entrancing the hardcore clubbers with their dancefloor anthem 'Temple Head' TGU raided their vast library of field recordings for more ethnic soundbites and grafted them to an insidious dance beat to create global fusion for those who wouldn't normally go near 'world music'. They use samples to spice up the tracks rather than as a substitute for their own melodic input before adding the vocal gymnastics of siren Natasha Atlas and a peppering of assorted percussion for an incomparable synthesis of acid house and ethnic influences. An album full of Eastern promise.

Rating:
Sound ★★★★☆ Content ★★★★☆
Also recommended:
'International Times' and 'Rejoice Rejoice' (Nation).
If you like this, why not try:
Fun-Da-Mental, Loop Guru.

Travis

'THE MAN WHO'

(Independiente) 1999

Track listing: Writing To Reach You • Fear • As You Are • Driftwood • Last Laugh Of The Laugh • Turn • Why Does It Always Rain On Me • Luv • She's So Strange • Slide Show

The Glaswegian group are living proof that you don't need to make big statements or a big noise to make an impression, provided of course that you possess a great deal of patience and you don't care a damn if the hits are forthcoming or not.

Travis are the creation of singer-songwriter Fran Healy who pens the kind of quiet, quality songs that no one seems to write anymore; songs which insinuate themselves into your head, resurfacing periodically to remind you that somewhere there is a sadder man looking for a shoulder to sob on. It seems inappropriate to talk about stand-out tracks when the strongest songs, 'Writing To Reach You', 'Driftwood' and 'Why Does It Always Rain On Me' are some of the most modest and unassuming moments in contemporary pop. Sometimes it pays to keep things simple.

Rating:
Sound ★★★★☆ Content ★★★★☆
Also recommended:
'Good Feeling' and 'The Invisible Band' (both on Independiente).
If you like this, why not try:
Coldplay, Moby, Radiohead.

Tricky

'MAXINQUAYE'

(Label) 1995

Track listing: Overcome • Ponderosa • Black Steel • Hell Is Round The Corner • Pumpkin • Aftermath • Abbaon Fat Tracks • Brand New You're Retro • Suffocated Love • You Don't • Strugglin' • Feed Me

Tricky was trip-hop even before the term was invented. After walking out on Massive Attack, Bristol bad boy Adrian Thaw resuscitated the ailing corpse that was dance and galvanized it into slow motion with an intravenous drip of narcotic dope beats and samples scavenged from sources as diverse as Shakespear's Sister and Smashing Pumpkins. He then led it down the dark alleys of his fertile imagination and scared the hell out of it. Each track is witness to his obsession with picking open the scars of his paranoid psyche while strident soul diva Martina acts as his angelic muse.

Dance has never sounded as psychotic as this, nor as atmospheric, intimidating and addictive.

Rating:
Sound ★★★★☆ Content ★★★★☆
Also recommended:
'Nearly God' featuring collaborations with Björk and Neneh Cherry.
If you like this, why not try:
Massive Attack, Soul ll Soul, Portishead.

The Triffids

'IN THE PINES'

(Mushroom) 1995

Track listing: Suntrapper • In The Pines • Kathy Knows • Twenty Five To Five • Do You Want Me Near You • Once A Day • Just Might Fade Away • Better Off This Way • Only One Life • Keep Your Eyes On The Hole • One Soul Less On Your Fiery List • Born Sandy Devotional • Love And Affection

Nirvana performed a version of Leadbelly's haunting homicidal blues 'In The Pines' as part of their 'Unplugged' set, but it was not as stark and unsettling as the version recorded earlier by cult Australian band The Triffids. The Triffids brought a bleak, brooding quality to their music that evoked the arid empty spaces of the outback which was made all the more eerie by the addition of a keening pedal steel guitar and violin. Unfortunately, the quality of their music was not matched by commercial or critical acclaim and they split in '89 to become a cult act after the fact. 'In The Pines' was recorded in a wool-shearing shed and is undermined by poor sound quality, but the songs are crucial. If The Velvet Underground had been raised in the Australian outback this is how they might have sounded.

Rating:
Sound ★★★☆☆ Content ★★★★☆
Also recommended:
'Born Sandy Devotional', 'Calenture', 'The Black Swan' and the compilation 'Australian Melodrama' (all on Mushroom).

If you like this, why not try:
David McComb's solo albums, **Giant Sand**, Green On Red.

The Troggs

'GREATEST HITS'

(Polygram) 1994

Track listing: Wild Thing • Love Is All Around • With A Girl Like You • I Want You • I Can't Control Myself • Gonna Make You • Good Vibrations • Anyway That You Want Me • Give It To Me • Night Of The Long Grass • Girl In Black • Hi Hi Hazel • Little Girl • Cousin Jane • Don't You Know • Together • Nowhere Road • I'm In Control • Summertime • Hot Stuff • Dust Bowl • I'll Buy You An Island • Crazy Annie • Jingle Jangle • Déjà Vu

In the year 1966 BC (Before Clapton) music hadn't progressed much beyond the point where primitive man had cracked his neighbour's skull with a club to produce the first top 'C', at least not if these old fossils are anything to go by.

The Troggs abbreviated their name from the word troglodyte, meaning a prehistoric cave dweller, and their music exhibited the same Neanderthal joy in noise that would have had our ancestors gulping down the grog and swinging their women folk around by the hair. Curiously enough, in the digital age the group's instrumental primitivism has been known to induce the same effect.

The Troggs' limited musical vocabulary made the garage groups sound sophisticated by comparison, but Reg Presely and his pals had the last laugh. 'Wild Thing' was covered by every punk outfit who could cobble together three chords, not to mention Jimi Hendrix, while Westlife's version of 'Love Is All Around' netted Reg a million in writer's royalties.

Rating:
Sound ★★★☆☆ Content ★★★★☆
Also recommended:
'Archaeology' (Phonogram) and 'The EP Collection' (See For Miles).
If you like this, why not try:
early **Who**, Small Faces, **The Kinks**.

Tina Turner

'PRIVATE DANCER'

(Capitol) 1984

Track listing: I Might Have Been Queen • What's Love Got To Do With It • Show Some Respect • I Can't Stand The Rain • Private Dancer • Let's Stay Together • Better Be Good To Me • Steel Claw • Help!

Madonna, Celine Dion, Janet Jackson and Whitney Houston have sold more records, but Tina beats them all for sheer lung power, dynamism and raw sexual intensity. After years in the wilderness, making ends meet by playing at conventions for McDonald's employees, she reclaimed her rightful place in rock with this album which was hastily recorded in two weeks, but which went on to sell five million copies. She opens her new account with an incendiary rocker 'I Might Have Been Queen' and earns further credit with her impassioned covers of Al Green's 'Let's Stay Together', Anne Peebles' 'I Can't Stand The Rain' and the title track, which had been

specially written for her by Mark Knopfler. The rest of the material is a pale imitation of the strutting, smouldering raunch 'n' soul that had hips shaking in the sixties, but she's still got what it takes to get your mojo working.

As for her band, they may be middle-aged session musicians, but there is nothing flabby about their sound. They've got muscle where it counts and pack plenty of wallop.

Rating:
Sound ★★★★☆ Content ★★★★☆

Tina Turner

'BREAK EVERY RULE'

(Capitol) 1986

Track listing: Typical Male • What You Get Is What You See • Two People • Till The Right Man Comes Along • Afterglow • Girls • Back Where You Started • Break Every Rule • Overnight Sensation • Paradise Is Here • I'll Be Thunder

In the sixties Tina was the very embodiment of earthy sensuality. She taught Jagger how to bump and grind like a pro and was blessed with a voice that could bring grown men to their knees. By the mid-seventies her marriage and her career appeared to be over, but then she clawed her way back with a series of slick, AOR albums which were aimed at seducing the lucrative mainstream market. To ensure success 'Break Every Rule' was co-produced with Bryan Adams and Mark Knopfler and it betrays their influence on every track.

'Typical Male', 'Two People' and 'Till The Right Man Comes Along' diffuse her animal magnetism in a soulless mix of synthetic disco and programmable drum machines, while the handful of up-tempo items aimed to market the one-time Queen of R&B as the soul sister of Dire Straits. Needless to say it shifted more copies than all of her classic sixties recordings put together and was followed by more of the same.

Rating:
Sound ★★★★☆ Content ★★★☆☆
Also recommended:
The double CD set 'Live In Europe' and the compilation 'Simply The Best' (all on Capitol).
If you like this, why not try:
Ike And Tina Turner, **Dire Straits**, **Whitney Houston**, Chris Rea.

Tyrannosaurus Rex

'A BEARD OF STARS'

(Castle Communications) 1968

Track listing: Prelude • A Day Laye • Woodland Bop • First Heart Mighty Dawn Dart • Pavillions Of Sun • Organ Blues • By The Light Of The Magical Moon • Wind Cheetah • A Beard Of Stars • Great Horse • Dragon's Ear • Lofty Skies • Dove • Elemental Child

This richly ornate tapestry of acoustic instruments embellished with electric guitar evokes scenes of a pastoral paradise inhabited by fabulous creatures drawn from the imagination of JRR Tolkien and the catalogue of children's authors whom Bolan used to credit as the main source of his inspiration. But even in this idyllic setting can be heard the faint echoes of Marc's heroes Hendrix, Chuck Berry and Eddie Cochran tempting the unsuspecting fairy folk to abandon their toadstools and bop by the light of the magical moon. 'Great Horse', 'Dragon's Ear' and 'Lofty Skies' are an intoxicating blend of fey folkiness, fanciful imagery and literally enchanting tunes delivered in the electric elf's exaggerated vibrato.

Rating:
Sound ★★★★☆ Content ★★★★★
Also recommended:
'My People Were Fair', 'Prophets, Seers And Sages', 'Unicorn', 'Best Of' (includes three previously unreleased titles) (all on Castle) and the radio sessions collection 'A BBC History' (Band Of Joy Records).
If you like this, why not try:
T Rex, The Incredible String Band, **Donovan**.

U2

'OCTOBER'

(Island) 1981

Track listing: Gloria • I Fall Down • I Threw A Brick Through A Window • Rejoice • Fire • Tomorrow • October • With A Shout • Stranger In A Strange Land • Scarlet • Is That All

U2's ascent from post-punk pub band to self-styled 'saviours of rock' began with this confident set which saw the realization of their desire to do something radically different with the traditional line up of bass, drums, vocal and guitar. While other rock groups of the time relied on block powerchords to reinforce the rhythm, U2 showed strength through a sparse and supple sound which was fortified by fragmented guitar harmonics. This is the way they sounded live and in the early eighties it was a breath of fresh air which almost cleared away the prevailing smog of stifling synth-pop at a stroke.

Rating:
Sound ★★★★☆ Content ★★★★☆

U2

'WAR'

(Island) 1983

Track listing: Sunday Bloody Sunday • Seconds • Like A Song • New Year's Day • Two Hearts Beat As One • Refugee • Drowning Man • Red Light • 40 • Surrender

By the time 'War' was released U2 could count Bruce Springsteen and Pete Townshend among their fans and yet, 'Sunday Bloody Sunday' and 'New Year's Day' sound like a band who are still hungry and determined to make their mark. After this their albums betrayed an increasing air of smug self-satisfaction although they also revealed a healthy appetite for new influences.

The strident, stripped-down sound is augmented with violin, sax and backing vocalists, but the evangelistic fervour is as intense as ever.

Rating:
Sound ★★★★☆ Content ★★★★☆

U2

'THE JOSHUA TREE'

(Island) 1987

Track listing: Where The Streets Have No Name • I Still Haven't Found What I'm Looking For • With Or Without You • Bullet The Blue Sky • Running To Stand Still • Red Hill Mining Town • In God's Country • Trip Through Your Wires • One Tree Hill • Exit • Mothers Of The Disappeared

After the group's three-year absence from the recording studio the release of 'The Joshua Tree' was eagerly anticipated and amply fulfilled the fans' expectations. Its combination of sincerity, soul-searching and concentrated strength touched a nerve with a generation who yearned for 'real music' to sweep aside the surfeit of synthesized production line pap.

It elevated the group to superstar status and gave them a global number one, putting them on a par with establishment figures such as Bruce Springsteen.

But it also marked the moment when everything they did took on an inflated significance, and songs such as 'With Or Without You' and 'I Still Haven't Found What I'm Looking For' strained under the weight of their new-found status as stadium anthems.

Rating:
Sound ★★★★☆ Content ★★★★☆

U2

'ACHTUNG BABY'

(Island) 1991

Track listing: Zoo Station • Even Better Than The Real Thing • One • Until The End Of The World • Who's Gonna Ride Your Wild Horses • So Cruel • Fly • Mysterious Ways • Tryin' To Throw Your Arms Around The World • Ultraviolet • Acrobat • Love Is Blindness

In 1991 U2 incarcerated themselves in the same Berlin studio in which Bowie and Eno had created 'Low' and there subjected themselves to musical group therapy in order to find their 'true selves'. Having left their emotional luggage at the door they presumably began by admitting that they suffered from a Messiah complex, were addicted to audience adulation and were out of touch with their 'inner child'. After which they must have indulged in an emotional catharisis involving lots of group hugging, positive affirmations and even a little chanting.

Having opened themselves up to new possibilities they were ready to assimilate more contemporary sounds such as hip hop, techno and grunge which resulted in their most personal and sharply focused statement to date. In contrast to the bombastic and superficial 'Rattle and Hum' songs such as 'One', 'Who's Gonna Ride Your Wild Horses' and 'Mysterious Ways' sound disarmingly sincere.

'Achtung Baby' is the sound of four grown men reborn in leather and shades grooving on the dancefloor, but without embarrassing the kids.

Rating:
Sound ★★★★★ Content ★★★★★
Also recommended:
'The Joshua Tree', 'The Best Of' 'All That You Can't Leave Behind' and the live album 'Under A Blood Red Sky' (all on Island).
If you like this, why not try:
Stiff Little Fingers, **The Rolling Stones**, **Simple Minds**.

UB40

'LABOUR OF LOVE VOL 1'

(DEP International/EMI) 1986

Track listing: Cherry Oh Baby • Keep On Moving • Please Don't Make Me Cry • Sweet Sensation • Johnny Too Bad • Red Red Wine • Guilty • She Caught The Train • Version Girl • Many Rivers To Cross •

'LABOUR OF LOVE VOL 2'

(DEP International/EMI) 1989

Track listing: Here I Am • Tears From My Eyes • Groovin' • Way You Do The Things You Do • Wear You To The Ball • Singer Man • Kingston Town • Baby • Wedding Day • Sweet Cherie • Stick By Me • Just Another Girl • Homely Girl • Impossible Love

UB40 took their name from Britain's unemployment benefit form, but soon chose to channel their energies away from political protest through pop into a sustained campaign for the popularization of reggae. Their records were frequently both danceable and intellectually arresting, although Ali Campbell's dour vocal delivery tended to make some of the slower songs sound perilously close to a self-pitying whinge.

'Labour Of Love' repays the debt they felt were due to the (mainly) Jamaican artists who had provided the inspiration for ten years of hits. In truth, not all of the chosen covers work as well as they might. Jimmy Cliff's spiritual anthem 'Many Rivers To Cross' is diminished by an uncharacteristically schmatlzy arrangement, but there are enough sufficiently spirited re-workings of Jamaican classics to ensure that the group's services to reggae will be rewarded in heaven by a seat at the feet of Bob Marley.

Rating:
Sound ★★★★☆ Content ★★★☆☆
Also recommended:
'Best Of Vol 1 & 2' (both on DEP International).
If you like this, why not try:
The Beat, Jimmy Cliff, **Bob Marley**.

The Undertones

'TRUE CONFESSIONS – THE SINGLES As AND Bs'

2 CDs (Essential/Castle) 1999

Track listing: Teenage Kicks • True Confessions • Smarter Than U • Emergency Cases • Get Over You • Really Really • She Can Only Say No • Jimmy Jimmy • Mars Bars • Here Comes The Summer • One Way Love • Top Twenty • You've Got My Number • Let's Talk About Girls • My Perfect Cousin • Hard Luck • I Don't Wanna See You Again • Wednesday Week • I Told You So • It's Going To Happen • Fairly In The Money Now • Julie Ocean • Kiss In The Dark • Beautiful Friend • Life's Too Easy • The Love Parade • Like That • Got To Have You Back • Turning Blue • Bye Bye Baby Blue • Chain Of Love • Window Shopping For New Clothes

The Undertones cast themselves as snotty-nosed street urchins from the back streets of Derry who, one imagines, spent their acned adolescence making faces at the poseurs on 'Top Of The Pops' and pressing their faces to the window of the music shops to ogle instruments they thought they never could afford. Their early singles betrayed an endearing naïvete and an addiction to simple pleasures like chocolate and chasing girls which was made all the more affecting by Fergal Sharkey's exaggerated vibrato. The group's apparent lack of ambition and artifice led to comparisons with The Buzzcocks and The Ramones with whom they also shared a knack for writing perfectly crafted three-minute pop songs, although 'Teenage Kicks', 'Jimmy Jimmy' and 'My Perfect Cousin' have an indefinable provincial quality that was unique to The Undertones.

Sadly, success led to an increasing sophistication and the loss of their musical innocence. By 1983 The Undertones had grown up after making an unlikely, but highly effective, foray into psych-pop with 'The Love Parade' and the members went their separate ways. But the cheeky charm and vitality of their early singles endures – acne and all.

Rating:
Sound ★★★★☆ Content ★★★★★
Also recommended:
'Hypnotized' (Essential/BMG).
If you like this, why not try:
Buzzcocks, The Only Ones.

Suzanne Vega

'SUZANNE VEGA'

(A&M) 1985

Track listing: Cracking • Freeze Tag • Marlene On The Wall • Small Blue Thing • Straight Lines • Undertow • Some Journey • Queen And The Soldier • Night Movies • Neighbourhood Girls

In the early eighties singer-songwriters were as scarce as an honest politician, and for that reason Suzanne Vega made a surprisingly strong impression with her moody acoustic sketches of life and love in the Big Apple. Her simple, understated songs invited favourable comparisons with Leonard Cohen, Lou Reed and Joni Mitchell and were given a sympathetic, suitably subdued setting by producer Lenny Kaye whose presence also lent Vega much-needed street cred.

Rating:
Sound ★★★★☆ Content ★★★★☆

Suzanne Vega

'99.9F'

(A&M) 1992

Track listing: Rock In This Pocket • Blood Makes Noise • In Liverpool • 99.9F • Blood Sings • Fat Man And Dancing Girl • (If You Were) In My Movie • As A Child • Bad Wisdom • When Heroes Go Down • As Girls Go • Song Of Sand • Private Goes Public

When UK techno act DNA transformed Vega's a cappella song 'Tom's Diner' into a chart-topping dance track, Vega saw a way to recapture the momentum she had lost with the disappointing 'Days Of Open Hand' album. For '99.9F' the sober folky puts on her party clothes and gets funky with a beatbox, a sampler and even those infernal, soulless synths. The amiable 'Liverpool' and its more brusque companion 'Blood Makes Noise' demonstrate two contrasting aspects of her personality and her favourite obsessions which she described as 'love songs and your basic mental health songs'.

Initial limited edition copies of this CD came with a free hardback diary.

Rating:
Sound ★★★★☆ Content ★★★☆☆
Also recommended:
'Solitude Standing' and 'Nine Objects Of Desire' (both on A&M).
If you like this, why not try:
Tracy Chapman, Joni Mitchell, Leonard Cohen.

The Velvet Underground

'THE VELVET UNDERGROUND AND NICO'

(Polydor) 1967

Track listing: Sunday Morning • I'm Waiting For The Man • Femme Fatale • Venus In Furs • Run Run Run • All Tomorrow's Parties • Heroin • There She Goes Again • I'll Be Your Mirror • The Black Angel's Death Song • European Son

The VU sounded a sour note in the Summer of Love by extolling the pleasures of fetishistic sex ('Venus In Furs'), transsexuality ('Sister Ray')

and drug addiction ('Heroin' and 'Waiting For The Man'). But they became an incalculable influence on punk and innumerable indie guitar bands of the eighties and beyond. So much so, that it has been suggested that rock sounds the way it does today because of the music that they made.

They were the protégés of pop art guru Andy Warhol who thought they might prove an exotic attraction at his multimedia parties, but record companies found their atonal freakouts and songs about the seamy side of city life as appealing as a contagious disease. Warhol financed the recording of this first album and created the banana logo for the cover. He even suggested that they recruit cadaverous German singer and model Nico to bring a sense of European decadence to what otherwise sounded like the soundtrack to a cheap porn movie, but he hadn't got a clue what to do with them after that.

Nico's presence appears to have been an afterthought, as indicated by the cover credit. Her lugubrious voice lends a sense of Berlin cabaret to the despairing 'Femme Fatale' and 'All Tomorrow's Parties', but the main event is Lou's descriptions of New York's festering nightlife and his duels with John Cale. Cale, a student of the avant-garde, pits his electric viola against Lou's droning guitar on 'European Son' and 'The Black Angel's Death Song' until the instruments seem on the verge of disintegration forcing Cale to concede defeat.

Thirty years on, 'The Velvet Underground And Nico' has lost none of its power to disturb, disorientate and delight.

Rating:
Sound ★★★★☆ Content ★★★★★

The Velvet Underground

'WHITE LIGHT, WHITE HEAT'

(Polydor) 1968

Track listing: White Light, White Heat • The Gift • Lady Godiva's Operation • Here She Comes Now • I Heard Her Call My Name • Sister Ray

Lou had once summed up his personal philosophy by stating, 'One chord is fine. Two is pushing it. Three chords and you're into jazz.' He obviously kept faith with his own ideals as none of the songs on The Velvets' second album appears to use more than a couple of chords, although sometimes it's hard to discern what the hell's going on underneath the screaming feedback. Take 'The Gift' for example, an everyday story of accidental dismemberment which is related by John Cale through a barrage of distortion that is presumably meant to illustrate the grinding chainsaw at work on the hapless victim. And then there's 'Sister Ray' with its graphic description of oral sex that must have had the marketing men foaming at the mouth. And we haven't even mentioned the necrophillic fantasy of 'I Hear Her Call My Name', or indeed 'Lady Godiva's Operation'. The VU were never going to make the top 40 daytime radio playlist with this material, but then they had no intention of playing the game. They were content to linger in the shadows, indulging in dissonance and distortion and liberal amounts of methedrine, which numbed them to the consequences of their addiction.

Needless to say, this is not an easy album to listen to. But it's essential if you want to know what rock can do when its makers don't give a damn for popularity. Just remember, if it's on when you're doing the dishes you'd better be prepared to break a few.

Rating:
Sound ★★★☆☆ Content ★★★★☆

The Velvet Underground

'VELVET UNDERGROUND'

(Polydor) 1969

Track listing: Candy Says • What Goes On • Pale Blue Eyes • That's The Story Of My Life • Beginning To See The Light • Murder Mystery • Jesus • After Hours • Some Kinda Love • I'm Set Free

This is the sound of The VU chilling out after a bad trip. Lou's instrumental duels with the recently departed Cale had evidently exhausted him and he appeared to be seeking relief in the introspection of languidly beautiful songs such as 'Candy Says', 'Jesus' and 'Pale Blue Eyes', although disturbing images continue to haunt him. 'The Murder Mystery' returns to the scene of the crime perpetrated by 'The Gift' to play games with stereo placement, panning one vocal to the extreme right and the other to the left.

But otherwise this is vintage VU contributing two more tracks to the punk's standard set list ('What Goes On' and 'Beginning To See The Light').

Rating:
Sound ★★★★☆ Content ★★★★☆

The Velvet Underground

'LOADED'

(Atlantic) 1970

Track listing: Who Loves The Sun • Sweet Jane • Rock & Roll • Cool It Down • New Age • Head Held High • Lonesome Cowboy Bill • I Found A Reason • Train Round The Bend • Oh! Sweet Nuthin'

The VU at their most accessible, purged of the subversive elements and formerly rehabilitated into rock and roll society. Gone are the derelicts, druggies, dealers and sexual deviants who inhabited the earlier albums. The band have taken the cure and are conspicuously clean. Lou gets high on rock and the band dutifully back him like old lags out to impress the parole board. 'Sweet Jane' and 'Rock And Roll' are lean, mean and a shot in the arm for the reformed offenders, but cold turkey has taken its toll and wrung them drier than a barrister's brief. At the risk of being accused of blasphemy it has to be said that they were pretty boring when they weren't stoned.

Rating:
Sound ★★★★☆ Content ★★★★☆
Also recommended:
'Another View' (previously unreleased out-takes from what would have been

their fifth album), 'Loaded – The Fully Loaded 2CD Edition' (Rhino) and the 4CD box set 'Peel Slowly And See' (Polydor).
If you like this, why not try:
Lou Reed, John Cale and **Nico**'s solo albums, **The Jesus And Mary Chain**, **Jonathan Richman**.

The Verve

'A NORTHERN SOUL'

(Hut/EMI) 1995

Track listing: New Decade • This Is Music • On Your Own • So It Goes • Northern Soul • Brainstorm Interlude • Drive You Home • History • No Knock On My Door • Life's An Ocean • Stormy Clouds • Reprise

The Verve shuffled out of Wigan in the early nineties with a host of other 'shoegazers' such as Ride and Slowdive, shaping surges of feedback and droning guitars into a vortex of ambient, antigravity soundscapes which gave their sonic explorations a sense of eager expectation. In contrast to their ethereal debut, 'A Storm In Heaven', which didn't seem to acknowledge structural conventions or even the need for the occasional chorus, the songs on a 'A Northern Soul' ride on a riff, charting their elliptical course from a point somewhere between Pink Floyd's 'Interstellar Overdrive' and Hawkwind's 'Master Of The Universe' to the black hole of infinite possibilities just over the horizon.

Rating:
Sound ★★★★☆ Content ★★★★☆

The Verve

'URBAN HYMNS'

(Hut/EMI) 1997

Track listing: Bitter Sweet Symphony • Sonnet • The Rolling People • The Drugs Don't Work • Catching The Butterfly • Neon Wilderness • Space And Time • Weeping Willow • Lucky Man • One Day • This Time • Velvet Morning • Come On

Two years after splitting, the band reformed under the baton of 'mad' Richard Ashcroft to create a suite of symphonic pop in the manner of early Floyd. Ashcroft's insistence of using an orchestral sample from the Stones for 'Bitter Sweet Symphony', instead of re-recording the part, cost him a small fortune in royalties, but one can understand why he wouldn't want to risk unravelling the fabric of what is indisputably a modern masterpiece sculptured in sound. Noel Gallagher claimed to have played it twenty times when he first heard it and presumably gave 'One Day' and 'Lucky Man', the other outstanding cuts, an equally good airing. The more spaced-out 'Come On' and its companion 'The Rolling People' supplied the perfect soundtrack for when the chemicals kicked in, while 'The Drugs Don't Work' scored big time when it was lifted for their second single and their first UK number one.

Rating:
Sound ★★★☆☆ Content ★★★☆☆
Also recommended:
'No Come Down' and 'A Storm In Heaven' (Hut).
If you like this, why not try:
Ashcroft's solo album, Spiritualized.

Tom Waits

'SWORDFISHTROMBONES'

(Island) 1983

Track listing: Underground • Shore Leave • Dave The Butcher • Johnsburg, Illinois • 16 Shells From A Thirty-Ought-Six • Town With No Cheer • In The Neighborhood • Just Another Sucker On The Line • Frank's Wild Years • Swordfishtrombones • Down, Down, Down • Soldier's Things • Gin Soaked Boy • Trouble's Braids • Rainbirds

Waits once claimed to have slept through the sixties. On 'Swordfishtrombones' he sounds like he's still in the process of waking up. His mumbled, gin-soaked vocal describes the barflies and the bums who are washed up on the outskirts of society like the minor characters who inhabit a Raymond Chandler novel. But for Waits it's these derelicts and the eccentrics who make life interesting and he portrays them with compassion and humour.

His band appear to have been equipped with an odd assortment of instruments redeemed from a pawn shop and were evidently doused in gin before they got to the studio. Waits rallies them as best he can, huddled over the piano and growling through the cigarette smoke as the band stagger like drunks from one song to the next. 'Swordfishtrombones' would have made the perfect soundtrack for a forties *film noir*, but you'll get an even better movie if you allow the images to form in your mind's eye.

Rating:
Sound ★★★☆☆ Content ★★★★☆

Tom Waits

'RAIN DOGS'

(Island) 1985

Track listing: Singapore • Clap Hands • Cemetery Polka • Jockey Full Of Bourbon • Tango Till Their Sore • Big Black Mariah • Diamonds And Gold • Hang Down Your Head • Time • Rain Dogs • Midtown • 9th And Hennepin • Gun Street Girl • Union Square • Blind Love • Walking Spanish • Downtown Train • Bridge Of Rain Dog • Anywhere I Lay My Head

'Rain Dogs' is the sound of American Gothic with Waits officiating at the funeral of a cast of colourful characters to the accompaniment of an inebriated New Orleans jazz band.

The songs are distilled from the usual cocktail of ingredients; Dixieland jazz, folk, blues, ragtime, vaudeville, off-beat rhythms and off-kilter imagery laced with the world-weary romanticism of the Beat poets.

Keith Richards' contribution is of academic interest only. No one upstages Tom Waits when the liquor kicks in.

Rating:
Sound ★★★★☆ Content ★★★★☆
Also recommended:
'Frank's Wild Years' and 'Bone Machine' (both on Island).
If you like this, why not try:
Captain Beefheart, Screaming Jay Hawkins, **The Sensational Alex Harvey Band**.

The Walker Brothers

'AFTER THE LIGHTS GO OUT – THE BEST OF 1965–67

(Fontana) 1990

Track Listing: Love Her • Make It Easy On Yourself • First Love Never Does • My Ship Is Coming In • Deadlier Than The Male • Another Tear Falls • Baby You Don't Have To Tell Me • After The Lights Go Out • Mrs Murphy • In My Room • Arcangel • Sun Ain't Gonna Shine Anymore • Saddest Night In The World • Young Man Cried • Livin' Above Your Head • Stay With Me Baby • Walking In The Rain • Orpheus • I Can't Let It Happen To You • Just Say Goodbye • Interview Excerpts

The Walker Brothers brought their sculptured Grecian good looks and sad sweet smiles to songs of doomed love affairs and turned them into epic romantic tragedies. Their biggest hits, 'The Sun Ain't Gonna Shine Anymore' and 'Make It Easy On Yourself' sound as if the three young Californians might be swept away any second by the tidal wave of strings that threaten to engulf their solemn ballads of lost love and loneliness – if the hordes of screaming girls don't get to them first. Scott is said to have played the tragic romantic to the last, living in an apartment with the curtain permanently drawn and Jacques Brel in endless rotation on the record player. Listening to these sumptuous sob stories one can believe it. These are the tracks Phil Spector must have wished he'd produced.

Rating:
Sound ★★★☆☆ Content ★★★☆☆

Also recommended:
'No Regrets' (Fontana) the best of Scott Walker's solo recordings and his Walker Brothers' hits.
If you like this, why not try:
Scott Walker's solo albums, Jacques Brel, Marc Almond, early **Bowie**.

Jeff Wayne

'WAR OF THE WORLDS'

2 CDs (Sony Music) 19??

Track listing: The Eve Of The War • Horsell Common And The Heat Ray • The Artilleryman And The Fighting Machine • Forever Autumn • Thunder Child • The Earth Under The Martians • The Red Weed • The Spirit Of Man • The Red Weed Pt 2 • Brave New World • Dead London • Epilogue

Bonus Tracks: The Spirit Of Man • Forever Autumn (2 alternate mixes) • The Eve Of The War

In the sad and sorry history of bad ideas Jeff Wayne's musical adaptation of HG Wells' seminal SF saga must surely rank as one of the worst.

Any record with a track entitled 'The Spirit Of Man' is asking for a one-way ticket to the bargain bins. But it's not the pretentiousness of the project alone condemns it. It's the paucity of musical imagination and invention that makes a stark contrast with Wells' own vision. Had Wayne attempted to adapt the story to a series of half-decent songs it might not have been so bad, but he chose to use the least promising of all musical forms, disco, as a basis. The result is roughly equivalent to having The Bee Gees sing the bible. Even the presence of Sir Richard Burton as narrator and fine performances by Phil

Lynott and Julie Covington cannot redeem this sacrilege. And yet… it exerts a perverse fascination in the same way that really bad B movies can do when you're in the mood to laugh at someone else's mistakes.

Rating:
Sound ★★★☆☆ Content ★★☆☆☆
Also recommended:
The single CD of 'Highlights' (Columbia) is only moderately more tolerable.
If you like this, why not try:
ELO, The Alan Parsons Project, The Moody Blues.

Paul Weller

'WILD WOOD'

(Go Discs/Polygram) 1993

Track listing: Sunflower • Can You Heal Us (Holy Man) • Wild Wood • Instrumental • All The Pictures On The Wall • Has My Fire Really Gone Out • Country • Fifth Season • Weaver • Instrumental Pt 2 • Foot Of The Mountain • Shadow Of The Sun • Holy Man (Reprise) • Moon On Your Pyjamas

Weller had a lot to live up to after disbanding The Jam and a lot to live down after forming the self-indulgent, coffee-jazz combo The Style Council. 'Wild Wood', his second solo album, restored his reputation as one of the sharpest songwriters of his generation and helped to make guitar pop fashionable again after more than a decade dominated by soulless electronic dance music. The disillusionment, 'self doubt' and 'deep despair' that he struggled to restrain on his self-titled debut gave way to a

mature self-confidence and a qualified optimism that was expressed in exhilarating sixties-styled R&B. The title track gave Weller his first solo top 10 single with 'Sunflower' supplying a second hit. The set was so strong that even the out-takes were collated for a companion set, 'More Wood' and the two formed the basis of a live album, not unsurprisingly titled 'Live Wood'.

Rating:
Sound ★★★★☆ Content ★★★★☆

Paul Weller

'STANLEY ROAD'

(Go Discs/Polygram) 1995

Track listing: Changing Man • Porcelain Goods • Walk On Gilded Splinters • You Do Something To Me • Woodcutter's Son • Time Passes • Stanley Road • Broken Stones • Out Of The Sinking • Pink On White Walls • Whirlpool's End • Wings Of Speed

It's evident from the conspicuous influence of Traffic that Weller spent as much time wading through Stevie Winwood's back catalogue before recording this as he did his own family snapshot album. Despite the pictorial and lyrical references to his childhood this is not a nostalgic trip down memory lane, but a guitar-fuelled graffiti spree across the anonymous architectural ghettos that have gutted Britain's inner cities of their sense of community.

Once he has appeased his social conscience Weller reflects on more personal matters in songs that confirm his growing insight and maturity, but also his continuing love for the songwriting values of the sixties. The cover of Dr John's 'Walk On Gilded Splinters' features a guest appearance by Noel Gallagher who lays claim to be the clown prince of Britpop, but Weller was clearly the authentic voice of British pop in the nineties.

Rating:
Sound ★★★★☆ Content ★★★★★
Also recommended:
'Paul Weller' (Go Discs) and 'Heavy Soul' (Island).
If you like this, why not try:
The Style Council, **The Jam**, **The Who**, **Traffic**, Small Faces.

The Who

'THE WHO COLLECTION'

2 CDs (Impression Records/Polydor) 1985

Track listing: I Can't Explain • Anyway, Anyhow, Anywhere • My Generation • Substitute • Legal Matter • The Kids Are Alright • I'm A Boy • Happy Jack • Boris The Spider • Pictures Of Lily • I Can See For Miles • Won't Get Fooled Again • The Seeker • Let's See Action • Join Together • Relay • Love Reign O'er Me • Squeeze Box • Who Are You • Long Live Rock • 5.15 • Magic Bus • Summertime Blues • Shaking All Over • Pinball Wizard • Acid Queen • I'm Free • We're Not Gonna Take It • Baba O'Reilly • Behind Blue Eyes • Bargain

The Who made music that was as British and brittle as Brighton Rock. From 1965 to '67 they were the violent sound of surly, disaffected youth with a destructive stage act to match. The first dozen tracks on this 2CD set capture the intense and obsessive energy of their core audience of that time, the Mods, whose moody, narcissistic preoccupation with looking sharp and staying awake all weekend on a diet of pills demanded an amalgam of 'Maximum R&B' and Pop Art.

The stuttering rage of 'My Generation' remains one of the most potent three minutes in pop, while the awkward sexual self-consciousness described in 'Pictures Of Lily' and the alienation articulated in 'Substitute' mark Townshend's accelerated development as a songwriter of singular perception. However, by '68 the group had taken sufficient quantities of acid to mellow out; tripping on 'I Can See For Miles' and 'Magic Bus' before Townshend became seduced by the fashion for oriental mysticism and a search for the meaning of life. He may not have found enlightenment, but he did find inspiration for 'Tommy', the first 'rock opera', from which 'Pinball Wizard', 'Acid Queen', 'I'm Free' and 'We're Not Gonna Take It' are taken. The remainder take The Who story into the seventies when they became stalwarts of the stadium circuit with hard-rock classics 'Won't Get Fooled Again' and 'Baba O'Riley'. There are even a couple of highlights from 'Quadrophenia' to whet your appetite for the original album.

This TV advertised collection is without doubt the best of the many Who compilations on catalogue. If you don't own this, you're not really trying.

Rating:
Sound ★★★★☆ Content ★★★★★

The Who

'TOMMY'

(Polydor) 1968

Track listing: Overture • It's A Boy • 1921 • Amazing Journey • Sparks • Eyesight To The Blind • Christmas • Cousin Kevin • The Acid Queen • Underture • Do You Think It's Alright? • Fiddle About • Pinball Wizard • There's A Doctor • Go To The Mirror! • Tommy Can You Hear Me? • Smash The Mirror • Sensation • Miracle Cure • Sally Simpson • I'm Free • Welcome • Tommy's Holiday Camp • We're Not Gonna Take It

So much gushing praise has been heaped on Pete Townshend's 'rock opera' that its qualities have become suffocated under the weight of it. But it was certainly a significant event at the time, making a strong case for pop to be taken seriously, and it was impressively consistent in terms of the quality of material.

Here can be found some of Townshend's strongest songs, namely 'Pinball Wizard' and 'I'm Free' in their simplified form without the cloying strings and synths that smothered the movie soundtrack. But it's still little more than an album of songs sequenced together to tell a plainly preposterous story, that of a deaf, dumb and blind boy who becomes a false messiah. It was a theme fully deserving of the garish comic strip movie that Ken Russell made of it.

A worthy effort to be sure, but if you want to hear the real 'oo', look elsewhere.

Rating:
Sound ★★★★★ Content ★★★★☆

The Who

'LIVE AT LEEDS'

(Polydor) 1996

Track listing: Heaven And Hell • I Can't Explain • Fortune Teller • Tattoo • Young Man Blues • Substitute • Happy Jack • I'm A Boy • A Quick One While He's Away • Amazing Journey • Sparks • Summertime Blues • Shakin' All Over • My Generation • Magic Bus

'Live At Leeds' has appeared in virtually every list of classic albums for as long as critics have been indulging in making such lists. But now it's an even more essential item thanks to the addition of eight extra tracks which take the total running time to over 70 minutes. Among these are 'Heaven And Hell', which the band always felt was infinitely preferable to the studio version and 'A Quick One', their early mini-opera which Townshend modestly describes as 'Tommy's parents'.

The Who excelled as a live act, cramming their pent-up power and personal animosity into a clenched fist of sound; punching through their set with so much energy that the only way they could release all their rage was to trash the equipment while the last chord was still ringing. But for all their in-your-face aggression 'Live At Leeds' reveals the depth of intuitive instrumental interplay between Townshend, Entwistle and Moon which justified their billing as 'The Greatest Rock And Roll Band In The World.'

Rating:
Sound ★★★★☆ Content ★★★★★

The Who

'QUADROPHENIA'

2 CDs (Polydor) 1973

Track listing: I Am The Sea • The Real Me • Quadrophenia • Cut My Hair • The Punk And The Godfather • I'm One • The Dirty Jobs • Helpless Dancer • Is It In My Head • I've Had Enough • 5:15 • Sea And Sand • Drowned • Bell Boy • Doctor Jimmy • The Rock • Love, Reign O'er Me

Townshend's ambitions evidently knew no bounds. Having created one of the first 'rock operas' he tried to top that achievement with this more personal tale of an angst-ridden adolescent whose search for his own identity leads to disillusionment with the Mod movement and alienation from his family and friends. Fortunately, Townshend had the creative energy to sustain the story which returned to the group's early days for inspiration, turning in songs which were alternately intimate and intense to reflect the youth's mercurial moods. When Jimmy is high, angry or pilled as on '5.15', 'Dr Jimmy' and 'The Real Me' the tracks erupt with Daltry leading the assault, Entwhistle holding down the chords, Townshend flailing powerchords and Moon bringing up a barrage of drums from the rear that threatens to split the speakers. But when Jimmy is pensive and vulnerable, as on 'Love Reign O'er Me' and 'Is It In My Head' the bass becomes more lyrical, Townshend reveals his subtle side and Daltrey's vocal melts into the melody. And Moon? Well, Moon the Loon goes for a pint.

Forget 'Tommy', this was The Who's finest hour.

Rating:
Sound ★★★★☆ Content ★★★★★
Also recommended:
'Who's Next' (the 1995 reissue has been remastered and features seven previously unreleased tracks).
If you like this, why not try:
Small Faces, **The Jam**, **Paul Weller**, **The Pretty Things**.

Robbie Williams

'LIFE THRU A LENS'

(Chrysalis) 1997

Track listing: Lazy Days • Life Thru A Lens • Ego A Go Go • Angels • South Of The Border • Old Before I Die • One Of God's Better People • Let Me Entertain You • Killing Me • Clean • Baby Girl Window

Robbie's larger-than-life personality towers over these tracks like a colossus, to such an extent that the songs become an extension of his affable image. There's no doubt that he's a very talented guy, with a knack for knocking off both perky pop tunes and emotive ballads which is matched by a flair for wordplay that must be the envy of many more 'serious' artists. But what keeps this album on the boil is Robbie's considerable personable charm. Musically speaking we're not exactly at the cutting edge of contemporary pop here, but he's obviously a gas to be around, with a sharp ear for a nifty tune and a shrewd eye for the talent that he cocoons himself with. Moreover, he keeps the promise he makes on 'Let Me

Entertain You'. And in the fickle, ephemeral music industry that's half the battle.

Rating:
Sound ★★★★☆ Content ★★★★☆
Also recommended:
'I've Been Expecting You' (Chrysalis).
If you like this, why not try:
Take That, **Pet Shop Boys, George Michael**.

Stevie Winwood

'ARC OF A DIVER'

(Island) 1980

Track listing: While You See A Chance • Second Hand Woman • Slowdown Sundown • Spanish Dancer • Night Train • Dust • Arc Of A Diver

Winwood was the great white hope of British pop, a prodigiously talented multi-instrumentalist with the elusive sound of a black soul singer, who showed limitless promise with The Spencer Davis Group, Traffic and briefly, Blind Faith, while still barely out of his teens. But during the eighties he settled for being a musician's musician and a career in AOR.

'Arc Of A Diver' took the term 'solo album' to a new extreme with Steve writing, playing and producing every track on his tod, although he commissioned lyrics from Elton John's partner Will Jennings and Viv Stanshall. It's an album which found favour with American FM radio and an audience in their 30s who demanded sophisticated, cerebral rock music and who were prepared to forgo a little spirit to get what they wanted.

Rating:
Sound ★★★★★ Content ★★★★☆
Also recommended:
'Back In The High Life' (Island), 'Roll With It' and 'Chronicles' plus 'The Finer Things' a 4CD retrospective compiling tracks from his time with The Spencer Davis Group, Traffic and his later solo career (all on Virgin).
If you like this, why not try:
Traffic, Blind Faith, **Family**.

Wishbone Ash

'ARGUS'

(MCA) 1972

Track listing: Time Was • Sometime World • Blowin' Free • King Will Come • Leaf And Stream • Warrior • Throw Down The Sword

Wishbone Ash will mean diddly-squat to anyone under the age of 40, but those who grew up in the heady days of prog-rock hold them dear. The twin lead guitars of Andy Powell and Ted Turner provided a blueprint for Thin Lizzy, but Ash didn't rock as hard as their Celtic counterparts and they tempered their boogie with smooth West Coast harmonies and fey English folkiness. The medieval imagery gives 'Argus' a heavier slant than their other albums which offer little more than endless variations on traditional 12-bar boogie.

Rating:
Sound ★★★☆☆ Content ★★★☆☆
Also recommended:
'Pilgrimage' (MCA).
If you like this, why not try:
Crosby, Stills, Nash and Young, **Horslips, Thin Lizzy**.

Stevie Wonder

'TALKING BOOK'

(Motown) 1972 Mid price

Track listing: You Are The Sunshine Of My Life • Maybe Your Baby • You And I • Tuesday Heartbreak • You've Got It Bad, Girl • Superstition • Big Brother • Blame It On The Sun • Looking For Another Pure Love • I Believe

In the days before he became a master of schmaltzy MOR mush Stevie was a funky young dude with a mission to bring soul to the mainstream rock audience. He began the decade by demanding complete artistic control over his recordings and by embracing the evolving technology, specifically the Moog synthesizer. Stevie gave the synth soul by writing the funkiest bass line for the clarinet in the history of black music. That riff for 'Superstition' alone justifies the purchase of 'Talking Book', but add 'I Believe When I Fall In Love It Will Be Forever' and 'You Are The Sunshine Of My Life' (which are just the right side of 'romantic') and we're talking a compulsive purchase order.

Stevie Wonder may be out of fashion now, but his early Seventies albums are required listening. Unfortunately, remastering has failed to make the muffled drum sound on 'Superstition' more distinct. Compilations such as 'Original Musiquarium' and 'The Essential Stevie Wonder' may have used better masters.

Rating:
Sound ★★★☆☆ Content ★★★★☆

Stevie Wonder

'INNERVISIONS'

(Motown) 1973

Track listing: Too High • Visions • Living For The City • Golden Lady • Higher Ground • Jesus Children Of America • All In Love Is Fair • Don't You Worry About A Thing • He's Misstra Know It All

By the early seventies black music had acquired a social conscience and daytime radio was wary of playlisting anything with a militant message. But Stevie Wonder had a knack for concealing his social conscience in elegant songs that radio simply couldn't resist.

The seven-minute 'Living For The City' is a striking centre piece, but it's complemented by several of his most sensuous ballads, 'Too High', 'Golden Lady', 'He's Misstra Know It All' and 'Don't You Worry About A Thing' plus the muscular funk of 'Higher Ground'. In retrospect the political element may be rather naïve, but both the lithesome dance tracks and the romantic ballads have lost none of their seductive power.

Rating:
Sound ★★★☆☆ Content ★★★★☆

Stevie Wonder

'FULFILLINGNESS FIRST FINALE'

(Motown) 1974

Track listing: Smile Please • Heaven Is Ten Zillion Light Years Away • Too Shy To Say • Boogie On Reggae Woman • Creepin' • You Haven't Done Nothin' • It Ain't No Use • They Won't Go When I Go • Bird Of Beauty • Please Don't Go

271

It's fairly safe to assume that the majority of record buyers in the mid seventies must have known that 'You Haven't Done Nothin' was a dig at 'Tricky Dicky' Nixon, but most of them were probably more impressed by the fact that the track featured backing by the The Jackson Five. Almost three decades later Stevie's political preoccupations are practically academic leaving the album to stand on the strength of sublime ballads such as 'Heaven Is Ten Zillion Light Years Away' and the supple 'Boogie On Reggae Woman'.

Forgive the repeated lapses of good taste that followed 'Ebony And Ivory' and give this a spin at least once a week.

Rating:
Sound ★★★★☆ Content ★★★★☆

Stevie Wonder

'SONGS IN THE KEY OF LIFE'

(Motown) 1976

Track listing: Love's In Need Of Love Today • Have A Talk With God • Village Ghetto Land • Confusion • Sir Duke • I Wish • Knocks Me Off My Feet • Pastime Paradise • Summer Soft • Ordinary Pain • Isn't She Lovely • Joy Inside My Tears • Black Man • Ngiculela Es Una Historia – I Am Singing • If It's Magic • As • Another Star

Stevie redefined the term prolific with this ambitious double album which required a bonus four-track EP to catch the surplus songs. Those who dipped into their wallets after hearing the mawkishly sentimental 'Isn't She Lovely' must have been surprised by the diversity of music on offer. There's the jump 'n' jive of 'Sir Duke', Stevie's tasteful tribute to Duke Ellington, the earthy funk of 'Black Man', the usual array of elegant ballads and even a soulful spiritual for the seventies, 'Pastime Paradise' which was transformed into the monster rap hit 'Gangsta's Paradise' by Coolio 20 years later.

Although two years in the making 'Songs' doesn't suffer from an excess of production polish, nor does it sound as if its spontaneity has been smothered by an over-protective artist. It's a remarkably consistent creation and the pinnacle of Stevie Wonder's extraordinary career.

Rating:
Sound ★★★★☆ Content ★★★★☆
Also recommended:
'Hotter Than July' 2CD set (Motown).
If you like this, why not try:
Smokey Robinson, Marvin Gaye, Sly Stone.

X-Ray Spex

'GERM-FREE ADOLESCENCE'

(Virgin) 1978

Track listing: Art-I-Ficial • Obsessed With You • Warrior In Woolworth's • Let's Submerge • I Can't Do Anything • Identity • Genetic Engineering • I Live Off You • I Am A Poseur • Germ Free Adolescence • Plastic Bag • The Day The World Turned Day-glo • Oh Bondage, Up Yours

With her prominent teeth in a brace and her angular body wrapped in a bin-liner the group's founder and spokesperson Poly Styrene was frequently featured on regional TV talk shows as some kind of freak symbol of the punk phenomenon. Much was made of the fact that she couldn't hold a note if it was stuck on with superglue, but to anyone who shared the joke X-Ray Spex and their joyful noise were the manifestation of punk's DIY ethos. They raged against crass consumerism and made an effort to articulate teenage obsessions in such accelerated anthems as 'Oh Bondage, Up Yours!' and 'Identity', trashing their tunes with the subtlety of a ram-raider as Poly's cracked vocal ranted against Laura Logic's squealing sax. But Poly had the last laugh by notching up three top 30 hits, 'The Day The World Turned Day-glo', 'Identity' and 'Germ Free Adolescence' and watching from the sidelines 20 years later as her album was taken to the hearts of the now 30-something part-time punks.

Rating:
Sound ★★★☆☆ Content ★★★★☆
Also recommended:
'Live At The Roxy' (Receiver).
If you like this, why not try:
The Adverts, The Damned.

XTC

'FOSSIL FUEL – THE XTC SINGLES COLLECTION 1977–1992'

(Virgin) 1996

Track listing: Science Friction • Statue Of Liberty • This Is Pop • Are You Receiving Me • Life Begins At The Hop • Making Plans For Nigel • Ten Feet Tall • Wait Till Your Boat Goes Down • Generals And Majors • Towers Of London • Sgt Rock • Love At First Sight • Respectable Street • Senses Working Overtime • Ball And Chain • No Thugs In Our House • Great Fire • Wonderland • Love On A Farmboy's Wages • All You Pretty Girls • This World Over • Wake Up • Grass • Meeting Place • Dear God • Mayor Of Simpleton • King For A Day • Loving • Disappointed • Ballad Of Peter Pumpkinhead • Wrapped In Grey

Although XTC emerged in the aftermath of punk they shared the art-school ambitions of early Pink Floyd and the Canterbury contingent (ie Caravan, Soft Machine etc.), which they tempered with a love of quirky rhythms and skewed side-glances at the absurdities of suburban middle-class life. They were frequently in danger of being seen as too clever for their own good, but time after time they redeemed themselves with eccentric but irresistible songs enhanced by Andy Partridge's off-the-wall observations and a sound that was as quintessentially English as garden fetes and scones.

Rating:
Sound ★★★★☆ Content ★★★★☆
Also recommended:
'Drums And Wires', 'English Settlement' and 'Rag 'N' Bone Buffet – Rarities & Out-takes' (all on Virgin).
If you like this, why not try:
Caravan, early **Pink Floyd**, Syd Barrett, **Julian Cope**, **Robyn Hitchcock**.

The Yardbirds

'BEST OF'

2CDs (Charly) 1996

Track listing: I Wish You Would • Certain Girl • Good Morning Little Schoolgirl • I Ain't Got You • For Your Love • Got To Hurry • Heart Full Of Soul • Steeled Blues • Evil Hearted You • Still I'm Sad • Shapes Of Things • Mister You're A Better Man Than I • I'm A Man • New York City Blues • Train Kept A'Rollin' • Paff...Bum • Mr Zero • Sweet Music • Someone To Love • Stroll On • Too Much Monkey Business • Got Love If You Want It • Smokestack Lightning • Five Long Years • Louise • Baby What's Wrong • Boom Boom • Honey In Your Hips • Talkin' Bout You • Let It Rock • Take It Easy Baby • Highway 69 • Putty In Your Hands • I'm Not Talking • I Ain't Done Wrong • My Girl Sloopy • Jeff's Blues • Like Jimmy Reed Again • What Do You Want • Here 'Tis

The Yardbirds began as Stones-styled R&B revivalists during the blues boom of the early sixties, but when they began dabbling with more commercial psych-pop their star guitarist, Eric 'slowhand' Clapton, considered that their credibility had been compromised and left the band in a huff.

His replacements, Jimmy Page and Jeff Beck, seized the opportunity for experimentation and took the group into a new dimension of exotic sounds and pseudo-classical stylings featuring harpsichords, Gregorian chants and backward lead guitar lines.

This highly desirable double CD set chronicles that development with the pick of their early R&B covers augmented with the psychedelic swirl of 'Shapes Of Things', 'Still I'm Sad' and 'Heart Full Of Soul'.

Rating:
Sound ★★★☆☆ Content ★★★★☆
Also recommended:
'Roger The Engineer aka The Yardbirds' (Edsel) their only complete studio album, 'Where The Action Is – Radio Sessions 1965–68' 2CD set (Burning Airlines), 'Train Kept A'Rollin' – The Complete Georgio Gomelsky Sessions' a 4CD set (Decal) and the budget-priced 'Very Best Of The Yardbirds' (Music Club).
If you like this, why not try:
The Rolling Stones, John Mayall's Bluesbreakers, early **Led Zeppelin**.

Yes

'FRAGILE'

(Atlantic) 1972

Track listing: Roundabout • Cans And Brahms • We Have Heaven • South Side Of The Sky • Five Per Cent For Nothing • Long Distance Runaround • The Fish • Mood For A Day • Heart Of The Sunrise

'Fragile' presents prog-rock, or pomp-rock, as they used to call it, in easily digestible segments with each song interspersed by the group's solo party pieces. Although no less ambitious, nor pretentious than their other work, it is at least more disciplined and the songs are strong – even if no one can be certain what on earth they're about! But no matter. Ian Anderson's pseudo-mystical musings are soaked up in the watercolour wash of sound created by Rick Wakeman's battery of keyboards and Steve Howe's spiralling sitar-styled guitar runs which are pinned down by the fractured jazz-rock rhythms of drummer Bill Bruford and

Chris Squire's percussive bass. This is as close to orchestrated rock music as any band was likely to come.

A little judicious use of the programme button on your CD player will enable you to skip the superfluous, self-indulgent segments and segue the songs into a satisfying suite.

This remastered issue is a significant improvement over the original CD release which suffered from noticeable distortion.

Rating:
Sound ★★★★☆ Content ★★★★☆

Yes

'CLOSE TO THE EDGE'

(Atlantic) 1972

Track listing: Close To The Edge – I. The Solid Time Of Change II Total Mass Retain III I Get Up I Get Down IV Seasons Of Man • And You And I – I Cord Of Life II Eclipse III The Preacher, The Teacher IV Apocalypse • Siberian Khatru

Side one of this ambitious prog-rock masterpiece consists of one long composition, the symphonically structured title track whose epic length effectively relegates the two remaining tracks to the role of the supporting programme. In a sense this is the definitive prog-rock concept album; it's ambitious to the point of almost over-reaching the abilities of those involved and it appears to be about something of great significance, although nobody has yet discovered exactly what that might be! Even the band later professed to being baffled. That said, it's certainly a worthy attempt to create a new genre of 'classical rock' by using rock instrumentation to create soundscapes as vivid as those of the classical impressionists, rather than merely providing backing for the singer.

The 18-minute title track grows organically, building on the main and secondary themes to bring a sense of completeness, while maintaining a pulse that keeps the track from being overwhelmed by a profusion of ideas and production ornamentation.

Depending on your age and point of view 'Close To The Edge' is either a grand musical folly or an imposing cathedral of sound. Perhaps it's just as well the impenetrable lyrics retain their mystery.

Rating:
Sound ★★★☆☆ Content ★★★★☆
Also recommended:
Their previous offering, 'The Yes Album', their magnum opus 'Tales From Topographic Oceans' which is a 2CD set, the last creditable release 'Relayer' and the compilation 'Classic Yes' (all on Atlantic).
If you like this, why not try:
Genesis, **Rush**, Jon Anderson's solo albums, **ELP**.

Neil Young

'AFTER THE GOLD RUSH'

(Reprise) 1970

Track listing: Tell Me Why • After The Gold Rush • Only Love Can Break Your Heart • Southern Man • Till The Morning Comes • Oh, Lonesome Me • Don't Let It Bring You Down • Birds • When You Dance You Really Love • I Believe In You • Cripple Creek Ferry

'After The Gold Rush' finds Neil disillusioned but determined to fight on at the fag-end of the sixties, consoling himself with a set of disarmingly simple songs delivered in that distinctive, plaintive singing style of his and performed with a faltering, ragged charm. There is a tender yearning in the title track for the Eden that eluded the Woodstock generation, but there is bitterness too in 'Southern Man' (a savage attack on Alabama governor George Wallace which was swiftly rebuffed by Lynyrd Skynyrd). This intrinsic tension between reflective ballads and brittle rockers has ensured that 'After The Gold Rush' remains one of the most consistently engaging albums of Young's lengthy and prolific career.

Rating:
Sound ★★★★☆ Content ★★★★★

Neil Young

'DECADE'

2 CDs (Reprise) 1977

Track listing: Down To The Wire • Burned • Mr Soul • Broken Arrow • Expecting To Fly • Sugar Mountain • I Am A Child • Loner • Old Laughing Lady • Cinnamon Girl • Down By The River • Cowgirl In The Sand • I Believe In You • After The Gold Rush • Southern Man • Helpless • Ohio • Soldier • Old Man • Man Needs A Maid • Heart Of Gold • Star Of Bathlehem • Needle And The Damage Done • Tonight's The Night • Turnstiles • Winterlong • Deep Forbidden Lake • Like A Hurricane • Love Is A Rose • Cortez The Killer • Campaigner • Long May You Run • Harvest

Throughout his wayward and erratic career Young has kept faith with the Woodstock generation while remaining hungry and determined to out-distance the young guns who shadow him, waiting for him to drop his guard. This retrospective boasts tracks chosen by Young himself who draws on his early folk-rock recordings with Buffalo Springfield and Crosby, Stills, Nash and Young before moving on to spotlight the best of his seventies output. It's hard to believe that the writer of the wistfully nostalgic 'Sugar Mountain' and the intense guitar demo 'Like A Hurricane' are one and the same person, but the dichotomy is what makes Young such a fascinating figure. However, it's just as well he didn't delay this release until the end of the eighties when it would have been necessary to include tracks from his rockabilly, R&B and electronic projects too.

Rating:
Sound ★★★★☆ Content ★★★★★

Neil Young

'RUST NEVER SLEEPS'

(Reprise) 1979

Track listing: My, My, Hey Hey (Out Of The Blue) • Thrasher • Ride My Llama • Pocahontas • Sail Away • Powder Finger • Welfare Mothers • Sedan Delivery • Hey, Hey, My My (Into The Black)

'Rust Never Sleeps' is Young's riposte to the punks who at the time were storming the barricades demanding the extinction of rock's dinosaurs. He puts up a sturdy defence for the preservation of the then unfashionable singer-songwriter format, delivering some of his strongest material for a decade. The albums that had followed 'After The Goldrush' had had their moments, but were patchy, while this mid-career highlight doesn't have a weak track on it.

The acoustic opener finds Young in the spotlight setting out his case with the classic line 'It's better to burn out than fade away', a line that Kurt Cobain was to quote in his suicide note, to Young's dismay. 'Thrasher', 'Pocahontas' and 'Sail Away' testify to the rustic poetry of country, while 'Welfare Mothers' and 'Sedan Delivery' demonstrate why Young was later adopted as the 'godfather of grunge'. We rest our case.

Rating:
Sound ★★★★★ Content ★★★★★

Neil Young

'RAGGED GLORY'

(Reprise) 1990

Track listing: Country Home • White Line • F*!#in' Up • Over And Over • Love To Burn • Farmer John • Mansion On The Hill • Days That Used To Be • Love And Only Love • Mother Earth

Young continues to surprise both himself and his audience well into the nineties. 'Ragged Glory' finds him and his compadres, Crazy Horse, barricading themselves in the stockade and making a last stand against the forces of compromise and stagnation. This is Young on a short fuse, sneering in the

face of fashion and redefining the term country rock in the process. Sounding like one mean, saddle-sore honcho with desert sand in his mouth and a burr under his saddle he tears through some of the rawest rockers in his repertoire. It is one of his most sharply focused studio offerings for some time and proof, if needed, that you don't have to be under 30 to kick ass.

Rating:
Sound ★★★☆☆ Content ★★★★☆
Also recommended:
'Harvest', 'Live Rust'.
If you like this, why not try:
Crosby, Stills, Nash And Young, **Pearl Jam**, **Patty Griffin**.

Frank Zappa And The Mothers Of Invention

'WE'RE ONLY IN IT FOR THE MONEY'

(Rykodisc) 1968

Track listing: Are You Hung Up • Who Needs The Peace Corps • Concentration Moon • Mom And Dad • Telephone Conversation • Bow Tie Daddy • Harry, You're A Beast • What's The Ugliest Part Of Your Body? • Absolutely Free • Flower Punk • Hot Poop • Nasal Retentive Calliope Music • Let's Make The Water Turn Black • The Idiot Bastard Son • Lonely Little Girl • Take Your Clothes Off When You Dance • What's The Ugliest Part Of Your Body (Reprise) • Mother People • The Chrome Plated Megaphone Of Destiny

Subversive, eccentric and controversial are the three most common adjectives that have been used to describe the late Frank Zappa who, for almost 30 years, cultivated an image as rock's resident weirdo.

In truth, however, he was much more. A more appropriate term might be 'genius', though his was a flawed genius because it was rarely focused in one direction for very long and he often sabotaged his own success by being provocative for the sheer hell of it.

His prolific output covers acid rock, pop pastiche, jazz-fusion, avant-garde classical compositions and all bases in between. Not surprisingly his discography is longer than the proverbial piece of string and it can be a daunting prospect to know where to start. This album is as good an entry point as any, though almost everything Zappa released has its moments of disarming brilliance.

'We're Only In It For The Money' is a stinging satire of the hippie dream, an extended Pythonesque skit on the mind-numbing nature of drugs (which Zappa abhorred) and a dig at the commercial music industry which he held in contempt. He clearly didn't need psychedelic substances in order to 'discorporate' and set his faculties free. From the merciless mockery of hippie counter culture on 'Who Needs The Peace Corps' and 'Flower Punk', through the surreal sound collages which link each song, right down to the packaging which spoofs 'Sgt Pepper', this has 'genius' stamped all over it.

Rating:
Sound ★★★☆☆ Content ★★★★☆

Frank Zappa

'HOT RATS'

(Rykodisc) 1969

Track listing: Peaches En Regalia • Willie The Pimp • Son Of Mr Green Genes • Little Umbrellas • Gumbo Vibrations • It Must Be A Camel

This largely instrumental album with a mild jazz-rock flavour helped to establish Zappa's reputation as a guitar virtuoso and 'serious' avant-garde composer, although it's essentially a series of extended instrumental workouts in search of a song. Great though, if you just want to chill out and listen to somebody else working up a sweat.

The one genuine song on the album, 'Willie The Pimp', features a vocal by the equally eccentric Captain Beefheart making this a rare feast for connoisseurs of auricular refreshment. A minor classic. This edition comprises the 1987 remixes which received the coveted 'FZ approved master' rating in '93.

Rating:
Sound ★★★★★ Content ★★★☆☆
Also recommended:
'Lumpy Gravy', the various volumes in the series 'You Can't Do That On Stage Anymore' and 'Shut Up And Play Yer Guitar' (all on Rykodisc).
If you like this, why not try:
Captain Beefheart, Soft Machine.

The Zombies

'ODYSSEY AND ORACLE'

(Ace/Big Beat) 1968

Track listing: Derelict • Devil's Haircut • High 5 • Hot Wax • Jack-Ass • Lord Only Knows • Minus • New Pollution • Novocane • Ramshackle • Readymade • Sissyneck • Where It's At

One of the great 'lost' albums of the sixties, 'Odyssey And Oracle' has since become a cult classic and a collector's item. The band, who were on the verge of being uneremoniously dumped by their record company at the time, were forced to finance the sessions themselves. And so to save money they opted to use a Mellotron instead of hiring an orchestra. It was a fortunate decision as the instrument's synthesized strings added a dreamy, ethereal quality and a soft-focus backdrop for Colin Blunstone's translucent vocal and Rod Argent's jazz-styled keyboard lines. The result is a uniquely ornate form of baroque pop which is as precious and ornate as a five-tiered wedding cake. 'Time Of The Season', an obvious highlight from the same sessions, became the band's second million-selling single, but they split soon afterwards and the album was allowed to sink into obscurity.

Rating:
Sound ★★★★☆ Content ★★★★☆
Also recommended:
'Singles A's And B's' (See For Miles) and 'The Zombies Box' (on Big Beat/Ace).

If you like this, why not try:
Caravan, The Left Banke, early **Pink** Floyd.

ZZ Top

'TRES HOMBRES'

(Warner Bros) 1973

Track listing: Waitin' For The Bus • Jesus Just Left Chicago • Beer Drinkers And Hell Raisers • Master Of Sparks • Hot, Blue And Righteous • Move Me On Down The Line • Precious And Grace • La Grange • Shiek • Have You Heard?

Have mercy! A decade or so before they hitched their hot-rod to MTV and seduced a generation with video dreams of long-legged ladies and gleaming automobiles, the Texas trio were knocking out albums of no-nonsense bar-room blues 'n' boogie. With a few riffs lifted from John Lee Hooker and Muddy Waters these good ol' boys stripped their sound down to the bare essentials and grew beards longer than Methuselah to hide the fact that they kept their tongues lodged firmly in their cheeks. If you're only familiar with the multi-million-selling hits of the eighties just imagine the same relentless riffing stripped of the synths and replaced with some finger-blistering solos and you have the sound of this record in your head. You can bet Ozzy Osbourne wouldn't have relieved himself at the Alamo if these tough hombres had been around!

Rating:
Sound ★★★★☆ Content ★★★★☆

ZZ Top

'ELIMINATOR'

(WEA) 1983

Track listing: Gimme All Your Lovin' • Got Me Under Pressure • Sharp Dressed Man • I Need You Tonight • I Got The Six • Legs • Thug • TV Dinners • Dirty Dog • If I Could Only Flag Her Down • Bad Girl

When the Lone Star State's most famous beards shrewdly roped in a battery of synths and allied themselves to the dance fraternity they bought themselves a one-way ticket out of the Saturday night roadhouse grind and into orbit on the stadium circuit. Their particular brand of swamp rock has been spruced up and the impurities airbrushed out for mass consumption, but beneath the surface sheen of multi-million-selling singles 'Gimme All Your Lovin', 'Sharp Dressed Man' and 'Legs' beats the greasy heart of Southern-fried rock and roll. The ideal album to listen to in the company of Jack Daniels and his friend Bud Weiser.

Rating:
Sound ★★★★☆ Content ★★★☆☆
Also recommended:
'Deguello' and 'Greatest Hits' (WEA).
If you like this, why not try:
John Lee Hooker, Lynyrd Skynyrd, George Thorogood.

THE ESSENTIAL COLLECTION:
200 INDISPENSABLE CDS

Ten Essential Roots Of Rock CDs

Willie Dixon 'The Chess Box' 2 CDs
(Chess/MCA)

John Lee Hooker 'The Best Of'
(Music Club)

Son House 'Father Of The Delta Blues' 2 CDs
(Columbia)

Howlin' Wolf 'Moanin' And Howlin''
(Charly)

Robert Johnson 'The Complete Recordings' 2 CDs
(Columbia)

Muddy Waters 'The Very Best' 3 CDs
(Charly)

Various Artists 'The Sun Story Vol 1 & 2'
(Charly)

Various Artists 'The Rhythm And The Blues'
(Charly)

Various Artists 'The Best Of Sun Rockabilly'
(Ace)

Various Artists 'Good News – 22 Gospel Greats'
(Charly)

Ten Essential Fifties Rock n Roll CDs

Chuck Berry 'Hail Hail Rock And Roll'
(Chess)

Eddie Cochran 'The 25th Anniversary Album'
(EMI)

Bo Diddley 'I'm A Man'
(Charly)

The Everly Brothers 'Original British Hit Singles'
(Ace)

Buddy Holly 'From The Original Master Tapes'
(MCA)

Jerry Lee Lewis 'Great Balls Of Fire'
(Charly)

Carl Perkins 'The Sun Years' 3 CDs
(Charly)

Elvis Presley 'The Sun Sessions'
(RCA/BMG)

Elvis Presley 'Elvis'
(RCA)

Little Richard 'His Greatest Recordings'
(Ace)

Ten Essential Soul CDs

James Brown 'Sex Machine – The Very Best Of'
(Polydor)

Sam Cooke 'The Man And His Music'
(RCA)

Aretha Franklin 'Queen Of Soul'
(Atlantic)

Marvin Gaye 'Anthology' 2 CDs
(Motown)

Wilson Pickett 'The Sound Of'
(Atlantic)

Otis Redding 'The Very Best' 2 CDs
(ATKO)

Smokey Robinson 'The Greatest Hits'
(Motown)

Sly Stone 'Greatest Hits'
(Epic)

Stevie Wonder 'Fulfillingness First Finale'
(Motown)

Various Artists 'The Ultimate Soul Collection' (Polygram TV) 2 CDs

Ten Essential British Beat CDs

The Animals 'Singles Plus' (EMI)

The Beatles 'Rubber Soul' (Parlophone)

The Beatles 'Revolver' (Parlophone)

The Kinks 'Something Else' (Essential)

The Rolling Stones 'The Singles Collection' 3 CDs (London)

The Pretty Things 'The Singles'
(See For Miles)

The Small Faces 'The Singles As And Bs'
(See For Miles)

The Yardbirds 'The Best Of' 2 CDs
(Charly)

The Yardbirds 'Roger The Engineer'
(Demon)

The Who 'Who's Better, Who's Best'
(Polydor)

Twenty Essential Singer-Songwriter CDs

Tori Amos 'Little Earthquakes' (Atlantic)

Billy Bragg 'Talking With The Taxman About Poetry' (Go! Discs)

Jeff Buckley 'Grace' (Columbia)

Kate Bush 'Hounds Of Love' (EMI)

Leonard Cohen 'Songs From A Room' (Columbia)

Elvis Costello 'My Aim Is True' (Demon)

Sheryl Crow 'Tuesday Night Music Club' (A&M)

Donovan 'Greatest Hits And More' (EMI)

Nick Drake 'Bryter Layter' (Island)

Bob Dylan 'Best Of Vol 1' (Columbia)

Bob Dylan 'Highway 61 Revisited' (Columbia)

Patty Griffin 'Flaming Red' (A&M)

Joni Mitchell 'Blue' (WEA)

Van Morrison 'Astral Weeks' (WEA)

Van Morrison 'Moondance' (WEA)

Beth Orton 'Trailer Park' (Heavenly)

Joan Osborne 'Relish' (Mercury)

Paul Simon 'Graceland' (Warners)

Simon And Garfunkel 'Tales From New York' 2 CDs (Columbia)

Neil Young 'After The Goldrush'

Ten Essential Psychedelic CDs

The Beatles 'Sgt Pepper's Lonely Hearts Club Band'
(Parlophone)

Captain Beefheart 'Safe As Milk'
(BMG)

Country Joe And The Fish 'Electric Music For Mind And Body'
(Vanguard/Ace)

The Grateful Dead 'Live'

Hawkwind 'Space Ritual' 2 CDs
(EMI)

Love 'Da Capo'

Pink Floyd 'Piper At The Gates Of Dawn'
(EMI)

Thirteenth Floor Elevators 'All Time Highs'
(Music Club)

The Velvet Underground 'The Velvet Underground And Nico'
(Polydor)

The Zombies 'Odyssey And Oracle'
(Ace)

Ten Essential Progressive Rock CDs

Emerson, Lake And Palmer 'Brain Salad Surgery'
(WEA)

Genesis 'Foxtrot'
(Virgin)

Genesis 'The Lamb Lies Down On Broadway' 2 CDs
(Virgin)

Jethro Tull 'Original Masters'
(Chrysalis)

Jethro Tull 'Thick As A Brick'
(Chrysalis)

King Crimson 'In The Court Of The Crimson King'
(Island)

Mike Oldfield 'Tubular Bells'
(Virgin)

Rush '2112'
(Atlantic)

Yes 'Fragile'
(Atlantic)

Yes 'Close To The Edge'
(Atlantic)

Ten Essential Hard Rock CDs

AC/DC 'Let There Be Rock'
(EMI)

Black Sabbath 'We Sold Our Souls For Rock n Roll' 2 CDs
(Essential)

Cream 'Live Vol 1'
(Polydor)

Deep Purple 'In Rock'
(EMI)

Deep Purple 'Made In Japan' 2 CDs
(EMI)

Jimi Hendrix 'The Ultimate Experience'
(Polydor)

Led Zeppelin 'Remasters' 2 CDs
(WEA)

Metallica 'Metallica'
(Vertigo)

Motorhead 'No Remorse' 2 CDs
(Essential)

Thin Lizzy 'Live And Dangerous'
(Vertigo)

Ten Essential Reggae CDs

Black Uhuru 'Black Sounds Of Freedom'
(Greensleeves)

Burning Spear 'Chant Down Babylon' 2 CDs
(Island)

Jimmy Cliff 'Best Of'
(Reggae Refreshers/Polygram)

King Tubby 'Dub Gone Crazy'
(Blood And Fire)

Bob Marley 'Natty Dread'
(Island)

Augustus Pablo 'Original Rockers'
(Greensleeves)

Sly And Robbie 'Reggae Greats'
(Reggae Refreshers/Polygram)

Toots And The Maytals 'Time Tough' 2 CDs
(Island)

Peter Tosh 'Legalise It'
(Virgin)

U-Roy 'Original DJ'
(Frontline/EMI)

Ten Essential Punk CDs

Buzzcocks 'Singles Going Steady'
(EMI)

The Clash 'Story Of The Clash' 2 CDs
(Columbia)

The Damned 'Damned, Damned, Damned'
(Ace)

Iggy And The Stooges 'Raw Power'
(RCA)

Sex Pistols 'Never Mind The Bollocks'
(Virgin)

The Stranglers 'The Hitmen'
(EMI)

The Ramones 'Ramonesmania'
(Sire)

Patti Smith 'Horses'
(Arista)

Stiff Little Fingers 'All The Best' 2 CDs
(EMI)

The Undertones 'True Confessions' 2 CDs
(Essential)

Ten Essential Seventies CDs

David Bowie 'Ziggy Stardust'
(EMI)

David Bowie 'Low'
(EMI)

Alice Cooper 'Billion Dollar Babies'
(Warners)

The Doors 'LA Woman'
(WEA)

Elton John 'Goodbye Yellow Brick Road'
(Mercury)

John Lennon 'Imagine'
(EMI)

Queen 'A Night At The Opera'
(EMI)

T Rex 'Greatest Hits – The A Sides'
(Edsel/Demon)

The Velvet Underground 'Loaded'
(Polydor)

The Who 'Quadrophenia' 2 CDs
(Polydor)

Ten Essential Eighties CDs

The Beastie Boys 'Licensed To Ill''
(Def Jam)

Guns n Roses 'Appetite For Destruction'
(Geffen)

Michael Jackson 'Thriller' 2CDs
(Epic)

Jesus And Mary Chain 'Psychocandy'
(WEA)

Madonna 'Like a Prayer'
(WEA)

Prince 'The Hits'
(WEA)

The Smiths 'The Queen Is Dead'
(WEA)

Bruce Springsteen 'Darkness On The Edge Of Town
(Columbia)

Talking Heads 'Remain In Light'
(WEA)

U2 'War'
(Island)

Ten Essential Nineties CDs

Blur 'Parklife'
(EMI)

Garbage 'Garbage'
(Mushroom)

Nirvana 'Nevermind'
(Geffen)

Oasis 'Definitely Maybe'
(Creation)

Oasis
'(What's The Story) Morning Glory'
(Creation)

Pearl Jam '10'
(Epic)

Primal Scream 'Screamadelica'
(Creation)

REM 'Automatic For The People'
(Warners)

Radiohead 'OK Computer'
(Parlophone)

Suede 'Coming Up'
(Nude)

Ten Essential Cult Independent CDs

Bevis Frond 'New River Head'
(Woroznow)

Björk 'Debut'
(One Little Indian)

Nick Cave 'Your Funeral, My Trial'
(Mute)

Cocteau Twins 'Heaven Or Las Vegas'
(4AD)

The Cult 'Sonic Temple'
(Beggars Banquet)

Dead Can Dance 'Axiom'
(4AD)

The Fall 'This Nation's Saving Grace'
(Beggars Banquet)

Joy Division 'Closer'
(Factory)

The Soft Boys 'Underwater Moonlight'
(Ryko)

Television Personalities 'Yes Darling, But Is It Art?'
(Fire)

Ten Essential Club Classics On CD

Chemical Brothers 'Exit Planet Dust'
(Virgin)

Happy Mondays 'Pills Thrills And Bellyaches'
(London)

Loop Guru 'Duniya'
(Nation)

Massive Attack 'Blue Lines'
(Wild Bunch)

The Orb 'The Orb's Adventures In The Underworld'
(Big Life)

Orbital 'Untitled'
(FFRR)

Portishead 'Dummy'
(Go! Beat)

The Stone Roses 'The Complete Stone Roses'
(Silvertone)

Trans-Global Underground 'Dream Of 100 Nations'
(Nation)

Tricky 'Maxinquaye'
(Island)

Ten Essential Compilations

The Album
(Virgin/EMI)

Atlantic Soul Classics
(WEA)

The Best Rap Album In The World...Ever! 2 CDs
(Virgin)

The Best Rock And Roll Album In The World...Ever! 2 CDs
(Virgin)

The Best Punk Album In The World...Ever! 2 CDs
(Virgin)

The Best Soul Album In The World...Ever! 2 CDs
(Virgin)

Chronicles – 70s Rock Classics
(Crimson)

Glam Slam
(K-Tel)

Motown Chartbusters Volume 1-4
(Motown)

Now That's What I Call Music [series]
(EMI)

Ten Essential Rock Soundtracks On CD

American Graffiti
(MCA) The pick of fifties hits from George Lucas' nostalgic cruisin' movie

Backbeat
(Polydor) Young guns re-recordings of the Beatles Hamburg set

The Commitments
(MCA) Lean-limbed re-recordings of sixties soul classics

Great Balls Of Fire
(Polydor) The life and times of Jerry Lee featuring scorching
re-recordings of his hits and more

The Harder They Come
(Island) Seventies' Jamaican gangster drama featuring indispensable
early reggae tracks

'The Last Waltz'
(EMI) The Band's farewell concert with celebrity guests

The Rocky Horror Picture Show
(Ode/Pacific) Glam-styled soundtrack to the ultimate cult movie

Saturday Night Fever
(RSO) Seventies disco drama featuring the Bee Gees

Stop Making Sense
(Fame/EMI) Talking Heads Concert film

Woodstock
(WEA) A historic record of three days of free love, mud and music

Twenty Essential Box Sets

(* = contains previously unreleased material)

James Brown 'Startime' 4 CDs
(Polydor)

Kate Bush 'This Woman's Work' 8 CDs
(EMI)

Eric Clapton 'Crossroads' 4 CDs
(Polydor)*

The Doors 'The Doors Box' 4 CDs
(WEA)

Bob Dylan 'Biograph' 3 CDs
(Columbia)*

Jimi Hendrix 'Stages' 4 CDs
(Polydor)*

The Jam 'Direction, Creation, Reaction' 5 CDs
(Polydor)

Janis Joplin 'Janis' 3 CDs
(Columbia)*

Led Zeppelin 'Led Zeppelin' 4 CDs
(Atlantic)*

John Lennon 'Lennon' 4 CDs
(EMI)*

Twenty Essential Box Sets (cont.)

Bob Marley 'Songs Of Freedom' 4 CDs
(Tuff Gong/Island)*

Elvis Presley 'The Complete Fifties Masters' 5 CDs
(RCA)*

Phil Spector 'Back To Mono' 4 CDs
(ABKO)

Various Artists 'Back To Black' 10 CDs charting the evolution of black music
from ragtime to rap (Atlantic)

Various Artists The Charly Blues Masters Box 4 CDs
(Charly)

Various Artists 'Hitsville USA – The Motown Singles Collection' 4 CDs
(Motown)

Various Artists 'Nuggets – Artyfacts From The Original Psychedelic Era' 4 CDs
(Rhino)

Various Artists 'Tougher Than Tough – The Story Of Jamaican Music' 4 CDs
(Mango)

Velvet Underground 'Peel Slowly And See' 4 CDs
(Polygram)*

The Who '30 Years Of Maximum R&B' 4 CDs
(Polydor)*

100 Essential Singles

The 100 records listed below are as indispensable as any of the albums described in the main text. To avoid duplication, none of these tracks appear on the CDs reviewed in the book. They can be found on various compilations or downloaded from the internet. Good hunting!

A

The Animals 'House Of The Rising Sun'
P.P. Arnold 'First Cut Is The Deepest'

B

Bauhaus 'She's In Parties'
Colin Blunstone 'Say You Don't Mind'
Booker T And The MGs 'Time Is Tight'/'Hang Em High'
Ken Boothe 'Everything I Own'
David Bowie 'Ashes To Ashes'

C

Gene Chandler 'Duke Of Earl'
Jimmy Cliff 'Many Rivers To Cross'
The Coasters 'Yakety Yak'
Edwyn Collins 'A Girl Like You'
Arthur Conley 'Sweet Soul Music'
Coolio feat LV 'Gangsta's Paradise'
The Crystals 'Da Doo Ron Ron'

D

Danny And The Juniors 'At The Hop'
Desmond Dekker 'The Israelites'
Destiny's Child 'Independent Women Pt 1'
Bo Diddley 'Who Do You Love?'

E

Easy Beats 'Friday On My Mind'
Dave Edmunds 'Girl Talk'
Electric Prunes 'Too Much To Dream'
Andy Ellison 'It's Been A Long Time'
EMF 'Unbelievable'

F

Marianne Faithful 'As Tears Go By'
Eddie Floyd 'Knock On Wood'
Fox 'Only You Can'
Frankie Ford 'Sea Cruise'
The Four Tops 'Reach Out'

G

Gary Glitter 'Rock And Roll Pt 2'
Golden Earring 'Radar Love'
Grandmaster Flash And Melle Mel 'The Message'

H

Isaac Hayes 'Shaft'

J

The Jam 'Down In The Tube Station At Midnight'
Elmore James 'Dust My Broom'
Etta James 'I'd Rather Go Blind'
Jan And Dean 'Surf City'
Joan Jett 'Hate Myself For Loving You'
Jefferson Airplane 'White Rabbit'

K

Katrina And The Waves 'Walking On Sunshine'
Killing Joke 'Love Like Blood'
The Kingsmen 'Louie Louie'
The Kinks 'You Really Got Me'

L

Left Banke 'Something On My Mind'
Little Eva 'The Locomotion'
Lovin' Spoonful 'Summer In The City'

M

Scott McKenzie 'San Francisco (Be Sure To Wear Flowers In Your Hair')
Mamas And Papas 'California Dreamin''
George McCrae 'Rock Your Baby'
Don McLean 'American Pie'
David McWilliams 'Days Of Pearly Spencer'
Van Morrison 'Brown Eyed Girl'

N

Nazareth 'Broken Down Angel'
Nilsson 'Without You'
Gary Numan 'Are Friends Electric?'

O

Orchestral Manouveres In The Dark 'Joan Of Arc'

P

Freda Payne 'Band Of Gold'
Bobby Pickett And The Crypt Kickers 'The Monster Mash'
The Pogues And Kirsty Macoll 'Lullaby Of New York'
The Police 'Roxette'
Procul Harum 'A Whiter Shade Of Pale'
Prodigy 'Firestarter'
Psychedelic Furs 'Pretty In Pink'
Python Lee Jackson (feat. Rod Stewart) 'In A Broken Dream'

Q

? And The Mysterions '96 Tears'

R

Radio Stars 'Good Personality'
The Righteous Brothers 'You've Lost That Loving Feeling'
Roy C 'Shotgun Wedding'
Roxy Music 'Pyjamarama'

S

Sam The Sham And The Pharaohs 'Wooly Bully'
Sam And Dave 'Soul Man'
Screaming Jay Hawkins 'I Put A Spell On You'
Del Shannon 'Runaway'
The Silhouettes 'Get A Job'
Percy Sledge 'When A Man Loves A Woman'
The Slickers 'Johnny Too Bad'
Soft Machine 'Do You Believe In Magic?'
The Sonics 'Psycho'
Shangri-Las 'Leader Of The Pack'
Patti Smith 'Because The Night'
The Smiths 'Panic'
Sparks 'No 1 Song In Heaven'

Edwin Starr 'War'
Suede 'Animal Nitrate'
Donna Summer 'I Feel Love'

Talking Heads 'Psycho Killer'
Them 'Gloria'
Thin Lizzy 'Whiskey In The Jar'
Tomorrow 'My White Bicycle'
T.Rex 'Ride A White Swan'
Ike And Tina Turner 'Nutbush City Limits'

Ultravox 'Vienna'

Ritchie Valens 'La Bamba'
Gene Vincent 'Be Bop A Lula'

Jackie Wilson 'Reet Petite'
Wizzard 'See My Baby Jive'
Link Wray 'Rumble'
Robert Wyatt 'Shipbuilding'

Neil Young 'Heart Of Gold'

Warren Zevon 'Werewolves Of London'
The Zombies 'She's Not There'